Tim Anstey
Katja Grillner
Rolf Hughes

ARCHITECTURE AND AUTHORSHIP

**black dog
publishing**

Contents

The Story of The Pool.
Madelon Vriesendorp.
Project by Rem Koolhaas, 1977.
Courtesy of OMA/AMO.

Foreword

Architecture and Authorship is a reader in architectural theory that explores how architects have operated historically and in contemporary contexts in relation to changing paradigms of authorship. Today, at a time of rapid change, discussions about the significance of technology for architecture, the nature of the architectural drawing, the impact of digital technology all question traditional ideas of architectural authorship. Although the professional identity of the architect, articulated through journals, publications and reviews, is still dominated by the pervasive idea of the architect as solitary author, creator of inspired and useful artefacts, contemporary definitions (affirmations, dislocations, translations, dissolutions) frequently question such established conventions through adopting collaborative, hybrid, open source, or 'emergent' paradigms.

This book explores the territory of architectural authorship through an introductory essay, *Architecture and Authorship*, co-written by the editorial team Tim Anstey, Katja Grillner and Rolf Hughes, and through essay contributions by Caroline Dionne, Carola Ebert, Penelope Haralambidou, Jonathan Hill, Sean Keller, Hélène Lipstadt, Stanley Mathews, Wallis Miller, Louise Pelletier, Charles Rice, Naomi Stead, René Tobe, Gernot Weckherlin, and the editors. These include on one side case studies and historiographical investigations, which examine how architects since the fifteenth century have staked their claims, defended their territories and maintained their status through appeals to the logic of authorship. On the other, the book presents critical/ theoretical analyses, and explores related concepts such as origin, intention, the ethics of signature, contract, disciplinary boundaries, authority, intellectual property or oeuvre. The essays, written specifically for this collection, are structured around four themed sections—'Affirmation', 'Dislocation', 'Translation', and 'Dissolution'.

Architecture and Authorship was initiated by its editors, as part of an ongoing interdisciplinary research project, Architecture and its Mythologies (www.auctor. se), funded by the Swedish Research Council and conducted at the Royal Institute of Technology School of Architecture and the Built Environment in Stockholm. The book builds on and develops ideas brought together at the year meeting of the Society of Architectural Historians held in Vancouver, Canada, in April 2005 where the editors chaired the session *Terms of engagement: defining the modern architect*. We gratefully acknowledge the support of The Swedish Research Council for Environment, Agricultural Sciences and Spatial Planning (FORMAS) for financially supporting our participation at this conference.

For inviting us at an early stage to give seminars and encouraging the development of this project, we would like to express our gratitude to Professor Kenneth Frampton and Professor Barry Bergdoll and the Columbia University Graduate School of Architecture, Planning and Preservation (GSAPP), Professor John Dixon Hunt and Professor David Leatherbarrow and the University of Pennsylvania, PhD programme in Architecture, and Professor Alberto Pérez-Gómez and the McGill University, History and Theory in Architecture programme.

This study would not have been possible without the generous support of The Swedish Research Council (Vetenskapsrådet), and The KTH Royal Institute of Technology, which we hereby acknowledge with our deepest gratitude. The editors would also like to thank the following for their generous support towards reproduction costs in the book: Adams Kara Taylor Engineers, London; Fielden Clegg Bradley Architects, Bath; and SHoP/Sharples, Holden, Pasquarelli, New York.

Introduction

Tim Anstey, Katja Grillner, Rolf Hughes

Fame and Architecture, guest edited by
Julia Chance and Torsten Schmiedeknecht,
Architectural Design, November 2001.
Courtesy of Wiley-Academy.

*Versioning: Evolutionary Techniques in
Architecture,* guest edited by SHoP Architects,
Architectural Design, January 2003.
Courtesy of Wiley-Academy.

Consideration of the nature of architectural
authorship began to affect the Architectural
Design publication series during the early 2000s.
Helen Hardcastle was the series editor.

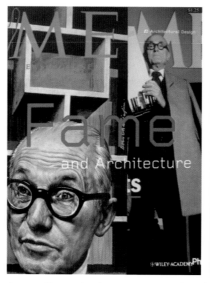
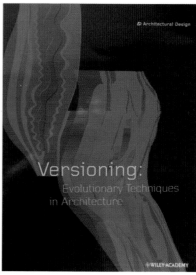

Among the myths that appear central to the development and maintenance of the
discipline of architecture from its modern beginnings is the notion of authorship. From
the fifteenth century, architects have staked their claims, defended their territories and
maintained their status through arguments modulated around subtly changing notions
of authorship and intention.[1] The professional identity of the architect, articulated
through journals, publications and reviews, is still dominated by the notion of a solitary
author – creator of inspired and efficient artefacts. At the same time, conceptual
uncertainties surround the authorial role of the architect and of the designer. If
architects claim to be authors, one might ask, exactly *what* are they authoring?

Authorship is once again being discussed within architecture—in magazine
publications, new forms of practice (and their accompanying rhetoric), or those apocryphal
stories that are exchanged and somehow bind together any group sharing and disputing
a common focus of concern. In all these cases authorship is one of those subjects over
which architects and those interested in architecture can argue, and by doing so define
relationships with each other without the need to concur or proclaim common agendas
or shared systems of values. Despite provoking a range of responses and attitudes,
authorship provides a kind of topography for architectural action, therefore, forming a
conceptual surface that allows architecture to develop as a coherent discipline.

This book brings together essays that negotiate this largely uncharted 'terrain'
of architectural authorship in order to produce not a complete map, but a series of
'journey accounts'—partial mappings which suggest the nature of the topography, and
which perhaps reveal where the fault lines exist that make authorship both fundamental
and unsettling for the discourse of architects. In order to provide a background for
these essays it will be necessary to say something more of the terms we use, and to
provide at least one starting point for the process of linking architecture to authorship.
In the context of this book architecture has been discussed primarily as a discipline
—in terms of discursive models and educational traditions—rather than as a product;
this distinction is important and should be born in mind. Architecture here cannot
be described as 'the magnificent play of forms in light' (or whichever other trope
one might deploy to describe the presence of architecture *qua* building). In this case
the archaeological level we seek is deeper—the underlying pattern of disciplinary

Facade of S Maria Novella, Florence, attributed to Leon Battista Alberti, c. 1470. The frieze that surmounts the facade, which was paid for by the Florentine merchant Giovanni Rucellai reads "IOHANES.ORICELLARIUS.PAV. F.ANSAL.MCCCLXX' ('Made by Giovanni Rucellai [...]. Year-of-our-Lord 1470). The tradition of architects claiming credit for structures is in part a translation of this other tradition, which itself originates in the identity of antique monuments with the name of their sponsors.

coherence that supports the articulation of such statements. At the same time, it is important to acknowledge that disciplinarity *per se* does not rest on a commonly accepted body of rules, but rather is defined by shifting frontiers between negotiable terms, appropriations, misunderstandings and misalignments that nevertheless allow certain identities to emerge.

When we join an inquiry into authorship with a definition of architecture as a discipline, we are prompted by the widespread habit of referring to buildings in the possessive—'Alberti's Tempio Malatestiano', 'Le Corbusier's Chapel at Ronchamp' —and the clumsy bifurcations to which such habitual discourse structures are inevitably subject—'Rem Koolhaas' Student Centre, designed through the Office for Metropolitan Architecture, sited around Mies van der Rohe's 'Commons Building' on his campus for the Illinois Institute of Technology.'[2] We are drawn to the complexities that exist every time an architect says 'I am building' or 'I built', a semantic structure that has survived, apparently entirely intact, from the renaissance patron's writing on the wall 'IOHANES. ORICELLARIUS [...] F[ECIT]'—or indeed from antiquity 'M. AGRIPPA [...] FECIT'—but one that holds an inherent ambiguity.[3] What mechanisms legitimise such claims of ownership? How do they negotiate the paradox that the material 'making' is conducted almost certainly by other hands than those of the claimant? A complex blend of assumptions, claims, and exclusions are packed into such apparently simple verbal constructions.

Modes of Authorship: Author Figures and Authorial Works

At its root, then, this book comes out of a wish to celebrate, criticise, dissect, and reinvent the long established habit of establishing a link between an architect and a set of material actions in the world—a link that implicates the trope of authorship. Such an objective introduces another set of complexities, for neither the notion of author, nor of the authorial work, nor indeed of the way these transient entities are related, can be seen to have any absolute definition.

What, for example, are the implications of assigning a specific body of work to a certain author? How does the epistemological status of the author shape that of the work (*oeuvre*)—and vice versa? The ambiguous nature of the link between author and work underlies Roland Barthes' "The Death of the Author", 1967, and Michel Foucault's 'reply', "What is an Author?", 1969, which posed problems within the field of literature and criticism that affect a broad range of disciplines. Barthes questioned the relevance of the author to the work, thereby liberating the text from the automatic presumption of its holding a fixed and unified meaning.[4] By this argument the act of writing becomes one of severance; it is the reader, for Barthes, not the author who endows a text with its meaning. While this position may lead to numerous impasses, contradictions and paradoxes in practice, the conceptual experiment it represents remains extremely important. Barthes understood the assignation of the link between works and authors, together with the confirmation of authorial status that it implies, as habitual— something socially produced and subject to challenge.

This understanding—developed further by Foucault in "What is an author?"— seems fundamental for contemporary analysis. Like Barthes, Foucault acknowledges authorship as a social construction; unlike Barthes, he also suggests that the mechanisms of authorship are enduring and might usefully reveal the mechanisms of society. "We should", Foucault writes, "re-examine the empty space left by the author's disappearance, we should attentively observe, along its gaps and fault lines, its new demarcations and the reapportionment of this void; we should await the fluid functions released by the disappearance".[5] To study how what he termed the 'author-function' operates differently across disciplines is to reveal much about such disciplines, their legitimising institutions and the allegiances in their discourses. Foucault accordingly historicises the author-function and its attachment to varying kinds of texts in different discursive cultures.[6]

"What is an author?" examines the forces that create the conditions for a public authorial persona and suggests that the mechanisms of authorship may persist without requiring the 'class' of authors or works as self evident species—it would be equally valid to assert that the author is a construction produced out of the work as vice

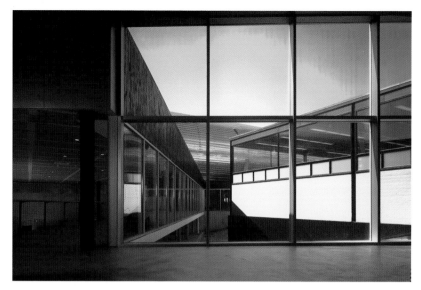

versa. For the essays in this volume Foucault is important, then, in that he provides a conceptual framework to account for the variety and vitality of 'author functions' that can be traced in literary and artistic production.[7]

The fluid nature of authorship as a category, or if one prefers the multiple nature of author figures that can be defined, is a matter of historical summary. A common criticism of Barthes' work has been how his argument forces him to construct an over-simplified (some would say idealised or even 'heroic') author, whose very existence prior to suffering a Barthesian death may be questioned. The essays in this volume show that figures of authorship vary greatly in architecture, not only over time, but also with context. This diversity reflects a much broader variety—cultural, discursive, personal and professional—which characterises the development of author figures through time.

In literary studies the author has appeared variously as a scribe, medium, prophet or genius (i.e. as a vessel for external inspiration that originates from the divine, from Nature or from recreational drugs, Coleridge's *Kubla Khan* being a celebrated example of the latter) or as an exceptional individual—a visionary, an embodiment of universal human spirit, a scientific experimenter, one capable of *creatio ex nihilo* (creation out of nothing), actively *shaping* the materials thus produced.[8] Seán Burke, a pre-eminent contemporary theorist of authorship, refines this distinction as dependent on whether cultural production is regarded as an *inspirational* or an *imitative* practice.[9] These points of view encompass a variety of figures. Within classical and medieval thought, *mimesis* —be it Plato's notion of an artist copying a natural world that is itself an inferior copy of the higher realm of Ideas or Aristotle's theory of imitation as the representation of a significant action—allows very little room for authorial inventiveness. Instead poets and tragedians were deemed to work within pre-established systems, rules or conventions of the sort specified in Aristotle's *Poetics*. As Burke observes, other manifestations of this paradigm of authorship include medieval designations of the artist as copyist working within long-established traditions, Russian Formalist notions of the author as craftsperson, the Structuralist concept of the writer as an impersonal assembler and arranger of literary codes, and traditional Marxist criticism of the Lukácsian variety wherein the author's primary duty is not to his or her inner feelings, but to allow the truth of a historical moment to find its expression within the text.[10]

Yet one is still tempted to look for underlying identities between this variety of figures, mimetic and inspired. There appears to be a paradox at the core of the Western concept of literary authorship; mastery of the materials of authorship in their passage from idea, inspiration or commission to audience involves a surrendering of self-mastery (to influences 'beyond one's control' such as divine afflatus or Romantic inspiration) combined with a highly disciplined command of materials (and therefore self).[11] Although one can point to author figures that seem to combine or transcend the categories set out above (the personifications of the artist, for example, as a *persona*

Bernard Rudolfsky, *Architecture Without Architects,* London: Academy Editions, 1965. The exhibition *Architecture Without Architects* opened at MOMA in 1964.

mixta, which arose out of the intersection of humanist discourse and jurisprudence in fifteenth century Italy and which fixed much of the modern idea of the artist as a producer of unique works, imbued that figure both with the facility to articulate *in terra firma* the divine beyond the confines of the world and, specifically, to use existing material to create 'something from nothing'), the paradoxical nature of authorship —simultaneous release and control—is one that seems to recur.[12]

In terms of the final flexible category outlined above, that of the 'work', one can also narrate a specific history. With changing economic conditions affecting cultural production in England, as elsewhere, the modern representation of the author as the originator and proprietor of a special commodity—the *oeuvre*—is held to derive from a blend of Lockean discourses of property and selfhood with the eighteenth century discourse of original genius. By the early nineteenth century, the author figure is increasingly 'liberated' from church or state patronage and instead obliged to sell his or her works on the open market. The figure of the Romantic author accordingly, by virtue of stamping the imprint of a unique personality on original works, takes them into ownership and thereby provides the paradigm and reference point for intellectual property law (as well as for author personality cults, a strategy that remains effective today for shifting units in saturated markets).[13]

As it emerged historically, therefore, the notion of the authorial work appeared to bind production to the individual creator, suggesting that there is something of the 'self' in the work—the work becomes in some sense the 'property' of the creator. (And it is worth noting, in this respect, that the patriarchal notion of an author 'fathering' his text, rather as God purportedly 'fathered' the world, has been an enduring myth in Western literary thought, metaphorically linking the male author with the authority of writer, deity, and *pater familias*.)[14] Yet relations between subject and work have never been easy. Copyright discourse has struggled from the beginning with the paradoxical notion of *incorporeal property* with its blend of corporeal and incorporeal, material and immaterial, body, identity and soul (or *Person, Man* and *Substance*, to use Locke's terms).[15] The problematic relationship between author and work, which Barthes and Foucault underlined, thus has a long history.

This ambivalent notion of the author's relationship to the work raises questions that can be applied to many disciplines. What remains of the notion of a 'work' if its link to an 'author' is uncertain (and what, by implication, remains of Literature, as such, or Art)? If one may transpose this question to architecture (although the validity of such a transposition cannot be taken for granted), one is confronted with a central disciplinary dilemma. Several of the essays presented here show how architecture is a discipline where there is a particular complexity in projecting that relationship between an author and a work; yet, once the uncertainty of the architect-work pairing is admitted, one must accept that there exists a threat to the understanding of Architecture—work or discipline—as such.

Authorship in Contemporary Architectural Practice

These fluid, linked and disparate categories—author and work—were of central importance to the development of the architect as a figure, and to the discourse around that development, from the mid-fifteenth century to the mid-twentieth. If one considers the subjects dealt with in this book within a chronological frame, one sees a pattern in which, from Leon Battista Alberti to Cedric Price for example, architectural figures and the debates and theories that surround them oscillate around paradoxes and ambiguities that emerge from the projection this 'classical' model produces of a link between a work and an 'authorial' creator. The context that produced the questioning of these categories in literary studies during the twentieth century was also of importance in architecture, and the rise of structural linguistics (from which both Barthes' and Foucault's respective positions developed) had a significant impact on the way in which authorship emerged as a central concern within architectural discourse. While in literature this shift was mortgaged to the development of post-structural theory, in architecture it was related on one hand to technology, particularly the growth of computer technologies, and on the other to the rise of user-oriented (participatory) design.

In observing the history of how architectural practice has negotiated and redefined models of authorship over the last 50 years, several questions or themes stand out. Firstly, what does an architect author? This is to investigate the nature of architectural action and the context for this action. Secondly, who is to be identified with the role of authoring in architecture—and who is excluded from such an account? This is to consider the challenges that exist to the hegemony of architects in the fashioning of the built environment. Thirdly, how is architectural authorship affected by the possibility of self-organising systems? Such discussions must include the ethical dimensions of human accountability in the design professions. And fourthly, how might different forms of architectural practice affect the constitution of architects as authors? This is to consider architects' modes of self-presentation, their complicity in the promotion of a certain type of author-centred discourse and the tendencies to deny authorial status to certain collaborators and fellow travellers (particularly women).

The first kind of challenge to architectural authorship—what does an architect actually author?—emerges in the tradition, stretching back at least until the 1950s but whose significance is only being admitted now, that questions the field or context for architectural action. This tradition might be seen to originate in certain design discourses emerging in the immediate aftermath of World War Two, that actively promoted the idea of architecture as 'service' and which questioned the status of the architect as artist.[16] The career and architectural rhetoric of the English architect Cedric Price, 1934–2003, can be seen as emblematic of the period.[17] Price contested the ground on which architectural actions take place, a challenge made particularly evident in the body of architectural production—drawings, diagrams notes and correspondence—that defines a project like the Fun Palace.[18] Price's work provokes questions both about how one should interpret architecture—permitting the beginning of an interrogation based on the notion of *field* rather than of *bounded object*—and about how the relationship between action, design and intention in architecture should be understood. Its legacy was a shift in perspective, exhibited particularly in the formative phase of the work of Richard Rogers and Norman Foster during the 1960s, that began to view actions of architecture as things that might take place in an arena outside that of the formal. That awareness of the centrality of contexts other than the formal or physical has continued to underwrite diverse types of architectural practice at the critical edge, whether made in student mappings of the invisible juridical boundaries of prohibition that rule a city like London, or the careful analysis of the context of contractual relationships and the technologies of digital production that informs the work of practices such as SHoP Architects in New York.[19]

The second strand that characterises redefinitions of contemporary architectural authorship, that which questions the status of the architect as an author, also raises questions about the nature of 'architectural action'. In this case the focus is not so much on the context for such actions—the possibility that judgement and intention in architecture might be played out in some field outside the formal—but on a rethinking of processes that govern the basic business of projecting formal arrangements for the organisation of physical material in the world. Again, one might refer here to Price, who established himself through a rhetoric that rejected the formulation of the architect as an author figure, and who early in his career described his role as that of 'anti-architect', calling into question the boundaries between architects and other actors in the production of the built environment.[20] This stance adumbrated a whole body of production that questioned the authorial hegemony of architects, which can be seen against the 1960s discourses in literary criticism mentioned above. In Barthes' desire to do away, not only with the author, but also with the 'work' (*oeuvre*), the 'text' was celebrated as "a multi-dimensional space in which a variety of writings, none of them original, blend and clash".[21] Similarly, notable architects and critics during this period replaced the notion of the 'architectural work' by that of the 'built environment', defined in multiple ways by its different inhabitants, whose authorship is equally multiple and impossible to define. From the mid-1960s, university-based movements within architecture began to advocate this view, developing methods for user-generated design, and pursuing detailed studies of vernacular 'nameless' architectures (refusing in many schools even to deal with the history of architecture as it had up until then been

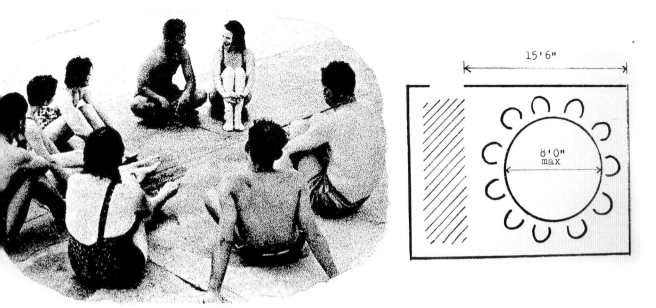

"Pattern 59 (Square Seminar Rooms)". From Christopher Alexander, Sara Ishikawa, Murray Silverstein, *A Pattern Language which generates multi-service centers,* Berkeley: Center for Environmental Structure, 1968.

taught, that is through the study of buildings whose authors could more often than not be named).[22]

These discussions which emerged during the 1960s around environmental design point to the third theme identified here as significant for recent architectural discourse— the challenge posed by self-organising systems to traditional notions of architectural authorship. Debate in this area is often inseparable from a discussion of technology, and several essays in this volume explore the ways in which traditional and cutting edge scientific paradigms have been advanced within architecture and architectural theory to question the centrality of authorial intention as a guide for production. Sometimes, as for Ernst Neufert, Lionel March, or Christopher Alexander, these influences resulted in instrumental theories (pragmatic handbooks, form-generating patterns, etc.) and at other times, as for Cedric Price, they proclaimed the possibility of a truly open-ended cybernetic gesamtkunstwerk.[23] Yet the exploration of how systems, rather than architects, order architecture is wide and informs the work of other figures studied here, such as Bernard Tschumi, Rem Koolhaas or Peter Eisenman.

Understandably experiments in authorial abdication and, more recently, self-generative design, are often located outside the established conventions of architectural practice and production, within the academy or the various sites of architecture exhibitions. Yet they are unlikely to remain exclusively theoretical. A fascination with 'datascapes'—3-D visualisations of geo-economic and demographical statistics—informs the prolific and importantly commercial production of practices such as MVRDV, UN Studio and the Office of Metropolitan Architecture, OMA.[24] This fascination at times appears to create a rhetoric that claims the possibility of turning informational analysis directly into architectural projection.[25] In this situation one must, inevitably, raise the question of whether there should be an ethical discussion in relation to such claims. Do they assert the possibility of a truly disinterested or 'scientific architecture', correct in its projections and unaffected by the mechanisms of its production? Do they suggest a return, either glorious or ironic, to the modernist era of social engineering? Is it, ultimately, desirable to forego the privileges and accompanying responsibilities that authorship confers?

In this last question 'desirable' can be understood in two ways: 'desirable' in terms of some Darwinian sense of species preservation among architects, or 'desirable' for the rest of the world that occupies architectural space. And in this doubling there lies a

11

clue, perhaps, to the fourth characteristic of discussions around architectural authorship that must be considered here—the necessity to consider architects' modes of self-presentation and their complicity in the promotion of a certain type of author-centred discourse. For it is very noticeable that despite radical experiments and exercises of erasure, despite abdications and crises, architecture, like literature, persists: architects, like literary authors, continue to flourish. Strong counter-forces continue to assign authorship, and to desire the persistence of the work. It is necessary then to study this continued vitality—to account for the survival of the architectural master.

What remains distinctive in architectural culture is the tendency of almost any kind of discussion to precipitate authors, individuals with names who stand for an intention or set of intentions realised in buildings or articulated through visual media and publication. It does not seem to us entirely accidental that the practice name of the most important group of early High-Tech architects warped rapidly back into its constituent (male) parts. Thus Team 4, established by Norman Foster, Richard Rogers with Wendy and Georgie Cheeseman in 1963, separated into Foster Associates, 1967–1999, and, via Richard + Su Rogers, 1967–1971, Piano + Rogers, 1971–1977. These were succeeded by Richard Rogers Partnership, 1977–, and Sir Norman Foster and Partners established after Foster's knighthood in 1990, name kept until his elevation to a peerage in 1999. This sequential change is no doubt the result of a number of parameters: shifts in style and mores that separated the progressive culture of 1960s Britain from a radically conservative one established during the seventeen years of right wing government after 1979; the increasing specificity demanded by operation in a global context. However the tendency, in which the increasingly precise naming of the single author exactly matched the expansion in practice size and project complexity, and surely also the increasing dissolution of responsibility for the actual authorial actions in any one project, remains intriguing. The phenomenon remains uncanny in part because of the simultaneous rhetoric of the parties involved; thus the volume 1 of the magnum opus *Richard Rogers* (three volumes and around 1,000 pages so far) celebrates the name of Team 4 as "a deliberate riposte to the cult of the individual which Rogers detested".[26]

The naming habit is of course subject also to the logic of branding and continues to change. Although the world may refer to "Norman Foster's designs for the Reichstag", the Foster office consciously emphasises the multi-authored nature of the work by Foster and Partners (the name of 'his' practice since 1999), as does Rogers.[27] Whether the final 'brand' of Foster will succeed in erasing the features of the world's most famous architect—whether Foster could ever become as faceless as Fosters—remains to be seen. Our guess is that it won't. As a kind of *coup de grace* among recent statements around architectural authorship, one that perhaps unsurprisingly binds together all the strands and paradoxes such statements can hold, one might return to the student centre designed by OMA, led by Rem Koolhaas, at the Illinois Institute of Technology. This building abuts and changes the context of an existing structure by Mies van der Rohe. The complexity of 'named' architectural authorship conditioned the way in which the building was reported, both in the general and specialist press; it self evidently conditions the design of the building in terms of strategy, and it finally conditions the way in which the building is self-represented by its designers and those who have documented it.[28]

At its worst this dominance of the single proper name obscures significant collaborations and important insights into the complex nature of architectural design processes. Not surprisingly the examples of architectural partnerships where the contributions of the female party have been either systematically erased or simply 'forgotten'—if not by critics and colleagues at the time, then certainly for long periods in the production of architectural history—are far too many.[29] If this particular kind of 'forgetfulness' most certainly has even deeper and more fundamental roots than the specific attraction of author figures to architectural discourse, it does raise the question what (or who) maintains the authority of an architect?[30]

The awareness of the problematic nature of naming in relation to architectural authorship, in part must explain the trend among contemporary practices to present their work in terms of an engagement in distributed forms of collaboration. While such strategies have resonances with the kind of 1960s thinking that spawned Team 4 and Archigram, we consider they negotiate a significantly changed context, both social and technological. Groups such as Servo, Ocean North and the Emergence and Design Group, all share the characteristics of a wide geographic distribution of their members, a particular interest for digitally-driven design processes and production technologies, and a near obsessive interest in the action of naming, thereby simultaneously escaping and reinforcing the logic of 'name-author'.[31] In a recent essay Chris Hight argues for the significance of network practices such as these, considering them examples of an importantly different mode of production, not only of architectural objects but also of architectural knowledge, and identifying their threat to "the presumed stability of the architect and his expertise".[32]

In one sense these organisations can also be read as 'brands' and their process of working as a kind of 'product'. Yet at the same time this brand or product is also granted some capacity of intention not usually associated with structures of this kind. The question "What is Servo doing?" can never be the same kind of question as "What is Marlboro doing?" or "What is Nike doing?"[33] Because the traditions of architectural discourse, with all its conflated conventions of social responsibility and personal fame, are deeply implicated in their actions, understanding their intention will always be a complex issue, and the nature of that intention will always be of prime interest.

Fields and Forces

The ultimate aim of this book is to discern the various forces that contribute to the constant precipitation of author figures out of the fluid statements of architectural discourse and practice, as well as to hint at the molecular level where such forces might suddenly change their direction, cease to act, reverse their polarity. Some of these forces are undoubtedly produced from within the discipline, from architecture's condition of negotiating its own disciplinary history; others from outside, from the interface between architects and society at large. At one level this 'external' context might be taken as the wider audience of those who must be convinced and cajoled, placated and persuaded in relation to particular strategies of architectural action, as discourse turns to specification and representation to action. But at another level, it is also implicated in the way that architecture has been 'remediated' through the use of terms and concepts taken from other disciplines. Those terms are sometimes translated from artistic or literary practices to define new architectural figures and new modes of architectural authorship, as happened with the development of theory around landscape and interior design during the eighteenth century; sometimes they emerge in theories of economic management, marketing or military strategy, as is happening today. In every case their translation into the discipline of architecture remains fascinating both for the redefinition of the terms themselves it implies, and for an evident potential to open up alternative readings, practices and actions in relation to architecture.

The acknowledgement that our view of architectural discourse, and indeed the very body of that discourse itself, is mediated through a screen of terminology that is as much borrowed as indigenous, has profoundly affected the way in which this book has grown. *Architecture and Authorship* is structured around four themed sections —'Affirmation', 'Dislocation', 'Translation', and 'Dissolution'. These consider the ways in which architects have operated in relation to authorship within the discipline of architecture —acting in ways that affirm authorship, or proclaiming its dissolution; and they consider how ideas of architectural authorship must be modulated by the cultural context around architecture—through dislocating pre-existing articulations, or through the translation of terms and categories just mentioned. The first and final sections, 'Affirmation' and 'Dissolution' are conditioned by the weight of a 'discipline' of architecture. They try to account for, as well as to criticise, the robustness of that projection; and they challenge the extent to which the notion of architectural authorship is implicated in it. The contributions in the second and third sections, 'Dislocation' and 'Translation', consider various 'parallel practices' which, from the perspective of architectural history and theory, can be defined in relation to, and must be seen to modulate, conceptual categories in architectural discourse itself.

In conclusion we say that the essays presented here constitute, if not an argument, then at least a convincing body of evidence for two important observations. First, that although the subject of authorship in architecture might seem to be one that has been projected recently into the limelight, the ambiguities and challenges that precipitate that emergence are long established. Architecture as a discipline is arguably defined by the complex issue of how we define architects as authors; if the issue of how we define authorship in architecture is currently 'at stake', this is merely to acknowledge that a long-standing ambiguity is again accorded the significance it deserves for architectural practice. Second, the essays in this book imply, some of them forcefully, that the new discourse on architectural authorship, and the new paradigms of authorship in architecture that are currently being suggested, are neither a clarification, an advance nor a solution to some traditional and clearly defined 'problem'. Rather, contemporary discussions around architectural authorship can be read within a complex fabric of accounts that both react to changing temporal conditions and that introduce conditions of change.

Spoorg, Gen(H)ome exhibition, MAK Centre at
the Schindler House, Los Angeles. Servo, 2006.
Courtesy of Servo/Joshua White/MAK Center.
Spoorg is a cellular network that attaches onto
the interior and exterior of glass facades and
windows to modulate climatic conditions. Spoorg
reacts to changing light levels and responds by
generating ambient sound. Behavior evolves over
time through the modulation of sound textures
based on a series of algorithmic rules. The
system has a distributed intelligence and
wireless radio communication.

Affirmation

What kinds of strategies have architects used to sustain the idea of authorial control? How has the idea of authorship been incorporated in architectural treatises and manifestoes? What role does art and architectural history play in the processes of reaffirming the image of the architect as author? The contributions in the first section consider the way in which changing social and economic conditions affect both architecture's self image, the image it projects to the world and the images that the world projects on it. The texts in this section are all conditioned by the weight of a 'discipline' of architecture; they try to account for, as well as to criticise, the robustness of that projection; and they try to uncover the extent to which the notion of architectural authorship is implicated in it.

Tim Anstey considers the long history of architecture's involvement with rhetoric and considers how this involvement conditioned architectural discourse and practice from Leon Battista Alberti in the fifteenth century to figures such as Colin Rowe and Cedric Price in the twentieth. The essay suggests that architectural authorship was endowed with an ambiguity in renaissance definitions of the architect as a figure. The significance of drawing for architects, their long habit of accounting for their actions in terms of appropriateness, and their concern with how their actions are seen all appear to derive from this condition. Particularly, Anstey suggests that the notion of 'context', which re-entered architectural debate in the late twentieth century, is also implicated in this renaissance definition and the rhetorical models on which it relies.

The significant developments that defined architecture as a profession during the nineteenth century, and the changing models of architectural education that underlined its intellectual character at the start of the twentieth, both appear central in accounting for the way in which architects deal with issues of authorship and creativity today. Caroline Dionne examines a nineteenth century context that can be taken as a microcosm of events unfolding on a much larger scale between 1850 and 1900. CL Dodgson/Lewis Carroll's architectural pamphlet *The Vision of the Three T's*, 1873, produced in the extremely insular conditions of academic debate within the University of Oxford, reflects contemporary debate about the role of architects and of architecture in relation to history, identity and experience. Without doubt the mirror Dodgson used to form this reflection was a highly distorting one, aimed at parody and caricature. Nevertheless, it provides valuable insights into the anxieties around architecture with which the nineteenth century endowed the twentieth. The text underlines the proximity of the expert and the monster, a problematic identity that emerges when architects claim both an authority over architectural actions that condition other peoples lives, and the expression of their own artistic personality through such actions ("it's my own invention").

This concern with 'monstrous' architectural authorship emerged clearly in criticisms of the modern movement that circulated in architectural discourse in the second half of the twentieth century. The third essay in this section, by Carola Ebert, considers two texts of operative criticism written during the 1970s, and speculates how practising architects involved in the discipline of architectural history and theory have simultaneously claimed the dissolution, and provided a rich reinvention, of the notion of this authorial figure in architecture. Bernard Tschumi's *Architecture and Disjunction* worked from the "margins" of architectural discourse to identify the possibility of a practice that needs "no inventor, no author... no architect". The work of Colin Rowe and Fred Koetter also emerges in a critique of the tradition of "the single central vision", and the rhetoric of *Collage City* prefers a Rome where "design and non-design qualify and amplify their respective statements" to a Versailles "where all is design, total and complete". How such ambitions survive in the projective world of architectural practice is a fascinating study. Tschumi presents his project of architectural disjunction as "a systematic and theoretical tool for the making of architecture". But in his practice this begins to imply a sovereignty in the system itself, a system that then turns out to be his 'own'; he becomes a name, a potential monster.

The tendrils of name-authorship thus cling tightly in architecture, perhaps because of the extreme difficulty the discipline has in escaping the rhetorical dimension that its renaissance definition imposed on it. And to examine the internal structures of architecture as a discipline is to consider only half the story. Concluding this section Naomi Stead illustrates both the resilience and the complexity of current constructions of architectural authorship that arise from outside the discipline. The Australian TV documentary *In the Mind of the Architect* which forms the case study for this analysis, exemplifies the problem of how architects are identified as author figures through the projections of external media in which they may, or may not be, complicit. Architectural authorship can never be considered alone, but must be examined within its wider cultural contexts.

Architecture and Rhetoric: Persuasion, Context, Action

Tim Anstey

Self-Portrait Medal. Leon Battista Alberti.
Bronze. National Gallery of Art,
Washington DC.
Alberti established fame, representation,
and authority as central issues for the
discipline of architecture.

Leon Battista Alberti's treatise on architecture, *De re aedificatoria* (*On the Art of Building*, c. 1452) asserts that an authorial link can be read between architects and buildings.[1] Today this assumption appears so domestic as to be inevitable, but it is nevertheless complex and needs to be 'seen again' in all its exotic complexity. Architects, in this projection, make judgements that result in 'works'—physical objects that can be analysed in terms of authorial intent. But their relationship to these objects is indirect: they do not 'make' the architectural work, they make representations in relation to it. This claim introduces an ambivalence about where an architectural project must be seen to lie. Is 'intention', that which is informed by the architect's judgement, to be read in the physical 'work' or the representations that are made about it? Are the architectural actions that reveal this intention only to be found imprinted into stone, or traced on paper, or written in digital projections, or can they be sought in other territories?

This essay considers what I will call the 'Albertian' model of architectural authorship (Albertian in that it appears to spring, almost fully formed, from the words of Alberti's treatise). The text suggests that Alberti endowed architectural discourse with a continuing relationship with rhetoric, which continued to condition the way in which architectural discourse developed through to the nineteenth and twentieth centuries. And it notes, finally, a potential shift in this relationship that modulates categories of intention and representation in contemporary architectural practice.

The 'Albertian' Architect

Authorship

> [T]o make something that appears to be convenient for use, and that can without doubt be afforded and built as projected, is the job not of the architect but of the workman. But to preconceive and to determine in the mind and with judgement something that will be perfect and complete in its every part is the achievement of such a mind as we seek.[2]

De re aedificatoria, which was produced in central Italy at a time when the relationship between patrons and builders was subject to dramatic change, can be seen as the place in which the modern idea of the architect was born.[3] As the current wealth of scholarship on Alberti makes clear, this treatise founded a genuinely new view of the discipline of building and marks a transition in thought that appears ever more marked over time.[4] Much of that radical quality emerges out of the way in which Alberti translated terms and ideas from one category of intellectual activity into another, in this case from the *studia humanitatis*, which addressed the complexities of contemporary life through the medium of ancient texts, to the 'Art of Building'.

Both Alberti's discourse on the architectural object, and that on the architect, have their origins in models and ideas adapted from antique texts on oratory, ethics and law, particularly those of Cicero.[5] Alberti explains buildings in terms of their ability to affect an audience, claims that reflect antique considerations of the potential (and value) of rhetoric and the art of speech.[6] This emotional power, which may even allow a building to "influence an enemy" and thereby act as a kind of protective shield, is attributed to the articulation in the building of a "divine sense of beauty".[7] It is clear that the articulation of this sense is dependent on the architect's skill at manipulating the material of a composition, rather as the power of an oration would depend on the skill of the orator in choosing and delivering words. In introducing this idea of beauty into his text on architecture, Alberti asserts the presence in the phenomenal object of a single persuasive

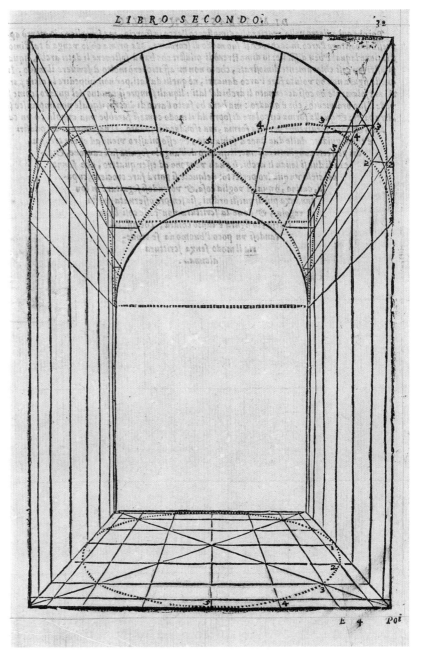

Perspective construction taken from Sebastiano Serio, *Tutte l'opere d'architettura et prospetiva*, Venetia: Giacomo de'Franceschi, 1619. Courtesy of the National Library of Sweden.
The long tradition of writing about architecture for an elite audience, which Serlio's work exemplifies, owes a debt to the discipline's involvement with rhetoric.

quality. This quality is distinct from the building's physical presence, and its existence is evidence of the will and mind of a (single) 'creator'. The architect-as-author/artist has arrived.[8]

To understand this fundamental binding characteristic in terms of persuasion is important. According to Alberti an architect may claim an authorial link to a work, but not necessarily an authoritative one. Architects are to be valued for their judgement, and this judgement will certainly be read in works created according to their decisions:

> [The architect] must calculate... the amount of praise, remuneration, thanks and even fame he will achieve, or conversely... what contempt and hatred he will receive, and how eloquent, how obvious, patent and lasting a testimony of his folly he will leave his fellow men.[9]

Rucellai Sepulchre, Florence, c. 1470, attributed to Leon Battista Alberti. Photograph, 1996. Courtesy of Thordis Arrhenius.

The Rucellai Sepulchre represents many of the difficulties in defining a 'frame' for authorial intention in architecture. Here authorship is habitually defined as controlling the outside of the 'internal' building (the figurative copy of the Sepulchre) and the inside of the surrounding Chapel. The 'project' in this sense defines a void rather than a solid, and has no exterior.

Yet these 'Albertian' architects are distanced from the two main sources of authority that traditionally ruled any architectural project—they have neither the master builder's authority over the building site or the absolute authority of the patron who commissions.[10] Alberti claims that there is a structural distinction between the building as physical object, over which the builder rules, and the building as idea, which is the architect's province and it becomes clear that architects do not 'make' buildings; they make representations of buildings.[11] And these representations have an uncertain authority. Alberti's letters preserved in relation to two buildings of which he is identified as the designer, the Tempio Malatestiano in Rimini and S Andrea in Mantua, clearly portray an architect who is physically separated from the theatre of construction (both letters are written from Rome) and who is equally clearly not in absolute control of the projects in question.[12] This authoritative 'lack' impinges also on the text of *De re aedificatoria*: "To have others' hands execute what you have conceived is a toilsome business; and who is unaware of the complaints that always greet any proposal to spend someone else's money as you think fit?"[13]

Alberti's declaration of distance introduces an uncertainty. Once absolute authority over the process of building is in question, there is a risk that other voices will condition the actions that make up the built work—that the knowledge, prejudices, limitations of other actors will effect the manifestation of the 'idea building'. Every architect, therefore, defined by Alberti's description risks the situation in which he or she is judged by results *not intended*. This condition—perhaps the defining condition of architectural practice—bears close examination both for its precedents and for its implications.

In terms of precedent, Alberti's description suggests an intriguing context for the adoption and exploitation of tropes taken from oratory in the development of architectural discourse. In order to cover the authoritative gap that results from their position, architects, according to Alberti's characterisation, will turn increasingly to rhetoric, its traditions and its practice, both to do all that can be done to exercise influence without authority and to lay claim to a vicarious authority through which they can exercise their own judgement. Thus in architecture, uniquely, one could argue for a doubling of the significance of the ancient discipline of oratory for the evolutions of renaissance and modern discourse. The power of the orator('s speech) to "send shivers down your spine", celebrated in texts such Cicero's *De oratore*, must be matched both by the emotional power of a building to "influence an enemy", and the capacity of the architect to persuade, rather than order, his Patron and the Patron's builders. Intriguingly, therefore, Alberti's training in oratory and law can be seen to condition not only an account of how artistic works function, but of how architects themselves must perform.

Representation, Decorum and Context

The architect who emerges from this kind of renaissance formulation, then, is a figure combining authorial ambition with a shadowy and uncertain authority. To acknowledge this condition is, perhaps, to shed light on a series of historical tendencies and discreet events that have characterised the development of architecture as a discipline through time. What is implicit in the argument of *De re aedificatoria*, yet remains invisible in the text, is the potential use of visual representation as a rhetorical tool. The history of the Renaissance architectural treatise, of writing about architecture for an elite audience, and the history of the use of illustration in such treatises, can both be seen as tied to the architect's pursuit of influence through rhetoric.[15] Through later history representation—architectural representation, that is; the whole mechanism of drawing and projection—became that piece of partial execution which the architect can directly control and which is offered as a guarantee of genius, a prosthetic device whereby architects increase the reach of their influence.

One can also suggest these ambiguities had a profound influence on the way in which architectural history and theory developed. The Albertian definition of the architect as a figure produces a tendency to read architectural intention primarily through an analysis of the architectural 'work'—whether built or otherwise. This reading of architecture introduced habits that can appear long-lived in architectural history and criticism. Once intention must be read in projected buildings the habit of reading works of architecture as *objects* (like pieces of art, things with discreet beginnings and ending points) becomes established.

The mortgaging of architectural discourse to the art of rhetoric has implications, finally, for ideas about the propriety of architectural action. So far I have noted how Alberti created an important equivalence between the architect and the 'work' in that he attributes to both a similar responsibility to define their places in the world through persuasion. Taken to its logical conclusion, this double responsibility created space in architectural discourse for a final notion that was to re-emerge during the late twentieth century—that of context. Being convincing in oratory relies on the internal logic and balance of a composition; but it also relies, and fundamentally, on the experience of that composition in its surroundings; either in terms of an immediate environment, or in terms of a wider tradition of actions and placement. In oratory the condition where the relationship between a composition and its context is convincing was called *decorum* (appropriateness).[16] In the best known accounts from antiquity, particularly that of Cicero, the persuasiveness of actions in oratory is thus read in terms of their appropriateness 'in context', and this context, as much as the content of the actions themselves, guarantees their decorous nature. It is this assumption that is moved over to discussions about 'appropriate action' in architecture—that what will be appropriate in one place is not correct in another (because of the relation between that architectural action and its context).[17]

Vitruvius, who introduced the class of the decorous into architecture and who appears to have drawn on Cicero in doing so, endows this principle of correspondence with an almost simplistic dimension: 'Manly' gods should have columns with 'manly' attributes; grand houses should have grand entrances; temples to healthy deities should stand in healthy places, etc..[18] This identification of the centrality of *decorum* with propriety may draw on one specific passage in Cicero's *De officiis* (*On Duties*): "in the home of a distinguished man, in which numerous guests must be entertained and crowds of every sort of people received, care must be taken to have it spacious".[19] Yet for Cicero both the principle and its potential implications for architecture have a further complexity that should be noted. "But if it is not frequented by visitors", *De officiis* continues, "if it has an air of lonesomeness, a spacious palace often becomes a discredit to its owner."[20] Appropriateness to context is compromised by considerations of sensory reception (what impression is made on an individual observer) and temporal performance (in this case the permanence of architecture confronted with the impermanence of occupancy).[21] Intriguingly, then, in antique texts on ethics, as well as in oratory and law, the notion of context goes beyond the fixed certainties of class or position.

Anticipated view of the Fun Palace on the banks of the River Lea. Photomontage. Office of Cedric Price. Fonds Cedric Price, Collection Centre Canadien d'Architecture/ Canadian Centre for Architecture, Montréal. The Fun Palace, indelibly identified with the practice of Cedric Price, upsets most of the productive tropes that architects of the mid-twentieth century had inherited.

LEA RIVER SITE

Criticism and the Twentieth Century Shift, 1950–1975

Cedric Price and Architectural Action

It can be suggested that the complexities unfolding from the definition of the architect in *De re aedificatoria* conditioned the way in which architecture developed as a discipline from the sixteenth, through the nineteenth and into the twentieth century. The class of the decorous appears to have had a long and lasting fascination for architects, who habitually frame their arguments around the trope of appropriateness.[22] The fact that architects during the gestation of and at the birth of Modernism used a moralised rhetoric of appropriateness, defined in terms of societal 'need', to argue their case, did nothing to undermine the authority of this category; modern debate and criticism was thus played out on a field that, to a certain extent, took the moral authority of 'the fitting' as its given topography. At the same time, the crucial changes that turned architecture into a profession in the middle nineteenth century, through the establishment national institutes, can be read in terms of a more or less clear reification of the shadowy authority that results from the Albertian definition of the architect.[23]

Camden Fun Palace. Network Analysis. Graphite and black ink on tracing vellum. Office of Cedric Price. Fonds Cedric Price, Collection Centre Canadien d'Architecture/ Canadian Centre for Architecture, Montréal. Architectural production around the Fun Palace included mapping the web of statutory and contractual forces that condition the decision-making process necessary before the construction.

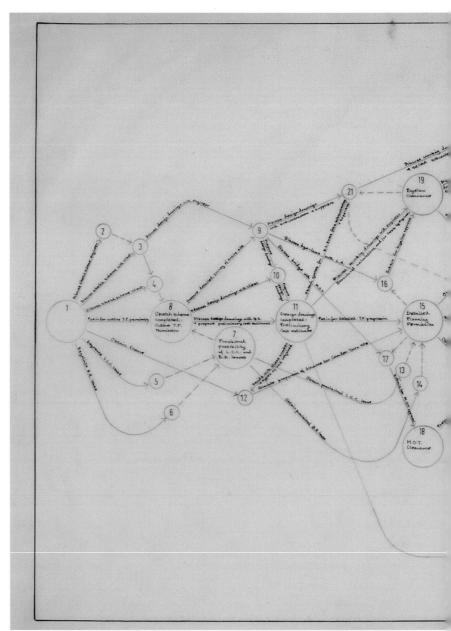

And the removal of architectural education ever more certainly into the university, a process completed in the Anglo-Saxon world at the start of the twentieth century, confirmed the status for 'design' that this uncertain definition first created.[24]

One might say, albeit tentatively, that these three modulations of the 'Albertian' model reveal the significant contours of the architectural figure associated with modernism in architecture and modernist planning in urbanism. One might, if one was feeling brave, suggest also that both Alberti's definition and its modulations continue to act on architects today. Yet the situation now appears to hold the possibility of a change. In order to give an account of what appears to be a 'long history' of the significance of rhetoric in architectural discourse, and to account for the possibility that this long history may now be subject to modulation, I will here consider the work of two figures who questioned how architecture should be conceived during the middle part of the twentieth century.

Cedric Price and Colin Rowe are intriguing specifically in relationship to the question of architecture's engagement with rhetoric.[25] The lines of thought developed in their work between 1960 and 1975 can be seen to operate on three similar fronts:

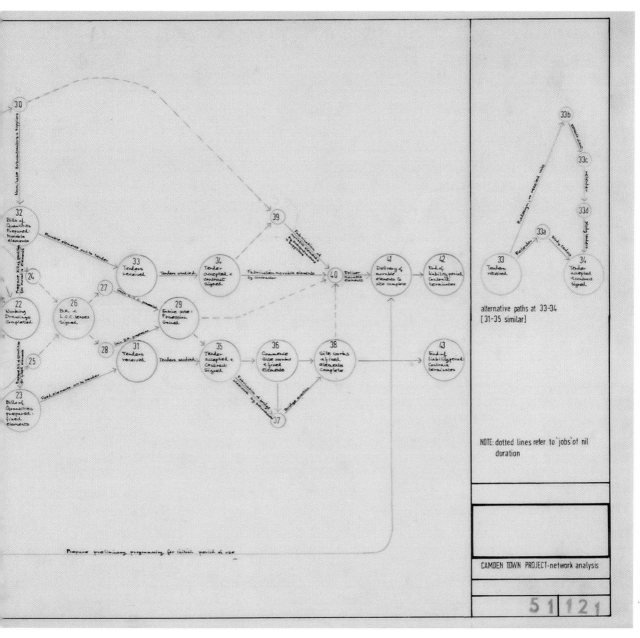

"Collage City", as presented in *The Architectural Review,* August 1975. Courtesy *The Architectural Review.*

to query what is the nature of architectural action; to question the sovereignty of the architectural 'work'; and to challenge the sovereignty of the architect as author of the work. Taken as a whole this questioning re-opened the gap between architectural representation, architectural intention, the projection of the building and the building itself. And it reintroduced, in varying ways, the issue of context back into architecture.

In the general culture of questioning and reassessment that followed the Second World War, the apparently structural disciplinary conditions outlined above were challenged. The 'Albertian' model of the 'authorial' architect as artist; combined with the nineteenth century reification of the architect's authority through the establishment of learned societies; and the twentieth century removal of architectural education into the world of the university; all produced a *status quo* in relation to architectural practice that, in the context of European and American discourse at least, appeared flawed and assailable.[26]

Price, who practiced in and was integral to the architectural life of London from 1960 until his death in 2003, was part of an architectural discourse that questioned this formulation of the architect as patriarchal creator. Early in his career he described himself as 'anti-architect' and he continued to attack central tenets of the discipline throughout his career.[27] "Small things, done with the best of intentions, can sometimes have devastating effects. Calling architecture a profession is one of these", runs a typical Price forray, delivered at the annual conference of the Royal Institute of British Architects in 1980.[28]

If one considers a project such as the Fun Palace, indelibly identified with the practice of Cedric Price, one realises that it upsets most of the productive tropes that architects of the mid-twentieth century had inherited.[29] Fun Palace was developed by an interdisciplinary team and was to be a building with an open programme, whose form and organisation should be steered and temporarily altered by its users. Its authorship was proclaimed as diffused in relation to the object, therefore, both in terms of promoting the notion of a team rather than an individual initiator, and in terms of the hoped-for relation between occupation and spatial definition in the building. Thus in the first instance the project challenges outright the 'artistic' nature of architectural production.

The critic Reyner Banham noted the general bafflement produced by Price's refusal to 'leak' any images of what the project might "*look like*": "that doesn't matter because it is not the point. Seven nights of the week it will probably look like nothing on earth".[30] In these terms the Fun Palace also questioned the status of visual imagery as the benchmark for defining architectural projects. This seems entirely logical given Price's position. As can be seen from the introductory sections to this essay, the rhetorical control of 'drawing' must be seen as one of the principle tools by which the traditional hegemony of the architect was maintained. To challenge that hegemony was inevitably to challenge the centrality of such means of representation.[31] Partly this challenge would question the kind of material that might be used to explain a particular kind of situation—in Price's case this led to the production of diagrams that explored fields that traditional drawing left unexplored. But it also questioned the role of representation per se. Price's activities began to suggest that traditional architectural drawing was no longer sufficient for the action of producing architecture.

Fun Palace also questioned, finally, the nature of architectural action. The material produced during the project (the drawing, events, happenings, films went on for over a decade) sheds fascinating light on the landscape of legislative control that surrounds architecture.[32] The project archives make clear that the authors—the interdisciplinary team just mentioned—made an effort to adjust this topography; to bend or revise rules; to lobby decision makers; to revise categorical boundaries. Thus the field in which these authors acted was proclaimed as being somewhere other than the space of formal projection: the project was to 'redesign' an invisible topography of contractual and institutional conditions that surrounds architecture as object.[33]

This assertion, that there are important fields upon which architectural intention must act that lie outside the realm of the formal, and that to make sense architectural actions must take account of, indeed must be conditioned by, such territory, was one to which Price adhered. In a very real sense, then, Fun Palace must be understood to have an importance outside the realm of its own individual construction. As a completed set

Hadrian's Villa at Tivoli presented as an exemplar in "Collage City", *The Architectural Review,* August 1975. Courtesy *The Architectural Review.*

of documented manoeuvres and exchanges, rather than as an unrealised architectural 'work' (the project was never finally built), it revealed a new kind of ground for thinking about architecture.

Colin Rowe and Context

Ultimately that ground has to do with 'context', although the connection might not seem immediately apparent. From its resurrection as a term during the 1960s, context was used to describe the physical, and often specifically historic, surroundings of a project.[34] It was as a term used within an extremely object-based interrogation of architecture and in this sense it might have apparently little to do with Price's uncovering of the subliminal forces that condition architectural actions, forces hard to register within the traditional modes of architectural representation and observation that contextualists held dear. Yet it is noteworthy that the discourse on context and Price's questioning of the nature of architectural action developed contemporaneously and that both see the experiential space around architectural projects—on one side the space of institutional and contractual relations, on the other the physical space of the city—as profoundly important. In this sense Price's iconoclastic challenges can be linked into the emergence of this discourse on context, in which Colin Rowe's engagement was central.

The key texts in the development of the discourse on context were Aldo Rossi's *L'architettura della città,* 1966 and, particularly in the English and American context, Colin Rowe and Fred Koetter's article for *The Architectural Review* "Collage City" (1975, revised and expanded as *Collage City,* 1978).[35] Where Cedric Price's position began to question the sovereignty of the architect as a figure, Rowe and Koetter's work reconfigured the idea of the 'project' produced by this figure as a category. This

Cedric Price. Portrait photograph.
Geoff Beekman. Courtesy of *Building Design*.

Colin Rowe. Portrait photograph.
© Valerie Bennett/National Portrait Gallery,
London.

Rhetorical figures: Price is identified partly
through his image, shown here in an original
photograph and as manipulated for the
monograph on his work. Rowe's pictorial
presence is more shadowy.

realignment can be seen in one sense as a shift in concern from single buildings to the city. Indeed, one of the fundamental and most stimulating aspects of "Collage City" is its reassessment of where one should draw the important 'lines' that read the built environment in terms of architectural compositions. The emphasis on collage readmitted to architectural thought the category of the fragment; and suggested a sophisticated means to evaluate the happenstance of reality according to its correspondence with a preconceived 'projection' of ideal architectural forms.

Rowe and Koetter shared with other proponents of contextualism a tendency to define boundaries in the city that reflected forces other than authorial architectural intention.[36] The emblematic example used to represent this condition in "Collage City" is the Villa Adriana, Hadrian's Villa at Tivoli outside Rome.

> The manifold disjunctions of Hadrian's Villa, the sustained inference that it was built by several people (or regimes) at different times; its seeming combination of the schizoid and the reasonable, might recommend it to the attention of political societies where political power frequently—and mercifully—changes hands.[37]

Rowe and Koetter's vocabulary developed within the Urban Design Studio at Cornell University, where Rowe taught from 1963 onwards, and its first theoretical formalisation in print occurred in 1971.[38] Much of Cedric Price's rhetoric that developed during the same period was formally collected in a six part series for *Architectural Design* between October 1970 and January 1972 (CP Supplements No. 1–5, *Architectural Design*, October 1970–January 1972). In these works the authors take similarly complex stances towards Modernist dogma; where the champions of context challenged the self-sufficiency of the architectural 'work', Price's interrogation challenged the myth of the modern architect as a self-sufficient author of that work.

Dissolution and Reinscription

These two debates make a similar identity between architects and 'works' of architecture to that which exists in Alberti—they turn a questioning of the contemporary 'model' of the architect, and a questioning of the status of the architectural project, on a single issue. If the sovereign architect is a myth (architectural actions are carried out in, and are subject to, a technical, political and institutional topography which conditions such actions) and if the self-sufficiency of the project asserted by modernism is a myth (projects have an equally large responsibility to the surroundings they cannot control as they do to the contents which they can) then in both cases the explosion of this myth is based on the significance of the surroundings for any architectural action.

Like Alberti's twinning, which relied on the categories of rhetoric, this identity places 'context' as a central issue for architecture. And in as much both Price and Rowe can be considered in a general sense as extremely good rhetoricians, one can begin, tentatively, to examine how their work can be linked into the long history of rhetoric in architectural discourse.

It is noticeable that Price, an architect with a 'practice', made skilful use of rhetoric in order to create a space in which his ideas could be heard and could persuade. This included an obsessive celebration of the possibilities of drawing and an almost iconographic attention paid, first by himself and later by his critics, to his image. In this sense Price simultaneously criticised and re-inscribed many of the traits that had marked the model of the architect he questioned. One shouldn't get too hung up on this apparent retrenchment, just as one shouldn't assume that its ironies would disappear if Price had not been a practitioner. The difficulties architects experience in escaping the categories of the discipline that binds them apply just as much to the 'critic' Colin Rowe as to the 'architect' Cedric Price. What seems more important is to underline the changes in the status of the architect that the work of both Price and Rowe potentially creates.

Price espoused a highly contingent version of authorship in relation to the control of architectural projects, particularly at the urban level. Partly this appears ideologically connected with the perception that architects in the mid-twentieth century pretended an authority over the built environment that they did not deserve and which

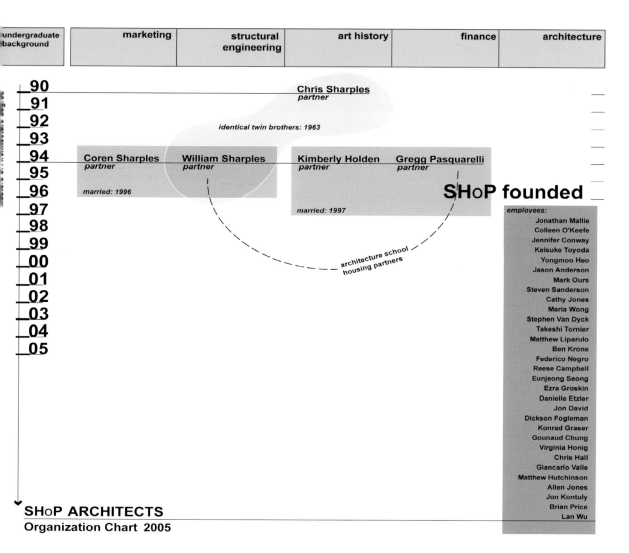

undergraduate background	marketing	structural engineering	art history	finance	architecture

SHoP ARCHITECTS
Organization Chart 2005

Social, institutional and aspirational diagram of practice. Digital image. SHoP Architects, August 2005. Courtesy of SHoP Architects: Sharples Holden, Pasquarelli.
SHoP identify both a problem and a possibility in relation to the kind of material that architects produce in relation to their practice.

did damage. Partly it appears the result of his acknowledgement of the fluidity of the context, political and social, in which architectural decisions must be made: "To maintain a valid role in a constantly changing society, continuous anticipatory design is required of architects. Instantaneous response to a single isolated architectural demand is too slow."[39] Rowe and Koetter, like Price, challenged the sovereignty of the architect at an urban level. *Collage City* asserted that the line around any authorial 'set piece' in a composition could not be considered to have any sure status of closure—that the region that existed outside that line, that was defined by the collection of many such lines, was of equal status for the success of failure of the work. And to take account of this condition they advanced the model of the architect as *bricoleur*, one who reacts to the situation at hand and who, although predisposed to a take a particular path, can act like "a dog straying or a horse swerving from its direct course to avoid an obstacle". The actions of this figure, like those of Price's architect, are likely to be contingent, a contingency that has much to do with a specific distrust of unilateral authorial 'vision' at the urban level.[40]

In this sense, then, it is important to acknowledge how both Rowe and Price begin to separate out the issues of authorial control over the 'work' of architecture, from the issue of rhetorical authorship and the production of persuasive representations. Self-evidently, neither figure had problems with being an 'author' in the latter sense. What is refreshing, both reassuringly familiar and radical about both Price and Rowe is the way in which they relax into the realm of rhetoric; they clearly eschew dictatorial authority for demonstration. In concluding this essay one has to affirm that this clarification seems

27

Detail of wall elements, Club Lounge
for Virgin Atlantic, John F Kennedy Airport,
New York. SHoP Architects, 2003.
Courtesy of SHoP Architects: Sharples,
Holden, Pasquarelli.
SHoP's work is based in a reassessment
of the 'context' of financial, production,
contractual and social relations that
surround architecture.

fundamental and that it potentially forms the ground for a radical shift. To underline this I will point to one contemporary practice that appears to owe a debt to the doubled discourse that emerges in the work of Rowe and Price, and which potentially modulates their anxieties, assumptions and theoretical positions in an interesting way.

For SHoP Architects, grounded in New York during 1996 by Christopher Coren and William Sharples together with Kimberly Holden and Gregg Pasquarelli, a fundamental question for architectural practice is how to regain, as opposed to dissolve, authority over the process of architectural production.[41] This desire operates both at the level of the overall project—the need to persuade clients, financiers, city planners—and at the level of building. At the level of the project SHoP use modes of architectural representation of the kind that architects always have, albeit the methods for producing this material embrace new digital technologies. Such 'representations' are 'persuasive' and follow the logic of rhetorical practice. But at the level of controlling building SHoP maintain that the architect's involvement requires another strategy, that is to say that it must be placed outside this rhetorical and representational practice. Authority over the building process, they suggest, is likely to emerge specifically through closing off the rhetorical dimension of architectural drawing. In terms of production architects should aim at providing 'templates' rather than 'drawings'. Such 'templates' directly control production, today frequently digital production, without needing 'interpretation' by others; they are thus importantly different to traditional architectural drawings in that they hold no rhetorical dimension whatsoever; the entire window of persuasion or potential disagreement is closed.[42]

SHoP's practice can seem both adoptive and subversive of the distinctions between persuasive rhetoric and authorial control implicit in Price and Rowe—adoptive in that they acknowledge the gap between rhetoric and direct control; subversive in their argument for the return of authority into the hands of architect, rather than the reverse. Yet if SHoP actively support a policy of assuming greater control in the realisation of architecture, it must also be noted that their claims in relation to the autonomy of the architect at an urban level are much more modest. Rather than emphasising the significance of formal invention, they advocate a "practice, that is pliant and reconfigurable," a strategy that is reminiscent of that proposed by Rowe and Koetter in their identification of the architect as *bricoleur*. And this practice relies on a special understanding of context, which must include "the context of financial, physical, social, temporal and legislative forces that prepare a thickened membrane within which an architectural intrusion can be inserted".[43] Although SHoP term this understanding as 'new', it reflects extremely closely the definition adumbrated by Cedric Price.

Thus in SHoP's work one could make a tentative reading of a practice that acknowledges an extremely sharp divide between the issue of authoritative control in building, which is something removed from the realm of rhetoric and in which the traditional modes of architectural drawing are subject to challenge, and the issue of persuasive representation in relation to the project as a whole. This acknowledgement returns one finally to the discussion with which I started this essay. The authoritative 'lack' in Alberti's definition of the architect can be linked, I suggested, to the development of architectural representation as a media. SHoP's challenge to the centrality of that system of representation emerges, logically enough, in the context of a proclaimed possibility of 'healing' this uncertain status of control. In this respect the questioning of the architect's position in relation to authorship, authority and representation, which began in the twentieth century discourse of *Collage City* and of Cedric Price, appears to have a valuable legacy. It allows historical conditions to be brought into perspective and forms the platform for new definitions of architectural action in the future.

Architectural Creativity in Lewis Carroll's *The Vision of the Three T's*

Caroline Dionne

The Vision of the Three T's is a pamphlet on architecture published by English author/ mathematician Lewis Carroll/CL Dodgson at Oxford, in 1873. The text, a short parody of a seventeenth century treatise *The Compleate Angler*, by Izaak Walton, conveys Carroll's critique of the project for a new belfry at Christ Church College, Oxford. Though Carroll borrows from Walton's "classic" both the shape of the treatise and some of its characters, a new figure appears in *The Vision*—Lunatic, the architect, is a mad man who, drunk and 'inspired', foresees the design of his future building as he contemplates a piece of cheese. As is often the case with Carroll's nonsense literature, interpretation of the work leads to a series of questions. How does Carroll, who depicts the architect so harshly—as a fool—see madness, or other altered states of mind, in relation to artistic and architectural creation? At another level, the shape and structure of Carroll's literary text generates a reflection on how textual accounts of 'moments of inspiration' in relation to architecture shape, or destabilise, the experience and understanding of a work. What is the status of the architect's 'vision' of the building, once transposed into language? Can it guide the interpretation of the work? What then is the position of the observer faced with an explanation conflicting with his own perception of the place? Does the gulf between the two textual 'visions'—the transcription of both the architect's and the observer's out-of-the-ordinary revelations— point to the limits of architecture's expressivity? Or does it not imply the need to rethink ways for architecture to "make sense" in the modern context? Lunatic's absurd position, through which he claims the novelty of his "creations", puts into question the authorial position of the architect in the context of the nineteenth century. This essay examines how Carroll frames his critique through a peculiar use of language and hints at the limitations of poetic madness in architectual creativity.

The Vision of the Three T's came out in 1873, a year after Carroll's first critical pamphlet devoted to the topic, *The New Belfry of Christ Church, Oxford*, which was published more or less anonymously in 1872.[1] The authorial credit for *The Vision of the Three T's*, "by the author of *The New Belfry*" installs a relationship between the two texts, emphasising how half-hearted the anonymity of their author may have been.[2]

To discuss Carroll's second architectural pamphlet, I will briefly describe the context of the architectural project at stake, that is, the construction of the new belfry of Christ Church. The fact that, in the context of the nineteenth century, an architectural intervention on Christ Church would provoke discussion, if not polemics, is not surprising. The College had been, since its foundation in the sixteenth century, celebrated, along with Christ Church Cathedral, as one of Oxford's most impressive architectural landmarks.

In founding Cardinal College (which was later to become Christ Church) at Oxford University in 1525, Cardinal Thomas Wolsey, who was at the time Henry VIII's chief minister, had high aspirations.[3] According to his plan, the college was to be the largest so far, surpassing all others both in Oxford and Cambridge, by its architectural features as well as its academic achievements. Construction began swiftly and though Wolsey's proposal was not executed exactly as planned, the building was largely completed before the Reformation, that is, within a few years of its conception, and has remained more or less unaltered to this day—it constitutes the core of Christ Church, the largest of Oxford older colleges. Built around the most spacious quadrangle of Oxford, Tom Quad, the plan of the college was laid out on the side of the three western bays of the nave of Christ Church Cathedral (originally the church of St Frideswide's Priory, which became a cathedral under Henry VIII in 1546). In 1529, Wolsey fell from power and work on the building was interrupted. The chapel he had envisioned was

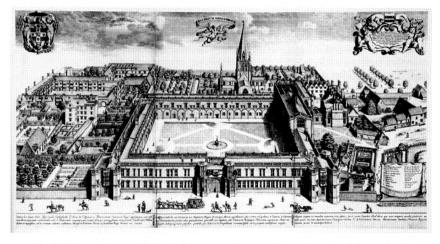

never built (Christ Church Cathedral is now both the college chapel and the main church of the city), nor was the gate tower of the main facade, which was only completed several decades later.[4]

The vault of the Hall staircase was the last major building undertaken in Oxford before the Civil War and can be roughly dated 1640.[5] It was carried out in the purest gothic style, probably following a lost design by Wolsey, and represents one of the most elaborate examples of such fan vaulting in England.[6] Eventually, in the late seventeenth century, the long symmetrical facade of Wolsey's original plan was completed, along with the tower above the main entrance to the college, Tom Tower, which is of Sir Christopher Wren's design and dates from 1681–1682. The College is essentially a renaissance building identified with a main author/patron whose plan unfolds and is carried out after his death. As it belongs to a genre, each decision that impacts on its composition is taken in the light of both the original project and the specific context of a late nineteenth century intervention on an existing—historical—structure.

The project commissioned in the 1870s by the dean of the College, Henry George Liddell, 1811–1898, was to end a 350 year long process of building at Christ Church.[7] The construction of a new bell tower was envisioned at the junction of the two major interior elements, Wolsey's impressive Hall of 1528–1529 and the vault over the staircase of 1640. From the beginning, Liddell's project was extremely controversial, as it touched upon the most pristine parts of the building, and was to alter the physical appearance of the college as it was experienced from the main quadrangle, Tom Quad. It also sought to resolve, and therefore had to deal with, a long standing ambiguity created by the history of the building so far. The absence of a proper college chapel, which left Wolsey's original composition unfinished and the situation of the existing church, which had to relate both to the closed world of the college and the profanities of the town, create a conceptual uncertainty with regard to the boundary of Christ Church, opening a centralised composition to the outside at an odd point on its perimeter. It is perhaps this tension that allowed Liddell to conceive a new project, with the intention of bringing the College to completion.

The architectural project that emerged from Liddell's initiative was designed by Sir George Gilbert Scott (1811–1878) and executed by his former student George Frederick Bodley (1827–1907) of Bodley and Garner.

Great Tom, the college bell which had been housed inside Wren's tower above the main entrance gate, had to be extracted from the structure and moved above the vaulted staircase, where the new belfry was to be built. To accommodate the bell tower, a breach was opened in the parapet above the Hall. This gesture is what Carroll and his colleagues at Christ Church referred to as the "Trench". Concurrently, it was decided that a new access to Christ Church Cathedral was to be provided. Following Liddell's commission, a student room on the ground floor was condemned by the architects in order to pierce through the east wing of the college all the way to the cathedral so that, from Tom Quad, visitors could have direct access to the church without actually entering the college. Two narrow vertical apertures with pointed arches were cut through the facade. This

Tom Quad, looking south towards the Hall. Photograph. Courtesy Oxfordshire County Council Photographic Archive Thomas Photos.
To the left of the Hall is GF Bodley's belfry (1876-9) over the Hall staircase. At the left of the picture (on the East side of Tom Quad) is the double passage leading to Christ Church Cathedral (the "Tunnel"). Notice also the circular pond at the centre of the quadrangle.

symmetrical double passage is what Carroll satirically refers to as the "Tunnel". These two stages of the project date back to 1872–1873; they were actually completed as Carroll is writing *The Vision of the Three T's*, and constitute the two first ts—i.e. the "Tunnel" and the "Trench", the third t being the "tea-chest", which refers to the new belfry itself.

A few years after it began, construction had to be halted due to financial problems. Bodley, then the architect in charge, was asked to design a temporary structure to house Great Tom above the Hall staircase until sufficient funding was gathered to complete the new belfry as planned. A temporary construction—a wood-enclosed scaffolding in the shape of a cube—was erected in place of the bell-tower as it now stands. The plain wooden box was quickly given the rather unflattering moniker of "tea-chest". It was unclear how long this temporary construction was expected to last, both due to its brittle nature and to the unlikely prospect of finding enough money to properly execute the project. It thus became a source of irritation and controversy. The actual belfry was completed between 1876–1879 but in 1873, as Carroll writes his second critical pamphlet, the wooden "tea-chest" had already been there a little too long and the future completion of the project was as yet uncertain.[8]

To present and structure his critique, Carroll, typically, adapted a well-known literary model. Most of Carroll's work effectively implies the recourse to a model or revisited genre, essentially inherited from the late middle ages or early Renaissance.[9] In this regard, his literary production is in line with that of many artists and writers of his time. His closest contemporaries include the Pre-Raphaelite painters, with whom he was closely acquainted, and architecture historian and critic John Ruskin.[10] Within Ruskin's wide body of work, the following points seem relevant here. On the one hand, Ruskin posited that the utmost care was necessary when dealing with ancient edifices—affecting their integrity or changing their appearance could alter their significance as providers of testimony of human history.[11] On the other, he believed that a building had to convey the appropriate moral, religious, and social significance for society as a whole. In that sense, architects had to find a way for the architecture of their time to be meaningful. In his "Lamp of Obedience" he writes: "Architecture never could flourish except when it was subjected to a national law as strict as minutely regulative as the laws which regulate religion, policy and social relations.... The architecture of a nation is great only when it is as universal and as established as its language."[12] This suggests that there were times when buildings and language were perhaps more closely connected, and that architects should draw upon such "great models". It also implies that different times most probably demand different buildings, thus raising the question of exactly how much one should rely on inherited rules—how far should the present depend on the past—and how much rule-bending is necessary for the result to be meaningful in a given context. In short, how can the architect create something 'new' within a context heavily, yet necessarily, conditioned by tradition and history? Carroll's pamphlet directly addresses these issues.

While *The New Belfry...* was presented as a 'monograph', mimicking a strategy proper to the natural sciences that aims at explaining any given topic in the most precise and exhaustive manner, *The Vision...*, as the title's word play "of the Three T's" announces, adopts a more traditional literary form, that of the treatise. His chosen 'model', however, does not come from the discursive architectural tradition. Rather, Carroll bases his pamphlet on the most reprinted book in English literature, Walton's *The Compleate Angler*, a treatise on fish and the art of fishing.[13] The book is shaped as a conversation between three main speakers, which takes place over the course of five days. Piscator (a fisherman), Venator (a hunter) and Auceps (a falconer) alternately discuss and commend their respective activities. This peculiar text serves a dual function: it is, on the one hand, a thorough, well-documented treatise on fishing and, on the other, a pastoral discourse that celebrates contemplation as a mode of accessing knowledge and wisdom. Though Walton's text was published in the mid-seventeenth century, the liveliness and open quality of its dialogue, which closely evokes a 'real' conversation, ties it to earlier Renaissance dialogues, as it strongly engages the reader in an active process of interpretation, as opposed to the more ordered, didactical dialogues emerging at that time.[14] Carroll's choice of this specific model as a point of departure for his pamphlet may be due to this open quality of the text, as much as its popularity. It is important to note that Carroll's literary experiments are almost invariably shaped as dialogues. There is, throughout his work, a constant emphasis on the spoken dimension of language—on orality—that connects to the ancient principles of oration, of Aristotelian rhetoric, and most especially to the notion of eloquence.[15]

If *The Compleate Angler* is a rather light-hearted celebration of fishing, *The Vision of the Three T's*, as the subtitle a "threnody" suggests, has a slightly different tone—it constitutes a complaint.[16] But despite this difference in tone, Carroll borrows extensively from Walton's text. Two of the characters Piscator and Venator, come straight from Walton's book, the style of writing as well as the structure of the dialogue are very similar. When the pamphlet came out, most readers would have been familiar with *The Compleate Angler* and thus their experience of *The Vision...* must have been quite different from that of today's readers. For most readers today, the weight of the historical precedent, as well as many references to the context of Carroll's life at Oxford, are not immediately perceived, but one can nonetheless grasp Carroll's criticism of the Belfry and its architects. The threnody, organised into three chapters, takes place over the course of an afternoon. The main characters, Piscator and Venator enter into conferences, or dialogues with three different protagonists. In this essay, focus will be on their encounter with Lunatic, the architect.

The opening chapter of *The Vision...* begins with the two sportsmen arriving at their fishing site, a perfectly circular little pond situated at the centre of a great quadrangle (there is actually a round fountain at the centre of Tom Quad). As they settle for fishing, they marvel upon the perfect geometry of their surroundings—indeed an ideal location for angling—and debate about the sorts of fish they may encounter as well as the best way to catch each kind. Fish being rare in this rather artificial setting, contemplation is facilitated and they begin to notice some modifications in the "noble Quadrangle". Venator asks: "Is all we see of a like antiquity? To be brief, think you that those two tall archways, that excavation in the parapet, and that quaint wooden box, belong to the ancient design of the building, or have men of our day thus sadly disfigured the place?" Piscator, having been there a few years earlier, can undoubtedly confirm the novelty of the three 'things'.

Unlike most of us when faced with a puzzling architectural setting, the characters of Carroll's pamphlet are lucky enough to meet the architect, and to ask him, personally, about his work. Lunatic, the architect responsible for the project, also goes by the name of Jeeby.[17] The rather convoluted conversation they have with him is interesting in two respects. First, as the sportsmen wonder about the nature of the garment that the mad architect is wearing, Lunatic's answer concerning fashion is telling. After having asked them if they read the Post, he goes on:

> Tis a pity of your life you do not. For, look you, not to read the Post, and not to know the newest and most commended fashions, are but one and the same thing. And yet

this raiment, that I wear, is not the newest fashion. No, nor has it ever been, nor will it ever be, the fashion.[18]

Jeeby's outfit, which looks like a cross between the outfits of a jockey, a judge, and a North American Indian, is completely gaudy and mismatched. For the architect, it is perfect since it is a-temporal, beyond the concerns of fashion and, just like his architecture, unique, eccentric and completely new. Clearly, Lunatic's architecture is unprecedented—that is, it entertains no relationship with the past (with history) or with its existing architectural surroundings.

This introductory passage, which already sets a distance between the "creator" and the observers, serves to destabilise the assumption that appreciation of a work requires an appropriate level of education and culture, thus introducing the problem of defining a common ground of signification. The second interesting aspect concerns more directly the question of authorship in relation to the work. In the story, the architect claims the entire responsibility for his work. When asked by Piscator and Venator about each of the wondrous architectural interventions, the architect wildly replies "'Tis mine! 'Tis mine!"—all three realisations are his deed. To somehow prove authorship over his work, Lunatic goes on to recall his vision for the "Tunnel". Though this constitutes a rather long passage, I reproduce it entirely.

> Tis mine sir! Oh the fancy! Oh the wit! Oh, the rich vein of humour! When came the idea? I'the mirk midnight. Whence came the idea? In a wild dream. Hearken, and I will tell. Form Square, and prepare to receive a canonry! All the evening long I had seen lobster marching around the table in unbroken order. Something sputtered in the candle—something hopped among the tea-things—something pulsated, with an ineffable yearning, beneath the enraptured hearthrug! My hearth told me something was coming—and something came! A voice cried 'Cheese-scoop!' and the Great Thought of my life flashed upon me! Placing an ancient Stilton cheese, to represent the venerable Quadrangle, on the chimney, I retired to the further end of the room, armed only with a cheese-scoop, and with a dauntless courage awaited the word of command. Charge, Cheesetaster, charge! On, Stilton, on! With a yell—another bound—another cavity scooped out! The deed was done.[19]

Logically, Piscator wonders, if the holes were done with a cheese-scoop, the apertures in the wall should have been round. To which Lunatic replies that they were at first, but that as he "wrought out that vision of beauty", he made some slight changes. "Oh, the ecstasy", he says, "when yesterday the screen was swept away, and the Vision was a Reality!"[20]

Lunatic's mad vision was made real. The nature of his vision, which occurred in a flash of insanity in the middle of the night, evokes an understanding of artistic genius completely detached from any other concerns than form. Lunatic can find inspiration while contemplating a piece of Stilton, as if the materiality of the building was irrelevant. If the experience of the building cannot, in itself, yield its meaning, that is, if the architect is unable to translate his vision skilfully into satisfying architecture, then cheese or stone, it is all the same; what matters is the idiosyncrasy of the gesture. The question of intentionality and the possibility for observers to make sense of the work are left unanswered. The wild architect will leave the site without providing his interlocutors with more information.

The two other attempts at explaining the building, gathered through the sportsmen's dialogues with Professor and Tutor, reveal little more concerning the signification of the building. What the two colleagues—a scientist and a specialist of unknown languages—propose as a means of explaining the wondrous architectural interventions is the use of strict rules. When asked about the belfry, that "unseemly box that blots the heavens above", Professor's answer is rather enigmatic: "Be you mad sir? Why this is the very climacteric and coronal of all our architectural aspirations! In all Oxford there is naught like it! ... And, trust me, to an earnest mind, the categorical evolution of the Abstract, ideologically considered, must infallibly develop itself in the parallelepipedisation of the Concrete!"[21] On the other hand, Tutor calls upon two Latin verses that he proposes as rules to justify the architectural interventions. The first one,

"*Diruit, aedificat, mutat quadrata rotundis*", Carroll borrows from Roman poet Horace's first Epistle to Maecenas.[22] Horace's line is quoted outside of its context and posited as a rule of Latin grammar. Tutor claims it as the motto of the Governing Body when commissioning the project. When asked by Venator about the relevance of using this grammatical rule as motto, he replies: "Sir, if we are not grammatical, we are nothing!" The second, "*In medio tutissimus Ibis*" (In the middle of things you go forth most safely) comes from another Roman poet, Ovid, and is misused in a similar way. A line in an ancient Roman poem becomes a mathematical rule, and, in turn, this mathematical rule is expected to shed light onto the architect's design of an oddly placed pillar "dividing" the "Tunnel". Tutor states the importance of these rules, the grammatical and the mathematical, as if they self-evidently led to an understanding of architectural interventions. The two collegians thus approach the work with self-referential frameworks of understanding having little to do with architecture. Carroll seems to imply that since there no longer are commonly understood rules regulating the practice of architecture, each observer is left facing the work, with his or her own knowledge baggage, which renders discussion of the work extremely difficult.

However, the irony implied in the absurd misquotations and use of such rules evokes a concern for language recurrent in Carroll's work. For him, meaning, and in this case architectural meaning, does not always take place within the rule, but more often than not, understanding happens in liminal conditions, as the rule is bent, within a temporary incursion at the limit of grammar, of mathematical formulas, of architectural form, and of language itself. This does not mean, however, that the regulating framework proper to a discipline can be denied, or that it ceases to operate. Rather (as can be found in Carroll's personal accounts of his own writing process) although some fragments indeed came to his mind in moments of *rêverie* that can be taken for momentary states of insanity—as the words that spur his mind do not seem to relate to anything or to make any sense—most of his work as a writer involved meticulous—even obsessive—hours of ordering, rearranging, and filling in when necessary in order to create literature.[23] In that sense, Carroll seems critical of the Romantic myth of the genius-artist held by some of his contemporaries that posit transitory altered states of mind as a form of supra-rationality—that is, as the precious 'gift' of a few highly creative individuals.[24]

Following this episode, Piscator falls asleep and has a strange dream. As he wakes up, he recalls his own vision of the three T's. In a tone that evokes the biblical apocalypse or some prophetic psalm, he retells his dream. The spirit of Cardinal Wolsey appears wearing a dress not dissimilar to that of Lunatic, with a cap and ribbons that defy gravity. He is surrounded by a myriad of other spirits howling and making loud noises.

> Darkness gathered overhead, and through the gloom sobbingly down-floated a gigantic Box! With a fearful crash it settled upon the ancient College, which groaned beneath it, while a mocking voice cried 'Ha! Ha!'. ... A darker vision yet! A black gash appeared in the shuddering parapet! ... Then a wild shriek rang through the air, as, with volcanic roar, two murky chasms burst upon the view, and the ancient College reeled giddily around me! ... Stand here with me a gaze. From this thrice-favoured spot, in one rapturous glance gather in, and brand for ever on the tablets of memory, the Vision of the Three T's! To your left frowns the abysmal blackness of the tenebrous Tunnel. To your right yawns the terrible Trench. While far above, away from the sordid aims of Earth and the petty criticism of Art, soars, tetragonal and tremendous, the tintinabulatory Tea-chest! Scholar, the Vision is complete![25]

This passionate retelling of Piscator's vision has apparently triggered the appetite of the two sportsmen who decide to have lunch and resume fishing. The story ends abruptly when the sportsmen see a fish and hook it.

The two visions, the vision (foresight or inspiration) of the architect and the quasi-divine revelation of the observer are analogous, yet very different. The two occur in a kind of dark, dream-like situation, and portray both architectural creation and the experience of a work of architecture as involving a momentarily altered state of mind (though in the case of Lunatic, his condition seems rather permanent). However, an

unbridgeable distance remains between Lunatic and Piscator's visions. Lunatic's vision is detached not only from any historical, cultural, social, economic or material concerns (c.f. the episode of the cheese), but, most importantly, from questions of architectural significance. Hearing Lunatic enthusiastically recounting his moment of inspiration, coupled with experiencing the space of the project itself, a space which, according to Carroll, possesses no architectural merit, leads, in Piscator's dream, to a vision of horror, the realisation that the architecture is entirely "other"—*une pure altérité.*[26] The two visions remain absurd attempts at explaining the work; Carroll's text raises more questions than answers. On the one hand, Lunatic's vision seems pathetic in light of the architect's inability to bring his project into material completion in a meaningful way. On the other hand, Piscator's dream presents the belfry as the College's *eschaton*, and Wolsey as the quasi-divine architect/patron imposing his last, posthumous authority over the work.

Here again, Ruskin's work on the nature of the grotesque seems to influence Carroll's work. The grotesque is seen by Ruskin as an important figure in works of art that deal with the symbol of the Fall or sin. Writing about the artist's state of mind when working, Ruskin asserts that there is an "uncontrolled" dimension tied to the phenomenon of inspiration. The vision of the artist does not come (solely) from within, but rather passes through like a wind, the divine breath or spirit, that at times seems to alter the mind, driving the artist toward madness. As Mark Dorian remarks, Ruskin associates the vision of the inspired artist to a mirror onto which the divine truth is reflected while, at the same time, it is blurred, or agitated, by his fallen (human) soul. The grotesque emerges through this movement, between the elevated divine truth and the base, natural nature of the human realm. Ruskin distinguishes several categories of grotesque, among which the noble grotesque is held to be most truthful. The noble grotesque is for Ruskin the product of a "healthy and well-proportioned mind", while the ignoble grotesque, the most ludicrous and monstrous, is the project of an abject mind that delights itself with the most base and vile aspects of human nature. But this dichotomy is problematised as Ruskin asserts that "in almost all cases, the grotesque is composed of two elements: the fearful and the ludicrous".[27] The former—fear—is crucial as it has the power to elevate the most ignoble grotesque, bringing the observer nonetheless to discern the truth, through its absence, by a strange detour of the mind pushed at its limit by terror and confronted with the imminent prospect of his own fall, or death.[28]

In Carroll's pamphlet, both visions fail to qualify as noble or terrible. Lunatic, with his unabashed creative 'madness', is not depicted as having a healthy, well-balanced mind. Piscator's vision, though perhaps horrific, does not lead the sportsmen to experience fear: as soon as it is recalled, they calmly resume to fishing. The two absurd visions posit the building far from the sublime, into the realm of the ludicrous. What Carroll's pamphlet also suggests, is that perhaps the categories associated with Renaissance grotesque no longer apply to the modern context of the late nineteenth century, as lapsarian symbolism has somehow lost its power to induce the kind of fear through which divine truth could be revealed. In his own writing, Carroll develops a new kind of grotesque that can be said to achieve a similar effect, yet, as nonsense, relying on the inevitable double distancing proper to artistic endeavours, as we now know them. In the episode entitled "It's my own invention" of *Through the Looking Glass and What Alice Found There*, as in many of the best nonsensical passages of his writing, Carroll stages a dialogue on the problem of sense, of meaning. Alice's interlocutor, the White Knight, is a sort of artist/inventor.[29] Carroll begins with a colloquial expression. In the story, the White Knight is not very skilled at riding his horse; he keeps falling off his mount, landing in front of it, behind it or on its sides. The Knight's *horse-sense* (good sense) is rather poor. Constantly off-balance, he eventually gets projected into the air and falls right onto his head. Whenever he falls, Alice diligently picks him up and places him back onto his horse. All this is happening as the two are discussing all sorts of things—from the Knight's inexhaustible hotchpotch of inventions (that are supposed to come in handy in all possible situations, but are rather absurd, though they all derive from a logical reasoning). Alice is puzzled by the fact that the Knight seems to be able to speak quietly even when he is standing upside down on his head. Apparently, the Knight tells her, this is the best way for inventing "things", as all the ideas thus come down to his head. One recalls how, in the same story, Humpty Dumpty, precariously perched on the edge of a wall in a rather temporary state of equilibrium, can claim mastery over words and their meaning.[30] The episode of the Knight represents another instance in which Carroll playfully questions the rules and limits of language, using a device that permeates the ensemble of his nonsense writing: the staging of serial paradoxes. Not unlike Humpty Dumpty's, the Knight's swaying manners also condition, or derive from, his own relationship to words, to language.

Two aspects of language are thus presented simultaneously: an event is stated in the text while it is, at the same time, actualised in the story—it takes place within the narrative flow of the tale. The event is thus presented *twice*. Carroll here brings together opposites in a way that leads to the formation of paradoxical sequences, one of the most 'modern' traits of his writing.[31] The White Night of Carroll's second Alice book may state as many inventions as come down to his head, he can never verify their validity through experience. He remains caught within language itself, tricked by his own way of playing with the rule, as his body and mind oscillate between "what is meant" and "what is said". But such oscillating is productive; it sets the mind of the reader in movement, through laughter, making him wonder about his own position in relation to language, to meaning, to truth.

Carroll constantly explores the transmission of possible meanings and, at the same time, what impairs that transmission. Like his other work, *The Vision...* is riddled with ambiguities. References to the model, as well as to the actual context of the project, are blurred; meanings are layered and multiplied. This process leads to the production of a form of literature—Carroll's nonsense—that, although it still relies on rhetoric, on the construction of literary figures and other historical principles of composition, nonetheless appears as something "new" and, in that sense, stands out from the nostalgic attitude usually attached to nineteenth century Romanticism.[32] As Jean-Jacques Lecercle tells us, nonsense is a literary genre that expresses a contradiction in the way one relates to language. "On the one hand, a language needs to be regulated and ordered, but the ordering process can only remain incomplete; the speaking subject needs to master his or her language, but such mastery can never be achieved. Nonsense dwells at the frontiers of language, where the grammatical and the un-grammatical meet, where the (always partial) order of language reaches the (never complete) disorder of its beyond."[33] In that sense, Carroll's nonsense serves to reaffirm the regulating framework of language while, at the same time, it destabilises it. Through this operation, Carroll's writing still manages to make sense for the reader, to convey meaning.

Ruskin wished for an architecture as universal and established as his nation's language. Throughout his work, Carroll plays with the limits of the English language of his time, allowing it to grow, from within, into something new. Using his invented form of literature to convey his critique of the romanticised notion of "genius", Carroll not only brings forth problems but proposes a mode of approaching processes of creation common to literature and architecture. If Carroll's lines on architecture do not exactly qualify as "standard" architectural theory, they nonetheless hint quite potently at the problem of architectural meaning; Carroll's pamphlet raises questions about the possibilities of defining a common ground of signification for the experience of a work of architecture in the modern context. As he writes about an architectural project that does not yet exist in its definitive form, Carroll's critique orients future understandings of the work (at least in the immediate context of late nineteenth century Oxford) while, at the same time, it limits possibilities for the 'real' architect to impose a unique, authoritative reading of his work. Carroll's text hints, albeit obliquely, at larger issues tied to historicism, that of approaching architecture via simple concerns of style, or of finding ways to manoeuvre between the authority of historical precedents and the imagination of the creative individual. The kind of poetic madness required from the part of the artist/architect, can no longer be approached via the same criteria that guided creation in mytho-poetic cultures, in which the production of a work was still framed by an acknowledged, although problematised, body of rules. Carroll's work reveals that the rules themselves are subject to alteration, and thus have to be constantly restated and defined by the author himself, only then to be bent and played with. How much bending is required from the part of the artist/author remains an open question. Contemporary architects are perhaps not in a better position than Carroll's Lunatic in the context of the Belfry project—a kind of White Knight with mismatched things hanging from his body on all sides, caught in this unstable, yet necessary position, between what is meant, what is said, and what can be understood.

Illustration of the White Knight. Engraving. John Tenniel. In Lewis Carroll, *Through the Looking Glass and What Alice Found There*, London: Macmillan and Co, 1897.

Post-mortem: Architectural Postmodernism and the Death of the Author

Carola Ebert

Introduction

During the 1960s and 70s, contemporary architectural discourse rarely addressed the issue of architectural authorship as such. At a time when the discipline was subject to intense external critique, struggling with different systems of architectural signification, and caught between social relevance and disciplinary autonomy, the emphasis lay predominantly on the significance of the architectural discipline and its methodologies. With the rising critique of architectural modernism after 1968 and a growing interdisciplinarity, various artistic and intellectual concepts were transferred into the architectural debate. *Collage City* by Colin Rowe and Fred Koetter, 1978, and Bernard Tschumi's early writings, 1975–1984, as assembled in his book *Architecture and Disjunction*, both explicitly employed modern artistic practices based on fragmentation as a critique of modern architecture.[1]

 This essay discusses the different implications of collage and montage as creative practices and as intellectual means of reconsidering architectural production, and it questions those significatory shifts that may occur during the transferral from one discourse into another. *Collage City* and *Architecture and Disjunction* reveal the implications of their criticism for architecture's protagonists when their lines of reasoning are considered in the light of Roland Barthes' seminal piece "The Death of the Author".[2] While *Collage City* and Tschumi's projects suggest different architectural analogies to Barthes' aims in "The Death of the Author", curiously such parallels are harder to identify in Tschumi's theory, despite its use of Barthes' terms. The analysis of *Collage City* and *Architecture and Disjunction* presents two different views about architecture's role as a postmodern discipline, defining thematic frameworks for the architect as author. A matrix of terms that distinguish different notions of modernity is useful to further differentiate those views and *Collage City*'s and *Architecture and Disjunction*'s positions towards cultural modernity.

 Although in both examples cited here the role of the architect as author is not addressed or criticised for its own sake, Tschumi, and Rowe and Koetter were able to revitalise the discourse around the architect as author in the wake of architectural modernism. Through their appropriation of terms and categories taken from other discourses, the arguments of *Architecture and Disjunction* and *Collage City* shed valuable light on the way in which the issue of architectural authorship was to re-emerge in architectural discourse during the last part of the twentieth century.

Against Modern Architecture?—Postmodern Conceptions of Architecture in *Collage City* and *Architecture and Disjunction*

Tschumi's early essays in *Architecture and Disjunction* challenge architectural modernism with methods inspired by French philosophy. His critique is immersed within a contemporary philosophical discourse that would be proclaimed as 'postmodern', and there is an intimacy in his translations of conceptual categories which relies ultimately on his personal acquaintance with the individuals who developed that discourse. Tschumi's attempts to formulate an interdisciplinary discourse of architecture are unthinkable without his knowledge of contemporary developments in art or his unusual literacy in poststructuralist thought, linguistic theory and psychoanalysis, whose concepts he translates into architecture.[3] Inspired by Derrida, Tschumi 'deconstructs' conceptual pairs in architectural thought that "have been accepted as self-evident and natural, as if they had not been institutionalised at some precise moment".[4] In *Architecture and Disjunction*, Tschumi leads architecture from the pyramid of reason into a Bataillean labyrinth of experience—a space that has "no inventor, no author [… and] no architect".[5] Tschumi's interest here lies in stressing the discontinuous nature of architecture beyond reason. Recurrent terms such as 'excess', 'non-sense', 'eroticism', 'sensuality' and 'pleasure' are his means to 'violate' and 'transgress' architecture's 'limits' in combinatory 'madness'. As Louis Martin argues:

> Following mainly [Philippe] Sollers (limits), [Denis] Hollier (Bataille), [Roland] Barthes (pleasure), [Julia] Kristeva (intertext), [Gérard] Genette (palimpsest), and [Jacques] Derrida (deconstruction), Tschumi introduced into his work the major themes developed by the most visible French literary critics of the 1960s and 1970s.[6]

In doing so, Tschumi's overt aim is the inclusion of a multitude of notions that he perceives as excluded and repressed into what is considered architecture—most importantly the subjective experience of space. His emphasis on the spatial experience of the human subject critiques architectural modernism for its non-experiential understanding of architecture and its preoccupation with the logic of form and function. *Architecture and Disjunction*'s writings work from the "margins"; from the initial disruption of architectural discourse in a confrontation with repressed notions such as the irrational, eroticism, and madness, to the conclusion that architecture "is… about… the conditions that will dislocate the most traditional and regressive aspects of our society and simultaneously reorganise these elements in the most liberating way".[7]

For the discussion of Tschumi's understanding of architectural authorship, it is important to consider the significance of the term montage here. A very general notion of montage aligns the term with collage and assemblage in that it contains "preformed natural or manufactured materials, objects, or fragments".[8] Peter Bürger characterised avant-garde artwork by the importance of the key principle of montage, in which discrepancies and dissonances are imported by way of its being constructed from fragments that are separated from a contextual origin and made to take on new relationships.[9] While this notion of montage may include collages, montage more specifically prioritises meaning and content over form and texture in its focus on the conceptual friction between its elements. This interest in the semantic/syntactic relationship between different fragments originated in early Dadaist photomontages that were conceived as motivated signs, and facilitated its appropriation for advertising and political propaganda. Most important for Tschumi's use of montage, however, is its aspect of resistance and subversion, in that montage, by isolating chosen fragments and arranging them to form a new single image, often is used to force the existing to

"Screenplays (The Fight)". Bernard Tschumi, 1977. Courtesy Bernard Tschumi Architects.

produce something new and to expose inherent contradictions and ruptures. Tschumi finds additional inspiration in Sergei Eisenstein's cinematographic montage, whose ideas about sequentiality, inter-shot conflict, and compositional abstraction he explores for example in the *Screenplays* series.

The concept of montage thus forms a vital part of Tschumi's architecture of disjunction. As Kate Nesbitt argues, "Tschumi's works must be seen in the light of surrealist and dadaist actions, especially because of his regular habit of juxtaposition."[10] With regard to the theme of architectural authorship, it is important to note how the postmodernist theories mentioned above are combined with the practice of montage, and seamlessly developed into a disjunctive approach to architectural design that is based on the idea of the fragment and on the formulation of various strategies for its superimposition, montage or collision with fragmented forms or unexpected programmatic contents. Tschumi's *Advertisements for Architecture*, for example, dramatically illustrate the postulated integration of the irrational by juxtaposing transgression (murder, decay) with institutionalised normality (the street/icons of modern architecture).[11]

> [T]he fear of decaying organisms—as opposed to the nostalgic search for the "outmoded purity of architecture"—appears in conservationist enterprises as much as in utopian projects. Those who visited in 1965 the then derelict Villa Savoye certainly remember the squalid walls of the small service rooms on the ground floor, stinking of urine, smeared with excrement, and covered with obscene graffiti.[12]

Tschumi's performance activities during the 1970s enacted his critique of architectural utility and gave additional emphasis to his concept of architecture as event. His strategy, then, is to further disjunction, via 'crossprogramming' or 'transprogramming', and he establishes a design method based on fragmentation and montage practices

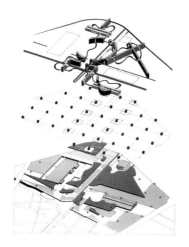

Parc de la Villette: Superimposition of three autonomous systems.
Bernard Tschumi, 1984.
Courtesy Bernard Tschumi Architects.

such as irrational combination and superimposition.[13] In particular, this method was constitutive of Tschumi's award-winning design for the Parc de la Villette in Paris in which the three different systems of lines, points and surfaces are each to represent "a different and autonomous system (a text), whose superimposition onto another makes impossible any 'composition', maintaining differences and refusing ascendancy of any privileged system or organizing element".[14] In his multiple activities, his writings, drawings, *Screenplays*, *Advertisements for Architecture*, actions and events, Tschumi thus not only claims the ground of criticism for architecture but also 'becomes' a new kind of author of architecture. The intellectual transgression of architecture's boundaries has its counterpart in an extension of the architect's authorial role and his products. By producing "[b]ooks *of* architecture, as opposed to books *about* architecture", Tschumi makes a claim for a critical architecture that operates outside and beyond traditional boundaries of the discipline.[15]

If the critique of architectural modernism articulated in *Architecture and Disjunction* relies upon the evolution of montage as a term of political resistance one can identify a similar tie between a critical position and a translatory term in *Collage City*'s argument. In *Collage City*, bricolage, and subsequently collage become a tool for the analysis, conceptualisation and design of architecture and urban space. Like *Architecture and Disjunction*, *Collage City* is acutely aware of the intellectual and artistic roots of the concepts it deploys for its critique. This critique is presented in a complexly woven text spiced with provocative questions, ironic references and bizarre analogies, often already self-consciously interrogating a stance within the process of positing it. The most important drive for *Collage City* lies in challenging architectural modernism's unitary vision and fixed signification process by confronting it with the artistic practice of collage:

> With... statements such as... Picasso's... one now enters a territory from which the architect and the urbanist have, for the most part, excluded themselves.... One is no less in the twentieth century; but the blinding self-righteousness of unitary conviction is at last placed alongside a more tragic cognition of the dazzling and the scarcely to be resolved multeity of experience.[16]

Rowe and Koetter add an architectural example to this critique by reading Le Corbusier's boldness and single-mindedness as an urbanist against Le Corbusier as an architect, "who sets up elaborately pretended platonic structures only to riddle them with an equally elaborated pretence of empirical detail, the Le Corbusier of multiple asides, cerebral references and complicated *scherzi*".[17]

Rowe and Koetter's more specific critique of architectural Modernism circles around two main points: the urbanistic isolation of Modernist architectural objects, and the failure of Modernism's unacknowledged utopianism. With regard to the latter, *Collage City* sets up an intellectual genealogy of architectural Modernism's world-view during the first decades of the twentieth century, which starts from architectural Modernism's Enlightenment roots via "the activist utopia... as a blueprint for the future" and "the threat of crisis", and which culminates in an analysis of the impact of a canonised Modernism on contemporary developments in architecture during the late 1960s, and most importantly, on the contemporary city.[18] This genealogy is important for Collage City since it constructs a history of how Modern architecture came to signify utopia; the good society, a better world, the city of tomorrow.

Rowe and Koetter criticise modern architectural discourse for its being bound by a significatory ideology—a Modernist phenomenon that Jonathan Hill describes elsewhere as "a uniform, organic system of meaning based upon mimesis, the belief that an... object is the carrier for a fixed message".[19] Rowe and Koetter suggest that the strategy of bricolage may present a way to liberate architecture from this restrictive ideology. For this discussion, they make use of the work of French structural anthropologist Claude Lévi-Strauss and his concept of *bricolage*. Lévi-Strauss terms bricolage "a 'prior' rather than primitive activity" on the level of speculation.[20] Rather than a specialist operating from a grand scheme, the *bricoleur* is a versatile 'odd-job-man' who works with material that is at hand and has already been used. "It might be said that the engineer questions

above
Le Corbusier: Marseilles, Unité
d'Habitation, 1946, roofscape

above left
Le Corbusier: Paris, terrace of the
De Beistegui penthouse, 1930-1

centre
Le Corbusier: house at Bordeaux-
Pessac, 1925, interior

below
Le Corbusier: Nestlé exhibition
pavilion, 1928

the universe while the 'bricoleur' addresses himself to a collection of oddments left over from human endeavours."[21]

When Rowe and Koetter thus employ the mind of Lévi-Strauss' bricoleur to challenge the modern architect's quasi-scientific methods and his self-understanding as the rational engineer of utopian goals, they aim to challenge the single-mindedness of architectural Modernism's unitary view in the self-understanding of its protagonist. Lévi-Strauss' discourse between the scientist's deductive logic and the bricoleur's improvised practice is characterised "by the inverse functions which they assign to event and structures as means and ends".[22] In this part of their postmodernist critique, Rowe and Koetter thus simultaneously rethink the authorial role of the architect, via the bricoleur, and suggest architectural appropriations of collage as potential new means of authorship. By arguing for an incorporation of bricoleur qualities into the role of the architect, *Collage City* aims not only for an extended responsiveness to the world but also for the ability to address problems individually without the need for a new meta-theory as 'blueprint'.

A close relationship between collage and bricolage is already suggested by Lévi-Strauss' description of collage as "the transposition of 'bricolage' into the realms of contemplation", and it also resonates in Werner Oechslin's critical statement that —despite more obvious suggestions that the term collage holds for architecture—*Collage City* "in the best tradition of art history" uses the term primarily as an abstraction;

collage as a state of mind.[23] If one allows that this abstraction also admits speculation about collage's more practical aspects, then collage holds a decisive advantage for *Collage City*'s critique: the way in which collage stresses the arbitrariness of signification and simultaneously favours incongruities, disjunctions and multiple meanings. Collage, since its experimental invention by Picasso in 1912, combined the experimental, open-ended nature of its quest for unexpected meanings with an interest in form and surface. With regard to aspects of signification in Cubist collage, it is interesting to note Christine Poggi's statement about the almost Saussurean understanding of the arbitrary nature of signs in Picasso's collages, and how it did not emphasise "the natural meanings of forms and materials... but a sense that representation is a matter of manipulating conventional signs".[24] By introducing collage practice, *Collage City* also counters the dominance of formal and functional aspects in canonised Modernism with a stimulating contemplation of materiality and a sensibility towards surface qualities innate to the visual syntax of collage. Furthermore, in Cubist collage and its overlapping and interpenetrating forms, a frame of reference is found, which—by "piercing the closed form"—allows for the contextualisation of Modernism's isolated architectural objects and a fluctuation of figure and ground, in which "planes assert a position in space along one clearly modeled edge only to bleed into the ground elsewhere".[25]

Colin Rowe's concern with a *Gestalt*-based analysis of the relationship between architecture and the spatial concepts of Cubism informed his earlier writings on architecture.[26] In *Collage City*, this spatial concept is employed at an urban scale: in their contextual discourse around the poché, Rowe and Koetter offer a middle ground for the opposition between the traditional city's fabric and Modernism's objects in space.[27] Facilitated by the strategy of bricolage and collage's potential for richness of both material texture and referential meanings, this middle ground may accommodate both concepts and suggests new formal objectives for urban design and the conceptualisation of urban space.

While Tschumi's writings in *Architecture and Disjunction* criticise architectural Modernism for its failure to address and express modernity's state of disjunction, *Collage City* argues against architectural Modernism because of the fixed role it assigned to architectural meaning in general and because of Rowe and Koetter's concern with the 'present urban predicament' more concretely. Both texts have in common that in their critique of architectural Modernism, drawn from innumerable sources outside the discipline of architecture, they employ fragmentary Modernist practices for a critical re-affirmation of architecture in the light of the 'postmodern condition'. It may be due to this focus on the architectural discipline that neither Tschumi nor Rowe and Koetter overtly discuss the role of the modern architect in their critique. However, the way in which *Collage City* reflects upon the architect as a means to redefine the architectural discipline and the consequence with which Tschumi's critique of architecture evades the question of its authorial subject both suggest that their reaffirmations of the discipline can hardly be assessed without reference to the question of architectural authorship.

The Death of the Architect?

Roland Barthes' essay "The Death of the Author", 1968, in its author-centred critique of Modernist literary criticism, lends itself as an ideal lever to unhinge Tschumi's and Rowe and Koetter's author-circumventing critiques of Modernist architecture, and to uncover how these two discourses about architecture respectively rely on certain assumptions about the architect as author. "The Death of the Author" is interesting for this discussion in that it presents three protagonists, the author, the reader and the scriptor, among whom the location of significance and meaning of any text is negotiated. In "The Death of the Author", Barthes questions literary criticism's obsession with the modern humanist subject of literature—a romanticised notion of the author—which he argues wrongly assigns primacy to the status of writing as the expression of an individual. Particularly, Barthes' seminal text gave priority to the reader's role in assigning meaning and therefore, in one sense, defining intention in a text. His text shifts focus onto the reader, who individually recreates the text in the act of reading, and onto a new writer or scriptor whose writing is based on the intertextual, and thus implicitly quotational practice of all reading and writing.

Palazzo Borghese, Rome.
From P Letarouilly, *Edifices de
Rome Moderne*, Liège, 1853/
Princeton Architectural Press, 1982.
The poché: mediating between figure and
ground and asserting "a postion in space
along one clearly modeled edge only to
bleed into the ground elsewhere".

Given Tschumi's intimacy with Roland Barthes' work mentioned above, evident for example in Tschumi's introduction of Barthes' concept of 'pleasure' into architecture, the various similarities to Barthesian thought in *Architecture and Disjunction* are not surprising.[28] Where Barthes proceeds to postulate the death of the literary author, Tschumi apparently follows and discards architecture's authorial subject. His discourse on architecture in general, and his design strategy more particularly, appear to be devoid of an individual voice. As Tschumi asserts with regard to the scheme for the Parc de la Villette in Paris: "when one system is superimposed on another, the subject—the architect—is erased".[29]

Yet the effects of Tschumi's project of architectural disjunction with regard to the figure of the author/architect are fundamentally different to those of Barthes' text. The poststructuralist literary critic Barthes implicitly expands his and other critics' scope of work by means of a new subject—who is clearly delineated in his argument. As Kate Nesbitt argues, "Barthes wants the critic, or reader in general, to take an active role as producer of meaning."[30] Tschumi's project, on the other hand, does not admit that a new role is created through its rejection of the established modernist notion of architectural authorship. When Tschumi, in one of the later essays, presents his project of architectural disjunction as "a systematic and theoretical tool for the making of architecture", and thus implies a sovereignty in the system itself, one comes to admit that, ultimately, this system is Tschumi's 'own'.[31] Barthes' argument results in an enlarged extent of critics' creativity. Tschumi's actions, even if he does not acknowledge it in his theory, have *de facto* a similar implication—they do not dispense with intention: rather they translate the site in which creative intention is seen to act, from the composition of forms in space to the creation of design methodologies and architectural systems.

Since the intellectual relationship between *Collage City* and Barthes' thought is not one of direct exchange, an obvious analogy for Barthes' author is not immediately apparent in Rowe and Koetter's book. On the contrary, rather than 'erasing' the architect, Rowe and Koetter focus their critique on his alleged state of mind. It is precisely a discussion of architecture's authoring subject that is their starting point, when they employ the mind of Lévi-Strauss' bricoleur as a challenge to the modern architect-engineer. However, upon investigation one notes a likeness between literary criticism's author as an interpretative concept that fixed the significance of a text to its authorial subject, and architectural Modernism's design ideology, which—according to Rowe and Koetter's analysis in *Collage City*'s first chapters—fixed the significance of modern architecture's objects to its utopian goals. The perspective of Barthes' text clarifies how *Collage City* argues for the 'death' of architectural modernism's ideology as a system of organic meaning. In rejecting this restriction of authorial intention, the book actively aims at a new notion of architectural authorship, on which Rowe and Koetter subsequently found their argument for "Collage City and the Reconquest of Time".[32] Almost diametrically opposed to Tschumi's argument, it is in the individual intention of the architect-author in particular that Rowe and Koetter locate the necessary shift with regard to the discipline. If we appropriated Barthes' terminology more fully for *Collage City*'s strategic argument, its authors would claim that it is only via the new authorial concept of the architect as urban 'scriptor' that the 'death' of Modernist ideology may 'give birth' to a new discourse of architecture and urban space.

Viewed against "The Death of the Author", *Collage City* and *Architecture and Disjunction* offer unexpected facets in terms of their concepts of authorship. While his theoretical writing seems to follow Barthes all too literally by 'erasing' the architect-author, Tschumi himself acts as a new kind of architectural author who aims to combine critique and creativity in one person and one activity. The former literal analogy may be intended by Tschumi, yet his literal 'erasure' would neither address Barthes' subtle camouflage of the author(-concept) as author(-individual) nor could it accommodate the former's own status as author of an architectural system.[33]

Collage City's portrait of the architect as critical scriptor on the other hand comes surprisingly close to Barthes' poststructuralist agenda for literary criticism in terms of the reflection about a discipline's perspective on creative and critical production: By challenging the restrictions of the design ideology canonised by Modernism, Rowe

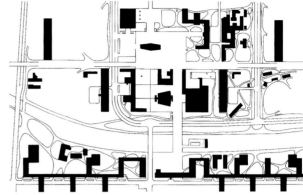

(left) Parma, figure-ground plan, and (right), Le Corbusier: project for Saint-Dié, figure-ground plan. Wayne W Copper. Presented in Colin Rowe, Fred Koetter, *Collage City*, Birkhäuser, 1984, pp. 88–89.

and Koetter reinvent the role of the architect. *Collage City* thus mirrors "The Death of the Author". Rowe and Koetter's aim is the integration of criticism into the architect's work (even if for them critical position and creative practice may not necessarily have to operate simultaneously) where Barthes, the literary critic, claims the 'dead' author's birth right to creative intention.

The comparative analysis against Barthes' text thus provides an interesting friction between the significance assigned to both Tschumi's and Rowe and Koetter's introduction of creative artistic practices on the one hand, and their concepts of architectural authorship on the other. Tschumi's own creative practice of a critical architecture is hard to reconcile with what his theory claims with regard to architectural authorship. *Collage City*'s argument on the level of architectural authorship suggests 'opening the writing' for architecture, despite its very concrete postulate of a "contextualist" approach to urban space and built form.[34]

Since neither of the texts directly addresses the issue of architectural authorship per se, this issue is to be analysed in conjunction with *Architecture and Disjunction*'s and *Collage City*'s critical propositions for architecture as a discipline and their respective view on (post)modernity.

Architectural Postmodernism and the Reaffirmation of a Discipline

The seamless continuity with which Tschumi's system of architectural disjunction aligns architecture with artistic and philosophical avant-gardisms suggests that his critique contains what Hilde Heynen has termed a 'counterpastoral' view on twentieth century architecture and modernity.[35] This view suspects a fundamental discrepancy between economic and cultural modernity, and regards modernity as characterised by insoluble contradictions. Indeed Hilde Heynen's matrix of terms, which differentiates traits in modern art and modern architecture by referring to 'transitory' and 'programmatic' as well as 'pastoral' and 'counterpastoral' concepts of modernity, provides a useful grid through which to consider the significance of Tschumi's and Rowe and Koetter's texts.[36] In terms of the first pairing, Heynen distinguishes a 'programmatic' sensibility, in which the final goal of autonomous domains such as art or science lies in their potential use for every day life, from a 'transitory' understanding, which stresses the transient meaning of the 'modern', and establishes change and crisis as positive values. A 'pastoral' understanding of modernity sees modernity as a concerted struggle for progress: underlying conflicts are ignored, when politics, economics, and culture are all united under the banner of progress. Within this matrix, Heynen claims that while many artistic practices of the early twentieth century avant-garde are based on counterpastoral views and express a transitory understanding of modernity, the views of the architectural avant-garde were programmatic and pastoral. She describes the founding moment of architectural Modernism in that an attempt was made to come up with a consistent but comprehensive response to the challenge of modernity. The Modern Movement saw itself as embodying a concept of architecture that constituted a legitimate answer to the experience of modernity and to the problems and possibilities resulting from the process of modernisation.[37]

According to Heynen's terminology, Tschumi's system of architectural montage and continuous disjunction, established in *Architecture and Disjunction* as a creative expression of modernity, is a clear departure from architectural Modernism's view on modernity: conceived from a transitory view that is combined with a counterpastoral understanding of modernity; characterised by "irreconcilable fissures and insoluble contradictions".[38]

Collage City, from the perspective of Heynen's matrix, aims to employ collage for a programmatic reinvention of architecture; its entire argument is "a project for progress and emancipation" from architectural Modernism's world-view, even if the suggested progress lies in the inclusion of history.[39] *Collage City*'s anti-avant-gardist argument, in its negation of the counterpastoral, implies something close to a pastoral view, in which the various autonomous domains "regain their common foundation"—for example when Rowe and Koetter insist on the interdependency of "the underworld of Haussmann's sewers and the superworld of Garnier's Opéra", of Superstudio's works, mystifying life on the grid, and Disney World's Main Street, or of Gordon Cullen's Townscape and Archigram's plug-in cities.[40] The book's first paragraph further supports the classification of its understanding of modernity as latently pastoral: "With these two statements... it might be possible to construct a theory of society and even a theory of architecture."[41] Bernard Hoesli refers to these lines when he argues that *Collage City* is not a book about architecture and urbanism only, but written for an audience beyond the architectural discipline—politicians, social psychologists, historians, etc.—since it contains "at heart torturing thoughts about the predicament of society and politics..., which are of great concern to the authors".[42] In its postmodern critique *Collage City* thus maintains and reaffirms architectural Modernism's programmatic understanding and its pastoral view.

From the perspective of the early twenty first century, certain limitations of Heynen's terminology are evident, since it cannot be severed from its origin in the age of industrial modernisation and its categories. In the later age of postindustrialisation and interdisciplinarity, a new complexity of culture and production challenges the traditional autonomy of individual disciplines. From this perspective the apparently obvious classification of Tschumi's architecture of disjunction as transitory and counterpastoral is once more called into question. While Tschumi argues that the non-coincidence between being and meaning, man and object have been explored from Nietzsche to Foucault, from Joyce to Lacan. Who then could claim, today, the ability to recognise objects and people as part of a homogeneous and coherent world?[43]

His theory of architecture assumes a homogeneous coherence at least for the cultural world. His critique and his architectural theory are grounded in the seamless applicability of other discourses' theories for the discourse of architecture. In the process of transposition, the content of each theory and its relevance for the architecture are not questioned, nor is the compatibility of different theories with each other at all addressed. Without this cultural coherence, those interdisciplinary transpositions would not be imaginable, and *Architecture and Disjunction* thus implies a pastoral view at least with regard to cultural production. A similar discrepancy exists between Tschumi's apparently transitory view of modernity, and his will to establish architectural disjunction as a systematic tool for the making of architecture. Contrary to his claims with regard to Bataillean uselessness for architecture, architectural disjunction itself must be categorised as Tschumi's 'project', and as such it maintains a programmatic understanding with regard to the architectural discipline.[44]

Rather than proposing the 'death of the architect', the postmodern critique of architecture in *Architecture and Disjunction* and *Collage City* offers a rich base for a discourse on the affirmation of the architectural author. If in *Architecture and Disjunction* the identity of the architect as author is mainly *defined through* an epistemological reinvention of architecture and its means of production, Bernard Tschumi's concern with the architectural author is evident in his own authorship and in the critical architecture he seeks to establish via this reinvention. While his theory is silent on his extension of the architect's authorial grasp, it is at the same time very clear about where it locates this architectural author: within a postmodern discourse of cultural interdisciplinarity. In *Collage City*, the architect is openly discussed, yet more as *an instrument for* a similar move of disciplinary reinvention than as an issue of primary

concern. *Collage City*'s argument reaffirms architecture as a societal discipline; its architect-author is neither the Modernist agent of societal utopia nor a postmodern cultural intellectual. Who this author is, or will be, remains a discursive question silently at the heart of the book's argument, put individually to each reader by its authors.

The analysis of architectural authorship in *Collage City* and *Architecture and Disjunction* gives a historical perspective to current debates about the location of intention for architects and their means of authorship by exposing a decade in the history of the architectural discipline and its authorial subject. It entails important questions with regard to the position of architects as authors within an extended discourse of architecture, especially important for architectural institutions and education. It sheds light on the emergence of sub-discourses within the discipline, and the different ties that relate architecture to the interdisciplinary discourse of culture and to the 'world of power and money', keeping open a field for the continuous discourse about the architectural subject—whether through the lens of the architectural discipline in the 1970s or more recently by way of the architect-author.[45]

'In the Mind of the Architect': Representation and Authorship in Documentary Film

Naomi Stead

This essay addresses the ways in which architectural authorship has been translated, represented and reconstructed through popular media, including narrative film, architectural awards, and especially through a specific, made-for-television documentary film: *In the Mind of the Architect*. Produced for the Australian Broadcasting Commission and first shown on Australian national television in June and July of 2000, this three part series and interactive web interface was broadcast to critical acclaim in the local press, won several awards for cinematography and architectural criticism, and is now staple viewing in schools of architecture throughout the country. There is no doubt that it was a milestone in Australian architectural culture, offering as it did a snapshot of national production at the turn of the twenty first century. It is also an extremely well made, visually stylish, thorough and sensitive documentary film. But it raises many important questions about authorship in architecture, in narrative film, in documentary film, in television, and each of these as they are reflected in one another.

In the Mind of the Architect is a work of applied criticism, didactic explication and exposition. Undeniably, though, it is also a work of narrative; it is as much the 'story' of a number of architects as it is a description of their buildings. Written and directed by Tim Clark, a non-architect, it is a story in which the many interviewed architects are cast, often somewhat equivocally or reluctantly, as agents, characters, and most pointedly as authors. Through a reading of this film as text, and also of some of the responses to it at the time of its first screening, I will examine the reception of architecture in the popular mind, and the ways in which notions of authorship are produced and maintained there. This reveals a conundrum: even as many architects and theorists might work to deconstruct the pervasive myths of architectural authorship, the world at large appears unwilling to let them go. And while this mythic stereotypical narrative is moderated in documentary film, with its pretensions to objective reportage and truthful representation, the tropes and techniques of filmic story telling remain.

It is often said that film is the only medium that is adequate to the representation of architectural experience, and documentary film seems to offer fascinating possibilities for a unique kind of applied architectural criticism. As 'popular' media, film and television also offer useful vehicles for public education, an exposition and explication

In the Mind of the Architect, Episode One. Film still. Courtesy of the Australian Broadcasting Corporation. Opening title sequence of the series.

In the Mind of the Architect, Episode Two. Film stills. Courtesy of the Australian Broadcasting Corporation. Architect Barrie Marshall as he drives through the Melbourne Gateway project, by his firm Denton Corker Marshall.

In the Mind of the Architect, Episode Two. Film still. Courtesy of the Australian Broadcasting Corporation. Architect Barrie Marshall sketching.

that could contribute to architectural culture by increasing the understanding and appreciation of buildings. This is particularly the case for a documentary commissioned by a publicly funded, free-to-air broadcaster such as the ABC, where the audience has a high interest and stake in what 'their' money is used to produce. Likewise, the status of the ABC as a national broadcaster also inevitably opens issues of a specifically or appropriately Australian architectural character.

Film has an established theoretical framework through which to understand authorship, and given the many parallels between film and architectural practice, this makes the lack of such a well-defined framework in architecture surprising. The *politique des auteurs*, as it was known amongst the group of film critics loosely aligned around the Parisian journal *Cahiers du Cinéma* in the 1950s, was famously translated and disseminated in English by the American critic Andrew Sarris, in 1962, as 'auteur theory'. His conception of the theory rested on three premises: 'the technical competence of a director as a criterion of value', 'the distinguishable personality of the director as a criterion of value', and most nebulously 'the third and ultimate premise of the auteur theory', which is concerned with interior meaning, the ultimate glory of the cinema as an art. Interior meaning is extrapolated from the tension between a director's personality and his material.[1]

While later critics such as Pauline Kael subjected these three premises (and the third one in particular) to a devastating critique, the notion of an 'interior meaning' deriving more or less directly from the 'director's personality' connects powerfully with historically determined notions of originary authorship, of 'the Romantic notion of the creative genius nurtured by an inner spark of inspiration.'[2] So while disciplinary arguments around auteur theory have occupied an enormous amount of theoretical and critical space in film studies over the past 50 years, the concept of the author as an anchor or locus of meaning remains, and remains pervasive.[3] As Peter Wollen writes, 'the *auteur* theory has survived despite all the hallucinating critical extravaganzas which it has fathered. It has survived because it is indispensable.'[4] Thus it is perhaps not surprising that the shadow of the auteur also persists in architecture—or at least in representations of it, as we shall see.

Paradigms of authorship are implicit in many areas of architectural practice and discourse, including the very concept of 'design' as conscious, singular intent. But these paradigms have rarely been as thoroughly excavated and examined in architecture as in film theory, and this opens a number of opportunities to draw parallels and contrasts. Of course, as soon as architecture is doubled and compounded by film in this way, one risks falling into a *mise en abyme* of representations of representations of representations. But it should be sufficient to say here that representations of architects in film are mediated, in turn, by film itself, and thus it is necessary to discuss concepts of authorship in both of these mediums together.

A good place to begin, then, is with representations of architects in fictive film. Numerous amusing examples can be found in Nancy Levison's essay "Tall Buildings, Tall Tales: On Architects in the Movies" where, in a rollicking descriptive trip through the many feature films that include architects as characters, she uncovers a whole range of absurd stereotypes, wishful thoughts, hoary clichés, and melodramatic characterisations of architects, in which Howard Roarke of *The Fountainhead* is only the silliest and most famous example. As Levison writes,

> Central to the mystique of architecture—in life and in the movies—is the idea of the architect as a person of marked creativity, creativity so strong it can seem a primal or religious force, allowing the architect to envision what does not yet exist, and so fundamental to his identity that others cannot help but acknowledge it, with various degrees of admiration, awe, envy, and fear. Central to the popularisation of this mystique—architect as artistic messiah—is *The Fountainhead.*[5]

There is not the space here to enter into a detailed discussion of this, King Vidor's turgid film of 1949, nor Ayn Rand's novel on which it was based. But despite the many problems with both book and film, the figure of Roarke, arrogant and virile hero architect, casts a long shadow over any discussion of authorship in the discipline. It is easy to see the 'mystique' that architecture continues to hold, despite the ugly or just plain banal realities of actual architectural practice. It is also easy to see both the cause and the stake of the mythology: this is the architect framed as artist, and by extension it is architecture licensed and authorised as high art. These are far more alluring and romantic conceptions, and they hold far more dramatic potential, than architecture conceived as a service profession, or architects as competent, organised, careful and risk-averse professionals. And as with all myths, no amount of demonstrating the 'truth' will completely dispel them. Instead the myth is amplified through popular culture. As Levison writes,

> That the dream-meisters of Hollywood, and even the more serious devotees of cinema art, should choose to disregard the exigent and adult realities of practice and fasten instead upon this seductive and adolescent mystique is hardly astonishing. One could even say that architecture, without this glamorous aura, would be an unlikely subject or setting for a motion picture. The highs and lows that mark the typically intellectual and sedentary lives of designers... do not percolate with dramatic intensity, and they lack the obvious political and social resonances, not to mention the life-and-death dealings, of courtroom battles, medical heroics, police sleuthworks, or even mobster musclefests. But the architect's mystique does offer filmmakers the chance to present wish-fulfilment fantasies in which charismatic and free-spirited personalities occupy a rarefied zone of high artistic creativity and enviable creature comfort.[6]

Thus, while actual architects may be aware of the mythic character of stereotypes about themselves, they may yet have a stake in perpetuating such representations. This brings us to the case of *In the Mind of the Architect.*

The film's publicity declares "this series is about politics, art, history, poetry, philosophy... about dreams and despair. The passions of complex individuals, their colleagues, detractors and admirers. These documentaries aim to trace the spirit and politics of these artists in our predominantly secular Australian culture."[7] This last reference is curious—does it imply that in a secular culture we must fall back on the metaphysics of art, rather than religion? Or does it imply that architects are in fact messianic creative author figures, bringing forth new worlds? The very title of the documentary series reinforces notions of authorship; and the complexities and difficulties of this, its challenge but also its drama, provides the film with its principal narrative thread. The film is loosely structured around four themes: 'Trust Me, I'm An Architect' (Issues of Faith)'; 'We've Got to Discuss This' (The Politics of Architecture)'; 'I've Got An Idea' (Inspiration in Design)'; and 'I'll Make It Work' (Confidence in Their Vision)'. While the documentary itself is more nuanced and equivocal than these rather corny titles might suggest, each theme opens a different aspect of the first-person author's role.

The vast majority of the documentary is constructed from interview footage, primarily of interviews with architects, but also institutional and domestic clients, building users, developers, politicians, planners, and members of the public. The film opens with a revealing sequence. An interview subject repeats the question he has presumably just been askcd: "A single word to describe architecture...?" What follows is a series of answers to this question, from the interviewees who will feature in the subsequent episodes. But what is most interesting about this somewhat awkward series of responses is that some answer as though the question was about *architects* rather than *architecture*. Thus 'improviser', 'collaborator', 'caretaker' and 'some kind of believer' are offered alongside 'creativity', 'richness', 'celebration of life', and the several descriptive terms that are negative, namely 'painful', 'hard', and 'tough'. This response might have been a misunderstanding of the question, or a variation in the way it was framed, but whatever the cause, the effect is that architecture and architects become interchangeable. The second thing to note about this opening segment is that the only person to describe architecture as 'high art' is not an architect at all, but a politician, in fact a former prime minister of Australia. The fact that a politician is willing to make this claim, when architects are clearly wary of doing so, is deeply revealing. Throughout the three episodes, in fact, it is conspicuous that the architects largely avoid speaking of their work in terms of art at all.

Two things complicate questions of authorship in *In the Mind of the Architect*. The first is the fact that it was made for and first seen on television. Television is often perceived as an 'authorless' or anonymous popular medium, given that "[t]he bulk of its output—news, documentaries, soap-operas, serials, adverts, come to us without any obvious 'organizing consciousness'".[8] Questions of creative agency and personal expression seem to have little relevance or currency there, even though, as with the earlier history of film, these qualities have been sought and pursued in the quest to elevate television to the status of a higher and more 'serious' art form. Another consequence of being produced for television relates to the imperatives of public broadcast programming: there is a whole branch of public television dedicated to the arts and culture, but much less of a space for general expositions of professional life.[9] The film thus sits within the field of arts magazine programmes, but it is an odd creature there—ostensibly an arts documentary, but where art is rarely explicitly mentioned.

The second complication is the complex relationship between authorship and truth within the filmic genre of documentary. If concepts of authorship revolve around the idea of an author's subjective and particular vision, then this is at odds with documentary's ideal of a transparent, 'pure' and unmediated reflection of the real. As James Naremore points out, 'the very word for the photographic lens in French is *objectif*', and there is an old argument that film, as a result of its technical nature, gives a coldly dispassionate and honest account of the world.[10] But of course this is not the case—documentary films by definition take messy, incoherent, and often contradictory events and situations in life, and transform them into a coherent, ordered, sequential visual narrative. As an inevitable part of this process, certain moments will be emphasised and made to appear more significant, others will be excluded or passed over. Documentary film is always a constructed version of reality, no matter how apparently spontaneous or truthful it might seem—it is always *realism* and never transparently the *real*.

This is of course also an historical issue, of changing understandings of 'truth' and 'objectivity' in the documentation and observation of the world, which has been subject to intensive interrogation through the disciplines of anthropology and sociology. As Allan Feldman writes,

> In the 19th century and earlier, "realism" was associated with modes of narration and visualization that presumed an omniscient observer detached from and external to the scenography being presented. It was linked to formal pictorial perspectivism and narrative linearity with all its assumptions about causality, space, and time. Yet during this period, aesthetic and scientific attention gradually detached itself from exclusive concentration on the scene observed in order to dissect and realistically depict the act of observation itself... Once perception itself became one object, among others,

of realist representation, the perceiving subject could no longer remain independent from the scene of visualization.[11]

In this context, and in the case of *In The Mind of the Architect*, this raises the question of how and why a documentary *filmmaker* can efface the position of author so effectively, but in doing so fetishise and amplify the authorship of *architects* as subjects. The relation between the invisible but all-pervasive filmmaker/author, and the very visible but rather ambivalent authorship of its architect subjects, is of key importance.

Feldman writes that "[w]hen Jean-Luc Godard declared that cinema is truth 24 times a minute, he was not asserting that cinematic content is reducible to pure information so much as noting that cinema makes truth claims 24 frames a minute. More importantly, it is the cinematic film frame that actually makes fast-forward claims to be truthful and real."[12] These truth claims are made most forcefully in documentary film, partly by an "absolute insistence... on cloaking directorial presence in signifiers of neutrality, distance, and objectivity".[13] This artifice has been explicitly challenged and uncovered, in recent years, in a new genre of documentary which foregrounds the subjectivity and auteur status of the documentary maker, and which blurs distinctions between standards of representation in fiction and non-fiction film.

The argument is that while the documentary genre dictates that the *content* should present unmediated truth, there is still considerable licence available in filmic *form*. Paul Arthur has argued that a 'new breed of non-fiction is edging ever closer to stylistic prerogatives of fictional cinema,' including the use of music to encourage emotional engagement, slow motion and other camera techniques which emphasise parts of the 'action', and the use of re-enactment.[14] These are all, in Arthur's terms, "in the process of forming a hybridized film language based not on conventions of factual argument or evidence but on the construction of spatial or temporal unities, suspense, character identification, and clearly-defined climactic action".[15] While this extreme is clearly not applicable to *In the Mind of the Architect*, with its careful journalistic standards, there is perhaps an inkling even here of a character identification akin to that we would conventionally find in narrative film. Michael Rabiger writes that:

> In character-driven documentaries, a particular character or group is chosen to generate the basic situation, then followed and perhaps interrogated over time to illustrate the situation's causes and its consequences. What emerges, after editing, is never actuality but an artfully constructed impression of it.[16]

On one level, the attention to architects in the film is not at all surprising. Following the art historical model, architectural discourse very often uses the names of architect-authors as an organisational or curatorial device, standing as a code-word not only for a particular body of work, but for the historicised set of ideas and techniques associated with it. Given that the subject matter of the documentary is loosely thematic, that it is not organised chronologically or regionally or typologically, then the device of using the speakers' own pronouncements to guide the arrangement of the material is conventional enough. But what is more unusual in this film is the close and explicit attention on these authors *prior to* or distinct from their work—one sometimes has the impression that the buildings featured are only an excuse or vehicle to hear more from the architects. This begs the question, of course, of whether an author is still an author if seen in isolation from their 'texts', and the further question of why anyone would want to make such a separation.

Many of the interviews are filmed with the architects standing, sitting, or walking in their own buildings. As well as the expected images of them sketching, examining models, talking on the telephone and being surrounded by the professional detritus of their offices, there are also a series of more dynamic scenarios. These include architect Barrie Marshall's black Porsche passing through the Melbourne Gateway project designed by his firm Denton Corker Marshall, architect Richard Leplastrier rowing his plywood rowboat on Pittwater near where he lives, and architect Kim Crestani at the wheel, discussing suburban mass housing as a succession of brick-veneer 'McMansions' glide by out the side window. 'Talking head' shots are interspersed with footage of interiors, facades, and spaces in use, and featured buildings are identified by title and architect through on-screen credits. There are also a series of aphoristic quotations interspersed throughout the film as section breaks, many of them also anchored by a canonical author, namely Le Corbusier with the house as a machine for living, Mies with less is more, Venturi with less is a bore, and so on. But aside from these overt structuring devices, the interviewees are very much at the centre of the film, and they speak for themselves. There is never any appearance of a presenter or reporter; an interviewer is never visible in the frame, and prompting questions are never audible. There is a narrator (the voice of the well-known Australian actor David Wenham) who makes a brief commentary between interviews, and this narrator's script bears some scrutiny, since it undertakes a wide variety of sometimes incongruous tasks. These include summarising and reinforcing what has been said in the preceding interviews, making provocative statements, posing rhetorical questions, making transitions between different buildings or ideas, and placing work in historical context. But in terms of an 'enunciative presence' or 'organizing consciousness', to use the language of auteur theory, this narration is a very mild intervention indeed. In spite of this, early in the film, the narration comes as close as the film ever does to defining its own set of aims and purposes. After a brief discussion of the utopianism of early modernism, with its ideal that 'the architect, cast as hero, would create a better life for everyone', followed by a series of interview snippets where architects discuss some of the problems of the modern movement, the narrator says that:

> Somewhere people lost faith in modern architecture. Today only three percent of new houses in Australia are designed by architects. Has architecture lost its way? Do architects still care about the big ideas…. And do those ideas still have the potential to change our lives?

In fact, it could be said that much of the film is dedicated to mourning the *lost* authorship of the architect in contemporary Australia, the apparent loss of creative agency and autonomous personal expression brought about by current institutional and commercial constraints. Its rhetorical question, "has architecture lost its way?" could equally be the question of whether architects have lost their authorship, and what is to become of architecture in its absence.

In this context, it is significant that auteur theory in film arose at precisely the time when film was attempting to carve a niche for itself in legitimate academic and philosophical discourse, and that one of the principal techniques for doing so was to distinguish serious, 'authorised', *art* film from the low, mass entertainment and escapism of 'the movies'. As Rosalind Coward writes,

> film was regarded as not worthy of serious study before the 1950s. Much of this attitude derived, as in the case of television today, from an unwillingness to treat an industrial, collective and popular medium as likely to be worthy of serious critical attention, and… it is worth noting here the way in which criticism inscribes the creative individual as the crucial factor, differentiating art from mass entertainment.[17]

The parallel to architecture, with its hierarchical elevation above and within building, is striking. One of the key denominators of architecture is its identification with and by an architect, unlike the anonymous or generic actions of builders. We might say that 'authored' architecture is analogous to 'art' cinema, with all its connotations of elite status and cultural capital, aesthetic inaccessibility, and the licence of art. This claim to singular artistic agency, the pure expression of the self in what appears such a mixed, technical, and collaborative art, is equally a claim to legitimacy as an art form. As Coward notes, 'it is an interesting reflection on the interdependency of the idea of art and the idea of the individual artist, that the higher the valuation of the medium *as an art*, the more likely you are to find the quest to establish an author for the work.'[18]

There are also significant parallels between architecture and film on the level of production—they are both industrialised, collaborative, and thoroughly inculcated within cycles of capitalist profit making. The problems with identifying one individual as the auteur of a film are similar to those of identifying one individual as the author of a

In the Mind of the Architect, Episode Two. Film still. Courtesy of the Australian Broadcasting Corporation.
Architect Richard Leplastrier rowing a plywood boat near his house outside Sydney.

In the Mind of the Architect, Episode Two. Film still. Courtesy of the Australian Broadcasting Corporation.
Architect Sean Godsell as he is interviewed in his office.

In the Mind of the Architect, Episode Three. Film still. Courtesy of the Australian Broadcasting Corporation.
Architect Kim Crestani as she drives through the suburbs of Sydney.

building.[19] But curiously, this question of attribution does provide a moment of contrast between the two—while filmic authorship most often rests with the director, it has also been ascribed to others—variously writers, photographers, composers, choreographers, and stars, have all been awarded the term at various times.[20] As Naremore writes, it "has even described the old-style corporate executives... who functioned as impresarios and wanted to keep their names before the public".[21] The equivalent in architecture, of the builder or engineer or client being ascribed authorship, seems unlikely. This is perhaps because of the perceived or actual level of 'creativity' in those professions—while film is widely acknowledged to be an accretion of creative works by several creative individuals, in architecture it is architects who claim, and guard, that privileged quality. Any focus on the authorial qualities of creativity, autonomy, singularity, and originality, will always coincide with the avant-garde architectural ideal of always breaking new creative ground.

In the Mind of the Architect seems to mediate then, sometimes uneasily, between the romantic mythical stereotype of architectural authorship represented so powerfully in narrative film, and the actualities of a highly equivocal, etiolated and in fact rather sheepish architectural authorship projected by the film's interviewees, as conditioned by actual contemporary practice. But it would be wrong to say that there was no projection or construction of architectural authorship here. Any canny architect knows that the projection of a stylish and creative persona makes good commercial sense in terms of publicity, and there was much to be read into the participants' manner of speaking and dressing. This was an image not lost on the audience, but it was not always well received, a reaction which extended to the visual style of the documentary itself.[22] Perhaps it is an instance of the reputed egalitarian streak in Australian society, but there was considerable audience antagonism directed towards the perceived elitism of the architects portrayed, and towards class and labour divisions in the wider architectural profession.[23]

One of the things that made the production unique was this ability on the part of the audience to respond immediately, in a series of 'web chat' discussions directly following each broadcast, and thus to interact directly with a panel of architects featured in the programme. These discussions, moderated by Janne Ryan the series producer, were then archived, forming a fascinating record of the immediate public reaction to each film. Thus it is not simply a documentary, but also an interactive interface.[24] More than three hundred posts were made in the web chat, which was a lively and immediate, if rather unruly, means of opening discussion on architectural matters amongst the general public. The curious thing was the occasional hostility of the audience reaction, which was particularly marked in its belligerence around issues of authorship—the point at which the architect's wishes take precedence over the client's. It appears that, for all the myth and mystique of architectural authorship in the public mind, it also has a dark side: that of the prima donna aesthete, out of touch with reality and recklessly spending other people's money towards their own self-aggrandisement. Of course, given the limited number and self-selected character of the respondents, there is a limit to the conclusions that can be drawn from this forum—it cannot be regarded as a representative survey. But on an anecdotal level, the discussions are revealing—many pressing issues surrounding the role, audience, and authorship of architecture were raised, in the language and terms of a lay public.

Perhaps less surprising was the reaction from the architectural profession, whose rather snide amusement was notable in the days and weeks after the broadcast. Much of the pleasure, for architects, stemmed from knowing (at least by reputation) the people portrayed, and comparing their mannered self-presentation in the documentary to what was known of them in 'real life'. The hilarity seemed largely *schadenfreude*, stemming from several revealing moments in the interviews, such as the wife of architect Sean Godsell explaining how, the night after moving into the newly completed family home designed by her husband, she realised that there was no privacy at all and she would have to get changed in the cupboard. Her patience and willingness to accommodate such an uncompromising design strategy in the name of her husband's profession seemed to only make the situation more absurd, and the scenario was also commented on in the public web chat following the episode.[25] But the pertinent thing to note here is the sense, among the architectural audience, that a spotlight had been turned on the profession;

there was suddenly a sense that the world (or at least Australia) was watching. The responsibility of these architects as spokespeople for the profession, introducing architecture to a national, popular audience, was keenly felt. Those architects who participated in the online discussion were clearly also aware of this new audience for architecture, and of the potential it held for a new architectural constituency, new clients, and new work. This is far from a trivial or incidental point: in a world where authorship is increasingly commercialised, it takes on a new range of meanings as a specialised mode of interaction and identification with an audience. Discussing the same issue in film, Tim Corrigan has noted that:

> Since the 1970s, the commercial conditioning of this figure [the author/auteur] has successfully evacuated it of most of its expressive power and textual coherence; simultaneously, this commercial conditioning has called renewed attention to the layered pressures of auteurism as an agency that establishes different modes of identification with its audiences.[26]

Likewise, architects' self-presentation as authors in documentary film is complicated by commercial concerns, the influence of public relations, and more fundamentally by its being a means of communicating and connecting with an audience which is also a body of potential clients.

Another direction through which these same issues of authorship and reception might be examined here, in closing, is through the study of architectural awards. It is worthwhile to zoom out for a moment to the more broad discursive context of the Australian architectural scene, and the way that it is viewed internationally. This was neatly emblematised in the awarding of the 2002 Pritzker Architecture Prize to the Australian architect Glenn Murcutt, who famously works alone, designing singular neo-Miesian pavilions in the bush.

As (arguably) the most successful architect in Australian history, Murcutt's influence looms large over the local scene, and his own personal mythology is thoroughly infused with the mystique of the author. He is one of the architects featured in *In the Mind of the Architect*, where he is described as 'the man most often identified with Australian architecture... the marriage broker between the Australian landscape and European occupation... between the old world and the new.' In light of this, it is evident that his work can be located at the centre of debates not only about architectural authorship, but also its imbrication with architectural identity and authenticity. Indeed, it could be argued that the mythology of (lone white male) authorship is particularly strong in Australia, where it is amplified—from the outside, at least—by a kind of frontier exoticism, and a fetishisation of site, climate, and place. This is both manifest and reinforced in the jury citation for Murcutt's Pritzker Prize, where at the same time as Murcutt's solo practice is celebrated for its singularity, his apparent uniqueness and small output is also imbued with a broad significance and applicability, one which seems able to stand for the identity of Australian architecture more generally.

The Pritzker Prize was established in 1979, and is awarded annually. With its generous prize money and reputation as the 'Nobel Prize for architecture', it is arguably the most prestigious award for architects in the world today. Its stated purpose is to "honor annually a living architect whose built work demonstrates a combination of those qualities of talent, vision and commitment, which has produced consistent and significant contributions to humanity and the built environment through the art of architecture".[27] The fact that the Prize is awarded *to an architect* is instructive. It is not presented to a building, as are many other architectural prizes, including the Australian national awards system administered by the Royal Australian Institute of Architects. It is the author who is recognised and rewarded by the Pritzker Prize, as much as the works themselves. In the jury citation for Murcutt's 2002 Prize award, J Carter Brown, the jury chairman, commented that

> Glenn Murcutt occupies a unique place in today's architectural firmament. In an age obsessed with celebrity, the glitz of our 'starchitects,' backed by large staffs and copious public relations support, dominate the headlines. As a total contrast, our laureate works in a one-person office on the other side of the world from much of

the architectural attention, yet has a waiting list of clients, so intent is he to give each project his personal best.[28]

This is a powerful image: the 'unique' master, working humbly alone, unaided by assistant or by computer, armed only with a pencil and a vision and giving his 'personal best' to the design of elegant pavilions on pristine rural or wilderness sites. There is also an irony here; in Australian circles Murcutt is perhaps the closest thing there is to a 'starchitect', he is certainly the most well known by the general public, and just because he does not have a 'large staff' or 'copious public relations support' does not mean he is not a celebrity. Clearly, though, he is seen by the jury as an *authentic* celebrity rather than one who has been framed and manufactured by spin merchants. Likewise, his marginal location, "on the other side of the world from much of the architectural attention", is upturned, in a curious dialectical reversal, to position him as a particularly deserving winner. It is as though the Pritzker Prize, itself a key instrument in the construction of architectural celebrity, has unearthed a genuine but little-known star, who gleams all the brighter for having been plucked from modest and marginal obscurity at the periphery of the known world. This is perhaps the most interesting irony of all: it is surely the Pritzker Prize, with its populist overtones and international pretensions, which is partly responsible for 'dominating the headlines' with 'the glitz of our starchitects in the first place. It could also presumably be expected to transform Murcutt, as laureate, into the exact opposite of the (modest, obscure, marginal) qualities he is here applauded for. Carlos Jimenez, another juror and professor of architecture at Rice University, writes of Murcutt's work,

> Nurtured by the mystery of place and the continual refinement of the architect's craft, Glenn Murcutt's work illustrates the boundless generosity of a timely and timeless vision. The conviction, beauty and optimism so evident in the work of this most singular, yet universal architect remind us that architecture is foremost an ennobling word for humanity.

Here again we see a reference to Murcutt, architect/author, as paradoxically 'singular, yet universal', with a 'timely and timeless vision'. The work appears to be secondary—or at least to be framed as entirely relative to and dependent upon the architect himself. The last line even leaves open the ambiguous possibility that it is the architect's own 'humanity', his 'conviction' and 'optimism', that infuses his work with such an 'ennobling' spirit. Slipping easily backwards and forwards between the characteristics of the built work and those of the architect, between subjective intention and objective form, the passage illustrates a very high level of identification between author and architectural work.

The idea of the architect as lone hero genius requires that the rosette of authorship be pinned on one lapel alone, and in Murcutt's case that is conveniently

In the Mind of the Architect, Episode Three. Film still. Courtesy of the Australian Broadcasting Corporation.
Architect Glenn Murcutt interviewed in front of the Arthur and Yvonne Boyd Education Centre, Riversdale, designed by Murcutt, Wendy Lewin, and Reg Lark.

In the Mind of the Architect, Episode Three. Film still. Courtesy of the Australian Broadcasting Corporation.
Designer Tina Engelen being interviewed within the Price O'Reilly House, Sydney, by Engelen Moore.

emblematised by his being a sole practitioner. This is surely part of the appeal of Murcutt's work: its scale is such that it *could* conceivably be all the work of one man, or at least its modest size makes it easier to overlook the inevitable industrial collaborative nature of architecture. The work is appealing, then, for the apparent equivalence or interchangeability it offers, between the independent, creatively autonomous designer and the spatially isolated buildings.[29]

On the basis of this case, it can be seen that the Pritzker Prize itself serves to reinforce and reconstruct architectural authorship in the popular mind. And there are no surprises here. The Murcutt citation is, in many ways, a classic projection of the architect as author, one that has often been reflected and refracted through popular culture, and in particular through narrative and documentary film as I have shown. The inference in all of these genres appears to be clear: without authors, architecture is not an art, and if it is not an art, then architecture is far less interesting to a general audience. The question, then, is whether there is anything more significant in this than simple romanticism, the enduring allure of the lone genius artist.

Such a privileging of the architectural author could be seen to instantiate the increasing convergence between non-fiction film and the subjects and techniques of narrative cinema. The special place that architects hold as characters in fiction film seems to support such a hypothesis, attesting as it does to a myth and mystique about architects that continues to subsist, even to thrive, in the world. It could be that casting architects as active and dynamic individual author/characters is a way of making the discipline itself attractive and interesting to a lay audience. Buildings are complex, uncommunicative, and sometimes unlovable. In explicating, describing, and making them engaging for a popular audience, architects are invaluable interlocutors and advocates for their work, this much is clear. What remains uncertain is whether this necessarily also entails taking and reinforcing the position of 'author', in the representation of architecture in documentary film.

Roland Barthes' essay "The Death of the Author" closes with the famous admonition that "to give writing its future, it is necessary to overthrow the myth: the birth of the reader must be at the cost of the death of the Author".[30] But what if the author in architecture never died? Or rather, what if that author's ghostly shade can be found as a character, stylishly dressed, sensitive, professional and creative, in any number of films past and future? Perhaps, in closing, it is useful to turn the question on its head, and ask why it is that in architecture the reader has refused to be born. And the answer to this must be that popular audiences for architecture, as reflected in awards like the Pritzker Prize, in narrative film, and in documentaries like *In the Mind of the Architect*, continue to perpetuate, reconstruct, and keep alive the mythical stereotype of the architectural author.

In the Mind of the Architect, Episode Three. Film still. Courtesy of the Australian Broadcasting Corporation.
Architect Harry Seidler interviewed in front of his own design for the Rose Seidler House, Wahroonga.

In the Mind of the Architect, Episode Two. Film still. Courtesy of the Australian Broadcasting Corporation.
Architect Richard Leplastrier.

Dislocation

If the first section brought together essays that consider the forces and processes that operate in different ways and through different media to affirm and solidify architectural authorship, the contributions in this section instead consider various 'parallel practices' which, from the perspective of architectural history and theory, can be defined in relation to, and must be seen to modulate, conceptual categories in architectural discourse itself. All these essays share an acknowledgement that architecturally conceived authorship might be disturbed by forces 'semi-external' to architecture, and all investigate this possibility through historical analysis. The section therefore includes essays that bring forth and critically discuss different kinds of dislocating discourses and practices of authorship in architecture. The contributions highlight the ways in which notions of authorial control in architecture are challenged by forces and figures external to the profession. They examine design processes that steer away from, or subtly dislocate, the idea of the architect as author, and that create new possibilities for outsiders as well as for 'marginalised' members within the professional community, and they investigate how such efforts have been received and retrieved in architectural criticism and history.

Katja Grillner's work investigates the emergence of the landscape designer as a figure in the eighteenth century and uses an analysis of the discourse that grew up around landscape gardening to reflect on issues of gender and authorship which condition contemporary practice both in architecture and landscape. In her essay "Nature's Lovers", she shows how, through eighteenth century landscape design discourse, an alternative authorial relation between designer and work is explicitly articulated, and an author position is constructed that is considerably more nuanced and sensitive than its architectural counterpart. But if landscape design discourse on the one hand can be argued to thus dislocate and slightly destabilise architectural discourse, as it concerns authorial engagement and control, Grillner's essay also points to the underlying strategies of control, objectification and domination that are arguably still in operation in the landscape paradigm that she examines.

Charles Rice's work examines the design history of the domestic interior, and considers how the interior has come to define the spatialities of contemporary life. His essay "Interior/Image", charts a brief history of architecture's relation to the interior since the beginning of the nineteenth century, and locates key points at which this relation becomes articulated in ways crucial for thinking about authorship. In this history, Rice argues, authorship becomes articulated less in terms of an individual will, whether it be that of an architect, decorator, designer or inhabitant, and more in terms of articulations of discipline and control that are enacted through particular regimes and practices of domesticity. The essay brings out the uncanny sense of doubleness, the co-creation of interior as image, and interior as domestic space, that marked its emergence, and that through the proliferation of new media, continues to resonate profoundly in our everyday lives.

Jonathan Hill's work suggests a multiplication of architectural authorship, through the acknowledgement of users, site- and weather-conditions, and a vast range of other forces, as authorial agents in the creation of architecture. His essay "Sweet Garden of Vanished Pleasures" tells the story of Derek Jarman's cottage and garden at

Dungeness, and brings out its affinity with a picturesque mode of reading and engaging landscape. By filtering his portrait of Dungeness largely through biographical detail and anecdotes, Hill on the one hand affirms the authorial convention which makes this place 'Jarman's' (that is—of his design); at the same time, however, he draws our attention to the subtle ways other agents have been brought into a continuous process of making the site, and are allowed to continue to transform the site after the death of its author.

The essays in this section identify the arts of landscape, interior, and gardening as three arenas external to architecture and yet closely connected in their effects or relations to questions of architectural authorship. There are a number of connections between landscape and interior design as spatial design practices. While they developed as independent art forms in the eighteenth and nineteenth century respectively, they remain closely intertwined with architecture today. Both 'landscape' and 'interior' are concepts that signified from the start an image as well as a physical space, they share a binding relation to questions of life-style and cultures of 'leisurely' (and excessive) consumption, and from the perspective of architecture 'proper' they are frequently looked down upon as secondary concerns.

Concluding the section, Hill's portrait of Dungeness and the filmmaker Jarman's creation of a 'precious' and 'vulnerable' home, brings the previous intertwining stories of interior and image, landscape and lovemaking, up to the present day.

Nature's Lovers: Design and Authorship in the Eighteenth Century Landscape Garden

Katja Grillner

Pont Chinois à Attichi à M. la Duchesse de la Tremouille

> In all, let Nature never be forgot.
> But treat the Goddess like a modest fair,
> Nor over-dress, nor leave her wholly bare;
> Let not each beauty ev'ry where be spy'd,
> Where half the skill is decently to hide.
> He gains all points, who pleasingly confounds,
> Surprizes, varies, and conceals the bounds.
>
> Alexander Pope,
> *Epistle to Burlington*, 1731[1]

In the eighteenth century, landscape gardening developed into a paradigmatic art—a privileged site for philosophical reflection. The figure who would act as a designer in the landscape garden often had a professional background as an architect, poet, painter or gardener.[2] In addition the independent land-owner was often strongly engaged in the role of designer on his own grounds. Despite such a variety of backgrounds, the significant body of garden theoretical publications that emerged in England, France and Germany in the 1770s, upon which this chapter builds its argument, invoked and described a very specific designer figure at work in the landscape garden, a character whose features we can already begin to discern in Alexander Pope's lines cited above.[3]

This chapter seeks to characterise the emerging landscape designer, his modes of operation and authorial status, and to examine how this figure differed from and represented a challenge to corresponding notions in architectural design. It will suggest that through this figure a potentially destabilising critique to the concept of the architect as author was launched. In contrast to the architect, the designer figure that emerges in the landscape garden is characterised by a series of *actions* that take place over time in a dynamic *process* of interpretation. These may be described as interchanging reading and writing the site—the landscape designer does not invent, but rewrites. This study builds on the discursive construction of this figure (i.e. how it was characterised by garden theoretical writers at the time), and not on studies of actual design processes at the time.[4] It presents the significant tropes that secured the features of this designer figure and further shows its firm inscription in a gendered power game that casts a troubling shadow over the softly spoken, sensitive gardener.

Authorship in the Landscape Garden

"What is an author?" asks Michel Foucault in his 1969 lecture and essay.[5] He asks this question in spite of the proclaimed deaths and disappearances of the author, not because he distrusts those proclamations, but because he believes in the continued significance of the 'author-function'—a notion that he argues needs to be critically understood and analytically applied both to historical and current discursive formations.[6] By shifting our attention away from the author, seen as a particular individual, to the function that is performed by the very attribution of a text, or a series of texts, to an author, Foucault provides a critical analysis not only of how and for what purposes these attributions come into being, but also of the controlling power that lies in the securing of an author to set the limits of a particular discourse straight.[7]

While Foucault's detailed analysis is limited to the world of textual discourse and of literary authors, the history and idea of the architect as author—and here the emerging landscape designer—may still be constructively analysed through the central notion of the author-function. This notion is directly linked to the idea of a bounded 'work' which can be explained and interpreted through its relation with its author, regarded as its point of origin. It further assumes a particular unity within the work, and between different works by the same author, i.e. the author is regarded a consistent source of expression. Foucault is keen to emphasise that, between different places and moments in time, the particular types of discourses that demand an author-function vary. Different cultural and historical contexts thus give rise to different understandings of what a 'work' may be, and how it is to be perceived as 'bounded'.

The attribution of authorship to architectural works has constituted an essential feature of the discipline of architecture since the Renaissance, and is closely linked to the process whereby architecture in the fifteenth century attained a more elevated position among the arts. In the eighteenth century the art of landscape gardening underwent a similar process. Through the formation of a new design discourse, independent from architecture and constructing a significantly different kind of designer 'author' than the architect, the emergence of the landscape designer raises a number of significant challenges—both with respect to the nature of the 'work' and the process of its design—and further opens up for alternative ways of discerning authorship even within architectural discourse proper.

This essay is structured around three intertwined narratives—the first relates the nature of the 'work'—how landscape becomes an object of design perceived as a gendered body for the designer to dress. The second takes the point of view of the 'author'—the designer—presenting the particulars of this 'dressing' process and its hermeneutical characterisation as one of humble interpretation. The third concerns the uneasy relation between landscape gardening and architecture—in the garden theoretical texts the architect was characterised as a counter-figure to the landscape designer. The dislocation of architecture in the landscape garden involved its shift to the realm of ornamentation (a beautiful button on the dress).

Landscape as an Object of Design

[T]he ground gently waves in both over easy swells and little dips, just varying, not breaking the surface; no strong lines are drawn; no striking objects are admitted.[8]

In Thomas Whately's *Observations on Modern Gardening*, 1770, the first comprehensive theoretical work on the landscape garden to be published, we are provided with a detailed vocabulary serving to describe landscape in terms of its spatial and material properties. An important objective of this treatise was to validate the bold claim of its opening sentence that "gardening/… /is entitled to a place of considerable rank among the liberal arts" by providing it with a proper theoretical foundation.[9] The treatise thus had to characterise both the artist and the particular skills that this art form required, as well as the nature of the work of art and its effects. While Whately's text greatly emphasises the work of art (the object of design), the artist, the designer figure, is rather articulated implicitly, as the primary addressee of the treatise. The reader becomes—understands—the artist through the act of reading. It almost exclusively addresses the *appearance* of nature's materials and forms, that is, it understands landscape primarily as a unified—albeit complex and varied—object of experience, not as a compilation of particular lawns, flowers and trees.[10] Whately's general descriptions are mostly very dry, while his accounts of actual parks and gardens activate the landscape for the reader in very particular ways. In the passage quoted above "the ground gently waves" over the "swells". The ground is one of the five "materials" that Whately teaches the designer to consider in the making of modern gardens, and it is also the first element to be characterised in the book: "The shape of ground must be either a *convex*, a *concave*, or a *plane*; in terms less technical called a *swell*, a *hollow*, and a *level*."[11]

The notion of landscape originally denoted (and still does in Scandinavian and Germanic languages) a political territory, a region that has a degree of independence. In the seventeenth century, however, the notion became a visual concept—denoting a perspective view of natural/rural scenery—which during the eighteenth century further shifts and expands to denoting in addition the actual physical grounds whose arrangement conditioned such a view. Landscape became an object of design in addition to its being an object of regard (for view). A figure that is frequently used to describe this new object is the body, a gendered body, sometimes a goddess (Nature), which we will discuss shortly. Whately's particular concern with the spatial and material effects of the different components of a real landscape composition, as well as with the effects of movement in the garden, reflects this transition. Once the physical, inhabited, landscape became an object of design, its four-dimensional appearance had to be articulated along these lines.

While one could articulate the French classical garden, in spite of its radical dimensions and magnificent scale, using an essentially architectural vocabulary and aesthetic, the landscape garden demanded a new language.[12] The spatial organisation of the landscape garden was structured upon *succession*, *transition*, and *contrast*, mediated through *paths* and *sightlines* which connected *scenes*, experientially and visually. These scenes were calculated to *strike* the eye and *please* the imagination. Buildings were subordinated to their situation in the landscape, considered decorative *objects*.[13]

The imagery presented to the eye in the landscape garden was however not radically new to the eighteenth century visitor—Arcadian landscapes had been presented in stage sets and paintings in previous centuries. The experience of purposefully spending one's leisure time inside those scenes was however quite new. The transformation of landscape representations into four-dimensional material reality, posed a difficult challenge. While the landscape painter or draughtsman might be skilled in finding the perfect view, and to twist it a little if needed, the landscape designer had to be skilled in the art of spatial transformation, rearranging physical grounds and structures of vegetation. In paintings and set designs from the previous century the illusion of landscape was created for an audience placed in more or less fixed positions. The landscape designer on the contrary had to address a moving subject. Movement was, according to Watelet, inscribed in the very idea of the landscape garden:

"movement, that very spirit of nature, that inexhaustible source of the interests she inspires, will constantly impel him to enliven the landscape he is designing". This in contrast to architecture where "the spectator perceives, guesses, but feels only a mild desire to alter his position".[14] Landscape gardening is here understood as a temporal art. The spatial experience is drawn out, extended, over time by the walking (or riding) body.

A different temporal aspect was the demand for designing within given situations. New gardens and parks were usually arranged within already existing sites such as old hunting grounds or previous garden designs. Existing trees on the grounds ought to be mapped and preserved as much as possible, since new plantations never would look their part from the start.[15] And the existing topography was the key to the laying out of efficient sightlines, unifying the garden within so called 'home-scenes', or expanding its boundaries out towards the countryside. And the existing topography was the key to the laying out of efficient sightlines. Even if a landscape garden was designed to completely rearrange (and erase) its given site (which would be the case, for example, when replacing an older formal park or garden, or if a site was simply barren or 'ugly') the designer would still consider his work in terms of 'improvement'—not 'invention'.[16] He would thus have to imagine the site in its unadorned, natural state as a point of departure. This might have been one of the most challenging novelties to the architectural designer in the garden: not the very notion of adapting his design in view of the existing site—any clever architect would be expected to do that, but the demand for a physical and seamless integration of the new design (the improvement) with what should be imagined as the unadorned 'natural' state of the site.

In the landscape garden, 'to listen to nature' implied specifically a concern with the *appearance* of nature. The object of design, the landscape garden, never stands *in relation to* nature but *presents* nature: "Of all arts", writes Jean-Marie Morel "this one will deviate the least from truth. It does not study nature to learn how to imitate her, but simply to assist."[17] A particular kind of realism is contained within the aesthetics of the landscape garden, a cult of the real that neither seeks metaphysical, nor scientific truths, but rather aims at capturing the poetic truth of appearance.[18] A complex balancing act is performed as the designer delicately frames the real, an act which may be closely related to the representational acts performed by painters and poets at the time.[19]

The landscape designers' actual background varied from painter, to poet, to architect, to gardener and landowner. Even though the designer role was increasingly professionalised towards the end of the eighteenth century, the designer figure described

Frontispiece to Jacques Delille, *Les Jardins —Ou l'Art d'Embellir les Paysages*, Paris, 1782. Courtesy of the Royal Library in Stockholm. Two muses in debate. The two women are surrounded by the attributes of painting and architecture; a palette on the rock to the left, and a pair of compasses, and rulers fallen to the ground by the feet of the two women. The woman to the left (Painting) points with her right hand up to the garden in the background; with the left hand she holds down a drawing on the rock. The woman at the right (Architecture) gestures down towards her lost instruments on the ground and behind her we see another drawing torn in the side showing what looks like a rectangular parterre with a circular pond in the centre. In front of the muses lies a piece of string the usefulness of which is unclear, even for Painting, as she is engaged in the art of gardening (Girardin specifically recommended the use of strings for 1:1 mock ups in the landscape). In the preface to this poem Delille clarifies that the landscape garden belonged to the domain of philosophy, painting and poetry, not to architecture (p ix).

in the garden theoretical publications of the 1770s essentially lacked a unifying title. Titles applied were as varied as: 'the designer' or 'the artist' (Heely); 'gardener' (Whately, Morel, Hirschfeld); 'the artist', 'the garden artist', or the 'composer' (Morel); 'the decorator of gardens' or 'the composer of pastoral scenes' (Watelet). Hirschfeld introduces yet another name in German; 'anlegern' which may be translated as a person who 'lays out' the ground.[20] The use of gardener is qualified by Morel in a telling way: "With gardener I mean the artist of taste who composes the gardens, not the one who cultivates them", a statement that clearly shows the need for a delineation of a proper author-function.[21] In order to promote the status of landscape gardening to a form of art in its own right it was necessary to define a controlling agent (composer).[22]

The Methodical Architect: Flat Papers and Symmetrical Forms

> It is not then as an architect or a gardener, but as a poet and a painter, that landscape must be composed, so as at once to please the understanding and the eye.[23]

> Architecture will seek precision in lines and neatness in detail; but the subtleties of garden art depend on a kind of charming indecisiveness and on a certain insouciance, so well suited to Nature.[24]

> ... to make symmetrical forms, and to calculate spaces, he [the architect] will want to subject Nature to his methodical combinations and will believe that he thereby embellishes her; but he will disfigure her.[25]

In the French writings quoted above, by René Louis Girardin, Claude-Henri Watelet, and Jean-Marie Morel, the landscape designer is articulated in relation to literary and painterly practices of representation, while the architect is positioned as an oppositional figure. Landscape composition is described as a representational practice of a particular kind, while architecture is portrayed as an art of rational precision, of stillness and of totalising control. With the ambition to establish landscape gardening as an independent art form, followed a need to distance gardening from its previously subordinated role as an essentially architectural art. By using the architect as a figure that stood for everything that landscape design essentially challenged (regularity, symmetry, order, stability, and stillness) its radical newness and its less easily definable counter-concepts (irregularity, variation, confusion, flow, and movement) were articulated.[26]

A particular source of unease for the architect in the landscape garden may have been the inappropriateness of the traditional tool for ensuring control of architectural design—the projective drawing. In Morel's opinion the geometrical plan gave no more accurate representation of a future landscape composition, than a direct foot-print of a painter's model provides a recognisable portrait of the man. "Here only the eye and the feeling may judge the effects, and exercise their sovereign power to decide."[27] The architect released in the garden found himself immersed, it would seem, in a landscape without a plan.[28] Did he get lost?

> [While] the architect will choose simple plans, symmetrical shapes, easily accessible proportions, and evenly balanced volumes, ... the decorator of gardens will favour designs full of mystery, dissimilar shapes, immediate visual impressions rather than underlying principles, and such surprises as resist uniformity.[29]

The landscape designer is continuously described by Watelet as something of a mystic in contrast to the rational architect. The crucial difference is located in the essential nature of these designers' engagement with their object of design. Watelet imagines an architect engaged in garden decoration: He stays inside his study, staring at a flat sheet of paper, and happily fills it with symmetrical terraces and walkways, as if the object might be created, as it were, *ex nihilo*.[30] The landscape designer, on the other hand, engages in his object, that is the existing site, in situ. The landscape is for him an object that is presented for the designer to be improved rather than invented.[31] The very term 'design' is used by Whately to denote in particular "choice, arrangement, composition, improvement, and preservation".[32] In spite of these seemingly soft and subtle instruments of control, the landscape (its topography, waters, grounds, and vegetation) does not escape objectification. In his own mysterious ways the landscape designer exerts the power that comes with intention. It is a rather complex power game directly modelled in disturbing ways on all-too-familiar, repressive gender determinations.

'And this Body will be Beautiful': the Designer as Lover

> In trees and flowers, smooth leaves are beautiful; smooth slopes of earth in gardens; smooth streams in the landscape; smooth coats of birds and beasts in animal beauties; in fine women, smooth skins; and in several sorts of ornamental furniture, smooth and polished surfaces.[33]

Edmund Burke's *Enquiry into the Sublime and Beautiful* had, as a populariser of the sensational aesthetics developed from philosophers such as Locke, Berkeley and Hume, a great influence on the garden theoretical writings at the time. Published in 1757 it offered a vocabulary and a conceptual framework by which to describe and discuss the landscape garden in terms of the experiential effects of its scenes and settings. In describing the role of 'smoothness' in the experience of beauty Burke, in the quotation above, juxtaposes objects of different scales and kinds such as animal furs, leaves, slopes of earth, water streams, fine women's skin, and ornamental furniture. The beauty that is perceived by the eye on encountering such objects is directly related by Burke to the pleasure experienced in touching smooth objects with the hand—"I move my hand along the surface of a body of a certain shape", he writes, and:

> [I]f a body presented to that sense [the eye] has such a waving surface, that the rays of light reflected from it are in a continual insensible deviation from the strongest to the weakest… it must be exactly similar in its effects on the eye and touch…. And this body will be beautiful.[34]

Burke's account of the beautiful shows the extent to which landscape—its slopes and waters—had become (in spite of its scale which made actual cuddling impossible) an aesthetically, but also erotically, charged object of experience and consumption. In Joseph Heely's *Letters on the Beauties of Hagley, Envil, and the Leasowes*, published in 1777, we find 'nature' appointed 'mistress' to the designer—her humble lover.

> But now, while you make her your mistress, and study only to humour her with the dress she knows will best become her, you cannot do wrong, nor need be under the least apprehension that perfection will not follow: Elegance will mingle with simplicity; everything will be lively, picturesque.—Attentively cautious of falling into the justly exploded errors, you robe her in the ease of careless dignity, follow her through all her sweet recesses with the hand of graceful novelty[35]

To design means along these terms to dress-up, beautify, and apply the make-up to the body/face of nature. The passage is highly sexually charged. The object being addressed, the woman, is never named explicitly as 'nature'. The metaphor becomes uncomfortably literal as we imagine the landscape designer in the act of making love —following "her through all her sweet recesses with the hands of graceful novelty". It reads as a filmic montage where we are simultaneously offered the double image of a voluptuous body and a sensual landscape and are further, in a semi-pornographic manner, invited to indulge. "But remember", Heely warns the designer, "she demands to be consulted with the most scrupulous attention; she is a rigid and peremptory goddess; the least insult to her charms, will drive her away; yet, approach her with modesty, she will suffer a thousand liberties, and stay with you forever."[36]

In the immensely popular didactic poem *Les Jardins*, Jacques Delille provides another telling example of the intricate love affairs that the making of a landscape garden demanded.[37] He stages a conversation between *La Nature* and *Le Genie*. Nature calls the genius to consider her "imperfect works" and the genius sets out to explore the land where he finds "a hundred beauties asleep":

He hurls himself forward, He approaches from all directions,
Foiling through these masses where a hundred beauties are asleep,
From valleys to ridges, from woodlands to prairies,
He touches up the varied scene in passing through.
[...]
He does not compose, he corrects, he purifies.
He completes the lines sketched out by nature.[38]

A forceful yet delicate lover at work. But who will in the end be the legitimate author of the improved grounds? There is no designer to firmly hold the pen. Neither does 'mother nature' have any control other than that of inviting the genius onto her grounds. A third entity—the genius of the place (genius loci)—rules in this metaphorical model. Nature is wild and raw and demands improvement. Only the genius, an entity we may understand as a site-specific spiritual force, can realise the full potential of the grounds. In a fluttering moment our genius materialises. We see a man. He is excited. Is he not familiar?

The designer as agent for the genius' force, has to put himself in the position of the genius, metaphorically taking his hand and allowing himself to be guided. Delille's model follows, as most popular garden writers in the latter part of the century, the concise advice offered by Alexander Pope already in 1731 to Lord Burlington: "Consult the Genius of the Place in all; That tells the waters to rise, or fall, ... Now breaks, or now directs, th'intending Lines; Paints as you plant, and as you work, designs."[39] Listening closely to the calls of 'mother nature', the designer learns to interpret her voice and to act out the genius' "touch-ups" on the ground. As Delille reminds us, he "does not compose, he corrects, he purifies. He completes the lines sketched out by nature." The eighteenth century notions of genius loci in landscape design and of genius in romantic literature bear interesting relations in the way they simultaneously reinforce and radically destabilise authorship.[40] Reinforcing by releasing a cult of the naturally gifted designer and poet possessing a talent that essentially could not be taught. Destabilising by the ultimate deferral of authority to an external force.

Both Heely and Delille perform in their texts a double strategy, carrying out a sober didactic mission while seducing their readers by ill-concealed erotic encounters. The first is however fully dependent on the latter seduction. The metaphors they apply follow the conventions of erotic and pornographic landscape descriptions. The long history of 'somatopic' descriptions—where a place is read as a body or part of one (and vice versa)—is traced by Darby Lewes in her study *Nudes from nowhere: Sexual Utopian Landscapes*. She notes the significant difference between the age-old gender-inscription of nature as female (mother earth), and of aestheticised nature (landscape) as 'mistress'. The latter has no reproductive function and provides 'mere' pleasure for her lovers.[41] By the application of stereotypically gendered metaphorical models, the landscape garden was constructed as a masculine arena designed by and for the pleasure of men. The woman, if present in the company of men, was imagined as a fairy muse, as a passage later in Heely's *Letters* confirms: "But what is your opinion", the letter-writer asks his friend, "of a *living* object as well, to grace such dainty Elysian bowers—such lady ground?—Don't you think a fine blooming girl like Maria *********, in Arcadian dress, with *her* easy graceful air, *her* exquisite shape, and delicate complexion—she, whose cherub lips, in enchantment pout luxurious...."[42] Maria, however pleased she might (or might not) have been in real life as the addressee of this verbal love-making, is in this fantasy a mere object for the eye, the 'greedy eye' (an expression earlier used by Heely at the sight of a Venus statue).[43]

While these erotic or even semi-pornographic metaphors and conceptual models were not uncommon in eighteenth century Europe, their repressive and alienating effects on a female readership both now and then, are crucial to acknowledge and examine along with their sustained discursive impact. In her study of eighteenth century women travel writers Elizabeth A Bohls describes the complex challenges that women were facing as they sought to engage as writers in an aesthetic discourse formed exclusively for a male

Woman on the swing; her 'assistant' to the left. Plate from Georges-Louis LeRouge, *Detail des nouveaux jardins à la mode*, Paris, 1776–1788. Courtesy of Collection Centre Canadien d'Architecture/Canadian Centre for Architecture, Montreal.

readership.[44] She further points to how, in contemporary aesthetic theory and historiography, this original exclusivity is sustained by a continued application (and even stricter reinforcement) of the conceptual limits set up in the eighteenth century.[45] Likewise it is apparent from a feminist critical theoretical perspective that the discursive formation related above, so remarkably present within the eighteenth century infatuation with landscape, is highly complicit in processes of gender inscription and control even today.[46]

Frequently invoked as a thought-provoking metaphor, the notion of landscape links very directly in our imagination to physical reality (and vice versa). This direct link between discourse and the physical world harbours a rich poetic and critical potential, but generates distinct unease when confronted with the gender-specific landscape discourse of the eighteenth century. Heely's invocation of Nature as his mistress translates into a real body that the designer and his friends walk upon. In following *her* demanding voice, whole villages could be erased—tolerating no 'mis-fits'—or in less dramatic cases simply hidden behind new vegetation.

Following in the Steps of Nature: Listening to Her Voice

In Delille's staged encounter between *la Nature* and *Le Génie*, only nature has a speaking part. The genius responds by direct action, forcefully, but silently. As discussed above this account implies a perceptive designer responding to the calls of nature, but carefully measuring his acts against the advice of a genius loci who *shows* the way but never reveals his secrets by *telling* them. In *Discourse Networks 1800/1900* Friedrich Kittler portrays the time-period from the mid-eighteenth to mid-nineteenth century as dominated by hermeneutical modes of operation, obsessed by the search for meaning. Voice gains primacy over text and in particular it is Woman's voice (the mother-tongue) which mediates the original spirit of nature to man.[47] The spiritual engagement with the search for meaning as presented by Kittler bears a striking resemblance to the activities ascribed to the landscape designer at the time.

Kittler begins his investigation by looking at changing pedagogical ideas concerning basic alphabetisation—how to learn to read (the ABC book). Towards the end of the eighteenth century the *mother* is urged into the study chamber to take on the role of teacher for her children. By play the child should effortlessly learn to read, and only by *meaningful* rhymes and verses. This in contrast to the old spelling method—coming to understand a word by summing up its individual discrete letters (s+h+i+p=*ship*)—which had produced ABC books filled with nonsense rhymes. Now, on the contrary, the child gets to listen to its mother's voice while watching the flow of language on the page. The written text becomes a mere 'vessel' for the 'mother-tongue'.[48]

The gender implications of this shift are drawn by Kittler far into the German politics of education and state bureaucracy. Here our main concern, however, is to consider some crucial connections to the landscape discourse generated in England and France: the triad of *woman-nature-mother*. By linking *reading* to the voice of the mother —the original woman—and erasing the material status of the text as a system of signs —significant letters—*language* became but a *channel* leading us back to 'mother nature' herself, as Kittler argues, quoting Herder: "Language is only a channel, the true poet only a translator, or, more characteristically, *he* is the one who brings Nature into the heart and soul of his brothers."[49]

Could the landscape designer be understood as such a poet? His language made up of slopes and bushes, waterfalls and clumps, temples and ruined castles? In *Théorie des Jardins*, published in 1776, Jean-Marie Morel portrays the designer's efforts:

> Without interruption the gardener will follow closely in the foot-steps of nature, contemplate her, question her, examine her with curiosity; step-by-step he follows & he will not be satisfied until he has captured her in all the purity of her lines, copied the forms with scrupulous precision, and presented her effects in their absolute truth.[50]

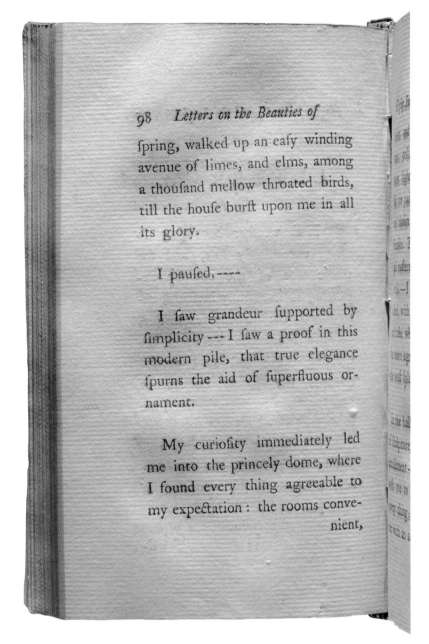

98   *Letters on the Beauties of*

spring, walked up an easy winding avenue of limes, and elms, among a thousand mellow throated birds, till the house burst upon me in all its glory.

I paused, ----

I saw grandeur supported by simplicity --- I saw a proof in this modern pile, that true elegance spurns the aid of superfluous ornament.

My curiosity immediately led me into the princely dome, where I found every thing agreeable to my expectation : the rooms convenient,

This poet/designer/lover is trained to listen, to seek the original voice of nature, and to translate for human eyes/ears/understanding—i.e. to re-write the text of nature. A 'text' that as much as the rhymes of the ABC book only gain their full meaning when the original voice is echoed by its material presence. The notions of interpretation, of reading and writing, that can be used to characterise the eighteenth century landscape designer are closely aligned with those pertaining to early modern hermeneutics. Interpretation moved away from divine to cultural forms of expression, a step towards modern secularisation.

Kittler describes an intricate dependency between reading-writing-re-reading-re-writing in which different agents take on different roles. The woman *reads* but does not *write* (she is a voice surfacing only in a text). The man *writes* and then *re-reads*. His muse, the woman, is his reader onto whom he, the poet, may reflect his *translation*, and consider its resonance with nature, his model.[51] This static system naturally had its rebels, but nevertheless many women who wrote poetry or literature at this time did so anonymously or under male pseudonyms. 'Real' authorship, Kittler argues, was essentially reserved for men.[52] Were these agents of reading and writing equally operational in the landscape garden?

Even though the experience of landscape gardening was something that took place *on site* by visitors immersed in 'real' nature the landscape discourse of the time had significant affinities with literature. Written descriptions operated as a crucial re-productive force for the landscape garden in the 1770s. Via text a particular mode of experience was communicated and taught.[53] Thomas Whately, whose *Observations on Modern Gardening*, 1770, constituted the first systematic effort to write a treatise on landscape gardening, applies the notion of *character* to discuss and qualify the expressive potential of different scenes in the garden, that is how the experience (the reading act) becomes meaningful and in turn how it may be produced (the writing act).

The most valued species of character is the *original* character. Less valued are in descending order the *imitative* and *emblematical* species. The *emblematical* character is achieved through allusions to history, poetry or tradition, made by rather crude devices such as sculptures or inscriptions.[54] The *imitative* character represents a "scene, or an object, which has been celebrated in description, or is familiar in idea".[55] Artificial ruins, lakes, and rivers are mentioned as examples of devices employed to create this type of character. According to Whately these objects are on the one hand nothing but representations (copies), but on the other hand special in that they are produced in materials and dimensions that are identical to their model (originals). The *original* character, in contrast to these two, aims for more than delighting the eye—it affects our sensibility. It is produced directly by "objects of nature"—certain properties and certain dispositions of them—and requires "no discernment, examination, or discussion, but are obvious at a glance, and instantaneously distinguished by our feelings".[56]

By discovering and framing original characters in nature the landscape designer achieves the power to affect our sensibility. Creating an experience where the representational distance is totally collapsed—we 'feel' magnificence, simplicity, cheerfulness, tranquillity or melancholy—these characters are present as such for our imagination. Whately does nothing to hide his excitement—"when the passions are roused their course is unrestrained".[57] The original character is a powerful vehicle. It pierces through the 'veil' of the representational landscape. It shreds a hole in the carefully crafted text, and it exposes, as it were, the skin of nature, undressed. This is for landscape gardening the equivalent of the 'poet's sigh', that introduces Kittler's *Discourse network*—*Ach!* in German, *Oh!* in English. An expression beyond language, the poet's sigh is the sign of the soul.[58] In the garden, the genius of nature breaks through.

A potential conflict surfaces in Whately's praise for the original character. To break through the veil dramatically, the veil needs to remain firmly in place. To open a 'channel for nature', to speak with Herder as cited above, through the 'language' of landscape gardening, the designer must continue to 'write' and the visitor to 'read' a largely representational landscape. Whately is aware of this and we can follow his attention to the different modes of expression in his careful descriptions of landscape scenery in the book. It is clear that landscape design in practice depends on a balanced orchestration of different expressive means operating in conjunction. In theory, however, it needs to be firmly anchored to a position outside of its universe. Landscape gardening demands an 'other'—is this nature as such?

While landscape discourse, following the general development of a sensationalist aesthetic in the eighteenth century, establishes a discourse that values immediate (unmediated) impressions ('obvious at a glance') over mediated (narrative or mythological) forms of expression, its practice remains highly dependent on mediation. Design (production) and experience (reception) is tightly woven together in the literal writing and reading practices of the landscape garden. In strikingly different ways the writers struggling with developing a theory of the landscape garden in the 1770s in effect *write* the landscape garden.[59] That is, they construct modes of experiencing it, ways of reading it. And for this they use language—text only—no images, no plans. From these descriptions the reader may construct his own models for measuring his future acts of landscape design and/or appreciation.

Dislocating Architecture? The Excess of Buildings

In architectural discourse over the last decade, landscape has repeatedly been invoked as a 'way out', a rescue, from the dead ends of Modern/postmodern architectural ad-ventures. The arguments set off in many different directions—from calls for site-specificity grounded above all in 'natural' conditions (climate, topography, light); to an awareness of larger urban and regional scales of interventions; to a recourse to mythical searches for genius loci as a new ground for architecture; to landscape as a story-teller fabricating instances of architecture.[60] While these different invocations ultimately share an acknowledgement of the crucial importance for architecture to act in the 'expanded field' which landscape art and design discourse may provide the tools for mapping and understanding, they also set up radically conflicting critical positions, reflecting different degrees of spatial control.[61] These conflicting positions can also be traced back to the landscape garden. Thomas Whately reveals in his treatise an ambivalent attitude towards buildings:

> Buildings are the very reverse of rocks. They are absolutely in our power, both the species and the situation; and hence arises the excess in which they often abound. The desire of doing something is stronger than the fear of doing too much: these may always be/.../bought by those who know not how to choose.[62]

In referring to the excess of buildings Whately implies that the rich believed they could buy their way to a stylish garden, by paying for the construction of a profusion of temples, seats, and Turkish pavilions. These people "know not how to choose" and therefore they aimlessly order buildings, the element in gardening that is "absolutely in our power". In the landscape garden design decisions were taken from the perspective of scenic composition and landscape experience in varying degrees of motion. "In a garden", Whately continues, "they [buildings] ought to be considered both as beautiful objects and as agreeable retreats; if a character becomes them it is that of the scene they belong to."[63] The process of designing a building thus never began with an isolated idea of a particular aesthetic to boast with, a function to fulfil, or an interesting technology to experiment with, but from an analysis of what the particular landscape scene demanded in terms of both expression and use. This did not imply that the buildings necessarily were mere scenographic devices, in terms of being designed only for visual consumption, and deficient when it came to real usability, materiality, and three-dimensional structure. As completed buildings they ought (if contributing to an original character of the scene) to bear all the marks of authenticity. The close affinity that has been pointed out between landscape design, literary and painterly practices, and their mutual engagement with imaginary worlds, does not imply that landscape design was ultimately withdrawn from the physical, material world of real experiences and uses. Rather its particular magic built on the arrangement of the 'real' (natural landscape) as 'art'.

The dislocation of architecture in the landscape garden, as referred to initially in this chapter, is thus a rather intricate affair. When Whately describes buildings as a material "absolutely in our power" this is not a singularly positive characterisation, but something to be rather suspicious of. In landscape design the ultimate challenge was importantly to be capable of operating *without* absolute power, to be receptive and intuitively adaptive. At the same time, on a much larger scale, the instruments of spatial control that were effectively actualised in the landscape garden through establishing sightlines, removing and adding vegetation, transforming the shape of slopes and boundaries, constructing lakes and rivers, erecting buildings on strategic locations and so forth, were immensely powerful. But while the landscape designer, on the one hand, in order to fulfil the expectations of a perfected work of nature, had to strive towards a radical taming of often vast expanses of land, the recommended design strategies did not mention the forcefulness demanded from this power-struggle. On the contrary, as has been shown, the designer was asked to always remain within the landscape scenery —a sensitive interpreter of nature rather than a commander in total control.

If architecture thus might have suffered a relative dislocation in the landscape garden, in terms of its buildings becoming subordinated as ornaments to the larger landscape composition, the ideal relationship it had established since the Renaissance between the architect as author, and his work, the building, as a controlled composition, remained in implicit operation on a much larger scale. Simultaneously however, as this text has shown, landscape, as a new object of design in the eighteenth century, profoundly upset conventional aesthetic notions (arguably still in operation in spite of repeated attacks) of the nature of a work of art. First the landscape garden was prescribed to be unbounded in a very particular way—remember Pope: "He gains all points who pleasingly confounds, / Surprizes, varies, and conceals the bounds."[64] This in itself, the evasive nature of the 'authored' work—the object of design—proved a particular challenge to the ways in which a proper author-function could be assigned. Then, all traces of art should ideally be concealed in favour of nature, an entity praised in its embodied form as a Goddess and mistress, but ruled by a genius. The designer should limit the use of his artfulness to simply embellish and improve—recall once more Pope's advice: "treat the Goddess like a modest fair, / Nor over-dress, nor leave her wholly bare." This means that the author-function, as constructed in the landscape theoretical discourse at the time, in relation to the designed landscape, is curiously two-headed in a very literal way as the landscape designer is credited with his skilful acts of design, while simultaneously guided by, *and* assuming the position of, the genius of nature.

An alternative authorial relation between designer and work was thus explicitly articulated through the emergence of landscape design. An author position was constructed that was considerably more humble, nuanced, and sensitive, than its architectural counterpart. In critical response to the high-Modernist architects' tabula rasa approach to urban as well as landscape contexts, this particular mythology was re-actualised in the late 1960s. This time with particular recourse to phenomenological foundations. In Christian Norberg-Schulz' appeal to the genius loci he urges the architect and planner to engage in a consensual friendship with the place, rather than a love affair.[65]

If this chapter has traced one point of origin for the critique of architecture that is implied in this Modern tradition, it has also pointed to the underlying strategies of control, objectification and domination that are arguably still in operation in this paradigm. A discourse grounded in Mother Nature produces, in the eighteenth century, a seductive landscape, a landscape of 'liberty' that poses as a democratic arena.[66] It belonged to the privileged who knew how to read it, and fully, only to those who could engage as designers—true lovers—in the landscape garden. It hid away anything that disturbed the happy scene.

Interior/Image: Authorship and the Spatialities of Domestic Life

Charles Rice

When architecture and authorship are considered in a domestic context, the relationship between architects and clients is immediately raised as an issue. This relationship is often characterised in terms of a mutual fear: architects fear that the integrity of their work might be compromised through the messiness of inhabitation, and the client as inhabitant fears that the architect's spaces will be too constricting, either not allowing the sort of domesticity hoped for, or denying that to which one had become accustomed.

Attempts to deal with this situation feed discussions about how architecture is perceived in broad cultural and societal terms. These range from the moralistically educative, whereby clients and 'the general public' should learn to respect and understand the 'particular creative approach' of architects, to the ethically populist, whereby the messiness and particularity of inhabitation should be embraced by architects in a relinquishing of the authorial imperative. The question of authorship is thus polarised around the figures of architect and client/inhabitant, and mostly articulated in terms of distinct and conflicting needs: those of the individual architect or the discipline as a whole, versus those of clients and society at large. This chapter seeks to think about the question of authorship outside of this unhelpful framework. It shall do so by considering in a new way a concept and material manifestation that has been ill-considered in its own right: the domestic interior. The interior is reducible neither to architecture, nor to the domain of the inhabitant. Historically, it emerged at the beginning of the nineteenth century and enabled the articulation of a specifically modern form of domesticity. The chapter charts a quick history of architecture's relation to the interior since the beginning of the nineteenth century, locating key points at which this relation becomes articulated in ways crucial for thinking about authorship. In this history authorship becomes articulated less in terms of an individual will,

The Drawing Room. Engraving. From Thomas Hope, *Household Furniture and Interior Decoration*, London: Longman, Hurst, Rees & Orme, 1807.

whether it be that of an architect, decorator, designer or inhabitant, and more in terms of articulations of discipline and control that are enacted through particular regimes and practices of domesticity.

The Emergence of the Interior

The domestic interior emerged as a new and distinct concept at the beginning of the nineteenth century. From the point of this emergence, it had significance as both a spatial condition, and an image-based condition. Semantically, it was only from the beginning of the nineteenth century that the interior came to mean "The inside of a building or room, esp. in reference to the artistic effect; also, a picture or representation of the inside of a building or room. Also, in a theatre, a 'set' consisting of the inside of a building or room." The meaning of 'interior decoration' corroborates the idea of its deliberate fabrication, its staginess, and its distinction from architectural construction: "The planned co-ordination for artistic effect of colours and furniture, etc., in a room or building."[1] The first use given is *Household Furniture and Interior Decoration*, the title of Thomas Hope's 1807 book, which, along with Charles Percier and Pierre Fontaine's *Receuil de Decorations Intérieurs* of 1801, marked the domestic interior as a site of professional struggle between architects and upholsterers. Indeed, the interior emerged as the newly articulated entity at stake in this battle, properly belonging to neither profession.[2]

A significant aspect of the emergent interior is its doubleness, the sense of its physical, three-dimensional spatiality, as well as its sense as an image, whether it be a two-dimensional representation such as a painting, a print in a portfolio of decoration, or a flat backdrop that could conjure up an interior as a 'scene'. This image-based sense also encompasses the interior as an imaginary or projected condition, one which could conjure the spatial from flat representations such as architectural plans, or which could transform a given spatial condition into something other.[3] Ultimately, the interior's doubleness has to do with the interdependence between image and space. Yet one is not simply transparent to or prior to the other. Both have particular effects as interiors, and a consciousness of the interior has been produced out of their often disturbing interdependence.[4]

Conceptually, the interior's emergence has meant that it is able to be considered as separable from the 'inside space' provided for it by domestic architecture. One lineage of this emergence can be traced through the problems architectural representations had with the internal conditions of buildings. As Robin Evans has shown, the interior attained a legibility in representation with difficulty. He notes that the 'room' became a new subject matter for architectural drawing from the mid-eighteenth century. This occurred in relation to the emergence of the developed surface drawing, a drawing type which could show all of the inside elevations of any given room folded out relative to the room's depicted plan. This was a more comprehensive representation of an internal decorative scheme than could be achieved through the traditional architectural section drawing, which could only show in detail one inside elevation of any given room at any one time.[5] Yet moveable furnishing that might give a sense of spatiality to such decorative treatment was a problem for such a flat representational technique, and tended to sit anchored to the wall, or floated awkwardly in quasi-perspective in the void-like space between walls.[6]

For Evans, the interior emerged in a spatialised sense in the early nineteenth century when the distribution of furniture became linked to the idea that there were a variety of ways of occupying a room. Such a notion of changing and variable distribution, both for furniture and for a room's occupants, began to outstrip the ability of the developed surface drawing to represent this condition adequately.[7] What emerged as a response to the inadequacy of the developed surface technique were representations that showed that "the *furniture* occupies the room and then figures inhabit the furniture".[8] These emerging representations, often rendered in watercolour, were, in an historically specific sense, interiors.[9]

Regimes of Domestic Discipline

Yet the role the emerging interior played in relation to architecture at this time cannot simply be given an account in representational or decorative terms. The interior figured in a far less obvious though no less pervasive way in architecture's interventions in social reform through the nineteenth century. The plan was the major device by which architects sought to reform housing, and thereby the living conditions of both rural and urban poor. As Evans has again shown, one of the failures of urban reform in particular was consequent upon "middle-class reformers and professionals who sought to re-mould the lower classes in their own recently crystallised image."[10] The middle classes' image of themselves crystallised around the interior, being grasped through the interior as itself an image. Architectural techniques of planning and the imagistic presence of the interior came together in a crucial way in Robert Kerr's well-known treatise *The Gentleman's House*, 1864, where the architect is directed to imagine a future interior that the planned distribution of rooms and functions would allow in a completed domestic building.[11] This imagination of a future interior condition, aided by the architect plotting furniture onto the plan, fed back into the planning process, guaranteeing the optimal arrangement in terms of how comfort, convenience and privacy might be imagined at the level of the interior. Hence a link emerged between the conceptualisation of suitable domestic plans, and the framework they afforded for imagining and eventually realising suitable interiors.

It was not class alone, but rather how class-based preferences were embedded in particular techniques applied to reform that led to the indifference of the lower classes to the sorts of reforms that were being instigated. The 'comfort' of the poor was to be found in a condition which Evans suggests predates a conscious uptake of the plan and its potentials for arrangement as an explicit architectural technique. This 'pre-interior' condition involved the commingling which confused divisions between families, ages and genders, precisely the conditions that bred immorality and disease in the eyes of reformers reflecting the mores of the middle classes, and precisely those conditions that an 'unstructured' sense of the plan allowed for.[12]

Later in the nineteenth century, a different sort of discipline went to work on the middle class image of themselves through the mechanism of the interior. The science and therapeutics of psychoanalysis made the middle class family the object of a particular sort of 'non-coercive regulation'.[13] As Michel Foucault has shown, this form of power arose from psychoanalysis' "deployment of sexuality" within the bourgeois family.[14] This deployment was not simply focused on the family as defined by the conjugal couple and their children. Rather, it worked through spatial articulations. Foucault writes of spaces haunted by sexuality, spatial conditions created to produce, regulate, separate and link multiple sexualities, and that derived from the planimetric reforms of earlier in the century:

> The separation of grownups and children, the polarity established between the parents' bedroom and that of the children (it became routine in the course of the [nineteenth] century when working-class housing construction was undertaken), the relative segregation of boys and girls, the strict instructions as to the care of nursing infants (maternal breast-feeding, hygiene), the attention focused on infantile sexuality, the supposed dangers of masturbation, the importance attached to puberty, the methods of surveillance suggested to parents, the exhortations, secrets and fears, the presence—both valued and feared—of servants: all this made the family, even when brought down to its smallest dimensions, a complicated network, saturated with multiple, fragmentary and mobile sexualities. To reduce them to the conjugal relationship, and then to project the latter, in the form of a forbidden desire, onto the children, cannot account for the apparatus which, in relation to these sexualities, was less a principle of inhibition than an inciting and multiplying mechanism.[15]

The import of Foucault's argument is that psychoanalysis is not simply reducible to the 'family drama', but must be considered in relation to a spatialisation of its power and effects. Considered in relation to the interior, this spatialisation figured at several moments and in different ways in psychoanalysis' development.

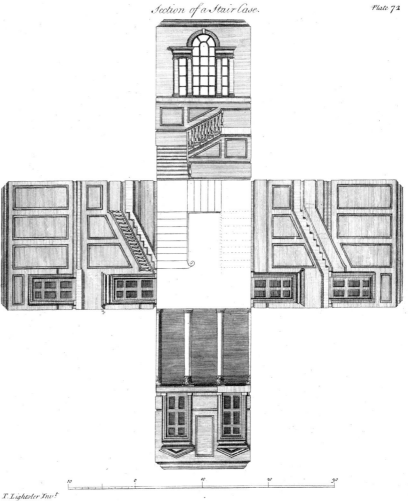

Section of a Staircase (also known as developed surface drawing). Thomas Lightoler. Engraving. From William Halfpenny, *The Modern Builder's Assistant*, London, 1757. By permission of The British Library.

T. Lightoler Inv.t

In *The Interpretation of Dreams*, Freud produced a litany of interpretations of the domestic scenes of dreams. In developing these interpretations, he drew on and critiqued earlier theorists of dreams who associated parts of a house, especially its interior, with parts of the body. The advance Freud made from these earlier theorists was in his suggestion that associations were made in dreams between unconscious impulses and domestic scenes, and further, that sexual imagery was hidden behind these supposedly innocent scenes.[16] In one particular example, Freud highlighted the association of a derogatory German term for woman, *Frauenzimmer* (literally 'women's room'), with the dream symbolism of rooms:

> Rooms in dreams are usually women ('Frauenzimmer'); if the various ways in and out of them are represented, this interpretation is scarcely open to doubt. In this connection interest in whether the room is open or locked is easily intelligible.... A dream of going into a suite of rooms is a brothel or a harem dream. But, as Sachs has shown by some neat examples, it can also be used (by antithesis) to represent marriage.[17]

This sexualised consideration of the domestic as dream symbol is augmented in the later theorisation of the psyche by what might be called an organisational consideration. In his introductory lectures on psychoanalysis from the beginning of the twentieth century, Freud used a suite of rooms to explain the structure of the unconscious:

> ... an individual process belongs to begin with to the system of the unconscious and can then, in certain circumstances, pass over into the system of the conscious. The crudest idea of these systems is the most convenient for us—a spatial one. Let

us therefore compare the system of the unconscious to a large entrance hall, in which the mental impulses jostle one another like separate individuals. Adjoining this entrance hall is a separate, narrower, room—a kind of drawing-room—in which consciousness, too, resides. But on the threshold between these two rooms a watchman performs his function: he examines the different mental impulses, acts as a censor, and will not admit them into the drawing-room if they displease him.... The impulses in the entrance hall of the unconscious are out of sight of the conscious, which is in the other room; to begin with they must remain unconscious. If they have already pushed their way forward to the threshold and have been turned back by the watchman, then they are inadmissible to consciousness; we speak of them as repressed. But even the impulses which the watchman has allowed to cross the threshold are not on that account necessarily conscious as well; they can only become so if they succeed in catching the eye of consciousness. We are therefore justified in calling this second room the system of the preconscious.[18]

What is striking about this spatial metaphor is the way in which it doubles the domestic situation experienced by Freud's clientele, a situation which, in many cases, had driven them toward the therapeutics of psychoanalysis: impulses held on the threshold of rooms, jostling between individuals, acts of guardianship that permit or deny access, the important eye needing to be caught. One gains a sense that disciplined behaviour in the bourgeois domestic interior offers a powerful explanatory tool in Freud's understanding of the structure and workings of the psyche, and also that this sort of domesticity was the context wherein psychoanalysis went to work. One of Freud's most celebrated and problematic cases, that of Dora, is a veritable psychoanalysis of the bourgeois family and its social relations, its theories and therapeutics intervening to restore proper inter- and intra-familial relations, and thereby psychological health.[19] The development of these theories and practices for many years took place in Freud's consulting rooms, which from 1908 were contiguous with the Freud family apartment at Berggasse 19 in Vienna. Domestic spaces by circumstance, these rooms were made into quintessential bourgeois interiors through the arrangement of Freud's vast collection of antique sculpture and imagery, resonating with Walter Benjamin's characterisation of the bourgeois interior as the space of the collector.[20] This space allowed the exteriorisation of Freud's own interior life, but also the interiorisation of Freud's science and therapeutics of the subject.

Modernism's Transformed Interior

Returning to the context of architecture and design at this point in time, one sees the ongoing 'battle' between architecture and interior decoration playing out in a new set of circumstances. The sort of intense, cultic relation to collected things that marked the interior's cultural prominence from around the middle of the nineteenth century became subject to a critique about the level of authorship that was being exercised by architects in this realm. While Freud's personal collection of antiquities mediated the psychoanalytic scene, marking the beginnings of a 'regulatory and non-coercive' form of therapeutic discipline, architects' relation to an interior of things was reaching a limit point. Benjamin outlined what he calls the interior's liquidation under the 'total art' of Jugendstil/Art Nouveau.[21] The individuality expressed within the interior shifted from being that of the inhabitant, mediated through the collection, and became that of the architect-turned-artist, whose artistic 'vision' constricted the inhabitant.[22] This sort of architectural approach to the interior was coming under attack from a nascent Modernism. In his parodic fable of the "Poor Little Rich Man", Adolf Loos attacked Jugendstil architects' authorial desire to provide a total artistic organisation for life. In the fable, a rich man decides to let art into his home as a response to his bourgeois ennui. The man goes to "a famous architect and says: 'Bring Art to me, bring Art into my home. Cost is no object.'"[23] The architect directs all of the interior decoration trades to create an entirely new interior for the man. The rich man is overjoyed, but soon discovers that he has to learn how to live in this new interior, that it is so tightly bound by the architect's vision of art and an artistic life that there is literally no room for him to accumulate his own belongings and have them placed within the interior. Significantly, the full impact of what the artist/architect has done to the man is communicated through the presence of his family, who, on the occasion of the man's birthday, for the first time come into the frame as inhabitants of the interior. They present the man with gifts, and the man then summons the architect to help him place these in an appropriate manner. The architect becomes irate, claiming that the man should not accept such 'traces', that through his design of the interior, he has given the man everything, and has 'completed' him. The interior spatialises a frozen image of the man, and the actions of his family show at once their exclusion from this image. In Benjamin's terms, at the moment of its total capture by architecture as art, the interior as a space of inhabitation is liquidated.

Aside from the immediate critique of turn-of-the-century architectural culture, the fable points to architecture's ineffectuality in regulating life. While the interior develops and links to wider powers of regulation and discipline, architecture makes an attempt to capture it in the name of art. But the hubris of this attempted takeover leads to the interior's liquidation, and a wider malaise of design culture, however short-lived. It was left to architects with a particular cultural commitment to pick up the pieces. Loos embarked on this process conceptually by positioning the family as that which bore the brunt of the ills of contemporary architectural culture; in this way Loos offered a kind of therapy for the poor little rich man. Architecturally, Loos divorced interior from exterior in order to go to work on the interior in a particular way. The field of intervention was not decorative but rather spatial. Loos' 'invention' of the *Raumplan* began to position the inhabitant in a different way, and also to set this very idea of positioning to work within the architectural material.[24] At this moment, the battle between architects and decorators was not simply about who should "consent to provide for the furniture", to use Robert Kerr's phrase, though Loos' built-in furniture implicitly organises the subsequent arrangement of furniture provided by the inhabitant.[25] Rather, the battle had to do with the spatiality of the interior being transformed and manipulated architecturally. Loos made a claim for the 'power of the example' in articulating the *Raumplan*, that is, the way in which an experience of the three-dimensionality of the space would act as a kind of instruction in domesticity.[26] Le Corbusier used the *promenade architecturale* to figure and direct movement through the free plan. The coherence of this plan was tied to the figuration of the promenade, and its legibility was provided through its enaction in movement. The world was reborn for the moving subject seeing in a new way from the vantage of the *promenade*. For Le Cobusier and for Loos, a modern subject submits to the authority of these new spatial manipulations, becoming modern in this submission.[27]

The Artist in Her Painting Room, York. Watercolour on paper. Mary Ellen Best, c. 1830s. © York Museums Trust (York Art Gallery)/Bridgeman Art Library.

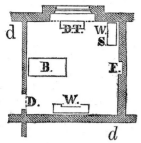

ENGLISH BEDROOM.

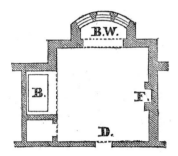

FRENCH BEDROOM.

Scale 1 inch to 30 feet.

B.   Bedstead.
D. T. Dressing-table.
W.   Wardrobe.
W. S. Washstand.

Plan diagrams of English and French bedrooms, indicating furniture arrangements. From Robert Kerr, *The Gentleman's House, or How to Plan English Residences from the Parsonage to the Palace.* London: John Murray, 1871 [1864].

Choice and Control

In articulating a further shift in architecture's relation to the domestic through the 1950s, Reyner Banham argued that industrial design's positioning within a consumer market meant that architects could not control the total design of domestic environments, but rather should act as mediators of this market on behalf of clients. Architects should be able "to exercise choice and background control over the choice of others".[28] Sylvia Lavin has recently allied this shift with one towards an affective environmental design, especially evident in the work of Richard Neutra.[29] This sort of environmental design developed in a close relation to what she characterises as a psychoanalytic culture that was ameliorative rather than regulatory. One could argue this difference in terms that suggest that the sort of 'interiorised' discipline present in a bourgeois Freudian psychoanalysis became broadened and more diffuse together with a reconstrual of design culture in terms of the affective environment. Following Gilles Deleuze, one might articulate this as a shift from discipline to control. The enclosed nature of the interior is no longer that which ensures regulated behaviour by virtue of the mechanism of enclosure. Rather, behaviour is tracked and variably adjusted through the extensive environment, which is as much informational as spatial. In this conception, the availability of choice, especially in a consumer context, becomes a different means of control. As Deleuze puts it: "Man is no longer man enclosed, but man in debt."[30]

For Lavin, the development of environmental design is coupled with a shift from the modern to the contemporary.[31] As a concept, the contemporary lies in the desire to make things 'of the present', whereas the modern is locked into a historical characterisation, even as conceptually it would purport to be 'the new'. The contemporary is changeable in terms of how one desires to provide a new 'look' or 'mood' for what might be an old (or even a modern) structure or set of relationships. The content of that look is precisely what is changeable. It is the subject of Banham's design by choice.

What is important to note here is how this category of the contemporary allows a different take on the image as part of the interior's doubleness. The image is the prime marker of the contemporary. The effects and affectivity of the contemporary, even as they involve a sense of an environment, are those of the image. This presages a further shift in considering how images constitute the domestic environment, and indeed the interior, currently.

The Spatialities of Contemporary Life

In a contemporary domestic context, the question of authorship has to do with the ubiquity of the image in culture, the way in which cultural identifications are made through visual media. To think of the interior as a formation of images (and what the spatial articulations of these might be) is to think through the way in which subjectivity and identity are bound up in the question of authorship, though not so much the authorship of a domestic environment as the authorship of a self. In this light it is instructive to sample from the range of contemporary media images of, and beamed into, the domestic environment. The range extends between the ominously but aptly-named Martha Stewart Living Omnimedia, and the reality TV of *Big Brother*. Framed conventionally, these examples might seem to be polarised around normalising versus perverting images of the domestic. Yet their mechanisms of mediation actually unite them, revealing regimes of control and echoing disciplinary structures that have been constitutive of domesticity since the nineteenth century. *Big Brother* doesn't bear witness to the collapse of an ideal domesticity so much as it tests, quite literally, powers of suggestion in a new mutation of the domestic beyond the nuclear family. The phenomenon of Martha Stewart belongs in the same category of the production of the domestic through regimes of control that direct self-fashioning, though her regime is perhaps more insidious in that the voice of Big Martha speaks through an illusion of individual choice. The ten month incarceration to which Stewart was sentenced in 2004 for misleading an investigation into her business affairs—half of this sentence was spent under 'house arrest', perhaps the ultimate example of the shift from a disciplinary society to a society of control—does not represent the irony of the supposed collapse of her vision of the domestic into that of *Big Brother*. Rather, it shows how they are intertwined from the start: Stewart's incarceration time will have reacquainted her with the mechanism of her own success.

There is also a way in which sites of domesticity have moved out from their traditional, interiorised enclosure. Where often the presence of media, and especially electronic media, in the domestic interior is conceived of in terms of an infiltration and a disturbance of that environment, there is a way in which the interior can be seen to be constituted through this very condition of transmission and reception.[32] The locations where interiors and their attendant domesticities might be created become variable. Paul Virilio has described a condition where house, automobile, and the speed and displacement of visual images mutate into a condition he terms the 'static vehicle', these becoming "extensions of domestic inertia".[33] This sort of condition does not signal the abandonment of architecture and architects in the face of interactive media and the proliferation of domesticities beyond the bounds of a conventional sense of enclosure. Rather, one discovers the ways in which the communication, reception and utilisation of images cuts across conventional architectural designations such as inside/outside and city/room. It even has the potential to confuse the difference between categories such as car and house.

Understanding the emergence of the interior, and the sense of doubleness that marks this emergence, means that one is able to think about the formation of domesticity in terms of this doubleness. Through the nineteenth century the relations between image and space managed a sense of enclosure for the interior. But repositionings of design and new conditions of media into the twentieth century have opened new possibilities for thinking about the construction of the domestic, and what forms and locations the interior might take and relate to in its imagistic and spatial doubleness. Above all, one gains the understanding that questions of authorship in the domestic context are not so neatly tied up or simply contested between the supposedly 'interested parties' of architects, designers, clients and inhabitants. While these parties figure in the historical circumstances that have been traced here, one must consider that the historical contingency and variability of their relations is but one aspect of how domestic formations might be understood.

Sweet Garden of Vanished Pleasures: Derek Jarman at Dungeness

Jonathan Hill

The Ness

Three thousand years ago Dungeness did not exist.[1] Today it is one of the largest shingle expanses in the world. Covering more than seventy square kilometres and nearly twenty metres deep, the headland is gradually moving north-east along the coast as the tides collect and deposit shingle. Attempting to counter this daily drift, trucks collect and carry shingle in the opposite direction.

Wind-swept and ignored, Dungeness developed without planning guidelines. Buildings, objects and artefacts litter the headland like detritus washed in on the morning tide. Dungeness is a laboratory layered with experiments past and present: each a memorial to a time and a technology.

> 100 wrecks, one a German submarine.
> 40 fishing boats.
> Two lighthouses, three more destroyed.
> A submarine oil pipeline to France built for Operation Pluto in 1944.
> A National Nature Reserve (NNR) and Site of Special Scientific Interest (SSSI).
> Railway carriages now used as houses.[2]
> "Acoustic mirrors" to detect incoming aircraft at sea.[3]
> A nuclear power station with two reactors.
> World War Two remains: anti-tank fencing, barbed wire, a concrete blockhouse, a giant timber "T" left over from radar experiments.
> A one-third scale miniature railway.[4]
> Pylons and power lines.
> Fishermen's cottages, some still in use, others now second homes.
> Two public houses.
> A bird sanctuary and observatory.[5]
> Gravel pits worked by rusting cranes.
> A lifeboat station.

The largest intervention is Dungeness nuclear power station. Dungeness A is a Magnox reactor that first became operational in 1965 and closed in 2006. Dungeness B, an Advanced gas-cooled nuclear reactor first operational in 1983, is due to close in 2018. Both will be subject to lengthy and costly site clearances. Financial and safety concerns—including operational failures, the decay of ageing reactors and long-term dangers of radioactive material—led recent British governments to reject further nuclear power stations. But, as a means to limit carbon emissions and reduce dependency on foreign energy supplies, the current Labour government is considering their revival. The proposal is highly contentious inside and outside the Labour party. The rising sea-level is a further deterrent to building a new nuclear power station at Dungeness. Marshes to the east and west are increasingly susceptible to flooding.

Centuries of disregard and sporadic development have made Dungeness abundant in nature, with over 600 plant-types and numerous coastal birds and insects, some very rare. But the situation is double-edged. Birds congregate around flooded gravel pits and the outfall pipes from the nuclear power station, which discard waste, warm water and sewage and encourage sea-bound biological growth. While, on land:

Sea Kale, Crambe maritima, is the Ness's most distinguished plant. There are more of them here than anywhere else in England—they come up between the boats. Crambe are edible, but a radiologist told me that they accumulate radioactivity from the nuclear power station more than any other plant.[6]

Prospect Cottage

In spring 1986, driving through Kent with Keith Collins and Tilda Swinton, searching unsuccessfully for a bluebell wood to film, Derek Jarman suggested a visit to Dungeness: "There's a beautiful fisherman's cottage here, and if ever it was for sale, I think I'd buy it."[7] Built in 1900 for the Richardsons, a local fishing family, Prospect Cottage had timber walls tarred black, bright yellow window frames, a black corrugated roof, black chimney and red clay chimney pots, colours that Jarman retained. Changing the windows to "old-fashioned" ones with smaller glass panes,[8] he stripped away carpets, wallpaper and plasterboard to reveal timber rooms: "The house is a gem. It has four rooms off a central corridor and is lined with rich tongue and groove."[9] In three rooms the timber boarding was waxed; the other room, at the front, was painted a "clear translucent Naples yellow"[10] with a white ceiling.[11] Jarman added simple furniture, "much of it created from bits and pieces from scrapyards and from beachcombings".[12] Gradually he moved in many of his favourite possessions. Noting that "The house is warm in the winter and cool in the heat",[13] Jarman's diaries describe familiar pleasures: writing, reading, listening to the radio, watching planes pass overhead and the weather change.

> Prospect Cottage is the last of a long line of 'escape houses' I started building as a child at the end of the garden: grass houses of fragrant mowings that slowly turned brown and sour; sandcastles; a turf hut, hardly big enough to turn around in; another of scrap metal and twigs, marooned on ice-flooded fields—stomping across brittle ice.[14]

Prospect Cottage Garden

Jarman was "always a passionate gardener—flowers sparkled in my childhood as they do in a medieval manuscript".[15] When he was just four his parents gave him a copy of the four-hundred page *Beautiful Flowers and How to Grow Them*, 1926: "*Beautiful Flowers* was to be my bible for many years: I pored over its exotic pages, scribbled in coloured crayon across its illustrations and made my first drawings of flowers by copying it."[16] His first garden commissions were for an opera, John Gielgud's 1968 production of *Don Giovanni* for the English National Opera at the London Coliseum, and a film, *The Devils* directed by Ken Russell and released in 1970. In 1973 he designed a garden at The Verzons near Ledbury, Herefordshire, for his sister and her husband, Gaye and David Temple. Each of these designs is for a formal garden with topiary, totems and obelisks.

At Dungeness he at first "had no thought of building a garden. It looked impossible: shingle with no soil supported a sparse vegetation".[17] A garden there is

Dungeness, looking along the headland towards the lighthouse.
Photograph, Jonathan Hill, 2006.

Dungeness, looking towards Prospect Cottage and the front garden.
Photograph, Jonathan Hill, 2006.

unexpected although many of its materials—natural and man-made—are indigenous to the area. Combining two long-held fascinations—beachcombing and gardening—Jarman remarks, "There are no walls or fences. My garden's boundaries are the horizon."[18] Lichens, plants, flowers, fruit; shells, stones, pebbles, flints, sea-ground bricks; driftwood, rusty metal, anchors, chains, fishing tackle.[19] All collected and combined into obelisks, totems and geometric shapes, the back garden loosely placed as though deposited by the tide, the front more obviously reminiscent of Jarman's earlier formal garden designs but on a smaller scale. The garden is arranged around the cottage—Prospect Cottage Garden—but, equally, the cottage is a feature of the garden—Prospect Garden Cottage. In its apparent informality, reaction to circumstance and combination of building and garden, Christopher Lloyd recognises a particularly English place:[20]

> Prospect Cottage is very much in the English garden tradition, showing a love of plants and growing them well as a personal satisfaction... The fact that he was not put off by being told that gardening at Dungeness was 'impossible', and of there being no protocol or guidance, is also in the English tradition.[21]

The Last of England

Jarman affirms the tradition in which Englishness is associated with its landscape. English people and places rank high in his influences and affections: "Blake and William Morris... all of them look backward over their shoulders—to a Paradise on earth. And all of them at odds with the world around them. I feel this strongly, chose a 'novelty' medium—film—in which to search."[22]

Jarman praises the English pastoral films of Humphrey Jennings and Michael Powell from the 1940s and 50s,[23] when a number of the arts used the picturesque and romantic to defend national identity and the "genius of the place".[24] In the eighteenth century, the design and appreciation of picturesque gardens developed alongside the increasing value given to personal experiences and opinions. In *Essay concerning Human Understanding*, 1690, John Locke argues that ideas are dependent upon experience.[25] In 1757 David Hume adds that "Beauty is no quality in things themselves: it exists merely in the mind which contemplates them; and each mind perceives a different beauty."[26] Consequently, perception is subjective and changeable. Any change in the weather, the time of the day or the position or mood of the viewer can affect perception, so that even an object seemingly as solid as a building may not seem the same from one moment to the next. Focusing attention on subjectivity transformed the visual arts, its objects, authors and viewers. Associated with political and personal liberty, the picturesque garden was designed the way it is experienced, by a figure moving through a landscape.[27]

Dungeness, looking along the headland.
Photograph, Jonathan Hill, 2006.

Dungeness, looking beyond the back garden at Prospect Cottage and towards the nuclear power station.
Photograph, Jonathan Hill, 2006.

Rather than being conceived and executed according to a fixed design more often it was altered and adapted as work progressed. As the eighteenth century progressed, immediate and intuitive experience was favoured to the extent that defined narratives became less evident in the picturesque garden.[28] Nikolaus Pevsner declares the relevance of the picturesque to Englishness and English architecture past and present: "the theory of the flowing line, the more general aesthetic theory of surprise and concealment, the way the Picturesque is tied up with English outdoor life and ultimately even the general British philosophy of liberalism and liberty".[29] Pevsner's promotion of the picturesque culminated in "The Englishness of English Art", the BBC Reith Lectures in 1955, which were published as a single volume in 1956.[30] In the early sixties at King's College, University of London, Jarman studied with Pevsner, who later became a friend.[31]

If the English landscape is synonymous with a way of life, mourning one means mourning the other: "In the short space of my lifetime I've seen the destruction of the landscape through commercialisation, a destruction so complete that fragments are preserved as if in a museum."[32] Released in 1987 and set in the near future Jarman's *The Last of England* depicts a derelict and decaying urban landscape ruled by the military.[33] The film's title refers to the 1855 Pre-Raphaelite painting by Ford Madox Brown, which depicts emigrants leaving England by sea. Opposed to the Modernist eradication of history Jarman identifies the continuity of the past with the present: "It's a love story with England. It's not an attack. It's an attack on those things that I perceive personally as things without value. Things that have invaded the mainstream of British life. That's not an attack on England. It's the opposite."[34] The film's colours are those of JMW Turner.[35]

Romanticism, which developed towards the end of the eighteenth century, did not represent a decisive departure from the late picturesque. But it equated self-exploration with the exploration of wild landscapes rather than gardens, focusing further attention on weather as a means to fully appreciate the qualities of a place and a person. John Dixon Hunt writes that Turner's "notebooks especially reveal how careful he was to record landscape subjects from different points of view or in different weathers, times of day, or even the moods in which he painted, for only in this way does a particular place yield its fullest genius".[36] Turner's depiction of weather extended to the city. Responding to the atmospheric pollution in nineteenth century London, then the largest industrial city in the world, Turner depicted the effects of its heady haze of smog and fog.

Jarman's paternal grandfather emigrated from Devon to New Zealand in the late nineteenth century but his father returned in 1929, 13 years before his birth. Many of Jarman's fondest childhood memories refer to the southwest of England. At Dungeness he was able to recall and recreate a number of the places found in his fondest childhood memories. One is the Isle of Purbeck, Dorset, a headland rather than an island.[37] Used as a military range since the Second World War, it has not been subject to extensive farming and contains some of the most varied wild plants and insects in southern England. Thomas Hardy is the author most associated with Purbeck.[38] In his novels, many written at the end of the nineteenth century, the landscape and weather are the principal protagonists, often intervening to determine events.

The Angelic Conversation, 1985, was filmed at Montacute House in Somerset, an Elizabethan mansion admired by Jarman.[39] Built between 1588 and 1601 it has a formal garden abundant in topiary and timber-panelled rooms ordered around a symmetrical plan. The most notable room is on the top floor. The 60 metre Long Gallery extends the full length of the house and has a bay window at each end, allowing the family to exercise and view the landscape when the weather was poor.

Jarman describes his visits to the home of a friend at Kilve in Somerset, where the Quantock hills meet the sea at an expansive shingle beach, as "the happiest part"[40] of his childhood. There he went beachcombing and completed his first landscape paintings, a practice he continued, however unfashionable. At the Slade School of Fine Art, University College London, in the early 1960s,[41] he recalls that while others were absorbed by Pop Art "I was painting landscapes, close to the red earth of north Somerset, the flowers, the butterflies in the meadows."[42]

Kilve is close to Alfoxden and Nether Stowey, where the romantic poets William and Dorothy Wordsworth and Samuel Taylor Coleridge made their homes at the end of the eighteenth century and produced some of their most influential work.[43] Jarman enjoyed the area's association with the Wordsworths and Coleridge and refers in particular to Dorothy Wordsworth's journals, a medium he enjoyed and practiced: "I too gathered worts on Danesborough, which she often climbed with Coleridge."[44] Also nearby is a nuclear power station with the same type of reactors as at Dungeness.[45] Begun when Jarman was 15, Hinkley Point nuclear power station was not a feature of his childhood but was important later. The Romantic tradition understands industrialisation as a threat to the English landscape and character. But Jarman made films—a medium synonymous with industrialisation—and throughout his life maintained a concern for desolate and portentous landscapes with a brooding presence, whether natural or man-made. Like other Romantic artists Jarman was repelled but also fascinated by the industrial landscape while he only had distaste for the manicured gardens run by the National Trust and the chocolate-box town of Rye, close to Dungeness.[46] Jarman visited Kilve once again just before he bought Prospect Cottage:

> The next week I drove to Somerset with Gerard to film on the beach at Kilve, where I spent afternoons as a child constructing driftwood sculptures for the incoming tide to sweep away. At Hinkley Point we took off the road to the nuclear power station which my Aunt Isobel and the village had fought from her cottage 'Great Beats'. Coming over the hill, it looked old and rusty: these power stations generate a strange atmosphere: the slight hum and the occasional whistle deepens the sense that those who ran them have left long ago.[47]

Sublime Prospect

Homeliness and other-worldliness drew Jarman to Dungeness: "the bleakness of Prospect Cottage was what had made me fall in love with it".[48] Influencing the picturesque and Romanticism, Edmund Burke's *Philosophical Enquiry into the Origin of our Ideas of the Sublime and Beautiful* was first published in 1757. His description of the sublime was not new; Joseph Adamson's *Pleasures of the Imagination*, published in 1712, was but one source. Burke's achievement was to compile the sublime and the beautiful into a system that provides a coherent argument for the sublime. While the sublime is magnificent, the beautiful is pleasant. The sublime is evoked by a desolate and expansive landscape subject to the uncertain drama of natural forces.[49] The pleasure of the sublime is first threatening and then reassuring as comprehension increases and fear diminishes:

> Whatever is fitted in any sort to excite the ideas of pain, and danger, that is to say, whatever is in any sort terrible, or is conversant about terrible objects, or operates in a manner analogous to terror, is a source of the sublime; that is, it is productive of the strongest emotion which the mind is capable of feeling... When danger or pain presses too nearly, they are incapable of giving any delight, and are simply terrible; but at certain distances, and certain modifications, they may be, and they are delightful, as we everyday experience.[50]

Dungeness is a landscape that evokes the sublime and the nuclear power station is one of its features; since the Industrial Revolution a terrifying and thrilling presence may be man-made as well as natural. And at Dungeness the sublime is experienced at home. Together, the headland, garden and cottage are sublime and beautiful, magnificent and pleasant, recalling Uvedale Price's claim in 1794 that the picturesque sits between the beautiful and the sublime and is able to combine the two.[51]

The Sunne Rising

Tony Peake argues that the nuclear power station provided "the best visual metaphor" Jarman "encountered for his own anger".[52]

> For the first twenty-five years of my life I lived as a criminal, and the next twenty-five were spent as a second-class citizen, deprived of equality and human rights. No right to adopt children—and if I had children, I could be declared an unfit parent; illegal in the military; an age of consent of twenty-one, no right of inheritance; no right of access to a loved one; no right to public affection; no right to an unbiased education; no legal sanction of my relationships and no right to marry.[53]

On 22 December 1986—the year he bought Prospect Cottage—Jarman was diagnosed as HIV positive, accentuating his anger and increasing his awareness of mortality. The garden at Prospect Cottage marks his life from diagnosis to death.

Describing his garden as "a therapy and a pharmacopoeia",[54] Jarman proclaims, "Like all true gardeners, I'm an optimist."[55] Gardening requires a confidence in the future but is so absorbing that the gardener may forget time: "The gardener digs in another time, without past or future, beginning or end. A time that does not cleave the day with rush hours, lunch breaks, the last bus home. As you walk into the garden you pass into this time—the moment of entering can never be remembered."[56] So dependent on the weather and seasons, the gardener also knows that life and death are necessary to one another. On the west wall of Prospect Cottage are the words of "The Sunne Rising", 1633, in which the English poet John Donne accuses the sun and asks for time:

> Busie old foole, unruly Sunne,
> Why dost thou thus,
> Through windowes, and through curtaines call on us?
> Must to thy motions lovers' seasons run?
> Sawey pedantique wretch, goe chide
> Late schoole boyes and sowre prentices,
> Goe tell Court-huntsmen, and that the King will ride,
> Call countrey ants to harvest offices;
> Love, all alike, no season knowes, nor clyme,
> Nor houres, dayes, moneths, which are the rags of time...
> Thou sunne art halfe as happy as wee,
> In that the world's contracted thus.
> Thine age askes ease, and since thy duties bee
> To warme the world, that's done in warming us.
> Shine here to us, and thou aret every where;
> This bed this centre is, these walls thy spheare.[57]

Attention given to the passage of time and the effects of weather and weathering is a recurring architectural tradition developed primarily from the picturesque, sublime and Romanticism. John Ruskin, another English author praised by Jarman and a noted advocate of Turner, in 1849 writes: "For, indeed, the greatest glory of a building is not in its stones, or its gold. Its glory is in its Age... it is in that golden stain of time, that we are to look for the real light, and colour, and preciousness of architecture."[58]

Describing Prospect Cottage as "more beautiful the older it becomes"[59] Jarman sees himself in his house and garden, vulnerable to the weather, subject to the seasons. In a section of his journals titled "Borrowed Time" he is "Like this old house in the gale... the clouds are blowing from the west, I'm drifting with them far away."[60] Seeing

Dungeness, looking beyond a discarded and weathered fishing boat and towards the sea. Photograph, Jonathan Hill, 2006.

Dungeness, looking along the headland towards the nuclear power station. Photograph, Jonathan Hill, 2006.

another season means living a little longer: "The day of our death is sealed up. I do not wish to die... yet. I would love to see my garden through several summers."[61] On 2 March 1994,[62] just eight years after he moved to Prospect Cottage, "The plain oak coffin was open. Jarman was dressed in a robe of glittering gold."[63]

> My gilly flowers, roses, violets blue,
> sweet garden of vanished pleasures,
> Please come back next year.
> Cold, cold, cold, I die so silently.[64]

Home Movies

At Prospect Cottage there are numerous references to other gardens, including Elizabethan ones such as Montacute. But the two English traditions it most refers to are the picturesque landscape garden and the cottage garden.[65] The pleasure of perception is the purpose of the picturesque garden. Looking out as well as in, the picturesque garden enforces clear power relations between those who own the landscape and those who work it and between a landscape of pleasure and one of production.[66] Jarman's garden looks out as well as in and the headland is its resource. But the views beyond are not framed and ordered and its labour relations are those of the cottage garden. Inward looking, the cottage garden is decorative and practical, growing fruit and vegetables to eat as well as flowers and shrubs to view. Pleasure and labour are combined; the owner is the designer and the gardener.

Whether beachcombing, gardening or filmmaking Jarman liked the ebb-and-flow of the creative process: "I don't really feel that I've ever been a big controller-director. I just let everything 'flow with the glue'. There are no big plans which have to be fulfilled."[67] Enjoying collaboration, he had no wish to be a figure of authority: "I never saw myself as a film-director, I've never seen myself as one, I'm not one."[68]

Jarman's longing for home-making and home-land combine in film-making: "The home movie is a bedrock, it records the landscape of leisure: the beach, the garden, the swimming pool. In all home movies is a longing for paradise."[69] Set around Prospect Cottage and released in 1990, *The Garden*[70] is "a home movie devoid of the innocent certainties of that form of film-making", writes Michael O'Pray.[71] Given that the film was "inspired by Jarman's love of his own garden" and contains "violence and sadism" that "surpasses anything in his prior work",[72] what sort of home is Prospect Cottage and its garden? One that is typical.

Gardens appear in many of Jarman's films, "where they are a metaphor for pain and pleasure, for Gethsemane and Eden".[73] The subject of Prospect Cottage and *The Garden* is the pain and pleasure of home, made especially poignant due to illness.[74] Jarman associates filmmaking with the sociability of home movies but home is synonymous with privacy and the self. Much of the time at Prospect Cottage he was alone. Jarman recalls the reaction of Swinton, a regular collaborator:

> Tilda said she experienced The Garden quite differently from The Last of England. It was as if she was "trapped" in my dream. She found the film intensely personal. The preoccupations of The Last of England were shared—here was something different. I feel the same way, can't really talk about the film. It's like talking about yourself![75]

A recurring theme in architectural discourse states that the home is the origin and archetype of architecture, the manifestation of its important attributes.[76] Defined by its separation from the world outside, the home is assumed to be the most secure and stable of environments. Banister Fletcher writes "Architecture... must have had a simple origin in the primitive efforts of mankind to provide protection against inclement weather, wild beasts and human enemies."[77] The apparent stability of the home may provide gratification but it can also, simultaneously, create anxiety because the home can never be safe enough and is not what it seems. In his 1919 essay on the uncanny Sigmund Freud describes the homely as "Concealed, kept from sight, so that others do not get to know about it."[78] The most uncanny and threatening experience occurs within the home, when the hidden and repressed returns unexpectedly, rendering the homely unhomely.[79]

Home-making

As the home-owner identifies with the home, mental unease and bodily disease—real or imagined—are easily projected onto the home. Jarman moved to Dungeness because a home there would be more vulnerable and thus more precious. The last of his 'escape houses' is as fragile as his first—made of grass, sand, turf, scrap metal and twigs—and also combines gardening and building, the natural and the man-made. The fragility of his garden and cottage—so like one drawn by a child—makes his achievements in home-making more profound. A home is made not found and home-making lasts as long as a life. At Dungeness, due to the extreme weather it is easy to understand that a building must be tended like a garden:

> Prospect has been re-tarred; it's shining and will remain so till the elements dull it. The west wall is the worst, sun and driving wet westerlies flake the paint in a year, so that it has to be painted continuously to keep the timbers in shape. Painting the house with tar varnish takes a day.[80]

Prospect Cottage was built in response to its site and weather. Equally aware of local conditions, Jarman added a garden where it was least expected. Prospect Cottage is now associated with one author: *Derek Jarman's Garden*. Reflecting Jarman's heartfelt knowledge of the natural and cultural landscape of England, his design developed and evolved as he collected new plants, artefacts and ideas. But a design may be intensely personal while acknowledging other protagonists.

Jarman enjoyed the camaraderie of filmmaking. At Dungeness his collaborators were natural as well as human. The cottage and the garden are subject to the forces that make and transform Dungeness. Winds and tides, human interventions past and present, unforeseen events, all determine the character of Dungeness, the cottage and garden. Dungeness is the model for the garden. And the garden is the model of Dungeness. On a smaller scale, the garden mirrors the arrangements, materials and conditions found at Dungeness.

Since the Italian Renaissance, it has been assumed that a significant building is the creation of a single architect—one who conceives at a remove from construction—because artistic, intellectual labour is associated with the individual; only occasionally is the contribution of a client, engineer or other architect acknowledged. But Dungeness reveals a condition that is widespread: there are always a number of architectural authors at work. At Prospect Cottage and its garden, architectural authorship is multiplied and juxtaposed, not dissolved. Multiplied because, rather than a sole author, a number of architectural authors are identified—such as the designer, builder, gardener, visitor, site and weather. Juxtaposed because—sometimes competing, sometimes affirming—each author may inform the other, as in a feisty dialogue of individual voices and unexpected conclusions. As natural and man-made forces affect each other on a global and a local scale, agents as well as authors are at work. An author is an initiating force while an agent responds, translates and transforms. As an author may also be an agent, the result is a complex interweaving of authorship and agency in which architecture and weather are connected rather than opposed and the production of architecture is shared and temporal.

Translation

If the texts in the section on 'Dislocation' are governed by a certain 'frontier mentality', and explore how the 'otherness' in other disciplines can critique existing architectural practice in relation to authorship, those in the section 'Translation' deal with cases where a fluid interchange can be achieved, where the practices of two disciplines visibly and easily enrich each other. This relaxed enrichment, these texts suggest, leads also to an enriched account of authorship in relation to architecture. While the first three essays by Pelletier, Miller and Tobe consider examples of trans-disciplinary enrichment within a distinct historical frame, Haralambidou's essay is more directly projective in its analysis of recent architectural examples that are suggestive of an alternative —'allegorical'—mode of architectural authorship at work today.

The first essay in this section, "Genius, Fiction, and the Author in Architecture" by Louise Pelletier, considers the close relationship that existed between architectural theory and literary practice in France during the eighteenth century. She shows how Nicolas Le Camus de Mézières, in his treatise *The Genius of Architecture*, 'writes' an architecture in direct analogy with the style of a 'boudoir novel' (and correspondingly how the writer Jean-François de Bastide staged in his novel an erotic drama through architecture). "Cultures of Display" by Wallis Miller explores the merging of architecture with display in the nascent tradition of exhibiting architecture at full scale, which developed in Germany at the beginning of the twentieth century.

Both Pelletier's and Miller's essays foreground sensationalist theories of architecture: with Pelletier in direct relation to eighteenth century philosophy and aesthetics (Condillac) and with Miller closely linked to turn-of-the-century empathy theories of architectural and spatial experience (Schmarzow). The eighteenth century occasioned a radical transformation of architectural design principles. Based on theories of emotional response and affect in man, rather than on correspondence (in a Neoplatonic sense), these new principles altered the role of the architect, of architecture theory, and ultimately of architectural representation. In her essay, Pelletier shows the great significance of literature and fiction in the search for articulations of this new mode of conceiving architecture. Correspondingly Miller connects the shift in the culture of architectural display where drawings and scale models of architectural projects were distinctly subordinated to 'experience itself', to the rise of empathy theory, in which the drawing was questioned as a mere 'specialist's' tool. But while in Le Camus, a representational medium remained at work to excite the imagination through the power of fiction, Schmarzow regarded only the full-scale experience of architecture as such to be of sufficient power to do the job. The conflation of architecture with display permitted however both the articulation of new conceptual categories in architecture (for example that of 'space') and a new form of authorial practice. The emerging notion of the exhibition as a new, independent, testing ground for architectural ideas, affected the operating definitions of architecture in profound ways that are still to be understood.

Renée Tobe's essay "The Inhuman One" surveys early examples of the free coupling between film design and architecture, exemplified in the work of Robert Mallet Stevens (in particular for the 1924 film *L'Inhumaine*, by Marcel L'Herbier) which also formed a new authorial persona on which the later 'heroes' of modern architecture relied. As popularised through film, the representation of modern architecture is discussed in terms of a political project, shaping a new and modern perception of the world. In the example of Mallet Stevens the figure of the architect is directly linked to the scenographer, staging an architecture that, as Tobe argues, 'authors' a new world and thereby a modern conception of life. If the boudoir novel in the eighteenth century may have staged for the reader an architecture of erotic drama, modern film correspondingly aroused a desire to live that life on display, and thus to inhabit those very same spaces. But the filmic 'lens', as directed in the case of Mallet Stevens towards early Modern architecture, did not exclusively serve emancipatory aims in its forceful propagation for a radically modern society, it also effectuated, as Tobe shows, the transformation of architecture into a desirable, and also potentially disposable, commodity.

In the closing essay "The Allegorical Project", Penelope Haralambidou seeks to define a territory of authorship in architecture that employs architectural design to articulate something 'other' than the description of a building. Drawing on projects by Jonathan Hill, Rem Koolhaas, Ben Nicholson and Mike Webb, she characterises this territory as allegorical, exploiting the articulation of a concrete set of ideas, images and words, to refer to an unrealised, informally and subliminally projected intention or reality. Taking the reader through the traits of the allegorical, such as the battle and progress themes; the reciprocity between the visual and the verbal; the figurative geometry formed between personages, objects, and sites; the duplicity of meaning; and the tendency to leave the allegory unfinished, Haralambidou provides a vocabulary for an architectural analysis that allows the architectural project to rest within the realm of the imaginary, whether existing in drawn, in modelled, in written or in built form.

Through its conjunction of allegory as a literary concept and contemporary architectural examples, Haralambidou's essay relates in interesting ways to Pelletier's and Tobe's essays as the architect in these texts comes forward importantly as a 'fiction-writer' or a 'realiser of dreams' (in Tobe's words). Whether these 'dreams' are utopian constructions or critical projections they stage a play between architectural space, as imagined in its full potential, and different fictional media—poetry, literature, film, drawings, models—that celebrates the very process of translation as a critical space in and of itself. Further, as Miller argues, in her discussion of Mies van der Rohe and Lilly Reich's exhibition *The Dwelling of Our Time*, even the full-scale architectural display can certainly be productive of a fictional site, though it may raise particular challenges for the critical mind to discern the status of the reality in which it finds itself immersed. Contemporary exhibition and publication cultures in architecture today offer important arenas for the recognition of architectures located sometimes outside of the built and the strictly buildable, at other times prototypical and suggestive of potential architectures to come. The four essays in this section offer through their respective analyses important models and ideas for how to understand and to conceptualise the different authorial territories which the architects that operate within these arenas are bound to negotiate, and which their critics often tend to confuse.

Genius, Fiction and the Author in Architecture

Louise Pelletier

LE GÉNIE
DE
L'ARCHITECTURE,
OU
L'ANALOGIE
DE CET ART
AVEC NOS SENSATIONS.

Par M. LE CAMUS DE MÉZIÈRES, Architecte.

Non fatis est placuisse oculis, nisi pectora tangas.
C'est peu de plaire aux yeux, il faut émouvoir l'ame.
POÈME de la Peinture par le P. MARSY.

À PARIS,
Chez {L'AUTEUR, rue du Foin Saint-Jacques au Collège de Maître Gervais.
BENOIT MORIN, Imprimeur-Libraire, rue Saint Jacques, à la Vérité.

M. DCC. LXXX.
AVEC APPROBATION, ET PRIVILÈGE DU ROI.

The Genius of Architecture. Title page from Nicolas Le Camus de Mézières, *Le génie de l'architecture: ou, L'analogie de cet art avec nos sensations*, Paris, 1780.
Courtesy of the National Library of Sweden.

The concept of authorship in architecture has always been tied to questions of architectural responsibility, but since the beginning of modernity, it increasingly raises issues of copyright, and underlines a blind quest for originality, somewhat shifting the emphasis from the work and its appropriateness to the individuality of the creative mind. A historical look at notions of responsibility, imagination and creation reveals some important transformations in the very notion of authorship that might help us understand the roots of the contemporary situation.

From the middle of the eighteenth century in Europe, understanding the creative process leading to the manifestation of an architectural intention became central to architectural discourse. Such creative processes were defined in terms of the expression of talent or taste, modulated by the application of rules. Many architects, however, became concerned with the potential mediocrity that plagued uninspired works that relied solely on imitation of proportions established by the Ancients, and tried to redefine the role of rules in architecture. A work of imitation came to have a definite derogatory meaning and its author was criticised for lack of imagination, while a mind of genius was celebrated for its ability to transcend rules and create new forms and ideas. Soon, the expression "fire and genius" had become a well-known expression of praise in architectural discourse.

Nicolas Le Camus de Mézières, one of the leading architects and theoreticians of the second half of the eighteenth century in France, even entitled his most important architectural treatise *The Genius of Architecture; Or, The Analogy of That Art With Our Sensations* in 1780. The recurrent discussion around the notions of talent, taste and genius, which indicated an intricate relationship between imagination and rules in the eighteenth century, was a central argument of Le Camus's treatise. Moreover, the genius of architecture for him also included the pre-Romantic notion of a creative fire.

Preceding Le Camus de Mézières by only a decade, Jacques-François Blondel also discusses at length the distinction between talent, taste and genius in his *Cours d'architecture*. The man of talent, he writes, is an individual who is well versed in the theory of architecture and in the practice of building construction, but who produces nothing that might depart from principles and proportions established by traditional authority. Most of his productions are fine in terms of composition, but tend to be "cold and monotonous" and often fail to attain "the perfection and sublimity of the art". The productions of a man of talent should be considered as nothing more than works of imitation. The man of taste, on the other hand, must not only be familiar with the secrets of his art, he is the one who can integrate to his creations the modulations determined by appropriateness, or cultural conventions. He knows when needed how to go beyond the limits prescribed by rules while remaining within the boundaries of good taste.

The man of genius, Blondel continues, also needs to be familiar with all the rules of the art, but is guided in his choices by a higher form of inspiration and an enthusiasm that will free him from enslaving rules. He knows how to create the different genres and assign the proper character to a building; he will take advantage of the natural conditions of a site and the available materials. Most importantly, the man of genius will produce creations that surpass the masterpieces they were meant to imitate.[1]

For Le Camus de Mézières as for Blondel before him, the inspiration of the man of genius was necessary to insure the highest accomplishment of the art, although rules could not be dispensed with. For Le Camus, however, rules were no longer dictated from Antiquity, but were drawn from other disciplines such as theatre, music, and literature. The subtitle of Le Camus de Mézières's treatise, which proposes an analogy of architecture with our sensations, was probably the most innovative dimension of his architectural theory. Le Camus's theory of architectural expression assumes that all shapes, colours, light, and texture employed in the design of a building convey to the senses specific predictable sensation in the observer. His primary aim in grounding his architectural theory on an analogy with human sensations was to ensure that the resulting architecture would not only speak to the rational mind but would also move the soul.

Accordingly, the article "Génie" from Diderot's *Encyclopédie* describes a mind of genius not in its rationality or its ability to formulate complex abstract concepts, but rather in its great sensitivity. A mind with a fertile imagination combines ideas to create new concepts, by transcribing abstract ideas into sensitive ones. The genius not only uses memory and association to create new meanings for a particular object, but also engages her/his mnemonic faculty to transform the tragic into the terrible and the beautiful into the sublime, to animate matter and to colour the mind by re-enacting every sensation: "In the heat of enthusiasm, [the genius] does not rely on nature, nor on the continuity of his ideas; he is transported into the situation of the characters he has created; he becomes these characters."[2]

The article "Génie" from the *Encyclopédie* also traces the origin of the word in classical mythology. The *genies* were beings whose bodies were made of an aerial substance and who inhabited the vast realm between the sky and the earth. These subtle spirits were considered to be ministers sent by gods to mediate in human affairs. As inferior divinities, the genies were immortal like gods but felt passions like humans. They were assigned to protect specific humans during their life and to guide their souls after death. From this interpretation, *génie* came to mean the human soul delivered and detached from the human body.[3] This notion of freedom of the mind and proximity to the divine remained the most powerful attributes of the genius, and still lingers—even if secretly—in the highest aspiration of the contemporary author.

With the surge of Newtonian sciences and empirical philosophy, eighteenth-century philosophers such as Étienne Bonnot de Condillac investigated the mind, the body, and the process by which ideas were carried from one to the other through the senses. When the soul is affected by an object, perception is intensified by the memory of specific events related to that object. This is one of the basic principles of Condillac's empirical philosophy. Memory behaves like a sixth sense, a bridge between sensation and understanding. In the act of remembering, imagination plays a crucial role because it combines different memories of sensations and creates new meanings according to the changing context. For a person of genius, this faculty is intensified: "He remembers these ideas with a feeling more intense than how he received them, because these ideas are merged with thousands more, that all contribute to arouse a feeling. The genius, surrounded by objects that concern him, does not remember, he sees; he is not restricted to seeing, he is moved. In the silence and darkness of his study, he takes pleasure from the joyful and fertile countryside; the whistling of the wind freezes him; the sun burns him; he is scared by storms."[4]

Poetic Language

According to Condillac's definition, the philosophical constructions of a mind of genius do not rest on reason, nor can they be appreciated in terms of truth or falseness. They are more akin to poems, revealing their meaning through the beauty of proportions. This analogy with literary works became an important model for artists and architects in the eighteenth century. Following the radical changes in the nature of architectural expression brought about by Claude Perrault's questioning of the Vitruvian canon, the proportions of the architectural orders lost some of their natural legitimacy as the shared language of architecture.[5] Although architectural intention was still conveyed in part through *measures and proportions*, it started to demand additional means of mediation. In various realms of artistic production, language and fiction became a favoured medium to further the intention of the author. Diderot's writings for the Salons are eloquent examples. For a few years between 1765 and 1769, Diderot used fiction to describe paintings exhibited at the Louvre, and momentarily transformed the spectators into active participants. Diderot's intent was to disclose the story hidden in the paintings, to reveal the author's true intention. In Jean-Baptiset Greuze's *Young Girl Crying Over Her Dead Bird* (Salon of 1765), for example, Diderot observes that the child is in tears over what appears to be the loss of her pet bird. He engages in a fictional conversation with the young girl from the painting, trying to console her over her loss. He speculates that her grief is due not merely to the fate of her bird, but perhaps also the loss of her virginity:

> Is it the loss of this bird that causes you to withdraw so strongly and so sadly within yourself? ... You lower your eyes; you do not answer me. Your tears are ready to run down. I am no father; I am not indiscrete or severe.... Well, I understand he loved you, he swore to you he did for so long.... That morning, unfortunately your mother was absent. He came; you were alone: he was so beautiful, so passionate, so tender, so charming! He had so much love in his eyes!.... He was holding one of your hands; from time to time you felt the warmth of some tears running down from his eyes, and dripping along your arms. Your mother still was not returning. It is not your fault; it is the fault of your mother....[6]

Two years later, in his description of Joseph Vernet's landscape paintings, Diderot went even further. His descriptions took the form of imaginary walks through pictorial worlds where the paintings themselves seemed to disappear. Instead of enumerating the elements that compose the landscapes, Diderot used fiction to literally enter into the paintings and visit places that seemed to unfold in the hidden corners of the pictorial compositions. Accompanied by an abbot, Diderot begins his journey through scenes that appear to be so authentic that Diderot's companion refuses to admit that any artist could have imitated nature so perfectly. However, for Diderot, the true work of art was not simply an imitation of nature but a translation that revealed hidden sensations and induced emotions in the soul that would otherwise remain unknown. His evaluation of the artistic value of a painting was determined by its capacity to touch and involve the spectator. His description of Vernet's sea storms and shipwrecks is most eloquent. Again imagining himself in the painted scene, Diderot describes the horror caused not only by reckless nature, but also by human cruelty. He is terrified at the sight of such commotion and mourns the fate of the unfortunate travellers. Through sympathy, he feels their suffering and desperation in his own flesh, yet he cannot take his eyes away from the painting due to his intense experience of the sublime. His literary descriptions of virtual promenades through landscapes were almost as evocative as Vernet's paintings themselves, and thus potentially raised art criticism to a new art form.

These original literary paintings epitomised the process of association and interpretation with which the genius creates a new world and new meanings. Never created *ex nihilo*, the work always refers to a shared context that grounds it and ensures that its speaks about a reality that extends beyond its author. Diderot's fictions created new potential paintings, and it becomes virtually impossible, once we have read Diderot's descriptions not to imagine his presence in the real paintings. As the author of these verbal scores, Diderot engaged a dialogue between different disciplines. If language became such an important mediator to experience works of art in the eighteenth century, it is because painting was not only a copy of nature, but man's own creation *from* nature.

Fiction and the Genius of Architecture

The power of language and fiction to recreate new worlds would have a direct impact on late eighteenth century architects such as Claude-Nicolas Ledoux, Étienne-Louis Boullée and particularly Nicolas Le Camus de Mézières. For these architects of early modernity, fiction and story telling became a favoured means of expressing architectural intentions. In *The Genius of Architecture*, Le Camus de Mézières described architectural spaces that followed a precise succession in an attempt to recreate an emotional climax typical of fictional story telling, making use of a famous boudoir novel of the time to structure his architectural theory: Jean-François de Bastide's *The Little House*, 1758.[7] As in other boudoir novels, architecture plays an active role in portraying the state of mind and emotions of its inhabitants. The fundamental assumption of both Bastide's novel and Le Camus's treatise is that architecture has the power to create feelings that are equivalent in essence and intensity to sensations induced by a lover.

The story of *The Little House* begins as a wager between Mélite, an educated young woman, and the marquis de Trémicour who believes he can seduce her solely through the architectural charms of his *little house*, a clandestine country house. The marquis knows that the gradual increase in ornamentation throughout the house creates a temporal unfolding that will gradually lead his guest to an emotional climax. Le Camus de Mézières describes the emotional structure of the plot in architectural terms: Because of the gradual increase of ornamentation, "each room makes us desire the next; and this agitation engages the mind, holding it in suspense, in a kind of satisfying bliss".[8] The admitted objective of architecture for both authors was indeed to create this culmination.

From the start, it is clear that the little house is an extension of the marquis' wit and a materialisation of his charms. As he guides Mélite throughout the house, the succession of spaces are qualified in terms of shapes, proportions, and various sensuous ornaments. The calculated placement of light is also most important in this lovers' abode, for it heightens the emotions of its inhabitants. The little house is a real "temple of genius and taste".

The long sequence takes the reader through the first vestibule, the living room, a bedchamber, and finally to a boudoir, "a place that needs no introduction to the woman who enters, her heart and soul recognizing it at once".[9] Here, more than anywhere else before, the lighting effects are carefully controlled to create the magic and optical effects of a natural grove enhanced by art. The walls of the boudoir are thinner than the partitions in the rest of the house, and in a wide corridor surrounding the boudoir the marquis has placed musicians who have been waiting for his signal to begin playing. In the little house, all the senses are addressed in an attempt to seduce its guest. As Mélite escapes from the boudoir where she fears for her virtue, she enters the bathroom where she is even more moved by the artistic beauty of the place. Mélite confesses that she is seduced by the charms of the little house, but Trémicour who senses his victory, delays Mélite's defeat and lightens his tone. Mélite is allowed to retreat as the marquis hopes that the architectural charms of the following apartments will convince her to concede his victory.

They return to the living room, where he opens the door to the garden. Trémicour guides his guest through the garden like a playwright directing spectators through a dramatic sequence. Nothing was spared to impress his young prey, including fireworks that introduced the gleam of a tender and submissive love into the eyes of the marquis. Mélite anxiously rushes back inside to escape the enchanted garden. She quickly passes through some cabinet, before entering the dining room, where a meal is waiting for them. By now, all of Mélite's senses are stimulated, and she becomes most vulnerable to the seductive powers of the place—and to the marquis de Trémicour himself. Suddenly aware that she can no longer resist the charms of the place and of its owner, Mélite attempts one last escape, but in her confusion, she takes the wrong door and finds herself in a green boudoir, where she ultimately loses the wager.

In boudoir novels of the time, architecture often played an active role in portraying the state of mind and emotions of its inhabitants. In *The Little House*, the succession of rooms and their gradual increase in ornamentation conveyed the idea of *gradation* of sensuous delight through the different kinds of voluptuous pleasures. Le Camus de Mézières compares this gradual progression of architectural ornamentation to the development of dramatic action in a play. He also uses the notion of "gradation", an explicit term of seduction, to explain the central concept of his architectural theory: "The gradation of opulence, as one progresses further into the interior, casts the spell and stimulates the senses."[10] The intimate connection between *The Genius of Architecture* and the sensuous architecture of Bastide's novel is based on more than their shared language of seduction, however. Le Camus's book includes a room-by-room description of the distribution and decoration of a *hôtel particulier* that follows the exact same sequence as the route described by Bastide in his novel. The reader follows the same progression that led to Mélite's seduction, which implicitly reveals an architectural space of desire in *The Genius of Architecture.*

As in Bastide's novel, the sequence of rooms in Le Camus's treatise begins in the vestibule, followed by a series of anterooms that best exemplifies Le Camus's notion of gradation. This first progression toward the main apartments of the *hôtel* is an extended threshold that delays the penetration of the visitor into the centre of the house while gradually increasing the level of decoration, and with it, the emotional tension. This sequence gradually leads the reader to the living room, which is used for festive occasions and must display the magnificence of the place. Then comes the bedchamber immediately followed by the boudoir, and there, the level of detail is developed to the highest degree. Its decoration appeals to all the senses, and invites a visitor to abandon any resistance to the pleasures of the senses: "Here the soul rejoices; its sensations are akin to ecstasy."[11] The general effect of the whole is better experienced than it can be described, Le Camus emphasises, which again confirms the distinctiveness of his architectural theory of expression: the specificity of distinct spaces can be perceived intuitively through the senses, but resists discursive identification.

Of all the rooms described in Le Camus's treatise, the boudoir most closely resembles the depiction in Bastide's novel; Le Camus's description of its ornamentation is taken almost word for word from *The Little House*, insisting on the sensuous qualities, the optical illusions and the lighting effects of this abode of sensual delight. The mirrors framed by sculpted tree trunks and arranged in a quincunx, the candlelight veiled with gauze, and the illusion of a natural wood artfully lit, are found almost literally in Bastide's novel, making evident the influence of the libertine novel on the architectural treatise. This unacknowledged borrowing of a literary description, however, was not necessarily perceived as a lack of imagination in the context of the Enlightenment. Rather it confirmed the need to operate within a shared reality using a common language.

In *The Genius of Architecture* as in *The Little House*, the bathroom is the main room that follows the boudoir. It is the apartment whose decoration is determined most specifically by its occupant, becoming an extension of one's clothing, an interface between skin and walls. Just like Mélite who escapes from the bathroom and runs off to the gardens for a moment of respite before returning to the house in Bastide's novel, Le Camus follows the same progression in the enumeration of the main rooms inside the *hôtel particulier* in his architectural treatise, and accordingly, he concludes with the dining room. He then returns to a final boudoir suggesting that the roof above the riding school would be an ideal location, for "Mars and Venus always agree".[12] A contrast of light and shade enveloping architectural elements in the most voluptuous way characterises this last boudoir. Le Camus describes the slow and sensuous movement of light softened by the roundness of the shafts, gliding voluptuously around columns, before falling plentifully on the ground where the surrounding peristyle reflects its brightness.

Le Camus's treatise implicitly addresses the architectural space of desire in a scheme of seduction as it shares the same "plot" as Bastide's story. Throughout his treatise, Le Camus insists that it is essential for the architect to determine the primary narrative that the house must convey. In *The Genius of Architecture*, the narrative is clear: the delayed fulfilment and extended threshold of the *hôtel particulier* evokes the erotic tension between two lovers, a tension that becomes palpable and that addresses all the senses while defying objectification. Even though Le Camus de Mézières appears to have borrowed deliberately the structure of his architectural treatise from a well known architectural novel of the time, this unacknowledged quotation points mainly at the importance of grounding one's discourse within a shared language, and ensuring that the work communicate a clear intention.

For Le Camus, the genius of architecture seems to depend on the architect's ability to convey the effects of fiction. In fact this reliance on fiction and erotic narratives to convey architectural meaning was part of a tradition in architectural theory that began with Francesco Colonna's treatise, the *Hypnerothomachia Poliphili*, 1499. *Hypnerotomachia* is an original narrative articulation of the architectural space of desire. It demonstrates the potential of architectural meaning to involve the individual not only intellectually but also in an embodied way.

Unlike Boullée or Ledoux, who were concerned with authoring architecture as "paintings" or as autonomous works, deliberately reducing the space between conception and execution, the implication for Le Camus seems to be that the "score" proposed by the architect demands "interpretation".[13] Like some of his predecessors, Le Camus was profoundly concerned with the analogy of music and architecture. In the concluding pages of his treatise he writes: "The sound of a trumpet animates the warrior and even his horses; and the tone, the proportions, and the harmony of Architecture have the same power over our souls."[14] Harmony of proportions in the elevations, in the volumes, and in the relations among all of the parts and the whole leads to pleasure and intellectual enjoyment, which is the ultimate goal of the fine arts. A lack of harmony among the parts of a building "offends the eyes, as the ears are offended by a false note in music".[15] Harmony can induce a wide range of emotions in both the listener and the beholder.

As stated at the beginning of this article, the question of authorship in architecture raises issues of ethical responsibilities that are closely tied with notions of imagination and originality. Prior to the nineteenth century, the author was defined less in terms of the individual who held most control over the end product than in the mind that generated the intention for a project. Consequently, the author of a medieval cathedral was more likely to be identified with the patron who ordered the construction than with the Master Mason who supervised the construction. In the Renaissance, with the development of tools of representation, the process by which an idea was conveyed—through drawings and their translation—became a determining factor. The architect, through his ability to convey the intention of a project, was considered the true author of a building even if the process of construction was delegated to a third party. In a revealing letter by Alberti to the acting architect at Rimini responsible for the construction of his Tempio Malatestiano, Alberti protested suggested changes to his design, arguing that it would "bring discord to all that music".[16] For Alberti, the intention of the work was conveyed through "the measures and proportions of the pilasters", and his responsibility as the author lay in insuring that such intention would not be compromised.

Le Camus de Mézières's analogy between music and architecture was coherent with the *modus operandi* of eighteenth century musical practice, in which the "work" was not autonomous from its performance and the function for which it was composed. Even though he does not prescribe proportions in his book, he assumes that through fiction the architect can modulate space and orchestrate erotic experience. Only a few years later, in the wake of Durand and Beethoven, architects and musicians would understand very differently the concept of "work". For these later artists, the work implies full control, as in planning or civil engineering, and the notations (scores and architectural drawings issuing from the "mechanisms of composition") leave little room for interpretation. Le Camus' concept of authorship, placed at the limits between the traditional world of the Ancien Régime and Romanticism, still allows for an important space of translation and participation, and thus may suggest strategies to negotiate our present predicaments.

Cultures of Display: Exhibiting Architecture in Berlin, 1880–1931

Wallis Miller

The winning scheme in the 1905 Schinkel Competition for the design of an architecture museum in Berlin was neither built nor influential, but it did mark a change in the culture of exhibitions dedicated to architecture. Rather than limiting their portrayal of architecture to small models and drawings, architects and curators started trying to use their displays to capture the experience of a building at full-scale around the turn of the century. While this change was immediately apparent in outdoor venues, where the large displays of architecture took the form of pavilions, reconstructions, and buildings, it seldom affected architecture exhibitions in exposition halls, galleries, and museums. But, in interior exhibitions framed by other disciplines, usually in museums, full-scale architectural constructions were more common. In Berlin, they started to appear in the archaeological reconstructions in the Royal Prussian Museums (beginning with the first Pergamon Museum in 1901), here the *Stilräume* (style-rooms) in the Kaiser Friedrich Museum (which opened in 1904), and the period rooms as well as the architecture of the regional Märkisches Museum (which opened in 1908). Emerging from a desire to replace the warehouse-like display of artefacts with a strategy that situated the artefacts within a context, the architectural constructions transformed the exhibit into a spatial experience of the topic at hand, making the exhibit legible to the general public.[1]

Because they only played a supporting role in non-architectural exhibitions, full-scale displays of architecture could slip into the gallery, avoiding the constraints of accuracy and authenticity that shaped exhibitions of objects. When architectural displays came into focus, however, it was clear that the displays confronted the constraints directly. The discussions that ensued, particularly about architectural displays in archaeological exhibitions, suggested that architectural constructions either had no place in the gallery (because of the various ways that they were considered to be inaccurate) or showed that the attempts to recreate architectural experience demanded a new set of standards that did not rest on the notion of authenticity, especially defined by building. Aside from

Design for an architecture museum in Berlin: courtyard. Alfred Boeden, winning proposal from the 1905 Schinkel Competition. Technische Universität Berlin, Universitätsbibliothek, Plansammlung.

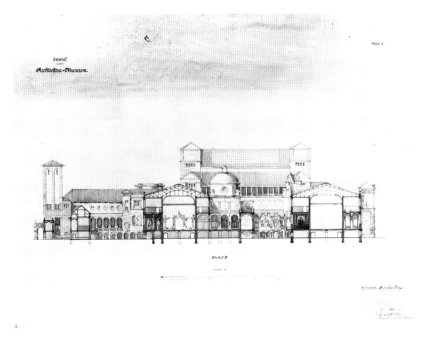

Design for an architecture museum in Berlin: section through the main space. Alfred Boeden, winning proposal from the 1905 Schinkel Competition. Technische Universität Berlin, Universitätsbibliothek, Plansammlung.

obvious logistical problems, this may explain why full-scale exhibitions of architecture were so rare. But it also may explain why the few early twentieth century examples of these exhibitions—such as the 1905 winning design for an architecture museum and the 1931 exhibition *The Dwelling of Our Time* (*Die Wohnung unserer Zeit*), which will be discussed later in the essay—displayed idealised versions of buildings and unbuilt projects, rather than actual buildings. One might say that they displayed architecture not building, finding a way to distinguish the two in the context of exhibitions and, more generally, in terms of aspects of professional practice.

In their program for the 1905 competition to design the architecture museum, a new institution, the Berlin Society of Architects and Engineers called for spaces large enough to accommodate triumphal arches and parts of Greek Temples, including their pediments and friezes. Following the model of Paris' Musée des Monuments Historiques in the Trocadéro, the program specified that the architects should make use of the objects on display—portals and colonnades, for example—rather than invent their own architecture to connect and subdivide large gallery spaces.[2] The winning entry by Alfred Boeden responded with interiors that were shaped by fragments of actual buildings, plaster casts, and elements of the architect's design. In the largest gallery, dedicated to Greek architecture, ancient portals defined the entries to the space, which then extended out into a temple landscape represented by a mural covering one of the gallery's multi-story walls. In each of the interior courtyards, which contained a display of architectural elements from a specific period, Boeden developed the perimeter as a corresponding collage of life-size building forms. Generally, it was hard to distinguish the content from the context of display or found objects from elements of Boeden's design. The complex exchange between the collection and Boeden's architecture was confined to the museum's interior, however, and did not determine the building's external appearance. According to the jury, the "early Renaissance" facades successfully performed the difficult task of unifying a building that was otherwise composed of many disparate parts.[3]

In 1905, the idea to exhibit architecture in a way that approximated the real experience of a building was not exactly new. As early as the Jubilee Exhibition of the Royal Academy of the Arts in 1886, architects had already avoided presenting their designs with elevations, sections, and plans in favour of an almost exclusive use of perspective, photographs, and large models of their buildings. The reporter from the *Deutsche Bauzeitung* was relieved to see what he called a "much wished-for change". Finally, according to the reporter, the architects had dispensed with the bleak and tiresome methods of presenting their work, methods that had only succeeded in scaring off the audience: professionals and the general public alike.[4]

Installation of the Gigantomachy Frieze
in the 1901 Pergamon Museum. From *Die
Skulpturen des Pergamon-Museums in
Photographien*, Berlin, 1903.
The Altar is identifiable at the far right
of the photograph.

Frontal view of the installation of the
Gigantomachy Frieze in the 1901 Pergamon
Museum. Zentralarchiv der Staatlichen
Museen zu Berlin—Preussischer Kulturbesitz.
Bildarchiv Preussischer Kulturbesitz / Art
Resource, NY.

The emphasis on three-dimensional representations of architecture (or those that suggested three-dimensions) in the Academy of the Arts exhibition responded to the opening of professional worlds to a public audience. Models are particularly important to this story. Architects had long used the model to illustrate a design for clients because of its legibility, but they had not always used it to represent themselves professionally. In the mid-nineteenth century, models had indeed been used at The Berlin Society of Architects and Engineers to illustrate lectures about various aspects of construction. But, at the same time, models were largely excluded from the architecture section of the Berlin Academy of the Arts exhibitions, which were geared toward architects although they attracted a public audience. Instead, the architecture section consisted primarily of drawings and was located after painting and sculpture. The models were exhibited in the last section of the show along with pocket watches, musical instruments, and rugs, and identified as the work of carpenters or their apprentices.[5] By 1886, when the yearly exhibitions had moved from the Academy's own building to pavilions at the exposition grounds, the architecture section included models and reconstructions as well as photographs. Freed from the confines of art academies and professional associations, exhibitions of architecture became public as well as professional events. As a result, architects became concerned about legibility and changed their representational technique. Now their work did not assume the form of painting and drawing and did not fit so neatly into the category of fine art.

The introduction of models and photographs indicated a shift from drawing to building as a way of representing architecture and suggested that exhibitions of architecture as a genre had grown much more complex. The freedom from the art academy galleries seemed to release the architecture models shown at the Berlin art exhibitions from some sort of constraint, and, very rapidly, the models grew so that by the turn of the century they were often extremely large, if not full-size.[6] It appeared that architects no longer felt limited to making what the Germans still call *Architekturausstellungen* (architecture exhibitions), the exhibitions composed of drawings and smaller than life-size models (the format used when architecture was included in an exhibition of art). Along with using large models at the art academy exhibitions in Berlin, architects around Germany turned to what Niels Gutschow and Johannes Cramer call '*Bauausstellungen*' ('building exhibitions'), exhibitions of complete buildings whose interior reflects the program indicated by the exterior of the building.[7] Using world fairs, open air museums, and model home shows as precedents, German architects began to show their work in the new context of the '*Bauausstellung*', the first one held at the Darmstadt Artists' Colony in 1901. Before 1927, the year of the *Werkbund* exhibition in Stuttgart and the famous *Weißenhofsiedlung*, *Bauausstellungen* were almost always found in Germany, but after that the spread of *Neues Bauen* (New Building) led to their emergence across Europe.

The emphasis on building over drawing marked architecture's appearance before a popular audience, a change echoed in architectural theory. In 1893, the art historian, August Schmarsow, declared that he was sceptical of architectural drawings ("plans, elevations, sections, and perspectives") because they only served the "specialist" whose "eye and trained imagination can piece together the whole". Implying, then, that he was thinking of the non-specialist, he worried that architectural drawings did not "preserve" the "original essence of a work of architecture", at least, he implied, for the general public.[8] Harry Mallgrave and Eleftherios Ikonomou explain that, for Schmarsow, "the essence of every architectural creation since the beginning of time [was] not its form... but the fact that it [was] a 'spatial construct'".[9] What essentially distinguished Schmarsow from predecessors like Bötticher, Semper, and Riegl, who also discussed architecture in terms of space, was that he claimed that the perception and understanding of space demanded movement. The others discussed space as if it were perceived from a fixed point of view.[10] The importance of movement underscored Schmarsow's emphasis on the bodily experience of space rather than a visual encounter with it in a representation, such as in painting or relief.[11] Considered in the context of exhibitions of architecture, Schmarsow's theory, as it was developed in various publications through the 1920s, could only have favoured the full-scale constructions that were emerging at the time.

The 1905 competition brief for an architecture museum showed that the members of the Society of Architects and Engineers were interested in embracing the new approach to display. As did the architects staging *Bauausstellungen*, the competition brief referred to world's fairs as well as museums as examples to follow: the Crystal Palace was cited as a reference probably because of the reconstructions in the Fine Arts Courts. In contrast, the South Kensington Museums were called "less relevant" because of the way in which the museum displayed fragments of buildings and useful items as isolated objects.[12] Like the full-scale models, the exposition pavilions, the displays of large scale fragments of buildings in exhibition halls, and the reconstructions (or constructions) of traditional villages and buildings at the world's fairs more generally, the reconstructions at the Crystal Palace originally served to provide a context for objects on display, but the members of the Society of Architects and Engineers made it clear in the competition brief that they valued them equally as the objects on display themselves. Their selection of Boeden's scheme, in which authentic, reconstructed, and idealised building fragments were engaged in the architecture, confirmed their view that the blurring of the collection and the exhibition environment was definitive for this new institution.

The example of the world fair indicates that the full-size architectural model appeared in exhibitions dedicated to subjects other than architecture, such as archaeology and ethnography. But the world fair was not the only context in which architecture appeared under the guise of other disciplines. Life-size architectural constructions also emerged in a museum culture likewise concerned about communicating with a new, non-professional audience. In the Berlin museums, this concern manifested itself around the turn of the century as a confrontation of ethnography and its strategy of presenting objects in context with the fine arts' emphasis on the autonomy of works on display. The confrontation affected curatorial practices in the Prussian State Museums into the 1920s, when it became known as 'The Berlin Museum Wars'. As curators attempted to resolve the situation by trying various approaches to presenting objects in context, some gradually turned their attention to the context itself. Ultimately, the museums found themselves in the business of showing architecture at full-scale, for example, constructing the public and private spaces of the collector's house in order to show a group of paintings, as von Bode did in the Kaiser Friedrich Museum, or constructing the Pergamon Altar to show its friezes.[13]

The history of the display of the Gigantomachy frieze, originally embedded in the Pergamon Altar, provides a good example of the struggle between object and context, which also characterised exhibitions of architecture. A collection of slabs and fragments from the frieze were first brought to Berlin in the late 1870s; in 1886 it was first presented to the public in the rotunda of the Altes Museum.[14] Although the frieze was exhibited as a series of objects without any hint of their original location, another approach to the frieze's display had already emerged. In many entries from the 1882 and 1884 competitions for a new Museum of Ancient Art (in the context of plans to develop the entire Museum Island in Berlin), the architects included a display of the frieze engaged within the Pergamon Altar.[15] When the first Pergamon Museum opened in

The 1930 installation of the Gigantomachy Frieze and Pergamon Altar. First floor, Collection of Antiquities, Pergamon Museum, 1934. Zentralarchiv der Staatlichen Museen zu Berlin—Preussischer Kulturbesitz. Bildarchiv Preussischer Kulturbesitz/Art Resource, NY.

1901, the architect Fritz Wolff indeed designed the altar as an armature for the frieze's display. His approach to this exhibit was possibly one of the reasons for the Museum's closure in 1908. While the claim at the time was that the unstable ground of the Museum Island could not support the structure, Can Bilsel points out that the museum that replaced it was much heavier. The better reason, Bilsel argues, is that the public could not get a good view of the altar, a complaint voiced by one of the museum's most important visitors, Kaiser Wilhelm II.[16] In fact, the guidebook did not mention the altar at all, describing the location of the frieze as a wall of the museum building (although this 'wall' appeared as an altar in the photographs).[17] With his attention turned toward using the architectural elements of the building to preserve the order of the frieze and, perhaps, make it possible for visitors to get a close look at it, Wolff had omitted the space necessary to complete the transformation of the wall into the altar, already started with the addition of architectural detail. The lack of space around the altar frustrated any attempt to view it as an imposing monument of ancient architecture and, instead, made it virtually invisible.[18]

The first Pergamon Museum was demolished in 1908 and reopened only in 1930 in a new building designed by Alfred Messel and Ludwig Hoffmann. After this long period of transition, the Pergamon Altar emerged, the backdrop for the frieze now transformed by its placement in the gallery as well as its design into an object in Berlin's collection of antiquities. Visitors entered the gallery to behold the main facade of the altar protruding into the space, complete with frieze and great staircase. The remaining course of the frieze, which originally wrapped the other three facades of the altar (shown as such in the first Pergamon Museum), now continued around the three walls of the enormous gallery, surrounding the visitors in one monumental gesture. Here the architecture was the focus of the exhibition and the frieze was an elaboration. Theodor Wiegand, the Director of the Antiquity Collection (which included other architectural reconstructions besides the Pergamon Altar) described the new museum as a "museum of ancient architecture".[19] In 1936, critic Adolf Behne took up this idea again when he hopefully described the museum in even broader terms: as the nucleus of a museum of architecture for Berlin composed of building fragments and spatial contexts that would express the monumentality of the original works.[20]

While architecture crept into the museum surreptitiously, it was rarely the subject of an exhibition there. Architecture exhibitions were (and are) problematic in institutions committed to collecting and exhibiting a nation's treasures as well as to educating its people. Drawings (and sometimes models) were valuable objects that a museum could display, but they were not accepted as a real work of architecture. They were not always the original or the final work of the architect and, consequently, they flaunted the museum's standard for authenticity. Buildings could not be brought into the galleries to help (and their collaborative character was also problematic), and, so, the attempt to offer museum visitors authentic architecture by giving them an integrated experience of space, mass, and detail at full-scale was frustrated from the beginning.

The royal collection of classical antiquities never became the seed for an architecture museum in Berlin, but it did establish a possible model for architecture exhibitions that answered the demands of the architecture profession for full-scale experiences of architecture and that of the museum for authenticity. Central to meeting these demands was the collection's introduction of full-scale artefacts—in some cases, authentic building fragments—into the museum. But equally important was the context set up around many of these fragments, which allowed curators to begin to reconstruct the building itself. In archaeological exhibitions, the authenticity of the display depended on the destruction of the original context. Without an existing referent and on a new site within the walls of the museum, building the display context could have only been a construction rather than a reconstruction; one that, at least, interpreted a lost original or, at most, an invented one.

When the Pergamon Museum opened in 1930, many archaeologists, curators, historians, and art historians criticised the Pergamon Altar as a fraudulent exhibit. Alone, the altar's placement at the centre of the exhibit and, then, its suggestion of completion contradicted the inconclusive state of the research. The critics argued that, instead, the character of the display should reflect the condition of the original objects at hand: it should be fragmentary and show the gaps in knowledge.[21] The demand for the display to be faithful to the research on the altar was supported by other complaints about the introduction of new materials used to construct the altar (and many of the other architecture exhibits), which, the critics claimed, devalued the authenticity of the original material. During the development of the design, critics had already called Wiegand's display "theater décor", not only because he relied on inauthentic materials to complete the invented context, but because the altar and frieze were no longer objects; they were now dramatic experiences, according to Wiegand's own description, that had lost their relationship to the authentic objects and their original situation.[22] The altar was only a facade, but it was positioned in the room so that it looked like a monument. The frieze, all but removed from its original context, was no longer viewed sequentially. Turned inside out and displayed on the interior walls of the gallery, visitors saw the enormous piece in its entirety from one point of view. Not surprisingly, Wiegand's critics called for an end to this approach to display.

For the public, however, the Pergamon Altar was a complete success. (There were about one million visitors the first year.)[23] For architects, the construction—or the invented nature of the context—should have been liberating. Can Bilsel restores some sense of authenticity to the 1930 altar display by referring to it as an early twentieth century German construction rather than as an attempt to reconstruct an ancient artefact.[24] And it is his approach, which rejects archaeology's preoccupation with an original as the sole standard for evaluating the authenticity of the exhibit and then casts the display as an example of contemporary architecture, that allows us to shift contexts from the archaeology to the architecture museum. The 1930 Pergamon Altar provided an example that could have freed architects from their frustrated attempts to show architecture in a museum context: from having to reproduce buildings with drawings and models in order to remain in the gallery and from having to remain outside of the gallery to show actual buildings. It demonstrated that authenticity could lie in the architectural experiences (however theatrical) newly constructed inside the museum rather than in concrete referents outside of it.

"Palaces of Foreign Rulers", Schinkel
Museum, 1931. left: Palace on the Acropolis;
right: Schloß Orianda. Zentralarchiv der
Staatlichen Museen zu Berlin—Preussischer
Kulturbesitz. Bildarchiv Preussischer
Kulturbesitz/Art Resource, NY.

Wall paintings and landscapes, Schinkel
Museum, 1931. Zentralarchiv der Staatlichen
Museen zu Berlin—Preussischer Kulturbesitz.
Bildarchiv Preussischer Kulturbesitz/Art
Resource, NY.
The wall paintings are from the Palais Redern
and the staircase of the Bauakademie, the
candelabra is from the Palais Redern.

Archaeology opened the door to architecture in museums (even as early as the first
Pergamon Museum in 1901), but the architecture museum as such never materialised.
The results of the 1905 competition were hardly publicised, perhaps because the
proposal was impractical. Perhaps the museum design was not convincing because its
architecture failed to engage the authentic fragments in a three-dimensional spatial
experience and, like the 1901 Pergamon Museum, offered its architecture only as a
backdrop to the collection. Or, perhaps, the results, which predated the 1930 Pergamon
Altar display by about 25 years, were ignored because invention had not yet entered
the museum, and the architecture of the courtyards was therefore only seen as false
compared to the museum's collection of artefacts. In general, the Berlin museums were
not inspired to produce exhibitions dedicated to architecture in the early twentieth
century, and very few architects or curators took advantage of the pressures of the
gallery on architecture to rethink the architectural exhibition at that time. The rare
example of an explicit exhibition of architecture in a museum surfaced only after the
opening of the Pergamon Museum with its contemporary German version of the altar
in 1930: the Schinkel Museum at the National Gallery, which opened in March 1931.

Although the Schinkel Museum made some attempt to construct an architecture
museum in the sense of the 1905 competition, it was still hemmed in by the art
institution that contained it. The museum was located in the *Prinzessinnen Palais*,
which visitors would have most likely entered on a bridge leading from the *Kronprinzen
Palais* that contained the National Gallery's collection of contemporary painting.
The Museum consisted of a sequence of rooms alternately containing Schinkel's oil
paintings and his drawings. In only one room, the room dedicated to his Berlin projects,
curators acknowledged that Schinkel's drawings referred to buildings: the drawings
were oriented to the projects they depicted.[25] The museum guidebook even suggested
that visitors look out the window to see the building—or at least the site—to which
the drawing referred. This attempt to escape the frame of the drawing united extremes
(drawings and buildings) but did not transform the presentation into something new
and, indeed, equivocated between two manifestations of authenticity already accepted
by the museum. In another room, however, there was evidence of a middle ground.
Over a group of landscapes hung a series of painted wall panels made for the Palais
Redern on Pariser Platz, a building razed in 1906 to make way for the Hotel Adlon.[26]
The panels were installed above the picture rail, as they were originally, making the
spatial apprehension of them at least as important as the appreciation of them as objects.
Although it was small and partial, the Palais Redern exhibit offered an experience of
Schinkel's architecture, echoing the exhibit of the Pergamon Altar across the street.

Unlike the Schinkel Museum, *The Dwelling of Our Time*, an exhibit that opened
a few months later, seemed to escape the struggle with the conventions of the display
of art. The exhibit formed a section of the 1931 German Building Exhibition and
consisted of a series of full-scale houses, fragments of apartment buildings, and
apartment interiors displayed inside an exhibition hall.[27] It succeeded in realising for
contemporary architecture what had been achieved by the 1930 archaeology display of
the Pergamon Altar, as well as what had been introduced by the first Pergamon Museum

in 1901 and the architecture museum competition for 1905: that is, the installation of an architectural experience in an indoor exhibition space. But, it emerged in a context very different from a museum: in the middle of a trade exhibition sponsored by the city of Berlin and the manufacturers and contractors in the building sector. *The Dwelling of Our Time* was largely controlled by architects; its director was Mies van der Rohe, and, while it was not officially sponsored by the *Werkbund*, most of the exhibitors were members of the organisation. *Die Form*, the *Werkbund* journal, devoted most of two issues to the exhibit right after it opened.[28] If anything, the commercial context, almost always the venue for *Werkbund* exhibitions, sanctioned the freedom to experiment with exhibition techniques, a freedom that had been so contentious in the museum.

Originally, *The Dwelling of Our Time* was planned as an exhibition of residential interiors, directed by Berlin architect Otto Bartning. When Bartning fell ill in 1930, Mies was asked to assume responsibility for the section.[29] With the assistance of Lilly Reich, Mies transformed a series of interiors lined up on the perimeter and down the central axis of a large exhibition hall into a collage of fragments of residential buildings, which he then inserted into a fictional site. The perimeter still contained interiors of various sizes (by architects such as the Luckhardt brothers, Walter Gropius, and Marcel Breuer), but it was now unified by a seamless elevation. Several freestanding units stood at the centre of the hall (by Mies, Reich, and Hugo Häring, among others), some identified as freestanding buildings and others identified as units whose intended building site was within a larger building. For example, two duplex apartment units stacked and placed on steel columns were described as being located somewhere in an apartment tower.[30]

The similarity of *The Dwelling of Our Time* to the Pergamon Altar exhibit, which opened the previous year, lay in the significance of the full-scale experience they provided rather than the objects out of which they were constructed. But they also shared a connection that was more profound: Mies's transformation of the original exhibition of residential interiors reiterated the process that created the Pergamon Altar exhibition: excising objects—thus rendering them as fragments—and reinserting them in the new context of an exhibition. He first redefined Bartning's free-floating

The Dwelling of Our Time, the architecture section of the 1931 German Building Exhibition, Berlin. Photograph. Baugilde, no. 10, 1931.
Mies's house is in foreground, right.

interiors, typical of the *Raumkunst* [interior design] exhibition, as fragments of larger
sites, whether the site was a building or a parcel of land. Visitors not only read that
they were looking at the interiors of a "single family house" or "a duplex in a residential
tower" but they saw it too.[31] After rendering the interiors as part of an architectural
context from which they were now separated, Mies used the overall exhibition design
to engage the fragments in a new and continuous site context. In this way, *The Dwelling
of Our Time* thematised the operations of collection and exhibition constitutive of not
only the Pergamon Altar but also museum practice more generally. The similarity of
The Dwelling of Our Time to the Pergamon Altar exhibit did not end here, however: the
reliability of both exhibitions was threatened by the very embrace of these operations,
which obscured any reference to existing buildings and their contexts. But, because it
was an exhibition about architecture of the future, The *Dwelling of Our Time* could
ignore this threat and assert the independence of the exhibition context from the so-
called 'original' context of its objects. The Pergamon Altar exhibition, however, had to
confront its origins because it was an archaeology exhibition. So, while the Pergamon
Altar display was committed at least to assembling the original frieze in its original
order (an issue which was not under discussion), the site design of *The Dwelling of
Our Time* wove together fragments with no previous relationship into a 'new world' of
architecture yet to come.

The inventiveness of Mies's exhibition design obscured any possible reference
to existing buildings made by *The Dwelling of Our Time* and, in doing so, gave the
exhibition the status of an authentic architectural experience. Not only did his design
avoid any general reference to an existing situation, but it also challenged the references
to the many different sites and contexts made by the individual units by literally
wrapping them in a 'new world'. In addition to articulating the continuity of the 'new
world' with a uniform exterior appearance, the exhibition design absorbed elements of
the exhibition hall itself into its architecture, and so rendered reality as part of Mies's
own vision. Spatial continuity was also a part of this 'new world'. It was a concept
that originally motivated the site design for the Weissenhof Siedlung in 1927, but
city officials in Stuttgart rejected the overlapping lots in the site design because they
feared that they would not be able to sell the units.[32] In *The Dwelling of Our Time*, the
freestanding units at the centre were linked by walls and the treatment of floors, which
extended from the space in and around one unit into that of another. This 'impractical'
aspect of the design, along with the openness of his own unit and the general lack of
detail in all of the schemes, suggested that Mies was offering visitors the experience of
an architecture that challenged existing conventions of ownership and privacy. As in the

case of the Pergamon Altar display, whose referent was lost to the past, the referent for *The Dwelling of Our Time* was inaccessible, not only because the design anticipated the future, but because the lack of construction detailing suggested that these projects could never be realised as such on a real site as a real building. Mies had been free to imagine the future, but he went further and constructed an experience of an ideal conception of modern architecture.

While the reactions to *The Dwelling of Our Time* were mixed, they all commented on the relationship of the exhibition to a notion of reality. Mies's supporters, many of whom were affiliated with the *Werkbund*, loved the scheme, excited that they could physically experience the essential aspects of a new architecture they hoped to realise at some point in the future.[33] His professional critics, however, discussed the exhibit as a series of real buildings on an existing site, and naturally found them problematic.[34] Likewise, the public searched for referents in the world of real buildings they knew or could anticipate but did not find them. Instead of accepting the units as fragments of works of architecture, they searched for complete buildings. But they found only "buildings on stilts", or, even worse, machines rather than homes for people.[35] The response was quite different than that to the Pergamon Altar, which was celebrated by the public. The Pergamon Altar presented visitors with a complete picture of the monument—however inventive—and, so, only caused problems for the experts, who viewed it in terms of the original building. The German public, however, had no knowledge of the original altar—or the theories concerning it—and no stake in searching for one.

The public not architects and archaeology (and other disciplines) not architecture opened up museums to architectural experience. In turn, museums opened up the possibility for architecture exhibitions and, ultimately, architects to establish their own position somewhere between the territories of fine art and building, both of which architects shared with others. The need to make scholarship accessible diverted the museums' focus from the objects in the collection to the conceptual and physical contexts that determined their importance and, in the process, produced more elaborate exhibition designs, which were often architectural, as a way to embody these contexts. But when the demand for a full-scale context encountered the pressure of the gallery, editing and invention became necessary. Consequently, the architectural context could not be an accurate reproduction of a building and, so, the integrity of the exhibition design had to rest in authenticity of experience it provided not in the design of the exhibition architecture itself. This echoed developments in architectural theory in the late nineteenth and early twentieth centuries, which recorded the increasing importance of space and the movement necessary to its perception. Along with the indoor site, the emphasis on experience rather than the object brought architecture exhibitions closer to letting architectural concepts rather than buildings shape displays and promised that architecture exhibitions might allow the public to understand a purely architectural discourse. Yet, the architecture profession mostly avoided the opportunity to present architecture as independent of art and building and the public generally rejected it when they did. On the one hand, Mies was one of the few architects to continue to exploit the museum context to create an approach to the exhibition of architecture outside of the models of art and building. Of course, he was also the one to claim (in 1928) that exhibitions were a site of practice and that the freedoms that they allowed rather than the constraints of commissions would advance the profession.[36] On the other hand, the public's struggle to understand his 'Dwelling of Our Time' suggests the general difficulty, if not the folly, of trying to present a new type of architecture exhibition, which offered an experience of architectural ideas independent of building. It also suggests the great irony of a project that emerged out of attempts by architects and curators at archaeology and art museums to be legible to the public and, yet, all but failed when it was finally realised in its most democratic venue: a trade exposition staged like a world fair.

The Inhuman One: the Mythology of Architect as Réalisateur

Renée Tobe

L'Inhumaine, Marcel L'Herbier. Exterior photograph. Art Director (this set): Robert Mallet-Stevens, 1923. Jaque Catelain as Einar Norsen in automobile in front of Claire's villa. Courtesy BIFI.

Introduction

Innovative in many ways, including its depiction of interactive electronic media transmission, *L'Inhumaine*, directed by Marcel L'Herbier and released in 1924, was the first film to display Modernist architecture through two sets designed by Robert Mallet-Stevens.[1] Although the narrative was taken from a novel written by the self-invented writer and sometime painter, Pierre Mac Orlan, the real author is Modernism itself.[2] Modernism manifests itself in the filming style, cast of characters both in front of and behind the lens, and is embedded within the story of how the film came into being, what it depicts, and how it was received. The sets of *L'Inhumaine* mark an important turning point in both Modernism and film set design and have been influential for both architects and filmmakers. For example, Alain Resnais acknowledges the influence of *L'Inhumaine* on the still figures moving across the perspectival landscape in his film, *Last Year at Marienbad*, 1961.[3]

Mallet-Stevens, with whom the film is most closely associated, collaborated on ten films in France between 1919 and 1929. For *L'Inhumaine*, he designed two sets, a villa, home of the female protagonist, an opera singer named Claire Lescot, and a laboratory for the hero, a Swedish engineer, called Einar Norsen. Both are distinguished by rectilinear compositions, sober ornaments, simple surfaces, and clear oppositions of shadow and light.

L'Inhumaine, Marcel L'Herbier.
Exterior photograph. Art Director (this set):
Robert Mallet-Stevens. 1923.
Robert Mallet-Stevens, Jaque Catelain, and
Marcel L'Herbier in front of Einar's laboratory.
Courtesy BIFI.

Photogénie

Three particular problems contextualise his influence on Modernism, architecture, and film design: architecture as photographed, 'real' architecture as filmed, and architecture as a set design. Mallet-Stevens worked with US fashion photographer Therese Bonney in the early stages of his career when his projects were mainly *macquettes* with few built works. Bonney's photographs of Mallet-Stevens' Modernist compositions, whether Bally shoe shops or Paris fashion house interiors, helped re-direct architectural photography from its documentary focus towards interpretive and abstract spatial compositions.[4] Mallet-Stevens hoped fashion would do for him what he also thought film would: promote him and his architecture.[5]

Mallet-Stevens suggests Modern architecture offers the best background for movement and to bring a scene to life.[6] As Beatriz Colomina demonstrates, film transforms architecture into a commodity—as both 'place' and object of consumption.[7] Mallet-Stevens' contemporary architects, such as Le Corbusier, or Adolph Loos who described *L'Inhumaine* as a stunning poem to Modernism and the birth of a new art, also suggested the media that frame buildings affect our understanding.[8] Loos disliked photographs for he felt they made architecture a two-dimensional artwork, to be looked

at not experienced, while Le Corbusier suggested a house could be like a camera, not an interior still, but a moving lens.[9] Mallet-Stevens' focus on *photogénie* creates photogenic architecture that is constantly being 'framed'.[10] In contrast to Le Corbusier's *promenade architecturale* where movement adjusts the image presented as the participant traverses the space, the biggest influence of film on Mallet-Stevens' architecture, was the use of *photogénie*, creating photogenic architecture that was aesthetically pleasing and looked to its greatest advantage in the photograph.[11]

Mallet-Stevens' ideas on style were put into practice in the rue Mallet-Stevens in Paris in 1926–1927. The rue Mallet-Stevens is designed as a street in the ideal Modern city and each of the individual houses or buildings represents an atelier home. The street offers the characteristic themes of Mallet-Stevens' work that include the relation of inside to outside, and shadow to light, as well as a complex ensemble of volumes punctuated by horizontal windows and roof terraces. Demonstrating the De Stijl influence on his work, his style includes the articulation of volumes around a central cube as well as the compositional openings and the filmic aspect offered by the different points of view permitted by the terrace design.[12] In 1921, influenced by his work on film, Mallet-Stevens designed an ideal town in which building archetypes (such as 'cinema' or 'town hall') in a single style were planned with sufficient space around and between each to accommodate the movement of the camera.[13] The title, *Dessins 1921 pour une cité moderne* as well as some of the intentions, were a double homage to both Antonio Sant'Elia's industrial thoughts and Tony Garniér's *Cité Industrielle.*

L'Inhumaine, Marcel L'Herbier.
Interior photograph. Design (this set):
Alberto Cavalcanti, Claude Autant-Lara, Pierre
Charreau, René Lalique, Jean Puiforçat,
and Jenan Luce. 1923.
Claire's villa, dining room surrounded
by moat, winter garden appears through
curtain in centre.
Courtesy BIFI.

L'Inhumaine, Marcel L'Herbier.
Interior photograph. Design (this set):
Alberto Cavalcanti, Claude Autant-Lara, Pierre
Charreau, René Lalique, Jean Puiforçat,
and Jenan Luce.
Costume design: Paul Poiret. 1923.
Georgette Leblanc as opera singer
Claire Lescot performs for her suitors
while accompanied by musician and
masked attendents.
Courtesy BIFI.

Chateau du Dé

Just as Charles de Beistegui commissioned Le Corbusier to design his Paris penthouse, 1929–1931, to act as a glamorous and imaginative backdrop for his own parties, the Viscomte de Noailles asked Mallet-Stevens to design a villa at Hyères on the Riviera in which he might entertain his friends, who included the artistic and cultural elite such as Pablo Picasso, Salvador Dali, and Balthus.[14] Although Mallet-Stevens was already a well-known media personality through writing exhibition articles and voicing radio programmes, by 1923, the time of its design, the Villa de Noailles was Mallet-Stevens' first piece of built work.

Noailles felt the villa at Hyères looked like a film set. He commissioned Surrealist artist, Man Ray, to make a documentary there in order to document what he felt was a new mode of life in the new Modern era. He also wished to leave his mark on the times.[15] When Man Ray saw the house, the Cubist forms reminded him of Stephane Mallarmé's poem *Un coup de dés jamais n'abolira le hasard* (A throw of the dice will never abolish chance), which provided both a title and theme for his film, *Les Mystères du Chateau du Dé*, Man Ray, 1928.[16] *Chateau du Dé* celebrates a predominantly exclusive and closed world. In Man Ray's short film (it is 20 minutes long) the actors that appear (in reality Noailles' guests) are as designed as the villa and the *mise en scène*. The film is an excellent expression of architectural dynamism; as in Mallarmée's poem, where the spaces between the lines are as important as the text, so the relation between different shots is crucial.[17] The film was shot largely in improvisation despite some general guidance concerning decision-making based on the throw of a dice. Mallet-Stevens suggested the actors should practice by acting in front of graph paper to measure the acceleration or deceleration of the relative gestures, in order to practice the fluid movement of the guests through the villa.

Other real buildings that have appeared in film in the Modern era include Michael Curtiz' *Female*, 1933 that opened with a shot of Frank Lloyd Wright's Ennis House designed in 1924, and his Robie House that appeared in several MGM films of the 1920s. Electrical engineer turned filmmaker Alan Dwan's film *What a Widow*, 1930, included Richard Neutra's Lovell House, 1927–1929 for exterior shots, and interiors designed by *Ecole de Beaux Artes*-trained (but proponent of bold Modernist design), Paul Nelson.[18] The first American film to have a Modern set was *Snow Blind*, made in 1924, a year after *L'Inhumaine*, with a set by Joseph Urban. Urban's set featured an entire room of faceted walls and shelves based on a square motif reminiscent of the designs of Charles Rennie Mackintosh and Josef Hoffman (who also influenced Mallet-Stevens).

Reciprocity of Architecture and Film

Mallet-Stevens declared that film has an undeniable and marked influence on Modern architecture which itself contributes its artistic share to film.[19] Modern architectural sets were not exclusively the efforts of Modern architects. Film set designers Cedric Gibbons and Richard Day had been among 100 designers selected by American President Herbert Hoover to attend the 1925 *Exposition International des Arts Decoratifs* in Paris, for which lighting designer Jacopozzi created illuminated Art Deco comets that darted about the Eiffel Tower.[20] Designers such as Gibbons and Day created Modernist film sets through the medium of books and exhibitions, rather than through first hand knowledge of Modernist buildings. Their fragmentary knowledge might be seen to produce a concern with visual detail and motif in their designs; yet one should also observe that a tendency to the fragmentary is perhaps a sine qua non of film sets, designed for the unilateral view of the camera rather than the experience of spatial enclosure.[21]

When Modern architecture appeared in film it acquired connotations far removed from the original Modernist intentions. The social context of Modern architecture was ignored and the focus turned to visuals and hints of excitement and adventure. Filmmakers contributed a sense of whimsy, fantasy, and drama to Modernism, qualities that animated the public's relation to Modern buildings that were often seen as sober and uninspiring. Modern architecture in film was the earliest introduction most viewers had to these radically new styles. Films were able to execute Modern designs on a grandness of scale that Modernism itself never attained.

Modern architecture in film epitomised the glamour of urban life. Film work offered architects a chance to design without conventions of structure, where stairs need not lead anywhere, and door and window openings are placed where they work best in the overall composition.

Mallet-Stevens' Instructions for How to Build a Set Design

At the time that Mallet-Stevens designed the film sets for *L'Inhumaine* he was a well-known, influential architect who had yet to realise a major architectural work. His most notable success was a life size model control building for the *aero-Club de France*, a design whose combination of science fiction and simple geometries, appealed to Fernand Léger with whom he collaborated on the film.[22]

Mallet-Stevens discussed Modernity in film set design in *Le Décor Moderne au Cinema*, the first book of the Modern era devoted solely to architecture and film. The book displayed a series of photographs of prominent examples of Art Deco and Modernist sets in an avant-garde and stylish layout.[23] Through his film work he became adept at working with recesses, and emphasising depth of field.

While other architects who contributed to film set design employed stairs to add verticality, Mallet-Stevens used planar elements such as placing Paul and Sonia Delauney paintings with their abstracted views of Paris over doors so the entrance becomes a vertical transition, not just a rectangle punched in a wall. Mallet-Stevens suggested L'Herbier move the camera to a higher position to better explain the set and takes advantage of the articulated elevation.

Just as the Delauneys made paintings inspired by aerial photographs, Mallet-Stevens' war-time experience taking aerial photos influenced his architectural design.[24] This manifested itself in the machine age ethos of simplicity in his designs, (that became less Vienna secessionist and more De Stijl), as well as his emphasis on three-dimensionality in his film sets. In the air, shadows are drawn out, and vertical elements, whether trees, bridges, airplane hangars, or buildings, emerge from the flat plane. When we move from the horizontal we see the world in a new way, just as the axonometric brings out dimensionality in a drawing.

While previously the actor moved and the set remained static, Mallet-Stevens suggests the set, that introduces the character, social position, tastes, habits, and lifestyle, must be dynamic as well. Mallet-Stevens suggests a more energetic set with repetition of planes, depth, and vertical design. One of the biggest contributions that Mallet-Stevens made to film was the use of open flowing expanse in the sets (that had previously been flats).[25] He encouraged straight and direct lines for ease of acting. His instructions included the height and movement of cameras, use of niches, use of both vertical and horizontal planes and white surfaces to set off a contrast of light and dark rather than colour, and compositions that work within the three: four aspect ratio of the screen.

He also warned designers and architects not to apply film set design to architectural projects as the proportions and ornament appropriate to film were not suitable to buildings, and he referred to the differences in lighting, colour, and the flattening of the image on the screen. With a strong Modern set and symbiotic relation between architecture and action, the set is as much a character as the actors—the latter therefore became appropriate components of set design and were set into relief by regular, preferably geometric, backdrops. The union of actor and setting—the notion of the performer and set alike as architectonic entities—emerges from the work of Adolphe Appia and Edward Gordon Craig in theatre set design.

Other Characters

Paris in the 1920s was a place of intrigue and scandal and looking directly at the individuals involved behind-the-scenes reveals an interactive network of influence and provides cultural context for the discussion of Modernity. For example, when L'Herbier needed a scene of an audience in an uproar (caused by Claire singing despite the tragic death of her lover), Leblanc's real-life lover, Margaret Andersen, created the riotous commotion by organising a concert at the *Théâtre des Champs-Elysées* for George Antheil (who also provided the score for Fernand Léger's film, *Ballet mécanique*, 1924) and asking

him to play his most controversial composition. Picasso, Eric Satie, Man Ray, Gertrude Stein, and James Joyce are reputed to have been in the audience at the *Théâtre*. Jane Heap helped bring both films to New York City where they were released together. Three years earlier Anderson and Heap published Joyce's *Ulysses* in the *Little Review.*

L'Herbier wished *L'Inhumaine* to be a sort of résumé of all that was happening in the visual arts in France, two years before the 1925 Paris *Exposition* for which Mallet-Stevens designed the *Société des Auteurs de Film* where French films were projected. With the exception of Le Corbusier, *L'Inhumaine* was the collaborative effort of those whose work at the Paris exposition would define the avant-garde of design: Mallet-Stevens created the exterior décor, Léger concocted the laboratory interior, Pierre Charreau designed the furniture, René Lalique, Jean Puiforçat, and Jenan Luce crafted the decorative objects, Raymond Templier the jewellery, and Paul Poiret produced the costumes.[26] Poiret, whose designs for Claire are superb, believed his *haute couture* creations to be a likeness of the wearers for whom they had been designed and that the bond between dressmaker and client should resemble the rapport between portraitist and sitter, just as the set designer wished actor, action and background to work together.[27]

Mallet-Stevens was a member of CASA, or the Club des amis du Septième art, founded by Ricciotto Canudo who included material from *L'Inhumaine* in his *Exposition d l'art dans le cinéma français* in 1924. Other members of CASA included filmmakers L'Herbier, Jean Epstein, Germaine Dulac, and Abel Gance as well as Léger, musicians Satie and Maurice Ravel and poets Jean Cocteau and Blaise Cendrars.[28] CASA's directive was to raise the cinema to its rightful place among the arts. They wished to use silent film (which depends on strong visual communication for its effectiveness) as a means to promulgate new ideas in design, and experimented with novel photographic techniques (such as soft focus, rapid-fire editing, opaque masks, and split screens) and Modern decor.

L'Inhumaine (L'Herbier, 1924)

The establishing shot of *L'Inhumaine* begins with a rapid tracking shot of a road above Clichy, followed by location shots taken from a high angle looking down on the industrial area, cuts to a *macquette* of Mallet-Stevens' Modernist villa, then a full scale set of the entrance. This front facade illustrates Mallet-Stevens' characteristic traits, such as glass doors, large horizontal bands, and the play of rectangular surfaces that remained constant throughout his career and appeared first in his film sets.

The house is a stark white Cubist construction that houses the enormous, elaborate, richly decorated and colourful interiors designed by Alberto Cavalcanti and Claude Autant-Lara.[29] The contrast between the cool lines of Mallet-Stevens' exteriors, and the ornate and elaborate schemes of the interior of Claire's villa, work against Modernity's notions of unity of design, while adding to the film's fascination.

Inside the villa, male suitors all try to woo her with different media, reflecting Modern sensibilities. For example, one suitor begs her to join him in leading a humanist revolution, an impresario suggests an alliance with him would mean endless theatre performances, and Einar proposes that she broadcast her voice electronically as the means to reach mass audiences. At first she seems to choose an attractive Maharaja. After some interesting romantic vicissitudes in which Einar pretends to drive off a cliff for love of Claire, L'Herbier presents location shots of the *Théâtre de Champs Elysée* where the singer performs, and is then attacked by a snake planted by the jealous Maharaja who spied on Claire and Einar outside Mallet-Stevens' other set for the film, the Engineer's laboratory. The laboratory stretches vertically with exposed electrical wires reflecting the energies within, and even has a satellite dish. The electric wires lead down to an underground machine room of vast proportions. As in the singer's villa, the *macquette* suggests proportion and organisation that does not appear in the interiors.

The laboratory's interior were designed and constructed by Léger. Léger's distinctively Modern sensibility of vision expresses itself as a dynamic, perceptual experience of space. Léger had been involved with film since Cendrars incited his interest with his book *L'ABC du Cinéma* in 1918 that had a direct influence both on Léger's paintings and his film *Ballet mécanique*, made with US filmmaker Dudley Murphy during the production of *L'Inhumaine*. Léger also advised Abel Gance on his epic 22 reel film, *La Roue*, 1922, that itself influenced Japanese filmmaker Akira Kurosawa, with its rapid montage, close-up of advancing railway tracks, and the wheel of the film's title as metaphor for the spirit of life.[30]

L'Esprit Nouveau

Mallet-Stevens' French *modernité* differs from Lang's German Expressionism in its depiction of the mechanistic human. As opposed to the malignant forces presented two years later by Fritz Lang in *Metropolis*, 1925, Leger's interior with its kinetic abstract forms, movement, and light offers a benign presentation of 'science' while Lang's perspectival geometry subsumes the human and emphasises the monumentality of his tale.[31] L'Herbier's sets and stylisation emphasise the spiritual and the spirit itself, in both humans and architecture.[32] In *L'Inhumaine*, the new spirit, the spirit of the age, lives not only in design but also in life. The machine that brings back the dead to life, or suggests it might come to life itself shows that there is a 'spirit' in the machines themselves.

Notions of Modernism infuse every scene of the film from the aerial view of the industrial city, the steel bridge, the moving car, to the media transmission of Einar's laboratory and the suggestion that electronic transmission will overtake painting and other visual arts, not just through sound but television as well. While we now see only the aesthetic and the visuals, the 'message' of modernity was equally important when the film was released.

L'Herbier was infatuated not only with modernity's style but its spirit as well, and carried the force of modernity over into his personal life with his Modern offices and Paris apartment complete with exercise equipment and punchbag, expressing Modern ideals that we must enter the future healthier and stronger than ever before.

L'Inhumaine, Marcel L'Herbier. Photograph. Design (this set): Fernand Léger. 1923. Fernand Léger in foreground of Einar's laboratory. Courtesy BIFI.

He had also many years earlier been infatuated with the film's star, Georgette Leblanc, who originated the use of Modernism in the film. Leblanc wished the film to be Modern in design in order to be contemporary, and to encourage the film's reception in the USA. As principal financial contributor to the film's production, Leblanc had a strong influence.[33] Leblanc contributed to the narrative, scripting the principal character, whom she played herself, as an 'inhuman', although also Modern, woman of independent means and character. Claire refuses marriage, pretends not to mourn her male suitor who killed himself on her behalf (reminiscent of post-war women who persisted with their careers). Women with qualities such as being inscrutable to men, independent of domestic expectations, were often characterised with sexual ambiguity in their appearances and presentation, or as in this film, as 'inhuman' or lacking human warmth. *L'Inhumaine* presented a kind of woman who did not appear in Hollywood films until ten and twenty years later. While the war may have upturned social and sexual orders, a woman's duty to have children was part of the ideology of French reconstruction and economic recovery.[34] The two 'revivals' in which on separate occasions both male and female protagonists are brought to life, plus the title of the film, show another link with *Metropolis* that also depicts the female as an automaton. Both films reflect the fear that the independent woman was lacking human qualities.[35]

After being poisoned by the jealous Maharaja, Claire arrives near death to the laboratory where she is revived by the engineer's newly invented life-saving device. *L'Inhumaine* with its 'primitive' inset scenes and sneaking dark skinned potentate, who represents the exoticism of the East, displays a disturbing post-colonial subtext not atypical for its time. The suggestion of media such as radio and television suggest that Claire can reach an international audience without travel. The audience the film depicts are urban masses and colonial subjects, including African and Egyptian, rather than the sophisticated elite present in Lescot's villa and diametrically opposite of the cool Nordic rationality represented by the Swedish engineer. The engineer's resurrection of the dead singer transforms the story into a metaphor for the uses of technology in the service of post-First World War reconstruction. In this sense Einar represents the masculinity of technology, and Claire's no longer independent sexuality comes under the control of his science.

Propaganda and Influence

The acceptance of Mallet-Stevens' atmosphere of Modernism leads us to look at the problem of 'directing' a Modern way of life, bringing together both architecture and plot, and raising the question why an architect should become a *réalisateur*. While Mallet-Stevens hoped the film would make Modernism acceptable to the French public, LeBlanc hoped that Modernism would help the film's reception in the US. The director, the writer, the main actor, the characters, the designers of the film's furniture, jewellery, and costumes, as well as the script itself configure the film in its time. Mallet-Stevens' inclusion of himself in production stills that he used for publicity shots for the film emphasises the question of his role, authorship, and foreground and background.[36] He described the purpose of cinema not to act as a role for architects to follow but as propaganda for introducing the public to, and educating them in Modern architecture.[37]

Propaganda originally suggested that which 'ought to be spread'. Propaganda did not, in Mallet-Stevens' time, have the same negative connotations it acquired during the Second World War and thereafter, although the contemporary political sense dates from the First World War. Propaganda techniques were codified and applied scientifically by a journalist, Walter Lippman, and a psychologist Edward Bernays (nephew of Sigmund Freud) who were hired by US President Woodrow Wilson to sway popular opinion to enter the First World War. Propaganda is often transmitted implicitly, and this is the power of film, which Mallet-Stevens fully realised.

Despite the propagandist use of Modern architecture in film sets, whether for aesthetic reasons, as with Mallet-Stevens, or for political purposes, most filmmakers ignored the Modern Movement's more radical underpinnings. In US cinema it came to represent the capitalist dreams of fame, glamour, money, and power, as advocated by Hollywood, the dream factory. Architects first originated the Modernist buildings and film sets that inspired Hollywood, then realised the dreams the films animated in the viewers.

The English term 'to direct' is in French *diriger*, which refers to telling people how to move or where to move to. The French term for director is either *metteur en scène* meaning the one who creates or constructs the scenario, or *réalisateur* the one who makes the scenario real. This is what architects do; we actualise dreams—our own or others'. However, architects are also famous for their inflexibility. Mallet-Stevens' mentor, Hoffman, even decreed what jewels his client should wear in which rooms. Mallet-Stevens himself used the language of control, of right and wrong, in both his discussion of design and of how the client should use the space and what it should and could be used for, a *réalisateur*, and an inhuman one indeed.

Architecture that provides an environment for 'lived experience' is particularly suggestive for the process of identification, whereby we, the viewer, identify with the hero.[38] Film adds another layer of appropriation than photography—we put ourselves into the film, projecting ourselves onto the character and into the architecture presented on the screen, architecture that, when Modern architecture was used as a set, represented the liberating lives one could lead by living, working, and playing within the new buildings. This means that the architect, as producer of architecture, is also the one who realises dreams—*réalisateur*—about a whole mode of life, not just invented three-dimensional structures. While a tenet of Modernity is that we are individuals thinking for ourselves, Mallet-Stevens suggests the influence of architecture and film as a way of directing a way of life, telling us how to live.

Film uses the 'language' of reality, and characters, even if their beauty, wealth, sophistication or wisdom are outrageously exaggerated, still supposedly represent the 'everyman', the man or woman on whom we project our own emotions, anticipations, aspirations. We empathise with the hero or heroine presented, bringing them, their lives, and the homes they live in, closer within our imagination.[39]

Réalisateur

Architects, such as Nelson in the USA and Mallet-Stevens in France, while they only contributed the sets to relatively few films, had broad influence on the collective dreams of film audiences of the Modern era. The architect becomes identified as one who realises dreams, not just of three-dimensional structures, but of a whole mode of life, which is the entire history of filmmaking.

The architect as the one who makes real the dreams and aspirations of the public, the client, and the culture in which we find ourselves, is also the *réalisateur* who forces and controls the way that we live within the buildings that are designed—thus contributing towards the lack of freedom for which Modernism is famous. There are many examples of this in the current era, where the architect's intentions can be at odds with the completed building and how it is used—not so much making real an environment of dreams, as in line with the English term, director, telling people how to live and move through their buildings. However, this does not necessarily diminish the building in any way—in fact, it often enhances it.

In conclusion, as Modernism grew more widely accepted Modern film décor no longer had to convince the public of Modernism's value. Through the familiarity gained in film, Modernism came to represent Utopianism, progress, and a future to be welcomed and embraced. Only the wealthy could afford Modern villas, but everyone could go to the movies. Modernism in film left a heritage of an enduring body of design that was seen and appreciated by an audience much larger than any architect would ever be able to reach.[40] But architects, the constructors of reality, had realised their own dreams in film, and turned them into dreams for everyone.

The Allegorical Project: Architecture as 'Figurative Theory'

Penelope Haralambidou

Introduction

According to Angus Fletcher, in the simplest terms allegory says one thing and means another. Deriving from the Greek *allos*, other, and *agoria*, speaking, it signifies a doubleness of intention that requires interpretation.[1] Consequently, Northrop Frye remarks that all commentary is allegorical interpretation and suggests the formal affinities of allegory with criticism.[2]

This paper seeks to identify and define a distinct territory of authorship in architecture which employs architectural design, the language of describing buildings, to articulate something 'other': a critical idiom combining drawing with text to reflect on architecture, art, science and politics. The allegorical architectural project is characteristically disconnected from the material construction of a building. The imaginative, sometimes poetic, bringing together of ideas in the design positions it closer to visual literature and, because of its high dependency on narrative, I see it here as a cross between a work of art, painting or sculpture, and a literary text.

Often the allegorical architectural project refers to another piece of work or site. The allegorical interpretation reveals an analytical inclination and the project becomes a vehicle for criticism. Allegorical design, therefore, is a critical method, which distances the architect from the construction site and redefines her as a commentator of spatial phenomena better grasped and analysed through drawing and text. A fusion between design and theory, the allegorical architectural project combines creative and critical traits and can be compared to a visual equivalent of literary or critical theory. This preoccupation with visual and spatial phenomena and use of drawing as a critical method, reveal a clear preference for the figure, making this alternative practice a 'figurative theory'. Here I use the term "figurative" inspired by Jean-François Lyotard's negotiating notions of discourse, related to structuralism, written text and the experience of reading, and figure, related to phenomenology, images/drawings and the experience of seeing.[3]

Allegory and the Architectural Project

The allegorical impulse is a mode of the human intellect linked to the origins of language and representation as the introduction of the "other", *allos*. Joel Fineman in "The Structure of Allegorical Desire" asserts that this other-discourse of allegory accompanies "the loss of being that comes from re-presenting oneself in language as a meaning... makes the psyche a critical allegory of itself, and... justifies psychoanalysis as the allegory of that allegory".[4]

John MacQueen in *Allegory*, part of a series entitled *The Critical Idiom*, provides a historical overview of literary allegory, where he recognises its origins as philosophical and theological, closely associated with narrative in the form of myths.[5] Examples from the classical world of Greece and Rome include the myth of Demeter and Persephone, an allegorical explanation of sowing and harvesting corn and inevitably of human mortality, and Orpheus, an allegory of the redemptive powers of the human soul. Furthermore, MacQueen recognises Plato as the founder of many aspects of the allegorical tradition; many of his dialogues include allegorical narratives, "which serve to image truths beyond the reach of the discursive intellect".[6]

Allegorical parables populate the Old and New Testament and allegory flourishes as a prevalent literary mode during the middle ages. In her *Castles of the Mind: A Study*

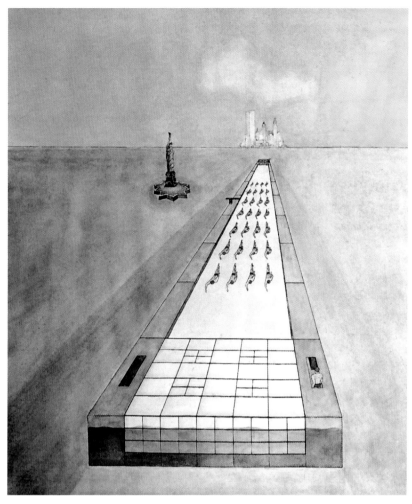

of Medieval Architectural Allegory, Christiania Whitehead studies the potential offered by architecture for allegorical representation and analyses how writers in the middle ages turned to the trope of the textual building, or 'scriptural architecture', to describe different themes from ecclesiastical truths to romantic love.[7] Furthermore, Dante Alighieri, author of perhaps the most famous medieval allegory, the *Divine Comedy*, offers the first theory of literary allegory in his *Convivio*.[8]

Walter Benjamin's analysis of baroque allegory, as Bainard Cowan asserts in his *Walter Benjamin's Theory of Allegory*, treats allegory as a literary theory, "casting it in cultural and ontological terms".[9] Indeed in Benjamin's analysis, allegory is primarily an experience; an experience of the world as no longer permanent, but fragmentary and enigmatic: "transforming things into signs is both what allegory does—its technique—and what it is about—its content".[10]

Departing from this brief historical overview of literary allegory, this paper seeks to specify its role in the architectural project. Although allegory exists in the experience of built architecture—for instance, Emile Mâle has shown how a medieval church is a historical allegory written in stone, glass and wood—we will focus on imaginary projects that use drawing to express something 'other' than the construction of a building.[11] Additionally these allegorical projects use figurative language and storytelling to articulate meaning through narrative structures. Use of narrative situates allegorical projects closer to a visual literature than pure architectural design, and allows them to be read in literary terms. I would like to suggest the allegorical architectural project as an alternative mode of authorship in architecture, one that uses drawing to contemplate spatial issues difficult to grasp through mere textual analysis. Blurring the distinction between two traditionally divided fields of authorship in architecture—the built work, in terms of the architect as designer and the theoretical/historical text, in terms of the architect as writer—we will study how certain authors' have used design as theory. Borrowing terms from studies of allegory in literature and fine art, the paper will reflect on allegorical designs by Jonathan Hill, Rem Koolhaas, Ben Nicholson and Mike Webb.[12]

Fictional Structures

Although chronologically close and clearly using allegory to structure and represent spatial ideas, the examples presented in this essay are not directly connected. While the authors are most likely aware of each other's work, they do not form a collective. Their critical use of drawing is fuelled by an individual desire for allegory, which for Fineman "is implicit in the idea of structure itself and explicit in criticism".[13] This critical tendency defines and separates the selected projects from their historical 'paper architecture' predecessors: from Piranesi's labyrinthine drawings through to the avant-garde architecture of the 1950s and 60s. An in depth historical tracing of the origins of this alternative architectural practice is beyond the scope of this essay. However, most architects presented here favour narrative as a vehicle for grasping and developing spatial ideas, a tendency originating at schools of architecture, such as the Architectural Association, Cooper Union and most recently the Bartlett, with which they are either directly or by approximation connected.[14]

Between 1972 and 1977, Rem Koolhaas worked on a series of imaginary collaborative projects sited in New York. Images and small descriptions of the projects were subsequently included in the appendix of *Delirious New York: A Retroactive Manifesto for Manhattan*, 1978. According to Koolhaas:

> The Appendix should be regarded as a fictional conclusion, an interpretation of the same material, not through words, but in a series of architectural projects. These proposals are the provisional product of Manhattanism as a conscious doctrine whose pertinence is no longer limited to the island of its invention.[15]

The Manhattan projects' pseudo-historical narratives add a fictional dimension to Koolhaas' critical historical analysis of New York. In his introduction, Koolhaas suggests the projects reflect analogous ideas to the ones explored in the main part of the book, by using architectural drawing instead of text. Sharing a similarly episodic manner, they point to, and accentuate a fictional tendency colouring the rest of his textual analysis.

Temple Island, a project by ex-Archigram member Mike Webb, was exhibited at the Architectural Association in 1987. The exhibition catalogue includes reproductions of his infectiously lyrical drawings accompanied by an elliptical and poetic text:

> Both in my memory and upon an islet in the Thames at Henley reposes a temple: i.e. the incorporeal and the real [one], and though the site of each remains intact, the incorporeal temple is fading, so that, were its façade to be precipitated on to a dimensional surface, a bit of "restoration" work would become necessary so as to provide an image you could read.[16]

Webb's poetic drawings critically investigate geometry and representation as the substructure of a fleeting childhood recollection. Precise graphic exercises in descriptive geometry contemplate projection as a means of not only drawing, but also remembering and imagining spatial phenomena.

In *Appliance House*, 1990, Ben Nicholson contemplates domesticity and the collector and offers a re-evaluation of architectural drawing through collage:

> Call the Appliance House a sub-urban home turned into a shelter from every kind of consumptive adversity the city is able to muster... Each room encloses an accentuated state of normal, everyday, sub-urban living, but the rooms have all changed their ceramic nameplates. Where there used to be the cosy nook with an open fireplace, there is a furnace to suit the pyromaniac within us all. Where there was once a study, in which the Toby Jug collection and family sports trophies were displayed, there

now exists the Kleptoman Cell, a room given over to the face-to-face confrontation of what it means to have in one's possession any object gleaned by any means, fair or foul.[17]

Nicholson's ironic critique of the nuances of contemporary life focuses on the pervasiveness of mechanical objects and appliances that "apparently nurture homeliness".[18] Splicing his raw material from the Sears and Sweets Catalogues, he employs collage as a drawing method and as a vehicle for his satirical renaming and redrawing of the rooms of a house. Satire is a subgenre of allegory, to which Fletcher attributes the role of awakening minds, lulled into routine inaction, by presenting behaviour in a grotesque, abstract caricature.[19] Nicholson's satire challenges social norms of inhabitation, but also those of architectural representation by questioning design intention and introducing the unexpected through collage.

In *Actions of Architecture: Architects and Creative Users*, 2003, Jonathan Hill discusses two projects, *The Institute of Illegal Architects*, 1996, and *Weather Architecture*, 1999, which are:

> ... metaphors of the outside pouring into the practice of architects. Each begins with a critique of an architectural idea and an architectural institution, in which the idea is manifest and leads to a counter proposition.[20]

Hill asserts that architecture is made by use and by design, considers the relations between the architect and the user, and argues for an architect aware of the creativity of the user. Two buildings become the focus of his critical analysis and the sites for his critical design interventions: the *Royal Institute of British Architects* by Grey Wornum, c. 1935 and the *Barcelona Pavilion* by Ludwig Mies van der Rohe, 1929/1986. In both cases, interventions are designed to reveal hidden assumptions and articulate counter propositions. Hill's critique of architectural institutions, therefore, originates in design.

We see from the above descriptions that these architectural projects resemble literary genres: Koolhaas' projects provide a pseudo-historical analysis, Webb's *Temple Island* reads as visual poetry, Hill's *Institute of Illegal Architects* has undertones of a manifesto and Nicholson's *Appliance House* bears a resemblance to satire, a genre he explored further in his recent allegorical project *The World: Who Wants It.*[21]

In parallel with the literary character of the work, these projects critically reconsider drawing as the underlying syntax of cultural spatial constructs in architecture.

Appliance House, Flank Walls. Drawing. Ben Nicholson, 1990. Courtesy of Ben Nicholson.
The Flank Walls are composed by collapsing the stretching action that took place to form the Cell Walls. The Flank Wall results from the compression of the Wall into approximately one-third of its total length, forming a reversed anamorphosis of the Wall This method of drawing, made into building, causes the Kleptoman, who walks between the Flank Wall and the Telamon Cupboard, to be brought up short.... The Kleptoman's body will be torqued by sensing the generating object, the Telamon Cupboard, and its three subsequent configurations. Spatially, the Kleptoman will have entered the Cell before he has even stepped inside, because the Cell's substance is recoded and presented to him bodily at the threshold.

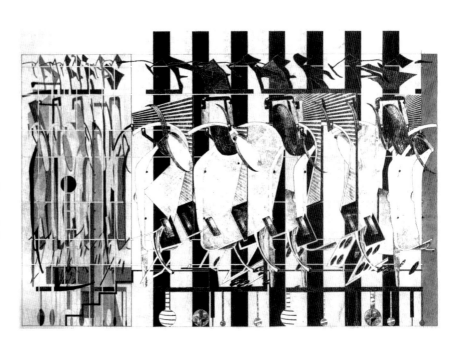

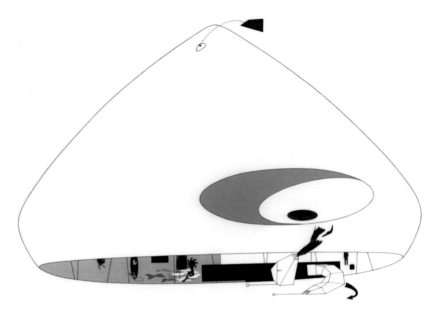

The Institute of Illegal Architects, Aerial perspective looking north of the sound production space.
Drawing. Jonathan Hill, 1996.
Courtesy of Jonathan Hill.
The rubber interior surface of the sound production space progresses from hard at the entrance to soft and upholstered at the rear. The south elevation of the sound production space consists of a 150mm wide void between two parallel sheets of glass. A pivoting hollow steel door with four recessed nozzles stores pigment, polystyrene and seeds, which are blown into and sucked out of the void, turning the facade from transparent to opaque and back to transparent. The periscopes on the storage door project the sights and smells of sound production into the Royal Institue of British Architects.

Allegorical Traits

In search of a theoretical background for this alternative architectural practice, we will now study analyses of allegory in literature and art to see if certain characteristics apply to the architectural allegories discussed here.

Battle and Progress

In *Allegory: The Theory of a Symbolic Mode,* Fletcher defines two broad categories of allegorical narratives: what he calls "battle", an opposition between two forces, or "progress", a description of a sequence of events that often takes the form of a journey.[22] Unsurprisingly, therefore, the allegorical projects presented here can be seen to belong to either one, and in most cases, both these two seemingly simplistic categories.

Hill's imaginary building contests the unchallenged authority of its neighbour at the other side of Portland Place:

> Sited directly in front of the Royal Institute of British Architects, the Institute of Illegal Architects challenges the idea that architects alone make architecture. Questioning the binary opposition of architect and user, it proposes a third entity: the illegal architect, a hybrid producer-user, who questions and subverts the established codes and conventions of architectural practice.[23]

From the above it is clear that Hill is setting up the narrative of his project as an opposition, a battle, between two forces—the RIBA and the IIA, the signifier of the architectural profession and its imaginary other.

Additionally, the project stages two simultaneous journeys—"one conceptual, from the architect to the illegal architect, the other physical, from the RIBA to the proposed IIA sited directly in front of it".[24] Similar to medieval 'scriptural architecture', the narrative of the journey through the forms and materials of the IIA provides the structure for the allegorical text. Hence, Hill's allegorical subversion is conceived as both battle and journey/progress.

In *Temple Island,* Webb describes the journey of a submersible travelling backwards on the regatta course. The "tripper" located inside the submersible is presented with four mathematically interrelated images of the temple via a circular periscope screen. Through complex geometrical calculations his projective act of looking "transmutes into solid", and when the submersible reaches the START the design for a new temple emerges:

If the design for a new temple has emerged, it is the result of the journey towards it... were the journey to be made in reverse, the new temple would revert back to the image of its incorporeal antecedent.[25]

Webb uses the parable of a journey to describe the design process and reflect on projection and representation through a series of geometrical exercises. The journey is therefore only an analogy, a narrative structure through which the underlying constitution of spatial representation and the way we mentally organise space is questioned.

Visual and Verbal

Craig Owens in "The Allegorical Impulse: Toward a Theory of Postmodernism" notes a reciprocity between the visual and the verbal in allegory: words are often treated as purely visual phenomena, while visual images are offered as a script to be deciphered: "In allegory the image is a hieroglyph; an allegory is a rebus—writing composed of concrete images."[26] All architectural projects presented here exist in book form, where drawing and text complement each other in the production of meaning.

In *Actions of Architecture*, Hill observes a difference between the use of words and images in his two allegorical projects. While in *Weather Architecture* words essentially affirm images, in *The Institute of Illegal Architects* one sentence may explain a drawing and another contradict it or add further information. Certain drawings offer the reader/viewer little opportunity for interpretation but in others "the relationship between signifier and signified is loose".[27] Drawings, photographs and texts are analogous to the buildings they describe but are also conceived as a "montage of gaps" where allegorical interpretation might take place.[28]

On the other hand, Nicholson describes the process of naming drawings and how a name, not necessarily associated with the things depicted, can be jarring. For the author the act of naming is part of the design process and offers the new forms

Temple Island, Regatta Scene.
Drawing. Michael Webb, 1998–2007
Courtsesy of Michael Webb.

Locate, O Observer, your Cyclopean eye at the focus of this circular painting. You'll find that the focus is, in fact, a vertex...
the vertex of a cone of vision...
whose axis will appear to you as a point and whose surface enwraps a volume of air, earth and water; the water being the waters of the River Thames at Henley.

I have divided the circle into two halves: the left half a romantic evocation of the landscape painted in the style of Claude Lorraine. It is late afternoon. The heat of the first weekend in July is oppressive; the still air heavily polluted. The right half is a mathematical examination of the landscape's perspective foreshortening using the posts that define the rowing lanes of the regatta course so as to form a grid; a grid being a necessary component of any such exploration.

Details of the grid:
I have divided the course into 24 equal units. Post 1 marks the Finish line and Post 25 the Start line. The Observer is at 0, one unit length away from the Finish. The course is depicted the course in perspective projection, but because conventional perspective is developed from an orthographic plan, I have positioned the plan projection alongside the perspective; so that Post 1 on the plan aligns with Post 1 on the perspective.
Now, if one measures the unit distance of each point from 0, on the ortho projection, so that post 1 is one unit away from 0, post 2 two units from 0 etc. and then record these unit measurements on the perspectival projection, a parabolic curve will result. This curve, if understood as a section cut through a cone, would establish 0, the Vanishing Point, as its vertex.

123

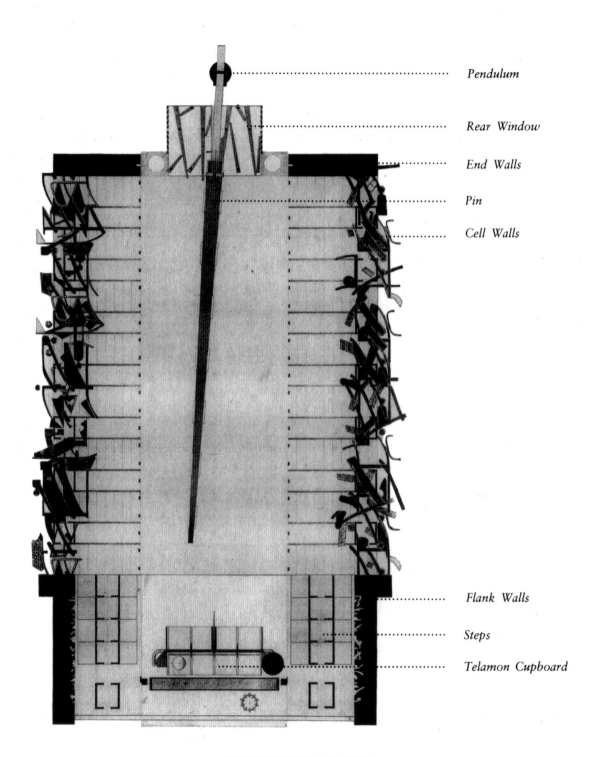

Pendulum

Rear Window

End Walls

Pin

Cell Walls

Flank Walls

Steps

Telamon Cupboard

THE KLEPTOMAN CELL

familiarity and plausibility. By naming a drawing, the thing depicted can be tamed.[29] Allegorical interpretation takes place within the gap created between the image and the name; this gap is where the reader performs a secondary creative act.

Furthermore, the counter-implication of visual and verbal in the allegorical project is most prominent in the use of extended captions accompanying drawings and images. Captions can be explanatory and descriptive, add further information or offer unexpected new ideas that make the drawings enigmatic.

Accompanying Webb's geometric explorations in *Temple Island*, the text exists in the form of numbered captions following a sequence of drawings in different scales. These interlinked captions compose the entire verbal account of the project, and read as a cross between poetry and a mathematical problem. Here, drawings and text appear in equilibrium: each double spread consists of drawings on the right and text on the left, a project equally engaging the two sides of the brain.

Figurative Geometry

Fletcher describes allegory as "figurative geometry". Allegorical narrative operates as a mathematical equation or geometric principle, which instead of abstract numbers and letters uses personages, everyday or sublime objects and sites to signify structural relationships. In this account of allegory there exists a bizarre contradiction: However particular its figurative elements, the allegory remains abstract—as if allegorical themes are emptied of their content by the structure that governs them.[30]

Elias Zenghelis, one of the founders of the Office for Metropolitan Architecture and Koolhaas' collaborator for the allegorical projects concluding *Delirious New York*, describes the design and function of *Hotel Sphinx*, which sits at the intersection of Broadway and 7th Avenue, facing Times Square where the dominant grid of the city is broken. This interruption defines a locus of ambiguity and a call for an alternative typology. *Hotel Sphinx* is a luxury hotel as a model for mass housing; the geometry of the building derives from the figure of the Sphinx, a mythical creature found in ancient legend, a winged monster with the head and breasts of a woman and the body of a lion. The legs of the Sphinx contain escalators ascending to a large foyer, a restaurant forms its wings, twin towers with north-facing double-height apartments shape the tail, the neck facing Times Square contains the residents' clubs, while the head is dedicated to physical "culture and relaxation":

> In response to certain important events, the face of the Sphinx can be directed to 'stare' at various points in the city. In response to the level of nervous energy in the Metropolis as a whole, the whole head can be jacked up and down.[31]

The early Egyptian version of the Sphinx appears in monumental dimensions as the largest sculpture in round sited on the Giza Plateau by the Nile River, with a small temple between its paws. *Hotel Sphinx* recalls this primeval form of an inhabited edifice and re-introduces it in the dense urban matrix of downtown New York, offering an ambiguous alternative typology for living in the contemporary metropolis. The name Sphinx derives from the Greek *sphiggein* (to draw tight or to bind together), in this instance perhaps referring to the hybrid typology of hotel and housing binding together two types of living, although the text accompanying the project offers no allegorical interpretation. The Sphinx, according to Greek legend, hid outside the city gate at Thebes accosting all visitors with a deadly riddle that only Oedipus was able to solve and thereby save the city. The legend allegorically alludes to the triumph of human intelligence over pure animal instinct; it is an encounter at the threshold between reason and a deceitful monstrous allegorical subconscious. As a reaction to the obliteration of all symbolism in Modernist architecture—a result of the Modernist aphorism: form follows function—OMA recalls the architectural figurative subconscious against Modernist reason. In *Hotel Sphinx* form follows an anthropomorphic figure found in legend, rich with allegorical interpretation.

Unfinished

Characteristically many allegories are left unfinished. Edmund Spenser's, *The Faerie Queene*, Franz Kafka's *The Trial* and *The Castle* and Marcel Duchamp's *The Large Glass* can be seen as examples of incomplete allegories.[32] According to Fletcher the unfinished form and fragmented nature of these works needs to be understood in dynamic terms: "all analogies are incomplete, and incompletable, and allegory simply records this analogical relation in a dramatic or narrative form".[33] Furthermore, Owens sees allegory as "consistently attracted to the fragmentary, the imperfect, the incomplete".[34]

Allegorical architectural projects are by definition unfinished, since they are never built. Physical realisation of the ideas in the drawings and texts is not the intention of the authors, who deliberately site their projects in the realm of the imagination. Often, however, the fragmentary, unfinished and incomplete trait of allegory exemplifies the critical rather than formal preoccupations of the author, and becomes an invitation for the viewer to become part of the creative act and complete the work. Webb's drawings for *Temple Island* dazzle the viewer with their apparent attention to detail, draughtsmanship and accuracy in plotting complex geometries by hand. A few reach a level of completion that makes clear the intention of the author, but they are never perfect or finished, polished. Smudges, creases and tears in the paper, unfinished lines, and erased parts reveal doubt, and hesitation. The drawings, still infectiously beautiful, remain unfinished—revealing glimpses of the process of thinking through the line. The wish for purity and accuracy of projection originating in the mind's eye is challenged by the gesture of the hand.

A project might occasionally appear reincarnated in subsequent configurations as in Nicholson's *Appliance House:* an allegory of contemporary living which starts as an exercise in collage, transforms into a set of elegant plans and sections, parts of which are subsequently built in life-size wooden models, only to find another transformation and new name as *Loaf House: Thinking the Unthinkable House*, a digital adaptation developing similar ideas.[35] One might say, the project is open to further interpretation; it is an allegorical set of associations and an open-ended equation, which has no final form and can appear in an infinite number of guises, under different representational techniques.

Double Meaning

By saying one thing and meaning another, in all allegories there is duplicity of meaning. But the link between what is articulated and its interpretation, as well as the intentions of the author, differ. Therefore, we find an intentional single secondary meaning in most Christian and medieval parables; ambiguity in baroque allegories; intentionally diverse multiple meanings when a work invites an open ended interpretation from the receiver; and a concealed meaning to be deciphered through a series of logical steps in an enigma or riddle. Finally, critical interpretation unearths meanings often not intended by the author.

Most of the architectural allegories presented here, use drawing as a critical tool to reflect on the architectural profession, buildings, architects, users, art or the city and urban living. However, on a secondary level they all challenge the underlying syntax of architectural representation itself and propose a reconsideration of accepted norms.

By exploring collage, Nicholson questions the closed circuit between intention and design and the unexpected juxtapositions of collaged elements become a fulfilment of the designer's desire to locate the unknown, or the "expectation of creating something that eludes forewarning or prediction".[36]

The projects presented in *Delirious New York* exist through representations, which would be more correctly described as paintings. Madelon Vriesendorp and Zoe Zenghelis were responsible for the production of a series of haunting images, ranging from bizarre caricatures—post-coital scenes of skyscrapers in bed—to axonometric compositions bearing distant resemblance to similar compositions from the 1920s by Theo van Doesburg and El Lissitzky.[37] A further reference to painting exists in the design of one of the elements: *The Raft of the Medusa*, a gigantic reproduction in three

Temple Island, Mosaic of nocturnal frontal
elevation. Drawing.
Michael Webb, 1989–2005.
Courtesy of Michael Webb.
What we see from our frontal vantage point
is that view which is privy to a floodlight,
located at the extremity of the folding angle
poise like structure circumnavigating the
dome on tracks. The picture plane related to
the floodlight is spherical, with the light at
its focus.

dimensions of the scene depicted in Theodore Géricault's famous painting by the same title. The painting depicts a dramatic scene of castaways on a raft after the shipwreck of the *Medusa*, a military vessel, which Koolhaas sees as a monumental expression of "loss of nerve" corresponding to the premature panic and loss of nerve in the contemporary metropolis. This architectural element made out of plastic is the equivalent of a nineteenth century public sculpture:

> When the weather permits it, the lifeboats leave the interior of the Hotel to go out
> on the river. They circle around the raft, compare the monumental suffering of its
> occupants to their own petty anxieties, watch the moonlit sky and even board the
> sculpture. A section is equipped as a dance floor, relaying the music that is produced
> inside the Hotel, through hidden microphones.[38]

In contrast to the fundamental purpose of the building as a protective shell excluding weather, Hill in *Weather Architecture* uses weather as an architectural material. Weather becomes a metaphor for the outside entering the discipline of architecture, an unpredictable force that challenges the watertight safety of architectural intention. Weather is also a manifestation of occupation and the passage of time, qualities that architects often disregard. The climatic conditions Hill chooses to install in the Barcelona Pavilion mimic the weather in Germany during the construction, short life and demolition of the first Pavilion between March 1929 and February 1930. Accordingly, the drawings describing the project include conventions familiar from architecture, combined with notations borrowed from weather maps. In Hill's work, therefore, the theme of the outside pouring into the profession applies as much to the architecture as to the drawing technique describing it. By introducing notation for predicting weather, Hill challenges the supposed precision of architectural representation and comments on the drawing's ability to predict. Although the form of the architectural object can be accurately anticipated, its occupation and further transformation by the user remains both predictable and arbitrary like the weather.

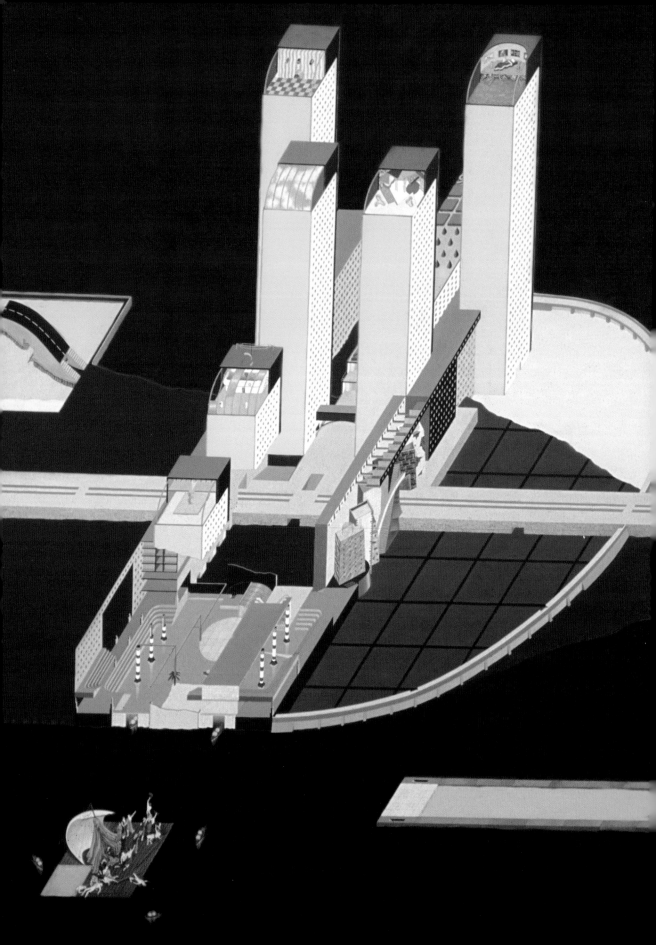

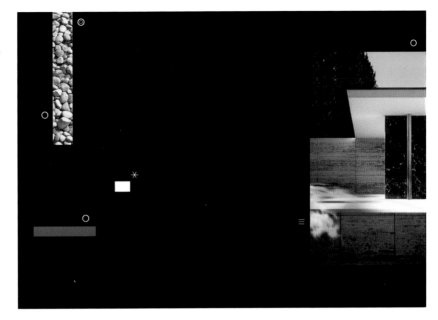

Weather Architecture.
Photographic collage. Jonathan Hill, 1999.
Courtesy of Jonathan Hill.
Berlin 2.55pm 18 December 1929—Barcelona
2.55pm 18 December 1999.
Large Pool: calm(Ba), clear sky(Ba); Small
Pool: snow(Be), clear sky(Ba); External
Travertine Floor: fog(Be), clear sky(Ba).

Welfare Palace Hotel, cutaway axonometric.
Painting. Madelon Vriesendorp; project by
Rem Koolhaas with Derrick Snare and Richard
Perlmutter, 1975–1976.
Courtesy of OMA/AMO.
In 'V' formation are 6 skyscrapers—each
with its own club (whose respective theme is
related to the mythology established on the
ground floor of each tower).
Tower 1: locker rooms, square beach
surrounded by circumferential pool; tower 2:
ship's bridge as bar; tower 3: Expressionist
club as climax of the mural; tower 4: vacant;
tower 5: waterfall/restaurant; tower 6: Freud
Unlimited Club.
The light blue in front of the hotel is
an artificial skating rink; to the left of the
hotel is a park with a 'Chinese' swimming
pool; in front of the Hotel is a gigantic Three-
dimensional Raft of the Medusa executed
in plastic (with a small area equipped
for dancing).

Figurative Theory

In an attempt to name this alternative vehicle for authorship in architecture we now look at Jean-François Lyotard's negotiating notions of discourse and figure in _Discours, figure._ Lyotard discusses discourse as related to structuralism, written text and the experience of reading and figure—which he introduces as an opposing force—related to phenomenology, images/drawings and the experience of seeing.[39] For Lyotard, discourse implies the domination of text over image, conceptual representation over unmediated perception and rationality over the 'other' of reason. On the other hand, the figural embraces rhetorical tropes, such as allegory, and implies notions of configuration, shape and image, without though the clarity and transparency that conventionally accompanies those terms. Part of Lyotard's aim is to defend the importance of the eye, but he then proceeds to deconstruct this opposition and attempts to show that ideally discourse and figure can be mutually implicated. He develops the concept of the figural as a violating force, which works to interrupt established structures in the realms of both reading and seeing.

I have attempted to describe here an alternative practice in architecture, whereby drawing is a critical tool articulating theory rather than the construction of a building. As we have seen, the allegorical architectural project combines design and theory, and its creative and critical traits make it a visual equivalent of literary or critical theory. This alternative type of theory, I would like to call here "figurative theory", inspired by Lyotard's definition of the figure. By naming this practice, the aim of this paper is to provide a ' lens' through which to understand and analyse recent experimental and critical architectural projects.[40] Rather than a description of new phenomena, the paper provides a new way of looking at these projects and offers novel tools for their evaluation. The introduction of the 'other', through the figure and allegory, is a mode of thinking and working in architecture that allows transgression of established modes, and defines "figurative theory" as an experimental practice, pointing to ideas impossible to grasp through the profession or in purely discourse-based theoretical investigations.

Dissolution

The final section of the book considers the possibility of a final release from the idea of discipline in relation to architectural authorship. Can radically new architectural ideas arise from a loosened attention to, or rejection of, authorial control? Are the limits of architectural expressivity defined by the gulf between an architect's original vision and the re-creative vision of an observer? What is the significance for architects of the shift from linear, deterministic systems of communication to interactive, networked and 'emergent' technologies? The texts in this section anticipate the freedom, and challenges, of disciplinary transcendence.

Rolf Hughes examines the issue of creative agency in contemporary practices that are characterised by no single disciplinary identity, such as algorithmic, generative or 'evolutionary' design, bioart and metacreation (the design of generative and creative processes). Contrasting two poles of contemporary authorship—autopoietic authorial erasure on the one side, and technoscience's seemingly unbounded pursuit of mastery over living matter on the other—his essay highlights the continuing centrality of authorship, in both its affirmed and disavowed guises, in projects that explore 'semi-living' creative processes using a fusion of organic, mechanical and electronic material. Disciplinary hybridisation, Hughes suggests, is reconfiguring our accounts of contemporary cultural production; it will also, inevitably, inform the evolution of practice in architecture.

The relation between dissolving disciplinary boundaries and revisionist accounts of architectural practice is a long one. Throughout the twentieth century, and particularly in its latter part, a number of writers, architects and commentators began to explore, by shifting attention away from the architect as an author figure within a closed discipline, the multiplicity of processes that condition how architecture is produced. The central essays in this section can be read as an account of five of these important figures and their work. More importantly, however, they take up varying themes that emerge out of the proclaimed 'loosening' of the ties of architectural authorship.

Perhaps the most marked characteristic of the essays in this book as a whole is the evidence they provide that, whatever modulations may occur, the discourse around a 'projective' practice such as architecture continues to project authors. In this final section, which concerns discussions and figures who looked towards a dissolution of authorship in architecture, and to an accompanying dissolution of the notion of disciplinarity around architecture, one is struck by the weight of the names involved. To be sure, these final cases point beyond the Siamese twinning of architect and work. All the figures studied endeavour to free architecture from the analysis that joins authorial intention, projection and formal expression together into a rigid construct. Yet, at the same time this last section presents a series of figures made monumental by their authorial status. Even without the need for their genius to be measured via the 'work', these authors of architecture—the Neuferts, the Eisenmans, the Alexanders—remain prominent. In some cases this 'authorial status' can be seen as evidence of the tenacity of certain internal habits that bind even the pronouncements that reject them. Thus Cedric Price's author status appears ultimately to rely on many of the disciplinary characteristics and traits of which he was critical and from which he tried to escape.

Hélène Lipstadt's essay, which concludes *Architecture and Authorship*, brings this discussion into the present and points to an ethical dimension. Lipstadt reviews some of the assumptions that inform the claims made by advocates of 'collaborative' or 'advanced' design practices, and applies the sociologist Pierre Bourdieu's notion of "exoticising the domestic" to examine the limits of authorial abdication and the re-emergent qualities of disciplinarity in architecture. This both questions the rhetoric around collaboration and salutes the vigour of the critique that accompanies it. It is important, Lipstadt argues, to identify how design practices based on self-generative systems can surreptitiously preserve traditional modes of authorship. Yet a critique of these models must consider not only the question of authorship per se, but also the issue of accountability. Indeed, this final notion of accountability is surely one of the reasons why authors endure in discussions around architecture. A central dilemma for those who acknowledge the complexity of the forces that condition architecture, who recognise the limits of architectural authorship and who point to alternative modes of architectural projection that respect such limits, is to define courses of action that appear both secure in their theoretical foundation and ethically responsible in their consequences. Acts that condition the built environment also condition people's lives, and there is a need, a political and ethical need, to identify responsibility for such acts. In architecture, the ethical dimension of authorial responsibility is hard to escape.

The Semi-living Author: Post-human Creative Agency

Rolf Hughes

I felt that blank incapability of invention which is the greatest misery of authorship, when dull Nothing replies to our anxious invocations. (...) Invention, it must be humbly admitted, does not consist in creating out of void, but out of chaos; the materials must, in the first place, be afforded: it can give form to dark, shapeless substances, but cannot bring into being the substance itself.

> Mary Shelley, Introduction to Frankenstein, 1831[1]

We see that in the organic world, as thought grows dimmer and weaker, grace emerges more brilliantly and decisively. (...) Grace appears most purely in that human form which either has no consciousness or an infinite consciousness. That is, in the puppet or in the god.

> Heinrich von Kleist[2]

Living organisms are nothing more than complex biochemical machines.

> Christopher Langton[3]

Who, or what, was the first author, the *auctor vitae*? Where (and when) did matter itself originate? Does nothing come from nothing—if so, is authorship inseparable from notions of chronology and historical sequence? What distinguishes truly creative practices from those that are merely mechanical? Architects, artists and authors are latecomers to this debate, which in Western accounts pits Plato's *Timaeus* against Augustine's *Confessions*, or the idea of a creator *either* giving pre-existing form to pre-existing matter *or* creating something out of nothing. As late arrivals, they can play the role neither of pagan prime mover nor of Christian God (Prime Innovator), but must rather begin with what has already been created and thereby accept historical traditions, which means they must suffer the fate of those condemned to speak a language that is always already spoken.[4]

To analyse the pairing of design and authorship demands a range of disciplinary perspectives on the essentially-contested concepts in both areas, their migration to and from other disciplines, and their relation to changing discourses of self, subjectivity, creativity, and intellectual property. Two recent projects—both "post-human" and of uncertain disciplinary origin—seem tailor-made to unsettle our understanding of authorship, creative agency and the relationship of the cultural artefact to the producing subject(s). I will therefore take these as my focus in the current essay.

Agency is a central concern in recent creative practices that exhibit a turn from analysing nature to its synthesis. These include algorithmic, generative or 'evolutionary' design, bioart and metacreation (the design of generative and creative processes). At one extreme, an 'author' would appear to have no role as such in work designed to *make itself*, thereby exhibiting the principle of autopoiesis or "self-making".[5] An autopoetic system produces not only self-sustaining patterns, but also, more significantly, its own *components*, the components that produce in turn the system's organisation.[6] Once the autopoetic system is up and running, the author would thereafter seem to be not so much dead (or terminally afflicted) as written out of the equation altogether. Whether this represents an abdication of authorial intention or its ultimate expression (a Promethean attempt to seize the original rights of the *auctor vitae*, perhaps) remains an open question.[7] What is clear is that in the creative disciplines, as elsewhere, such practices are already altering familiar forms of cultural production, relationships between producers and consumers, distribution models, and, above all, discourse.

When teams of artists and scientists create artificial systems that simulate or synthesise the properties of living systems, they instantiate a wider drive towards the modelling, simulation, degeneration, engineering and manipulation of biological life—in effect, the triumph of the designer's will over everything from stem cells to human reproduction via genetically manipulated species, food crops and mammalian cloning.[8] By examining these two poles of contemporary authorship—autopoietic authorial erasure on the one side, and technoscience's seemingly unbounded pursuit of mastery over living matter, on the other—I will explore the continuing centrality of authorship, in both its affirmed and disavowed guises, within contemporary cultural discourse while examining how the hybridisation of disciplinary practices is spawning new metaphors within author-related discourse. As the practitioners of art, science and design increasingly seek each other out, exchanging aims, technologies and methods in the process, the problems afflicting concepts such as attribution, contract, intellectual property, rights, teamwork and creativity multiply and spread like a virus through the new constellations of professional networks. Thus it is not only collaborative *cultural* practices such as architecture or film-making that explicitly unsettle our understanding of the modern author-figure and the modern subject.[9] The allocation of authorship and ownership rights within contemporary scientific culture (a factor that often determines how scientific research is financed and distributed) shows that the question of authorial attribution is a vexed issue here too as there are no agreed standards of authorial conventions between different laboratories, between academia and industry, nor even between different departments, disciplines and industries all of which might separately contribute to a specific, shared research goal such as decoding the genetic language of early life.[10]

Today's many disciplinary convergences have contributed, as Julie Thompson Klein has noted, to reversing "the differentiating, classificatory dynamic of modernity" and creating instead an "increasing hybridisation of cultural categories, identities, and previous certainties".[11] This means that there exists a growing number of professional issues that cannot be tackled with the tools available within existing forms of disciplinary practice. "Many of the problems professionals face are neither predictable nor simple", Klein notes. "They are unique and complex. (...) As a result, the art of being a professional is becoming the art of managing complexity."[12] This "art of managing complexity", made necessary when formerly distinct fields (architecture and cybernetics, biology and art, for example) decide to cohabit the same conceptual space, requires that the metaphors, analogies and references (as well as the tools and methodologies) to be used are carefully negotiated within the interdisciplinary group. So far so good. But can metaphor successfully connect ideas from distinct fields when both (or more) disciplinary domains have to agree to the *appropriateness* and *usefulness* of the linking in question (and do so at a time when it is generally accepted that metaphor today has no absolute stability, not even within a single discourse)?[13] Isn't it more likely that metaphor (or the use of tropes more generally) may lead from order to disorder in an *unproductive* sense, by creating a maze of cross-disciplinary terminological confusion? Or is this precisely the point? Rosenberg writes:

> When questions become unanswerable within a single domain, innovators seek analogous questions in foreign realms in order to resituate their lines of inquiry, and even to pursue several lines simultaneously, hoping, through juxtaposition, to find answers or more powerful questions in between, or beyond.[14]

My first example aligns contemporary neuro-science research with art, performance and the interdisciplinary study of artificial life (a-life) to raise important epistemological questions concerning how we define human/post-human creativity, intelligence, and representation. "MEART—The semi-living artist" is a geographically detached, wetware/software/hardware hybrid, described as "semi-living" because it comprises both living and artificial components—its culture of neurons and glia are grown and nurtured, whereas its robotic elements are constructed.[15]

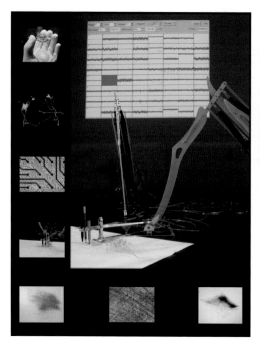

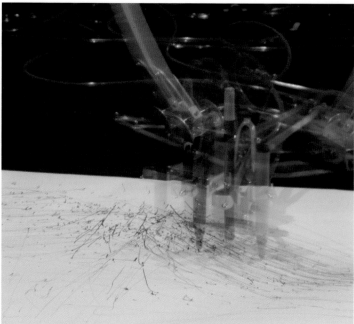

Meart: The semi-living artist. SymbioticA
Research Group (SARG) in collaboration
with the Potter Lab.
Photograph courtesy SARG and
the Potter Lab.

The robotic arm, Biofeel, 2002.
Meart: The semi-living artist, SymbioticA
Research Group in collaboration with the
Potter Lab. Photograph courtesy
Phil Gamblen.

Conceived by Philip Gamblen and Guy Ben-Ary of SymbioticA Art and Science
Collaborative Research Lab at the University of Western Australia as a bio-cybernetic
research and development project to investigate aesthetic outcomes when living
neurons communicate with a physical body, the installation takes to extremes the
putative Cartesian separation of mind and body. The artist's 'brain' (neurons from
mouse cortex grown over a "Multi Electrode Array") is nurtured in Dr Steve Potter's
neuro-engineering lab at Georgia Institute of Technology, Atlanta; its 'body' (a robotic
drawing arm capable of executing two-dimensional drawings) is set up at the location
of each exhibition (to date exhibitions have been held at Linz, Perth, New York, Bilbao,
Moscow, Melbourne Atlanta and Shanghai). The geographical remoteness of the
'wetware' and 'hardware' is surmounted by two software modules: one in Atlanta and
one at the location of each exhibition with the internet operating as a form of 'nervous
system' to interface between brain and body. As MEART has developed, it has begun
to explore the cognitive dimensions of 'seeing' and converting what it 'sees' into
representation. Thus the robotic arm can send an image from a digital camera, which
is converted as it arrives at the 'brain' into a thumbnail of 60 pixels, each correlating to
60 electrodes that then stimulate the neurons grown on an electronic chip. This image
is then compared with what the robotic arm has already drawn on the paper (spaces
that are dark in the photo and blank on the paper are identified as areas to correct, for
example); the neurons process this information, the electric signals on the electrodes are
measured again and this measurement becomes the basis for guiding the robotic arm.
The digital camera records what the arm 'draws' and sends a signal back to the neurons,
which is evaluated as before and further modifications are sent back to the arm. Thus the
optical element (the digital camera) monitors the progress of the drawing. The result
of this activity is then converted into a stimulation map that is sent to the neurons.
These stimulations inform the neurons about the state of the drawing (and, in the next
iteration of MEART, additionally reports about events occurring in the gallery, which
sounds ominously like a potential semi-living surveillance system). Unlike human artists
and designers, there is no knowledge in the arm itself, although both of MEART's
arms carry sensors (controlled by the local software, which is instructed in turn by the
neurons) that register the position of both arms at every point in time.[16]

MEART is an example of how an interdisciplinary team, exploring the conceptual space
where scientific and cultural experiments converge, can generate compelling subject-
specific research questions alongside resonant metaphors of broader philosophical

significance. At Georgia Tech's Laboratory for Neuro-engineering, where Steve Potter is Assistant Professor in the Department of Biomedical Engineering, the project is part of a pursuit of greater scientific understanding of the behaviour of neurons, research that according to research assistant Douglas Bakkum may be directly applied to the study and design of neuro-prosthetics such as a mechanical arm connected to the brain, cochlear implants for the hearing impaired, or visual prosthetics for the blind.[17]

At a more performative level, MEART appears to be, as one commentator remarks, "a collage of contradictions" designed to inspire in its beholder maximum "cognitive dissonance":

> Its authoritative complexity simultaneously convinces us of its technological reengineering of cognitive processes, while also calling attention to just how far it has strayed from generally held conceptions of life, intelligence or creativity. [...] It offers us the actual biological substance of the thinking brain yet out of its biological context and system of developmental ordering. It offers us seeming proof of its responsiveness by two way signaling yet begs the question 'is it merely a closed circuit in which captive neurons simply return electrical signals to the 'arm' that were previously sent to them via the camera?' Are the differences between the image sent and the image drawn by the arm merely low-level 'noise' in the system or even configuration inaccuracies in the complex process? Or conversely, are the slight variances and exaggerations in the images sent to the neurons and the image drawn by the arm evidence of complex neural network beginning to form in the plated neurons?[18]

The project team claim that MEART suggests a future scenario in which "humans will create/grow/manufacture intuitive and creative 'thinking entities' that could be intelligent and unpredictable beings. They may be created by humans for anthropocentric use, but as they will be creative and unpredictable they might not necessarily stay the way they were originally intended."[19] Here the project team (characteristic of a-life artists more generally) equate creativity with unpredictability; what is valued is the artefact's escape from authorial intention (and robotic predictability) towards emergent excess and autonomy. One question here is whether such an automated unmooring of human intentionality, if left unchecked to play out its own logic, may ultimately lead to a point of dissolution. Mitchell Whitelaw, somewhat apocalyptically, suggests that it might:

Neurons on the Multi Electrod Array, MEART's 'brain'. Meart: The semi-living artist, SymbioticA Research Group in collaboration with the Potter Lab. Photograph courtesy Dr Steve Potter.

The robotic arm, Australian Culture Now, 2004. Meart: The semi-living artist, SymbioticA Research Group in collaboration with the Potter Lab. Photograph courtesy Phil Gamblen.

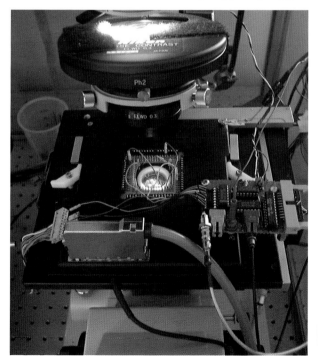
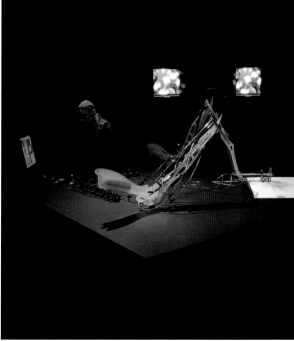

Any system capable of autonomous ongoing emergence could move outside the bounds of its host system, across domains. A work of a-life art that succeeds might be conceptual or cultural as much as robotic or computational; it might be imperceptible, subsisting within and across existing structures but changing, adapting itself and them. There is no reason why it should stay in the gallery or in the computer. If the coevolutionary processes observed in biological life are any indication, emergent a-life would sustain itself in processes that span strata of media, culture, technology, and biology. [...] Thus if a-life art were to fulfil its desire for excess, it would cease to be identifiable (and functional) as art. It would be unbounded and unintentional, an adaptive pattern indistinguishable from the wider dynamics of its environment.[20]

As a conceptual artwork, the questions MEART raises can illuminate a number of important questions for a discussion of post-human creative agency. These include: Can 'semi-living' technological systems ever learn human qualities, such as experience, intentionality, memory, irony, interpretation, creativity—i.e. the evolved wisdom of living systems?[21] In the absence of any external feedback, how can MEART 'learn' from its artistic activity? Lacking a system of goal and reward, can MEART be said to be engaging in creativity, an activity that involves the capacity for critical evaluation? The discourse-related questions include: Can we talk about MEART as a *single* cyborg/organism/author/artist when its components are distributed across such geographically remote locations?[22] Other questions concern the economic/legislative implications of 'post human' intellectual property (in 2006, four of MEART's drawings were sold to the MEIAC museum in Spain): Does MEART's artwork challenge the basis of intellectual property rights? What defines its 'signature'? Should its output be subsumed under existing copyright formulations?[23] And, not least, what of the relationship between experience, representation and aesthetic judgement? Can we 'represent' that which we have not experienced? Can there be creativity without consciousness? Can a conscious point of view exist in a purely autonomous state (a 'brain in a vat' that is nonetheless conscious of its surroundings)? MEART suggests we must acknowledge a shift from a traditional economy of art in imitation of nature, to one that subsumes or incorporates nature self-reflexively, resulting in an artistic medium which is itself (partly) alive. One way of looking at these issues, the participants themselves propose, is to consider creativity along a spectrum—"from a reductionist mechanical device, to an artistic genius" (ironically, the genius figure thus returns as the pinnacle of creative endeavour).[24] Another important conceptual 'lens' for examining the issues at stake is that of the question of *embodiment* and its relation to experiental knowledge.

Like other information artists, MEART's artistic emphasis is on *process, practice,* and *skill,* an emphasis shared by *practice-based research.* Yet whereas practice-based research in art and design privileges *experiential knowledge* (including its epistemic siblings 'embodied', 'situated', 'practical' or 'tacit' knowledge), the work of information artists is frequently characterised by a concern with *disembodiment,* which we may define as "the technologically driven unmooring of human cognition".[25] To mimic living matter, however, is not the same as creating a compelling parallel for human experience in creative practices. Design-based experience (and, importantly, its *communication*) is arguably what nourishes the processes and outcomes of the creative disciplines—it is surely what distinguishes creative processes from those that are merely mechanical. In this respect, the debate regarding authorship as a trope for describing cultural production rests on a claim for, or disavowal of, the centrality of human experience in creative acts. According to Peter Eisenman, post-humanism no longer views the human subject as the originating agency, but rather as "a discursive function among complex and already-formed systems of language, which he [*sic*] witnesses but does not constitute.... It is this condition of displacement which gives rise to design in which authorship can no longer either account for a linear development which has a 'beginning' and an 'end'... or account for invention and form".[26] What is at stake here is thus far more than an opposition between "technological formalism" and "human content and values" (the latter being threatened by the former).[27] With designers using algorithms and heuristics to encourage computers to actually compute, to manage complex behaviour and become active proponents of design, architecture (or its wider design family) has now entered a distinctive phase in relationship to authorship, one that will make significant demands on our critical resources. Do we possess the aesthetic, ethical and methodological tools and terminology to engage satisfactorily with such developments? If not, is it sufficient to *adapt* existing critical tools? As Stephen Wilson notes, such approaches, while useful for specific purposes, barely touch upon the critical significance of the work in question; as a consequence, artists, audiences, art historians and critics alike will need to become 'literate' in the disparate research areas that emerging 'information arts' explore.[28] Like early computer pioneers, many current 'metacreationists' or 'information artists' (these are the terms Wilson uses in the absence of more compelling descriptive tags) are interested less in the final image or artefact produced, than in devising abstract generative processes, new kinds of artistic skills involving the development of innovative algorithms, and understanding and experimenting with organic matter such as cell manipulation or working with the constraints and possibilities of genetic materials. Evolutionary algorithms, which mimic biological evolution by generating many different designs, rejecting the less fit in order to select the most promising within given parameters, are one step in this passage from computation to living matter, from code to cells.[29] But whereas evolutionary algorithms use fixed sets of instructions to manipulate information, a related field —genetic programming—seeks to improve performance by applying Darwinian evolution principles to software development. The computer processes millions of possible solutions to a specific problem, progressively evolving over several generations until eventually it identifies what it regards as an optimum solution. In some respects, evolutionary simulations can be said to replace design, since artists can use this software to breed new forms rather than specifically design them. At the same time, as Manuel de Landa points out, deliberate design is still a crucial component in the deployment of genetic algorithms—for the evolutionary results to be truly useful as visualisation tools, the range of possible designs that the algorithm considers needs to be surprising and extensive as well as qualitatively rich. This means that software needs to be designed for which all the possibilities cannot be considered in advance by the designer.[30] W Ross Ashby has termed this "Descartes' Dictum" and noted that for a device to achieve better performance than its initial specification it would need to be informationally open and capable of interacting with the world independently of its designer—in other words, it must display characteristics of both epistemic and structural autonomy.[31] Hence, perhaps, the current turn from code to 'wetware'—a shift that may be characterised historically as a displacement of Modernism's use of technology to *control* nature by postmodernism's use of living matter ('nature') to *'enliven'* technology, to escape its monotonous and repetitive logic and pursue instead the unpredictable, 'emergent' and creative capacities of a meeting between organic, mechanical, and electronic impulses.

Such technologies raise important questions for design theory: is an invention, invented without the presence of a human inventor, really an invention? If so, who is the inventor/author (who is accountable if it goes wrong or causes unforeseen damage)? If the invention works and serves the purpose for which it was created, does it matter if we don't understand *how* it works? There are evolved designs, such as the evolved electronic circuits of Adrian Thompson, a researcher at the University of Sussex, that defy explanation, could not be reproduced in a simulation, and are described by their creator (the term here is intended to denote those who initiate and then witness the artefact's coming-into-being i.e. Thompson and his colleagues) as "bizarre, mysterious and unconventional".[32]

Gordon Pask's work on electrochemical computing devices with emerging sensory capabilities explored (in the late 1950s and early 60s) the promise of 'growing' active evolutionary networks by electrochemical processes, improving on their initial designs by evaluating past performance and altering their decision processes accordingly.[33] Pask's devices were able to adapt and construct their own sensors and thus influence the relationship between their internal states and the external world. As such, they were conceived and specifically designed to discover their own "relevance criteria".[34] More than 40 years later, Pablo Miranda began pursuing "a new type of architectural aesthetics which are no longer grounded on the architect's privileged point of view, but on the relentless accumulation of unintelligent calculations, mindless arithmetics

The Dendroid electrochemical computer cell connected to a light sensor array. Pablo Miranda and Arijana Kajfes, 2004. Photograph Per-Erik Adamsson. The Dendroid was set up as part of the Occular Witness project, Smart Studio, Interactive Institute. exhibited at Farg Fabriken, Stockholm, 2004. In this case the dendritic growth device works as recorder of the light received from the sensor array.

performed by computational armies of clerks", and thereby became drawn to Pask's work on chemical computers.[35] *Dendroid*, a collaboration between architect Pablo Miranda and artist Arijana Kajfes as part of the Occular Witness project, comprises an electrochemical bath, a microcontroller circuit and software running on a standard computer.[36] In this electrochemical hardware the system does the typical transformations involved in projective geometry and characteristic of CAD programs, such as rotation, scaling, and all the different types of parallel and perspective projections. In *Dendroid* geometric data in the form of three-dimensional vectors (X, Y, Z) is translated into electric signals which pass through the dendrites in the electrolytic bath, are then read, and subsequently translated again into geometric information. Signal transformations are equated to geometrical transformations. As with an apprentice architect, the device can be trained (if given a set of geometric transformations such as those corresponding to architectural drawings, it can be 'indoctrinated' to produce the standard, average architectural projective transformation), or—again like its human counterpart—it can be left to grow arbitrarily, without learning. In the latter case, after a period of formation and growth, the device is capable of geometrical transformations and becomes effectively "a serendipitous machine, suggesting different 3-D transformations according to the growth patterns of the dendritic machine".[37]

Here design practice impacts directly on our metaphors and terminologies not least the constellation of concepts clustered around authorship and design itself. The widening attractiveness of both complex systems and interdisciplinary (or even *adisciplinary*) ways of working, means that the ideas of interdisciplinarity and complexity have become increasingly bound together over recent decades, sharing (as Klein has charted) a range of disciplinary practices and concepts such as breadth of knowledge, integration, and synthesis, as well as the capacity to exercise judgment in complex and rapidly changing situations.[38] Disciplinary cross-traffic of this kind invites us to review the interplay of cultural practice and technical innovation, to examine again pillars of authorship such as origin, intention, and authority, as well as collective paradigms such as 'open source' with its anonymous dispersal of diverse operations.[39] Complex systems are open to influence and change from external *and* internal factors, and are therefore fundamentally unpredictable, despite their apparently deterministic character. Such unpredictability presents a challenge to a notion of authorship founded on the reassuring archival and stable logic of print. Katherine Hayles' phrase *orderly disorder* may be one appropriately paradoxical way of describing the complex structure of order and disorder within such complex systems—tiny deviations can produce radically divergent behaviour. "Emergence", Hayles writes, "implies that properties or programs appear on their own, often developing in ways not anticipated by the person who created the simulation. Structures that lead to emergence typically involve complex feedback loops in which the outputs of a system are repeatedly fed back in as input. As the recursive looping continues, small deviations can quickly become magnified, leading to the complex interactions and unpredictable evolutions associated with emergence."[40] Self-organising, emergent or generative systems do not merely reproduce themselves unchanged—this would be merely the neurotic monotony of repetition—but within them forces of disorder lead to order, and order similarly mutates into disorder at a fundamental level. As Hayles argues, this implies a *politics of the representation of order* but it also suggests a form of *cyberpoetics* in which noise (defined as the *unexpected*, or in Gregory Bateson's formulation "any difference that makes a difference") is seen to enhance informational value by resisting information's entropic, homogenising tendency, whereas routine information degenerates into sameness and predictability and thus devalues informational currency.[41] In other words, innovation is valued and continuity (repetition) devalued, which means that cybernetics and information theory share the Modernist values of originality, individuality, and *making it new*. Maturana and Varela's aforementioned concept of autopoiesis treats noise as being crucial to the development of complexity in self-organising systems, once again because it is used to counter informational entropy and enhance complexity. Literature is information rich, according to this view, whereas clichés are informationally impoverished.[42]

As both Hayles and Whitelaw discuss, the most successful manifestations of emergence appear to involve systems that operate outside the formal, technological grammar of designed robotics and computation.[43] The introduction of biological materials or influences unhooks artificial life from design, human intentionality and conceptual modelling and effects a transition from the known to unknown, from the formal and familiar to the strange, unpredictable, mysterious, autonomous and open. Hence a kind of reverse reductionism operates—artificial life, as a scientific epistemological project, uses known components to create mysterious, ineffable results (or, as Mitchell pithily expresses it, "Instead of dissecting the frog, it tries to build one, although the goal, an enhanced knowledge of a living thing, is the same.")[44] The aims of a-life artists, in comparison, tend to be more synthetic, focusing on the absolute emergent result—the excess—rather than the relationship between the formal

The Dendroid electrochemical computer cell connected to a light sensor array. Pablo Miranda and Arijana Kajfes, 2004. Photograph Per-Erik Adamsson. Metallic ion aggregation and first experiments with an aqueous solution of copper sulphate (CuSO4).

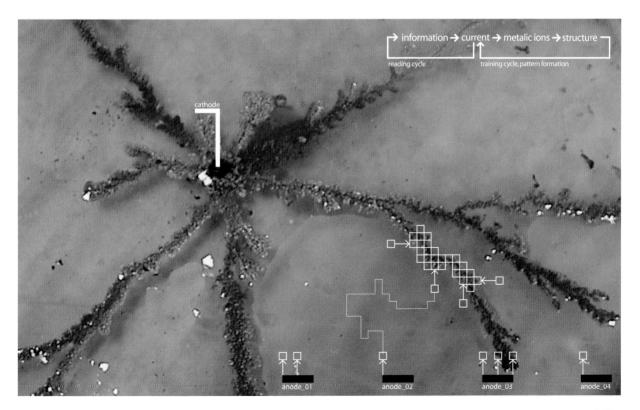

infrastructure and the emergent phenomenon. With such motivations, Whitelaw observes, a-life art becomes a *"metacreative"* endeavour—"it wants to create creation, variation, otherness. If a-life science is about knowing and understanding, a-life art is very basically about making and becoming, becoming-other, and becoming-unknown." Such an orientation, Whitelaw continues, puts a-life art in a paradoxical position—to devise increasingly sophisticated a-life systems, systems that will exceed the designer's intentions and knowledge, demands an increase in design, control, and intentionality as well as technical knowledge. This means that a-life art is closely following the approach of a-life science, whereas if it is to attain what its practitioners apparently seek—"a becoming-other, an endless excess"—it will need to "surrender its intentionality" at some point:

> The question is whether this point of surrender, the point of emergence, will arrive when technological and formal innovation reaches a certain crucial point, or appear in another domain, on another axis altogether.[45]

Complex systems and emergence discourse are thus generating metaphors that will permit different articulations of the theory and practice of authorship in architecture and design. From Hayles we have already heard the paradoxical pairing of *orderly disorder*. The metaphor of *chaos* is defined by Stuart Kauffman, whose focus is on biological networks, but whose analysis can also be applied to social and cultural domains, as "the compromise between order and surprise".[46] The moment of complexity within such dimensions of experience is a medium "[p]oised between too much and too little order" and, as such, one that facilitates the emergence of network culture.[47] With too much order, systems become static and do not change, whereas too little order means that things fall apart—the systems (cultural, political, or economic as well as technical, informational, or biological systems) cease to function.

It is not only in the discursive terms of metaphor that complex systems present profound challenges to the culturally privileged notion of authorship. As one commentator remarks, the shift from linear, deterministic communications to interactive, non-linear, complex, networked and 'emergent' communications, accompanies a shift of techno-scientific paradigms from the 'hard' mechanical sciences of the early twentieth century to the 'soft' biological sciences (and informatic technologies) of the early twenty first century, alongside a corresponding "decentralisation of human perception and individual creativity as the core evaluating criteria for an authentic work".[48] Nonetheless, this process of decentralisation invariably impacts on the way we articulate knowledge and our choice of metaphors for describing it:

> The complexity of knowledge is suggested by the current rhetoric of description. Once described as a *foundation* or *linear structure*, knowledge today is depicted as a *network* or a *web* with multiple nodes of connection, and a *dynamic system*. The metaphor of *unity*, with its accompanying values of universality and certainty, has been replaced by metaphors of *plurality relationality* in a *complex* world. Images of *boundary crossing* and *cross-fertilisation* are superseding images of disciplinary *depth* and *compartmentalization*. Isolated modes of work are being supplanted by *affiliations, coalitions,* and *alliances*. And, older values of *control, mastery,* and *expertise* are being reformulated as *dialogue, interaction,* and *negotiation*. Changes in the spatial and temporal structures of knowledge also call into question traditional images of knowledge as a cognitive *map* with distinct *territories and borders* or a *tree with different branches*. They are too linear. In their place, images of *fractals*, a *kaleidoscope*, or a wildly growing *rhizome* without a central root have been proposed.[49]

Seán Burke's observation that "the inability of theoretical models to encompass the disruptive enigmas of authorship strengthens rather than weakens its claim on our attention" is therefore timely.[50] Although the modern author concept—as solitary creator of original representations—is increasingly irrelevant to contemporary authoring practices, Western educational, industrial and legislative institutions continue to promote it at the expense of other possibilities, perhaps as a means of retaining a more or less enforceable logic of intellectual property. How then might we re-conceive the role of authorship across disciplines while avoiding the *impasses* of the Romantic conception of author-as-creator and the author as absence (or, worse, as deceased pseudo-deity)? One way must be pragmatic, based on study of practice, and the accurate description of such practice (irrespective of the sometimes inflated claims of those whose interests are served by mystification of their methods). Such an approach may adapt Paul Watson's proposal for a *practice-based model of art*—a "pragmatic redescription of cinematic authorship", which involves applying multi-faceted critical perspectives to understanding a range of labour, creative and commercial considerations:

> In locating the study of film authorship in a practice-based model of art it is not only possible, but desirable to study the work of stunt directors, production designers, visual effects supervisors, concept illustrators, computer animators, costume designers, sound engineers, fight co-ordinators, composers, specialist post-production houses, studios as well as screenwriters, producers, editors, actors and directors in terms of film aesthetics and comprehension.[51]

Within such a collaborative mode of cultural production, the specific creative, expressive and artistic input of the various agencies working together on a project (and their individual contributions to the project's 'style') can thereby be analysed, alongside "the socio-cultural practices of contemporary media culture which constructs the auteur as a commodity, a logo so to speak, which stands not behind the text as in Romantic notions of authorship, but rather in front of it precisely to explicate, expand and legitimise the marks of individuality, expression and style in a film."[52]

We might also contrast the Benjaminian notion of a cultural artefact's 'authenticity' to its capacity to convey 'operational' or 'projective' meanings, as these represent two critical lenses that produce significantly different perspectives on the same object of inquiry, depending on whether the critical gaze is oriented backwards or forwards in time.[53] Work such as MEART or Dendroid actualise philosophical, scientific and artistic investigations, of human cognition, creativity and originality. How we respond to such "realities that emerge from handwork", to use Rilke's pregnant phrase, depends if we celebrate such "operational fiction" as "a cyborg of representation and reality, art and science... flesh and transistor" or lament the loss of authenticity and authority and, with these, the authorial role as a narrator—more or less reliable—of historical testimony.[54]

Cedric Price as Anti-architect

Stanley Mathews

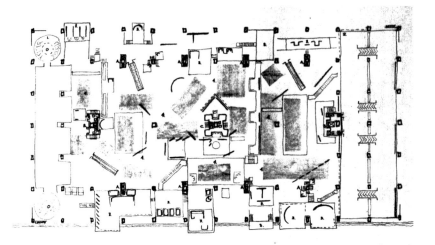

The Fun Palace, a 1965 design attributed to the late British architect Cedric Price, was an unusual project. Not only was the design novel, but Price's architectural role in the project was equally unconventional. While researching the Fun Palace in the Cedric Price Archives at the Canadian Centre for Architecture, I discovered a yellowing note written in Price's hand, on which he describes his role in the Fun Palace as that of the "anti-architect".[1] My first thought was that this might refer to Price's lifelong delight in challenging and provoking what he regarded as an often pompous and self-important architectural profession. Yet, this was more than simple professional provocation, and the assertion was Price's attempt to disavow architectural authorship of the Fun Palace. This is not to say that Price was uninvolved or somehow stole his ideas—rather, it is a repudiation of the mythology of the Author as quasi-divine and paternalistic progenitor of design. In the Fun Palace, Price hoped that authorship, origin, and programmatic determinism would recede, while the building itself, as an architecturally performative language, would speak and be 'read' and understood differently by the individual users. We find in Price's 'anti-architectural' note one of the many paradoxes and ironies it contains: that the passage was discovered in the Archives of the Canadian Centre for Architecture, and thus the record of Price's disavowal of authorship is forever ensconced within a named repository whose sole purpose is to preserve a paradigm of authorship.

The Fun Palace project began in 1962 as a simple collaboration between Price and avant-garde theatre producer Joan Littlewood. From her beginnings in the 1930s working class agit-prop street theatre to her string of successes on the London stage, Littlewood had long sought to create a truly Brechtian theatre—not of stages, performers, and audiences, but a theatre of pure performativity, a space of cultural bricolage where people could experience the transcendence and transformation of the theatre not as audience, but as players themselves. Her vision of a dynamic theatrical experience which demolished the invisible 'fourth wall' of conventional theatre, provided the conceptual framework on which Price began to develop an interactive, performative architecture, endlessly adaptable to the varying needs and desires of the users.

The Fun Palace would not be a museum, school, library, fun fair, or theatre—and yet, it could be any and all of these things. Specific activities were never fully encoded in the form or incorporated in the design. It would be like a vast shipyard, an open-ended matrix of constant change and activity. Using huge cranes and prefabricated modules, the users could assemble their own learning and leisure environments, creating an improvisational architecture where they might escape from everyday routine and monotony of serial existence in one-dimensional society, and embark on a journey of creativity and individual fulfilment. Although it would serve as a model for the 1976 Centre Pompidou in Paris, the Fun Palace was very different from that building. The Fun Palace was there to respond to people, to be what people wanted and needed, not to offer prepackaged exhibits and events. The Fun Palace was a far-sighted venture which utilised nascent computer, cybernetic, and information technologies to create a virtual architecture, capable of temporal transformation, of being reprogrammed and becoming an entirely different building at various times and in different situations. It was to be a socially interactive machine, highly adaptable to the shifting cultural, social, and economic conditions of London in the 1960s. The Fun Palace would be a space of possibility rather than direction, a 'text' of empty signifiers, each awaiting 'reading' by an army of 'readers': the individual users.

Unlike the colourful speculations by the Archigram group, the Fun Palace was no mere paper architecture or science fiction fantasy. It was a real project, carefully designed and very nearly realised. But, after years of planning, and just as construction was set to begin, the project was halted on a minor technicality by mid-level bureaucrats in the London planning office and the Fun Palace was never built.

While the project had begun with the vague dreams of Joan Littlewood of an interactive theatre and in Price's idea of an additive, variable architecture, the Fun Palace grew far beyond these formless, intangible origins. The design emerged gradually through countless suggestions and contributions, so that the final design bore little resemblance to the 'original' ideas of Price and Littlewood. Price and Littlewood recruited a small battalion of engineers, sociologists, cyberneticians, and scientists to help design the innovative structural and mechanical control systems essential to the success of the project. By 1965, the Fun Palace had become something of a *cause célèbre* for scores of English intellectuals who saw in it the germ of a new way of building, thinking, acting, and being. More than thirty seven people, including Buckminster Fuller, Yehudi Menuhin and Tony Benn, volunteered their services and contributed to the evolving design. In this sense, Price was never the sole "author" of the Fun Palace. Authorship was dispersed across the many designers, contributors, collaborators, and consultants, such that the final design amounted to an architectural *cadavre exquise* which represented something different to each member of the Fun Palace design team. In the end, it became so collaborative that it is difficult to say exactly who designed what, and its very authorship must be considered as fluid and indeterminate as the design itself.

In other essays, Price enlarged on the concept of the anti-architect, explaining his conviction that architects must take their place "in the ongoing process as provider of opportunities for experience and change, not as a master builder of immutable monumental structures".[2] His challenge to the centrality of the architect as author went against the grain of the convention, but how successful was his attempt? Despite Price's efforts to disavow authorship, to disperse authorship across a collaborative team, and to create a 'readerly' architecture, the Fun Palace continues to be inextricably identified with Price. This is perhaps not surprising. Since the days of Alberti, architecture has been identified with the persona of the architect. The modern concepts of genius and authorship have applied with equal force to literature, art, and architecture, and histories of modern architecture tend to be organised by architect, rather than by region or type. Certainly it is more seductive and less challenging to speak of heroic architects and their buildings in the quasi-Frankensteinian terms of creator and progeny than it is to consider buildings as the de-personalised narrative of collaborative design teams.

The notion of authorship, so central to Modernism, remained largely unchallenged until the 1960s, when author Roland Barthes wrote his landmark essay, "The Death of the Author".[3] This essay, which signalled a shift in Barthes' thinking from structuralism to post-structuralism, concisely and elegantly deconstructs and historicises the concept of authorship as an ideology of fetishised individuality, genius, and the mythology of pure creativity from the conceptual tabula rasa of the human mind. Barthes identifies the Author as a uniquely modern figure who is "the epitome and culmination of capitalist ideology, [and] has attached the greatest importance to the 'person' of the author".[4]

Barthes notes the emergence of a new kind of writing characterised by a displacement of the authorial persona in favour of a dispersed notion of the work or text, focused more on the reception and interpretation by the reader than on origination and intentionality. He sets out a multivalent argument, challenging both the notion of authorial voice and the singularity of intention.

The concept of the Author focuses the mythology of individuality on the person of the writer. Barthes counters the fetishised construct of the Author with the concept of the scriptor: the mediator whose role is to compile the elements of the text from the lexicon of pre-existing cultural meanings, and then withdraw from the space of the text, which henceforth stands as an autonomous and multivalent system of signs. As Barthes explains, "a text is not a line of words releasing a single 'theological' meaning (the 'message' of the Author-God) but a multi-dimensional space in which a variety of writings, none of them original, blend and clash. The text is a tissue of quotations drawn from the innumerable centers of culture".[5] Authorial intention thus recedes as the text opens a space of multiple readings and interpretations, according to the particular experiences and insights of the individual reader.

Anticipating Derrida's concept of *différance*, Barthes notes that the text is itself an ordered assemblage of pre-existing ideas and texts, rather than the emergence of a wholly original and unprecedented creation out of nothing. Similarly, although the design of the Fun Palace was undeniably 'novel', it was essentially a collage of parts in which users could play out their own cultural *bricolage*. It was an assemblage of ready-made, off-the-shelf components, from computerised control systems to the escalators and structural elements. This aspect of a DIY assemblage was even more pronounced in Price's highly successful 1976 Inter-Action Centre, which unlike the Fun Palace, was actually built, and has the look of a bargain basement version of the Centre Pompidou.

While architecture is clearly distinct from literature, I would like to draw a further analogy between Barthes' concepts of the author and writing, and those of the architect and architecture. Parallels between literary theory and architecture are hardly unique, since Barthes himself offers a broad interpretation of 'writing' and the 'text' beyond a narrowly constructed concept of literature, and his essay on the death of the author appears in a volume entitled *Image, Music, Text*.[6] Moreover, architects and critics such as Robert Venturi, Aldo Rossi, Peter Eisenman, and Geoffrey Broadbent have similarly identified strong affinities between the function and practice of architecture and the structural and post-structural linguistic theories set forth by Ferdinand de Saussure, Roland Barthes, and Jacques Derrida. Within the analogical correspondence between the author and the architect, between the text and architecture, Price's involvement in the Fun Palace, as we have seen, was authorship at a remove. His role would not be that of Author, but that of mediator, a role which Barthes describes: "in ethnographic societies the responsibility for a narrative is never assumed by a person but by a mediator, shaman or relator whose 'performance'—the mastery of the narrative code—may possibly be admired but never his 'genius'".[7] This would seem to describe the role that Price envisioned for himself in the Fun Palace.

Yet, as we have seen, histories and criticism of modern architecture tend to enframe architecture as part of a quasi-autobiographical sequence of creative and original works identified with the person, the life, and the passions of the architect. As Barthes notes, "the explanation of a work is always sought in the man or woman who produced it, as if it were always in the end, through the more or less transparent allegory of the fiction, the voice of a single person, the author 'confiding' in us".[8] The persona of the Author is the supposed key to deciphering a work, and therefore of defining and delimiting its meaning.

Barthes notes that when the Author is considered central, he or she is conceived as the paternal antecedent, origin, and past of their creation. Writing, or in the case of architecture, design, is regarded as the recording, representation or depiction of the original thought of the Author. But once written, Barthes argues that the Author's presence fades, while the text remains present in an eternal "here and now". Thus, once

Interior of the Fun Palace. Drawing.
Nicholas Bawlf, 1965. From the 1964
Civic Trust publication, "A Lea Valley
Regional Park".
Fonds Cedric Price, Collection Centre
Canadien d'Architecture/Canadian Centre for
Architecture, Montréal.
Price worked with avant-garde theatre
producer Joan Littlewood to create an
improvisational architecture endlessly in
the process of construction, dismantling,
and reassembly. Users would rearrange wall
panels to create new spaces from old spaces
as the program changed and evolved. The
Fun Palace was to be a "university of the
streets", providing educational opportunities
in the guise of leisure entertainment.

complete, the meaning of the text no longer dwells within the person of the author,
but within the consciousness of the beholder, the reader. The text is complete and
"out there", as an autonomous, neutral space, detached from origin, disconnected from
the voice of the author. Ultimately, Barthes suggests, it is the reader, not the author,
who determines the meaning of the text: "The reader is the space on which all the
quotations that make up a writing are inscribed... a text's unity lies not in its origin
but in its destination."[9] Thus, Barthes describes a new interpretation of writing—that
of the "readerly" text, devoid of directed, determined, and intended meanings, and
complete only in the consciousness of the reader. Once writing comes to light, the
author, according to Barthes, "enters into his own death". Yet, in their novel proposition
of the substitution of the elite figure of the author by a textual anonymity, both the Fun
Palace and Barthes' essay have paradoxically become elevated to the status of canonical
texts, inextricably associated with their respective, if reluctant authors.[10]

The design of the Fun Palace was not 'language' in the usual sense of an
architectural semiotics of form and symbol, but envisioned instead as an architectural
performative. It would be the Fun Palace itself, not Price, which would 'act' in
unmediated relation to the 'reader'. The neutrality of architectural performativity was
to be assured within the mechanisms of the building itself—not specifically dictated by
the authorial prescriptions of the architect—but through the impersonal actions of the
cybernetic and computerised self-regulating systems at the heart of the structure.

The Fun Palace was not intended to have any directed meanings. In the first place,
there are myriad ways of understanding and interpreting the project. It can be regarded
as an early foray into the realm of High-Tech formalism, or as a novel attempt to create
a technologically interactive architectural mechanism, as an effort to give physical form
to Bergsonian temporality, as a manifestation of Bertolt Brecht's theory of theatrical
alienation, as an expression of Price's deep-seated preoccupation with uncertainty
and indeterminacy, or as a political statement about the unpredictable socio-economic
conditions of the post-war English Welfare State. Any of these interpretations might
be equally valid, yet none would exhaust the meaning of the Fun Palace. It is all of
these things and probably more as well. Yet any attempt to establish a singular meaning
for the Fun Palace diminishes the project and impoverishes its significance. I myself

Inter-Action Centre, Kentish Town. Office of Cedric Price, 1976 (demolished 2003). Photo the author, 1999. Price's Inter-Action Centre incorporated many of the concepts and features of the ill-fated Fun Palace on a much-reduced scale. The Inter-Action Centre provided community services and creative outlets for local citizens until its demolition in 2003. In 1977, Reyner Banham commented on Price's influence on the design of the Centre Pompidou: "the concept of a stack of clear floors that can be adapted to a variety of cultural and recreational functions seems to recall the... Fun Palace of Cedric Price and Joan Littlewood, even if the project was never as radical as the floorless Fun Palace, or as casually innovatory as Price's Inter-Action Centre". Reyner Banham, "Centre Pompidou", *The Architectural Review*, May, 1977.

have written half a dozen essays, all different, on various aspects of the Fun Palace. None of these fully explain the project; none has exhausted or fully defined it. I have found the Fun Palace to be so richly enticing precisely because it cannot be exhausted and can easily support a multiplicity of readings. Of course, the capacity for endless interpretation is true of virtually any building or artefact, since it is probably impossible to design something with a single, unchanging meaning. What seems unique in the case of the Fun Palace is the *intentionality* of creating a readerly ambiguity that would support a multiplicity of readings. Yet what is *intentionality* if not an aspect of authorship?

The real revolutionary import of the Fun Palace seems to lie in its opposition to any quasi-theological attempt to fix absolute meaning in reason, science, or society. Yet, the "theological" aspect of authorship to which Barthes refers encompasses more than the authority of the text, to include the mythologies of creation and origin in the person of the author whom he seeks to destroy. Before his involvement with the Fun Palace, Price was a young, unknown London architect. It was only as Price began to enjoy a degree of fame and notoriety that he chose to adopt his anti-authorial stance. As with Barthes, this suggests that in order to dethrone the auteur, one must first elevate him to magisterial status. One might wonder, if a bit cynically, if the motivation for Price's gesture of selflessness might not in fact have been a further and paradoxical gesture of magnanimity and self-aggrandisement, if for no other reason than to go down in the history books as the first anti-architect.

Of course, this present reading of the Fun Palace is not in itself exhaustive, for the meaning of the constantly changing Fun Palace would itself ceaselessly shift for each 'reader', and no two experiences of such a place would ever be identical. Still, whatever elusive meaning the Fun Palace might have comprised only approaches totality in the user, the reader of this architectural text—never in the author or authors, or in myself as critic. For, as Barthes points out, there is one place where this shifting multiplicity is focused. That place is the reader, not the author.[11] In the Fun Palace, it is the user who gathers all of the elements constituting the work into a whole.

Yet, neither did Price and his associates seek to create a Degree Zero architecture, which would consciously avoid meaning and association. What they were after was a place of endless signification and function, in which meaning would oscillate ceaselessly in a rhizomatic field of shifting meaning. As a 'text', the Fun Palace is comprised of multiple and ambiguous signifiers, 'writings', and possible 'readings', drawn from many aspects of architecture, science and culture and entering into an endless dialogue. The deliberately anti-aesthetic form of the building, described as if it was like a "shipyard", was an attempt to resist specific associations and achieve an architectural stylelessness. Nevertheless, as the unwitting progenitor of the subsequent High-Tech style, the Fun Palace does define and connote an aesthetics of process, indeterminacy, 'industriality' and Constructivist ideologies. The result is clearly in Piano and Rogers' 1976 design for Centre Pompidou, which is as much homage to the Fun Palace as it is a canonisation and domestication of its anti-aesthetics. Despite the superficial formal similarities between the two buildings, the connotations of anarchic interchangeability in the Centre Pompidou are largely rhetorical pretense. It is another of the ironies of the Fun Palace that the deliberate narrative stylelessness and readerly ambiguities of the design would give rise to High-Tech aesthetics as a new stylistic canon.

Was the Fun Palace a genuinely neutral and 'readerly' architecture, in which form and function were determined not by the author/architect, but by the individual users themselves? Or did the resulting design and cybernetic programming encode a stealth 'directed' reading, which guided activities and shaped the public's reception of the Fun Palace? Might the motivation for such a 'readerly' architecture be regarded as Price's pursuit of a new social and political paradigm of democracy and individual agency?

Price's goal was to enable architecture to adapt to the changing needs of society, and hopefully, to enhance the quality of life as well. Yet, his unqualified faith in technology at times blinded him to certain inherent dangers. Despite his deep commitment to individual freedom, he seemed unaware of the latent Orwellian implications of cybernetics and social control in the Fun Palace, and the prospects of technology run amok undoubtedly cost him the support of people on the Left.[12]

It is equally worth asking whether the attempt to establish users as creators of their own architecture was a genuine effort to erase social boundaries, or if it was merely a paternalistic gesture motivated by philanthropic compassion. Was the Fun Palace the same kind of patronising—and elitist—architectural philanthropy that produced Walter Besant's 1887 *People's Palace* in London?[13]

Price clearly regarded the Fun Palace design team as an intellectual elite, while considering the Fun Palace as an artefact destined for the 'masses'. This would seem to indicate a persistent class-consciousness that belies the otherwise seamless pretext of classlessness in the project. Could it be that Price felt that such a democratic and 'neutral' architecture of the 'readerly' could only be realised through the beneficent agency of the informed elites? It is striking that the lists of Fun Palace consultants are representative of the educated elites, with virtually no representation by the masses for which the project was intended. Price was quick to explain that the project was not exclusively for the working classes, yet its locations (both the Isle of Dogs and Lea River Valley sites) were squarely in what would have been recognised as London working class districts, and the intended audience were those disenfranchised members of society who had neither the means nor the education to receive the benefits and advantages promised by the Fun Palace on their own. Despite the fact that the Fun Palace was planned for an underprivileged social group by their 'betters', it would seem that the absence of determined programmatic direction and patriarchal authorship in the Fun Palace would seem to deflect the brunt of such criticism. At the very least, the Fun Palace would not be encoded with the values of high or elitist culture. Price and his team seemed comfortable with the spontaneous emergence of ad hoc cultural expressions in the Fun Palace, and regarded the Fun Palace as a "cultural launching pad" where people from all classes would be free to determine their own destinies. Although it would have undeniably been set in motion by a class of elite intellectuals, it is arguably a valid example of socially activist architecture. Nevertheless, this adds to the paradoxical problematic of the Fun Palace.

To paraphrase Barthes, Price made a valiant attempt to give architecture its future and give birth to the 'reader' by overthrowing the myth of the Author.[14] Ironically, despite the dispersed responsibilities of design, and his deliberate attempt to create a 'readerly' architecture, Price continues to be indelibly identified as the 'author' of the Fun Palace, and the building has itself become a canonical text on anti-authoritative architecture. As an artefact of the tantalising yet elusive goal of an anti-authorial 'readerly' architecture, the Fun Palace has continued to fascinate architects in the forty years since the demise of the project.

Ernst Neufert's Architects' Data: Anxiety, Creativity and Authorial Abdication

Gernot Weckherlin

Drawing. Ernst Neufert, *Bauentwurfslehre*, thirteenth edition, Berlin, 1950, chapter on "Design Studios"—"drawings are to be stored appropriately in drawers not on the table".

6   Zeichentisch in Verbindung mit Schrankkörper erleichtert die Ordnung bei der Arbeit

7   Zeichnungen liegen zweckmäßig nicht auf dem Tisch, sondern in Zügen

Artists have an interest in our believing in sudden flashes of insight, in what we call inspirations; as if the idea for a work of art, for a poem, for the fundamental thought of a philosophy shone down like a gleam of grace from heaven. In truth, the imagination of a good artist or thinker continually produces good, mediocre, and bad things, but his power of judgement, highly sharpened and practiced, rejects, selects, ties together; thus, we now see from Beethoven's notebooks that he gradually gathered together the finest melodies and selected them, as it were, out of multiple beginnings. Someone who sorts things less rigorously and likes to give himself over to imitative recollection can in certain circumstances become a great improviser; but artistic improvisation stands low in relation to seriously and laboriously selected artistic thoughts. All the great artists were great workers, tireless not only in inventing, but also in rejecting, sifting, reshaping, ordering.[1]

The architect, like any other artist, is not a magician. However, he or she builds up a reputation as an artist if seen by non-professionals as a genius creating architectural form almost unconsciously out of nothing sitting in front of a blank sheet of paper. Occasionally Modern architects, like Alvar Aalto in his autobiographical texts, 'explain' such a working-method:

> When I personally have to solve some architectural problem, I am constantly—indeed, almost without exception—faced with an obstacle difficult to surmount, a kind of 'three in the morning feeling.' The reason seems to be the complicated, heavy burden resulting from the way that architectural design operates with countless, often mutually discordant elements. Social, humanitarian, economic, and technological requirements combined with psychological problems, [...] all this builds up into a tangled web that cannot be straightened out rationally or mechanically. [...] This is what I do—sometimes quite instinctively—in such cases. I forget the whole maze of problems for a while, as soon as the feel of the assignment and the innumerable demands it involves have sunk into my subconscious. I then move on to a method of working that is very much like abstract art. I simply draw by instinct, not architectural syntheses, but what are sometimes quite childlike compositions, and in this way, on an abstract basis, the main idea gradually takes shape, a kind of universal substance that helps me to bring the numerous contradictory components into harmony.[2]

Yet the idea of the solitary author creating architectural forms by mere imagination has not much in common with the reality of design processes in modern architecture. It does not even work in Aalto's case, as Bruno Reichlin outlined in an article investigating in detail Aalto's design process for the famous 'Senator's Dormitory' (Baker House) in Cambridge, Massachusetts. Reichlin demonstrates how Aalto focused on systematic compositional research of a project's data—from the number of rooms required to the best position for the cafeteria.[3]

Architectural design practice in general demands inspiring and at times extensive sources of information, a sense of order, routine knowledge, principles of composition and the highly complex faculty of judgement trained from the first day of architectural education onwards. The self-image of architects, emphasising the creative faculty of judgement alone, however, is deeply disturbed by an ever-increasing quantity of books, catalogues, architectural magazines, manuals (being replaced today by electronic media), in use and necessary for almost any architectural design work from the early nineteenth century onwards. The drawing table was never as empty as the popular image of the solitary artist-architect makes us believe. The earthly act of collecting and evaluating data—from building regulations to pattern books for a design project—is, however, in general played down by modern architects as a derivative aspect of their work as 'divine' creators of an autonomous art.

It is intriguing to ask whether this self-image of architects is a particularly modern myth. To find an answer it might be helpful to examine those various data sources and to find out what they reveal about the 'episteme' of a design practice. Is it possible to describe the effects of these sources on the actual decisions of designing architects? And do these sources have an impact on their self-image? Although one might think that it would not be hard to find traces of such discourses, protocols of readings, practices of re-readings and arrangements of data from various sources, those traces are rarely tracked down in written texts or in any other form of representation such as drawings.

One of the most intriguing books of this strange genre, which could be named "standard books of reference rarely mentioned by modern architects", and one almost completely forgotten about in architectural history and theory, is Ernst Neufert's *Bauentwurfslehre* (*Architects' Data*).[4] Significantly the book was introduced to English 'readers' as 'not literature' in the second English edition:

> This book is not literature; it is a practical manual. The text is telegraphic and predicatory; in this it follows the practice of Ernst Neufert, who wrote in his first edition that his aim had been to reduce, schematise, abstract the elements of design basics so as to make simple imitations difficult and to oblige the user to create form and content out of data...[5]

A careful examination of this 'non-literature' heavily used by designers on the drawing table thus is particularly appealing. Ernst Neufert's *Architects' Data* is here but one popular modern example.[6] A closer look on Neufert's manual reveals that it provoked reactions from architects seeing the book as an incredibly useful aid for everyday design work, and, simultaneously, as a threat to their authority as individual authors of a building. The history of Neufert's book and the reaction to its success within the profession give some insights into the "nature" of the paradox of Modern architecture looking functionally inevitable and artistically inspired at the same time. The architect creating "form and content out of data" is bound to the particular structural logic and form of the data available. Artistic freedom in Aalto's sense, however, i.e. the privilege of an artist to reduce unconsciously the various elements of a design into a mysterious 'universal substance'—bringing them into harmony—becomes more and more a myth as books or magazines like Neufert's provide hundreds of examples ready to be copied at least in parts into new projects. The way out of mere imitation is the abstraction of the information given by Neufert and the faculty of individual creativity. Consequently, Neufert's manual is a good example for examining the concept of autonomous authorship in Modern architecture.

Neufert's *Architects' Data* (first published in 1936) was a major commercial success. It was the best-selling architectural publication in Germany in the last century. Notwithstanding the fact that Neufert, as a student from the early Bauhaus period, published his book in pre-war Nazi Germany and later worked for Albert Speer's planning committee for the future capital Berlin as an expert on technical norms and standards in architecture, his book remained extremely successful even after 1945. In 1949 the first post-war edition (12th edition) came into print, proudly announcing in the publisher's preface that to date (the latest edition, the eleventh, had been published in 1944) 123,000 copies had been sold. The work was revised and re-edited 32 times within the author's lifetime. Recently the 38th German edition, revised and updated by Johannes Kister, hit the bookstores.[7] It has been translated into 17 languages.[8] Currently authorised editions are available in Bahasa-Indonesia, Chinese, Czech, English, French, German, Greek, Hungarian, Italian, Japanese, Polish, Portuguese, Russian, Serbo-Croatian, Slovenian, Spanish, and Turkish.

As early as 1950 and 1960 the architectural magazine *Bauwelt* dedicated articles to Neufert celebrating his birthday and his famous book simultaneously. These articles illustrate the acceptance of this strictly 'functionalistic' standard manual for architects. In a 1960 article Neufert's *Bauentwurfslehre* was compared to a widespread German college dictionary named after his first author, Duden. The *Duden* is a standard dictionary, as popular as, say, *Webster's Dictionary* is for American English. Which school child, who now habitually picks up the *Duden*, knows that, in fact, Professor Konrad Duden was a human being? In a similar manner, one could ask how many of our young and conscientious building professionals, to whom the 'Neufert' has become a daily tool just like a pencil, parallel rule, triangle and compass, know at all, that behind this *Bauentwurfslehre* stands a former resident of Weimar and Berlin and now a Darmstadt-based university professor, Ernst Neufert?[9]

The author's name gained international recognition with the translations of his book into several European languages in the late 1940s. Paul Klopfer reported in his 1950 *Bauwelt* article that Spain's architectural community misunderstood the verb "to neufer", as a translation of the German word "entwerfen"—"to design".[10] These articles, and the unavoidable "Editor's Preface" in every new updated edition of the book, demonstrate its widespread popularity. "Der Neufert"—the book's short title even today has become a synonym of the book for most architects in Germany. His success as an architect of large industrial complexes and other buildings has been eclipsed by this literary success story.[11] This fusion of the author's name with his magnum opus is certainly more than a grotesque anecdote. It rather shows the widespread popularity of a book and the acceptance of a rationalised design process propagated by Neufert in his text, which was in use in architectural education and practice from the moment it was on sale. It is worth noting that the book was highly regarded as a manual by both traditionalist and modern architects in Germany. As an everyday tool of the design studio it introduced a new and faster 'rhythm of work', as Klopfer put it in his article in *Bauwelt*.[12]

To understand the book's tremendous popularity and the reactions it provoked within the architectural profession, it is worth examining its origins. Neufert's *Architects' Data* was written—or, to be more precise, drawn and written (it mainly comprises thousands of small drawings resembling comic strips, rather than text)—by a former student of Walter Gropius during the early days of the Weimar Bauhaus. What motivated the author between 1933 and 1936 to compile such an unparalleled encyclopaedic volume with more than 3,600 black and white drawings illustrating the everyday situations of modern architecture? Certainly Neufert as an author writing for various architectural magazines such as *Bauwelt* or *Wasmuths Monatshefte für Baukunst* knew an article by Werner Hegemann, "Das Dänische Handbuch der Bauindustrie".[13] Hegemann mentioned the American *Sweet's Catalogue Files* published by the American building industry, and another Danish publication: *Haandbog for Bygnings-Industrien*. Both publications' chief characteristic was a clearly arranged and illustrated collection of the most recent advertising material for architects published in architectural magazines by the building industry. The main idea of these catalogues to Hegemann and certainly Neufert appeared extremely persuasive: architects received updated information on building technology in one volume and the advertising departments were able to avoid direct mailing to architects, which was extremely ineffective as many of them, as Hegemann observed, threw direct mail directly into the waste paper basket.[14]

However, this was only one source of inspiration for Neufert. As a talented architect, but one lacking any academic formal education, he published his famous *Bauentwurfslehre* in March 1936, some years after teaching at the Weimar School of Architecture.[15] The earliest origins of this book date back as far as to the years from 1926 to 1930. After the Bauhaus (the director of which was Walter Gropius) moved from Weimar to Dessau in 1925, Neufert was appointed to the Weimar school (director Otto Bartning) as a professor for *Schnellentwerfen* or 'rapid design'. Neufert, aged 26 at the time of his appointment, developed a radically new concept of teaching at this new school *Staatliche Bauhochschule Weimar* (Weimar State College for Building).

Design classes for his students, most of them with a professional background as builders, involved designing small projects within an extremely limited time frame —within three hours a complete housing project had to be developed. Neufert (employed at Gropius' office between 1921 and 1924) was a talented manager of his master's building sites. However, he did not approve of the design process practiced by Gropius and his studio architect at the time, Adolf Meyer. Neufert many years later gave an account of frequent delays on building sites caused by ever changing drawings done by Meyer and revised by Gropius' comments. In many cases, Neufert later reports, the decisive drawings of the studio had been sent to his building site, when the building was completed long ago.[16] The experience convinced him of the need to avoid such an ineffective design process in architectural education. On the other hand, the work for the studio of Walter Gropius, the 'spiritus rector' of the early Bauhaus period, made Neufert familiar with some of the most urgent issues architects had to deal with after the First World War. Gropius published and lectured at that time on industrialisation and rationalisation and on the development of norms and standards for an industrialised housing production.[17] Henry Ford's car industry was a particularly shining example for a productive building industry and was frequently quoted by Gropius and his contemporaries. Neufert realised the contradictions between Gropius' visionary literary promises and his master's less promising architectural practice. The pedagogic concept of Neufert and the Weimar School was based on two elements. The design process itself was subject to a more economic method of planning, as the example of the "rapid design" course shows, and an architectural training in closer contact with building practice than in any other architectural school in Germany between 1925 and 1930.[18]

The 'active building atelier' ('aktives Bauatelier') of the school formed the second year of the program directed by Neufert, and addressed real building projects, two of them realised in the nearby University town of Jena. Generally speaking, the most spectacular difference of Neufert's pedagogic concept, in comparison with other schools of architecture at the time, was the introduction of the latest scientific findings in industrial engineering and industrial management (the latter was part of the timetable and featured in lectures given by the engineer Max Mayer) into the design process itself. For his first year 'rapid design' courses Neufert worked out the idea of a standard card-index box of 'typical' design solutions. His idea was to develop a standard library from experiences made by the active building atelier, from questions of the building owners and his and his students' own expert skills in the design studio. The painful experience of a designer sitting anxiously in front of a blank sheet of paper was to be avoided with this collection of typical solutions.

Neufert's concept of architectural education was a radical departure from the established teaching methods of his days. His idea of the standard card-index box was to assemble a supplementary 'open source' catalogue of ready-to-use samples to be copied by his students and assembled whenever needed for new architectural projects: "the school assembles from productive work a rich store of expertise, available not only to students and teachers but to the whole building world, a true storehouse for students".[19] Neufert later published some of those 'standard projects' of the school's 'active atelier', including a student house in Jena, a university cafeteria including administration premises or the Abbeanum university building in Jena, demonstrating the logic of procedural efficiency as a rational basis for any design task and avoiding waste

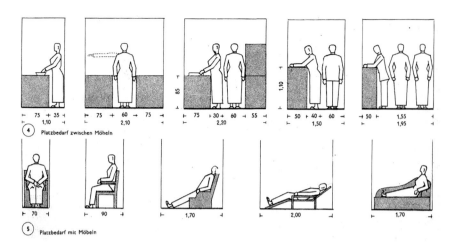

of space in a rather 'Fordist' manner. His concept of architectural authorship thus is radically different from his contemporaries: Neufert sees the architectural object more as product of an effectively organised architectural service, whereas other Modernists like Le Corbusier tended to emphasise the role of the author as an inspired interpreter of eternal mathematical laws—for example, his Modulor.[20]

Neufert's Weimar career unexpectedly ended in 1930 when the first Nazi-state government in Thuringia decided to reorganise the school. Otto Bartning resigned as a director of the school and Ernst Neufert and the other teachers were let go.[21] During the next six years Neufert worked on his encyclopaedic manual; he received a commission for this job from *Bauwelt* publishers in 1933. Consequently Neufert had to give up the idea of an 'open source' library of architectural standard solutions because he had to earn his living by publications and architectural work. In this respect the form of a book was definitely more promising. The book (published in March 1936) was so much in demand that within the first three weeks the first edition was completely sold out. Neufert was at the time travelling to the USA, considering emigration, when he received notice of his incredible success. He visited Frank Lloyd Wright in Taliesin and proudly reports how impressed Wright was by the book; indeed, the extent of the sales even made him change his plans for emigrating to the USA (if we choose to believe his confessions in Gotthelf's small monograph on Neufert published in 1960).[22]

What are the main characteristics of Neufert's *Architects' Data* compared to other manuals of his time? A subtitle of truly baroque proportions gives us an insight into the intentions of the author: *Architects' Data: Basics, Standards and Regulations on Layout, Construction, Design, Spatial Requirements, Spatial Relations, Measures for Buildings, Rooms, Fixtures and Utensils with Man as a Measure and Objective. Manual for Building Professionals, Building Owners, Teachers and Students.* The subtitle informs us of Neufert's intended audience and concisely defines his quite extraordinary new concept of a book based on the logic of a time-saving design process. The book does not follow the logic of a traditional systematic seminar or treatise in architecture (unlike, for example, Durand's famous proto-functionalist *Cours d'Architecture*); neither is it a compilation of exemplary building types.[23] It is a book for everyone interested in building, not merely a book for the professionals alone. Neufert's aim was to help those unable to imagine the real size of future buildings or building elements. This lack of imagination was, of course, a problem for architectural students as well. Long texts were regarded as a waste of the reader's time and space in the book, as the complete basic knowledge required by designing architects had to fit into one single volume. This concept of a one-volume edition obviously is an adaption of the *Sweet's Catalogue File* or the Danish *Haandbog for Bygnings-Industrien* mentioned in Neufert's list of references.[24]

Its main idea is extremely simple: The designing architect in the author's view is an expert who:

> ... has to know the dimensions of the devices, garments, etc. which surround him in
> order to determine the appropriate sizes of receptacles and furniture. He must know

how much space a person needs between pieces of furniture in kitchens, dining rooms, libraries, etc. in order to ensure adequate interaction with and the comfortable use of the furniture—without wasting space. Ultimately, he must know the minimum dimensions of the spaces within his everyday environment—such as: Trains, trams, cars, etc. He has fixed ideas based on these typical and narrow spaces. From these dimensions, he derives, often unconsciously, his other spatial dimensions.[25]

Consequently the book is an encyclopaedic manual showing in abstract and reduced drawings the whole universe of modern man and his modern life, sitting in a restaurant or in an armchair at home, working in an office, travelling in airships or playing tennis. In fact it is a strange and at times quite curious collection of domestic requisites, loosely classified by the logic of building 'types' from table size (apartment houses) to runways (airports).

Neufert opened up a completely new field of knowledge for architects although one indebted to the work of Alexander Klein (and many others) and his own "scientific" experiments with minimum housing and optimum floor plan layout in the years around 1930.[26] At the same time, in *Dei Neufert* the previously secret know-how of the discipline is made open and accessible to the public, only requiring the purchase of this—admittedly expensive—book. Perhaps because of this Neufert did not face political reprisals in Nazi Germany, even though he—a rather self-confident Bauhaus-architect—never made a secret of his enthusiasm for an undesirable (in 1936) Modern architecture, and although his book contains examples of projects from many emigrant architects who were later forced to leave Germany, such as Alexander Klein, Ludwig Hilberseimer, Erich Mendelsohn, Mies van der Rohe, and even truly Bolshevist communal housing projects by Moissej Ginzburg in Moscow.

Neufert's attitude towards the role of an architect as an author however remained strangely conventional. He described at length a strictly functionalist approach to a design program, beginning with an extended program and a series of questionnaires to be answered and followed by a schematic layout of rectangles with minimum dimensions of the floor plan requirements. Anticipating criticism, he then added, "In the end the personality of a designer—and his building owner—finds its expression in every building, as it depends on him [the building owner] whether he puts his building into the hands of a real man (*Kerl*) or a 'rubber man' (*Gummimann*)."[27] Neufert regarded 'born' architects, more as 'real men'. For 'real men' there is no such thing as a 'canned wisdom' and no ready-made architectural solution. For them, in Neufert's view there exists only:

> ... elements and methods of combination, construction, composition and harmony. A born architect or an architect with the desire to build in his heart, will close his ears and eyes, as soon as a solution to a problem is given to him, because he is so full of his own imagination and ideals, that he only needs the elements to put his back into the job, to make a whole from it. [28]

This attitude the author expressed for the first time in a publication *The architect at the point of dismemberment* with a text titled "The Formation of Creative Competence of Architects" in 1947.[29] Neufert filled a teaching position from 1945 at the Technical University of Darmstadt. Neufert's moderate, almost traditional image of the architect

Drawing. Mies van der Rohe, presented in Ernst Neufert, *Bauentwurfslehre*, third edition, Berlin, 1936.
The ground floor plan shows the "house of the year 2000 with thin load-bearing steel-columns, and independent, non-load-bearing, thin partition-walls and exterior walls, best weather protection, noise and heat-insulation guaranteed. Between living room, dining room and entrance hall no doors, only spatial separations."

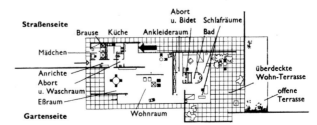

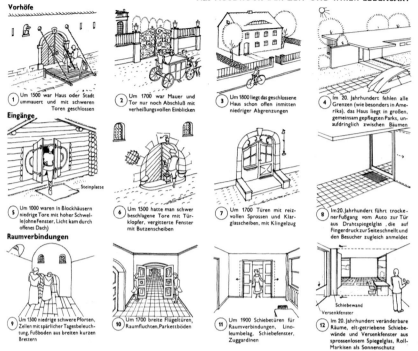

HAUS UND FORMEN
ALS AUSDRUCK DER ZEIT UND IHRER LEBENSART

Vorhöfe

(1) Um 1500 war Haus oder Stadt ummauert und mit schweren Toren geschlossen

(2) Um 1700 war Mauer und Tor nur noch Abschluß mit verheißungsvollen Einblicken

(3) Um 1800 liegt das geschlossene Haus schon offen inmitten niedriger Abgrenzungen

(4) Im 20. Jahrhundert fehlen alle Grenzen (wie besonders in Amerika), das Haus liegt in großen, gemeinsam gepflegten Parks, unaufdringlich zwischen Bäumen

Eingänge

(5) Um 1000 waren in Blockhäusern niedrige Tore mit hoher Schwelle (ohne Fenster, Licht kam durch offenes Dach)

(6) Um 1500 hatte man schwer beschlagene Tore mit Türklopfer, vergitterte Fenster mit Butzenscheiben

(7) Um 1700 Türen mit reizvollen Sprossen und Klarglasscheiben, mit Klingelzug

(8) Im 20. Jahrhundert führt trockener Fußgang vom Auto zur Tür aus Drahtspiegelglas, die auf Fingerdruck zur Seite schnellt und den Besucher zugleich anmeldet

Raumverbindungen

(9) Um 1500 niedrige schwere Pforten, Zellen mit spärlicher Tagesbeleuchtung, Fußboden aus breiten kurzen Brettern

(10) Um 1700 breite Flügeltüren, Raumfluchten, Parkettböden

(11) Um 1900 Schiebetüren für Raumverbindungen, Linoleumbelag, Schiebefenster, Zuggardinen

(12) Im 20. Jahrhundert veränderbare Räume, elt-getriebene Schiebewände und Versenkfenster aus sprossenlosem Spiegelglas, Rollmarkisen als Sonnenschutz

as an author "full of imagination and ideals" in the year 1947 is less surprising when we read this statement in context with fierce public reactions after 1945 to another book Neufert published as a supplementary volume to his *Architects' Data* in 1943 with the title *Bauordnungslehre*, a title translated best as "Dimensional Coordination".

In this book the author went one step further in architectural rationalism and the time-saving, working methods efficiency-based concept of Neufert's first book. In the eyes of many architectural colleagues of his time the author went too far.[30] The "born systematician", as Neufert was called in the architectural press in Nazi Germany, now aimed at a totalitarian dimensional standardisation for many building types, from factory shops, military sheds to completely industrialised housing.[31] The main editor of the book was Albert Speer, then *Generalbauinspektor* (Chief of Staff) of the capital Berlin. Speer's intention was to establish a completely rationalised building industry for the period of 'total war' and after.

It is unsurprising that Neufert's reputation as author of the *Bauentwurfslehre* became tarnished after 1945. In a debate published in *Neue Bauwelt* and other architectural magazines such as *Baukunst und Werkform*, many of Neufert's colleagues such as Georg Leowald in an article on "Sense and limits of standardization: A late discussion of Neufert 'Dimensional Coordination'" repeatedly expresses his highest respect for Neufert's *Bauentwurfslehre*, but criticises the official character of Neufert's less famous *Bauordnungslehre*.[32] In fact with totalitarian control of building production during the war, standards and norms became more and more legally binding regulations for architects and building contractors alike.

The intensity of this debate is illustrated by a synopsis of 46 articles published in 1947 on norms and standards for architects and the building industry in *Neue Bauwelt*.[33] Technical standards and building 'types' for a long time had been subject of voluntary agreements between building professionals, brick manufacturers and other interest groups. Within the total war economy, norms lost their voluntary character and became obligatory for the German building industry, and Neufert's wartime definition of technical standards established the trend which governed the post-war reconstruction period. The traditional role of the master builder now faced threats from many sides. The standardisation of modular dimensions such as in the brick industry

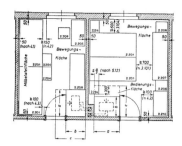

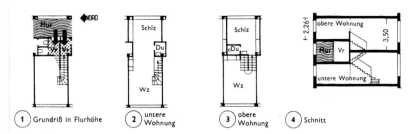

Drawing. M Ginzburg, Moskow presented in Ernst Neufert, *Bauentwurfslehre*, Third edition, Berlin, 1936.
"Russian type of apartment house. Small apartment with lower bedroom and higher living room. One exterior corridor serves two floor levels."

Norm DIN 18011 in Hanns Frommhold, Siegfried Hasenjäger, "Stellflächen für Möbel und Öfen im sozialen Wohnungsbau", *Wohnungsbau-Normen*, 1967.
Norms for social housing projects in Germany (introduced August 1951), showing minimum space required for pieces of furniture and stoves. The illustration shows obvious similarities to *Architects' Data*.

(DIN 4172) based on Neufert's octametric modular coordination of his *Bauordnungslehre* was introduced first in 1944. Other norms e.g. for social housing projects during the reconstruction years recommending minimum (spatial) dimensions for standard flat types were not compulsory. However, public funding was closely associated with the obligation to observe those norms in (western) Germany.

If one were to ask contemporary architects to estimate the influence of books like *Architects' Data* on architectural design practice today, their answer is invariably: None. Despite this, the book has lately reached its 38th German edition, and so one is inclined to question such answers. Why do students and architects buy such an expensive book, if they do not need it? The influence of those secondary sources piling up on the drawing tables of designing architects cannot be easily analysed. But it is worth looking closer at those traces of a discourse without stable units as authors and their "work". This is particularly fascinating as the field of secondary literary sources has changed dramatically. Libraries and catalogues have moved to the Internet or to CAD-software. But the number of elements given to the architect as a solitary genius is not unlimited and the elements themselves are deeply linked with other discourses. The width of the drawing paper or the standard elements of the CAD software are given in advance and have an impact on his or her modus operandi.

In conclusion, we should note that 'non-literature' like Neufert's handbook is rarely mentioned in the discourses of architectural history and theory. Both disciplines for a long time concentrated on architectural authors. Even today almost any recent catalogue of the architectural press recommends monographic or even biographic books presenting more or less famous architects and 'their' masterworks. The author and his or her 'work of art' are apparently stable units within a discourse of architectural history, avoiding analysis of the impact of virtually anonymous design sources, such as catalogues, manuals for architects, etc.. A closer analysis of manuals and other secondary literature, however, threatens such categories of the author and a work of art; it is impossible to describe the impact of a manual in terms of authorship, as the reader/user producing "form and content out of data" in Neufert's sense does not create by personal imagination alone. The architect making use of non-literature either does not mention its use or does not care about it. The reason for this behaviour is obvious—if references and the modes of composition are transparent, the logic of the design process becomes at least partly reproducible. The data from such sources introduce their own logic. They challenge the idea of a producer inspired by exclusively personal ideas and help to develop a slightly different concept of architectural authorship, pointing to the significance of the conditioning frame in which architecture unfolds.

Systems Aesthetics, or How Cambridge Solved Architecture

Sean Keller

Introduction

If today we are often told that architectural authorship will be revolutionised by digital technologies, we should remember Mark Wigley's warning that much recent talk about architecture in a digital age is perhaps only "an echo of an echo" of ideas explored decades earlier.[1] After the Second World War the University of Cambridge came to play an important role in this historical echo chamber. There ideas about architectural authorship taken from strains of pre-war Modernism (Functionalism and Constructivism) were adapted to post-war developments (the computer, operations research, structuralism) in an effort to solidify architecture's intellectual and social standing. Examination of this historical context will help us see that—despite unprecedented computational power and often fatiguing claims of novelty—present attempts to reformulate architectural authorship are actually variations on a theme as old as architectural Modernism itself. A look at post-war Cambridge will also reveal that approaches to architectural authorship that today seem widely disparate have grown out of a common background. I also hope that this account may discourage further echoing of naive myths about scientific, mathematical, and computational solutions to the inescapable dilemmas of architectural (or any other) authorship.

In 1972 Lionel March, the head of the University of Cambridge's Centre for Land Use and Built Form Study, proposed that architecture should be designed by what he called "the systems aesthetic".[2] Based on newly available computer modelling and sophisticated mathematics, the systems aesthetic was envisioned as a scientific method that would overcome the "private pranks" and "empty images" created by architectural intuition.[3] By somehow reaching beneath the surface of architecture, systems aesthetics would reveal a deep logic of buildings and cities. March's phrase "systems aesthetic" resonates historically as a description of a wider trend in early computer age architecture that attempted to replace the subjective architect-as-author by an objective and systematic design process. I want to explore this trend by bringing March's work together with that of two other influential Cambridge graduates—Christopher Alexander and Peter Eisenman. For despite important differences, these three men have all been driven by a desire to produce architecture through systematic methods that dramatically reconfigure the role of the architect.

Fundamentally this desire has been provoked by a question of authorship: how is architectural authorship authorised? From what authority is an architectural design derived? While in special situations this question can be asked about other arts, the technical, political, and economic scope of architectural work makes it unavoidable. The long-echoing answer that runs from Constructivism through the systems aesthetics of the 1960s and 70s and down to present models of emergence is that architectural authority—the justification for forms—can only be secured through design methodology. Rejecting both intuition and historical precedents, the variations of this approach have all aimed for design processes which would be rational and systematic enough to be self-justifying. They also have shared a belief that such systematic methods would connect architecture to mathematics and science. Indeed, architects like Alexander, Eisenman, and March seem to have always been thinking of something else. When they looked at buildings they saw mathematics, biology, geology, and linguistics. When they read mathematical and scientific theories they imagined architecture. Repeatedly they have turned to other disciplines (mainly sciences) to justify their work, as if, perhaps, architecture itself had no authority to offer.

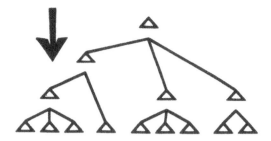
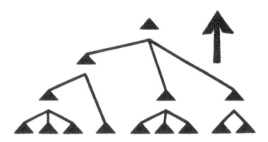

Analysis of program and synthesis of form. Christopher Alexander. *Notes on the Synthesis of Form*, Cambridge, MA, 1964.

The Analysis and Synthesis of Form

Christopher Alexander first completed a mathematics degree at Cambridge before migrating to the architecture department in 1956. He did not, however, leave his mathematical mindset behind, and was immediately frustrated by what he saw as the "sheer absurdity" of the instruction in architecture.[4] After publishing his first paper on the Golden Section and modular building systems, he decided to pursue a PhD at Harvard University. His dissertation, published in 1964 as *Notes on the Synthesis of Form*, became the founding text of a movement that attempted to bring mathematical and scientific methods to architectural design.[5] In brief, Alexander argued that traditional approaches to design were inadequate in the face of the rapidly shifting complexities of post-war society, and that the recourse to individual artistic intuition, which he understood Modernism to propose, was hopelessly unaccountable. Conveniently, developments in mathematics and the newly available electronic computer provided an alternative. Using these tools, complex architectural 'problems' could be broken down through analysis into manageable pieces and then 'solved' through a complementary process of 'synthesis'. The result would be designs that 'fit' their environments perfectly, having grown like sand dunes simply out of their requirements, with no interference from the architect. Alexander's bold claim was that, through the use of the most advanced technology and mathematics, architecture could return to a prelapsarian world in which all of the cultural, political, and aesthetic dimensions of design as both an intentional and an interpreted act could be fully naturalised. Apparently, this vision was attractive to architects of the 1960s, for, despite the many theoretical and practical flaws in Alexander's book, and despite his own subsequent rejection of its main argument, it sparked a wave of similar work throughout Europe and America. For a technical tract on design methodology, the book was hugely popular: it was translated into Italian in 1967 and French in 1970 and is now in its fourteenth English printing.

After emphasising that his mathematical approach was required by the unprecedented novelty and complexity of modern demands on architecture, Alexander chose to demonstrate his method with the design of a fictional 600 person village in India. This is perhaps the least novel, least modern architectural program he could have selected. The contradiction makes clear that it was not the demands of the architectural problem that required computer analysis, but an independent desire to use mathematical techniques—and especially, somehow, the computer—that determined Alexander's methodology. This computer-envy also explains the level of complexity displayed in the example. Alexander lists 141 requirements that will define his hypothetical Indian village, such as:

> 20. People of different factions prefer to have no contact...
> 67. Drinking water to be good, sweet...
> 92. House has to be cleaned, washed, drained...[6]

From a theoretical view, it seems impossible to say why Alexander hit upon these 141 requirements and not others. It also seems impossible to know why there are 141 and not 14 or 1,410. A good explanation is that 141 gave Alexander a number that was too

A1

Diagram resolving a subset of requirements for an Indian village. Christopher Alexander. *Notes on the Synthesis of Form,* Cambridge, MA, 1964.

large to be analysed by hand, yet small enough to be sorted by an IBM 7090 within a reasonable amount of computational time. Again, it was the desire for the computer that shaped the requirements, not the requirements that demanded a computer.

Alexander uses a number of terms for the organisational structure he is trying to discover through his analysis: "form", "conceptual order", "organization", "pattern", "abstract structure", "logical structure", "logical picture", "diagram of forces", "field description", "formal picture", "constructive diagram", and, finally in his mathematical treatment, "the graph G(M,L)"—where M is the set requirements and L the set of connections between these requirements for a particular design problem. All of these terms are used by Alexander to suggest that at a fundamental level, hidden from intuition, architecture is organised by logical relations that can be revealed only by mathematical analysis. However, the connection between these logical relations and the physical forms of the material objects they are supposed to describe remains entirely ambiguous. The strategic role played by this ambiguity is revealed by a scattering of diagrams near the back of the book.

After sorting by the IBM 7090 the requirements of Alexander's Indian village were organised into subsets containing between seven and 23 parameters that could not be further disentangled. At this most critical point the computer drops out and it is a long-established sort of architectural sketch, the *parti pris*, rendered with a broad pen, that is brought in to 'solve' the conflict among these remaining requirements. Alexander never explains how he arrives at these diagrams, and whether these are the only possible solutions. Instead, the sketches seem to come from exactly the sort of private, intuitive, visual language Alexander had promised to overcome. Buried deep in Alexander's mathematical and iconoclastic method it is the cocktail napkin sketch that is left to perform the crucial trick. In a work apparently dedicated to mathematical clarity, it is the diagrams' ambiguity that makes them indispensable. The diagrams hover between representing abstract relations and representing concrete plans. The wide strokes and irregular forms appear to record very abstract patterns—what Alexander would call the logical structure of the problem—and yet also very tentatively suggest ground plans for the proposed village. The implication of the diagrams is that the detailed, concrete, design is yet to come. However, his brief explanations reveal that Alexander is actually proposing very specific configurations of wells, roads, fields, trees, and buildings, but without venturing to show how these would actually be laid out, at what scale, with what geometry, and in what materials. The diagrams give the impression that Alexander's method has in fact produced a design for an entire village, but without showing what that village would look like.

The function of these images within the methodology attracted critical attention and Alexander's introduction to the later paperback edition focuses on their role. There, in a surprising inversion, Alexander argues that it is the diagrams that have "immense power" and that "once the book was written, I discovered that it is quite unnecessary to use such a complicated and formal way of getting at the independent diagrams".[7] Instead, "you can create, and develop, these diagrams piecemeal, one at a time, in the most natural way, out of your experience of buildings and design".[8] This amounts to a complete rejection of the book's fundamental argument that the torturous mathematical analysis was needed precisely because the intuition of the individual designer could no longer be trusted—a radical, but perhaps impossible, rewriting of architectural authority that apparently even Alexander himself could not sustain.

Architectural Science

Like Alexander, Lionel March began studying architecture at Cambridge in 1956 after transferring from mathematics (he had entered with a recommendation from Alan Turing, the famous computing theorist). Also like Alexander, March later spent time in the other Cambridge conducting research at the Joint Centre for Urban Studies run by Harvard and MIT. March, however, returned to England, and in 1967 received funding to establish the Centre for Land Use and Built Form Study (LUBFS) at the University of Cambridge. Modelled on a scientific research centre, LUBFS was devoted to the use of mathematical methods in architecture and urban planning. March's goal was to establish an 'architectural

Models of Environment, guest edited by Lionel March, Marcial Echeñique and Peter Dickens, *Architectural Design*, 41, 1971.

science' that would meet the challenges of post-war society with objective, quantitative methods. As he was proud to report, many of the researchers working at the centre came from mathematics or the sciences. The computer quickly became a focal point for the centre's work. New, expensive, technically advanced, and inherently mathematical, the computer was an ideal symbol for the seriousness and rigour that March and his colleagues hoped to bring to architecture through their reforms.

The LUBFS approach reached a rhetorical highpoint in May of 1971 with the publication of a special issue of *Architectural Design*, titled "Models of Environment", edited by March, Marcial Echeñique and Peter Dickens, and filled exclusively with the work of Cambridge researchers and graduates. The one-page introduction to this collection, subtitled "Polemic for a structural revolution", argued that the use of mathematical methods in architecture was part of a general "structural revolution" taking place in the social and behavioural sciences. This mathematical approach was intended to replace the "intuitive skill", "confusion", "sophistical sciences", "individual hunches", "court jesters and acrobats", "private pranks", "pricey prima-donnas", "hallucinations", "extravagant and empty images", "individual expression", and "personal prejudice" that threatened architecture and planning. This polemic was most radical in its rejection of artistic intuition and in its deep iconoclasm. Intuition was condemned on two counts: first, that it was unequal to the complexity of post-war politics, economics, and technology; second, that it was private and opaque and, thus, unaccountable. Instead, the Cambridge researchers sought an explicit, quantified design process that was open to criticism and gradual improvement. Regarding architectural images, the damnation was concise: "Draughtsmanship is a drug." In the LUBFS work texts, formulae, diagrams, and computer code replaced plans, elevations, and photographs as the proper tools of architectural research; and the long-held understanding of the building as an object of sensory engagement was replaced by the idea of the building as a system of functional relationships. An architectural theory that rejected images was rejecting the profession's dominant medium of communication—both internally and with the general public—as well as the profession's established methodologies, all of which were image-based. That the long history of drawing could be replaced by mathematics was not obvious— 'revolution' was a fair term.

The computer was at the centre of this methodology that March dubbed the "systems aesthetic". Not unlike Alexander, he proposed that all of the factors affecting a design proposal could be brought together in a mathematical model run on a computer. However, he was at pains to distance himself from Alexander's view that such models could automatically yield successful designs. Instead, he viewed the computer model as an environment in which the 'artificial evolution' of architectural types could take place.[9] This digital evolution would occur though a "cyclic, iterative procedure" (like most computer programs) passing repeatedly through three phases: production, deduction and induction:

> We conceive of rational designing as having three tasks—(1) the creation of a novel composition, which is accomplished by productive reasoning; (2) the prediction of performance characteristics, which is accomplished by deduction; (3) the accumulation of habitual notions and established values, an evolving typology, which is accomplished by induction.[10]

March believed that implicitly this had always been the way designs were developed, whether by individuals, offices or entire building traditions. Like Alexander however, he argued that there was a new need, and a new capability, to make the process explicit:

> If internalized personal judgement, experience and intuition alone are relied upon, the three modes of the PDI-model become inextricably entangled and no powerfully sustained use of collective, scientific knowledge is possible. Design will remain more or less personalistic and a matter of opinion, albeit professional. If the design process is externalized and made public, as it evidently must be for the team work to be fully effective, then the three stages of the PDI-model are worth making explicit so that as much scientific knowledge can be brought to bear on the problem as seems appropriate. In this externalized process it is feasible to experiment with artificial

Production/Deduction/Induction Model. Lionel March. "The Logic of Design and the Question of Value", in *The Architecture of Form,* edited by Lionel March, Cambridge, 1976.

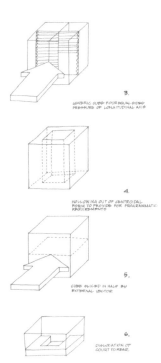

3.
ANALYTIC CUBE FOUR EQUAL SIDES
PRESSURE OF LONGITUDINAL AXIS

4.
HOLLOWING OUT OF CENTROIDAL
FORM TO PROVIDE FOR PROGRAMMATIC
REQUIREMENTS

5.
CUBE SLICED IN HALF BY
EXTERNAL VECTOR

6.
DISLOCATION OF
COURT TO REAR

Diagram showing external forces influencing
a cube. Peter Eisenman. *The Formal Basis
of Modern Architecture,* PhD dissertation,
University of Cambridge, 1963, reprinted by
Lars Müller, Baden, 2006.

evolution within the design laboratory using simulated designs and environments. New, synthetically derived stereotypes may emerge, and old ones may be given new potential without having to wait for practical exemplification. Design comes to depend less on a single occasion of inspiration, more on an evolutionary history, greatly accelerated as this iterative procedure can now be—a prospect opened up by recent advances in computer representation.[11]

For March the success of this 'artificial evolution' depended on the creation of broad, sophisticated computer models that could simulate the demands of the world and that could unite the disparate concerns of architecture in one design space. In effect March anticipated the collaborative computer models used by architectural offices today which contain ever-greater quantities of information and simulate an ever-expanding range of characteristics. Practically then, March's work has been shown to be quite prescient. However, while March avoided the main problem with Alexander's methodology by allowing a place for unquantifiable value judgments, he nonetheless left open all questions of architectural aesthetics. For it remains entirely unclear what would drive March's artificial evolution, what would determine the selection of one 'stereotype' over another. The rhetoric of architectural authorship in the late 1960s and early 1970s was, as ever, surely confused and hyperbolic, but that situation could not be clarified simply by providing more detailed architectural models. March's characteristic avoidance of aesthetics effectively ceded the field at precisely the moment his computer models were about to open an unexpected flood of formal possibilities.[12]

Conceptual Architecture

In 1960, at the same time that Alexander left Cambridge, England for Cambridge, Massachusetts, Peter Eisenman was headed in the opposite direction, moving from Cornell University to the University of Cambridge to continue studying architecture. There, he came under the influence of Colin Rowe, with whom he travelled to Italy and first saw the buildings of Giuseppe Terragni that would haunt his future career. There too Colin St John Wilson passed on an early draft of Alexander's dissertation. As Eisenman tells the story, his reaction was decisive: "The text so infuriated me, that I was moved to do a PhD thesis myself. It was called "The Formal Basis of Modern Architecture" and was an attempt to dialectically refute the arguments made in his book."[13] This dissertation, completed in 1963 was never published, although a greatly condensed summary of its argument appeared the same year in *Architectural Design.*[14]

As in many contemporaneous polemics, Eisenman's first point in his dissertation is that post-war architecture lacks a proper theoretical basis. The modern climate, he says, is "factual rather than rational: the atmosphere being so saturated with the actual, that the theoretical is easily passed over".[15] Reason and logic, he claims, have been replaced by history. "Actual" here has an unusual meaning. In one sense, the term is used to describe the demands of function that Eisenman sees as overtaking architecture—particularly Modernist architecture—and that he will later reject more thoroughly in his essay "Post-Functionalism".[16] At the same time "actual" refers to the "demands of the age", the *Zeitgeist,* with which Modernism claimed architecture must be synchronised, a goal Eisenman rejects as overly "historical". (This second use indicates the influence of Karl Popper's critique of historical determinism, which Eisenman surely would have known through Rowe.) To avoid the twin threats of the "actual", Eisenman sets out to develop an architectural theory that is thoroughly "conceptual":

It is the desire here to consider buildings as a structure of logical discourse, and to focus attention on consistency of argument, on the manner in which spatial and volumetric propositions may interact, contradict, and qualify each other. This dissertation therefore is concerned with conceptual issues, in the sense that form is

Analytical diagrams of Giuseppe Terragni's
Casa Giuliani Frigerio, Como, 1939–1940.
Peter Eisenman. "From Object to Relationship
II: Giuseppe Terragni: Casa Giuliani Frigerio:
Casa del Fascio", *Perspecta,* 13, 1971.

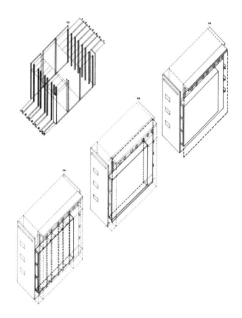

considered as a problem of logical consistency, in other words, as the logical inter-action of formal concepts. The argument will try to establish that considerations of a logical and objective nature can provide a conceptual, formal basis for any architecture.[17]

So, while aspects of Eisenman's methodology may differ from those of Alexander or March—the demands of architectural program and of computer programming have no place here—Eisenman's motivation is nonetheless similar: he wants to obtain a logical and objective basis for architecture. Eisenman too rejects intuitive composition in favour of systems:

systems provide a discipline rather than a limit.... They are not rigid but allow for growth; they accommodate the scherzo; they can be elaborated to encompass infinite variations and complexities. Systems deny only the arbitrary, the picturesque and the romantic: the subjective and personal interpretations of order.[18]

The dissertation thus refuted Alexander in so far as Eisenman argued it was the very attempt to satisfy functional requirements—which Alexander had placed at the centre of his method—that prevented post-war architecture from attaining a firm foundation. However, Eisenman's description of this refutation as "dialectical" was perhaps unwittingly appropriate because he retained a belief in the possibility of a logical, objective, and systematic architectural methodology.

What emerges in Eisenman's dissertation is essentially a system of rules for determining the interaction of cubic solids, in which "pressures" caused by the site or by programmatic needs produce supposedly necessary reactions and deformations of initially pure original forms—a pseudo-physics of form similar to that underlying Alexander's model of environmental fit. The system is demonstrated through the analysis of the work of four Modern architects: Le Corbusier, Aalto, Wright and Terragni. During the later 1960s these analytical studies were extended into the generative processes used in Eisenman's early houses, and the interest in quasi-autonomous processes for the creation of forms continues to be developed in his subsequent work and that of the many younger architects he has influenced.

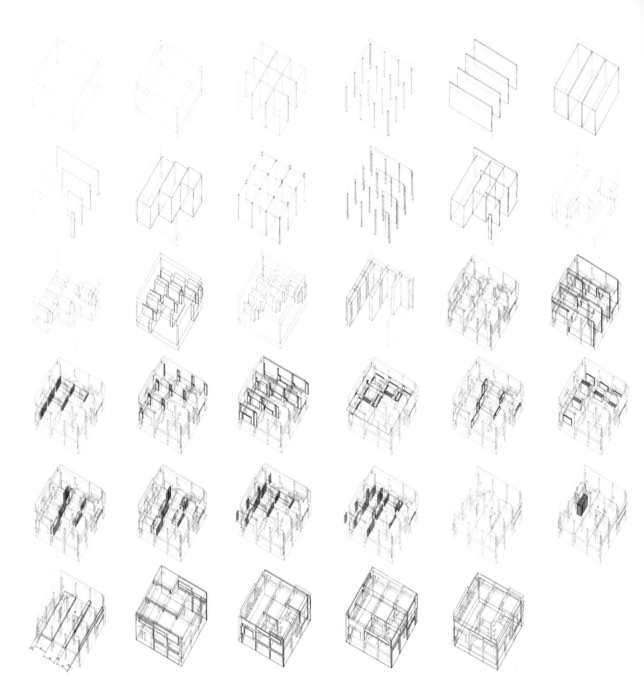

Diagrams of House II, Hardwick, Vermont, 1969–1970. Peter Eisenman. *Houses of Cards*, 1987.

Eisenman's Platonism and formalism, which show Rowe's influence, clearly set his work apart from the empiricism and functionalism of Alexander and March. Compared to Alexander, and particularly to March, he was also more conservative: he did not attempt to replace, or ignore, the primacy of formal considerations in architecture, but to create a system of rules for forms. Nonetheless, his work at Cambridge and immediately after reveals that even on the formalist side of the fence, the desire of the time was for systems, and for logics, that could redefine architectural authorship. Wisely recognising architecture's inherently representational aspect, Eisenman, at the time, avoided the literal engagement with computers and mathematics taken on by Alexander and March. Instead, he attempted to construct a logic of architectural forms which, at most, stood in a metaphorical relationship to its historical context. Which is to say that Eisenman's early analyses and designs unfold *like* logical proofs, or *like* computer algorithms, without actually being anything other than architecture.

Conclusion

The common desire of these three Cambridge graduates to reject received notions of architectural authorship and to develop instead systematic approaches to architectural design reflects a number of historical influences. In 1956—the same year that Alexander and March began studying architecture—Leslie Martin was made head of the department of architecture at Cambridge and the university's first professor of architecture. Martin was a powerful figure who had been closely involved before the war with a British variant of Constructivism. In 1937 he, along with artists Ben Nicholson and Naum Gabo, edited *Circle: International Survey of Constructive Art*, an influential one-time journal which included contributions from Piet Mondrian, Le Corbusier, Henry Moore, Marcel Breuer, Richard Neutra, Siegfried Giedion, Walter Gropius, Laszlo Maholy-Nagy, and Lewis Mumford.[19] *Circle* called for the synthesis of science and art through the study of form, and after the war Martin was able to reshape the architecture department at Cambridge toward this end. Prior to Martin's arrival, architecture "was considered to be a soft option, along with estate management and geography. If you were good at sports, were active in the theatre or journalism, or enjoyed the full social life, then these were the subjects to go for."[20] Martin was determined to make architecture "hard": to make it an intellectually rigorous discipline. A later, but more comprehensive, connection to Constructivism was established through the groundbreaking historical work of Catherine Cooke, who completed her PhD on Soviet town planning at Cambridge in 1974.[21] Cooke's work gave a detailed description of Soviet Constructivist thinking about architecture, with which the Cambridge researchers came to feel "a sense of intellectual community".[22]

More widely, all of the social sciences took a mathematical turn during this period as they attempted to incorporate new computer-based approaches in their work. Colin Rowe recalls a visiting scholar complaining that "The university itself... should get a different name. Not the University of Cambridge, it really should be called Fenland Tech; and we should all go out and get T-shirts to advertise this message."[23] March has noted the influence of work coming out of other Cambridge departments: Mary Hesse's *Models and Analogues in Science*, 1963, Richard Stone's *Mathematics in the Social Sciences and Other Essays*, 1967, Richard Chorley and Peter Haggett's *Models in Geography*, 1967, and David Clarke's *Analytical Archaeology*, 1968. When this work was read by researchers in architecture "there opened up the prospect of disciplines merging together through the form of approach, despite the ever-increasing specialisation of content".[24] Needless to say, the unifying "form of approach" was mathematics.

Finally, all three of these architects were closely tied to universities and academic research, and the need in such a setting to produce rigorous, or apparently rigorous, frameworks for their work cannot be underestimated. Faced, by the late-1960s, with the dissolution of the Modern Movement, these men sought more stable foundations for architecture in mathematics. Searching for authorial authority in logic and mathematics, they handled the disruptive act of architectural intuition in three distinct ways: Alexander attempted to bury the form-making gesture at the bottom of his analytical process where it was presumed to influence decisions at only the smallest scales; March attempted to discipline subjective form-making by placing it within a continuous cycle of assessment and revision; and Eisenman displaced subjective choices to a higher level, so that he was designing systems rather than forms (he also cloaked these choices by claiming that the systems were objective and logical).

In retrospect, Eisenman's work has had the greatest influence: as Stan Allen has said, because of Eisenman "since the 1970s an attention to process has been the explicit sign of a conceptually ambitious, theoretically-driven work".[25] Paired with increasingly sophisticated computational tools this trend has begun to alter our notions of architectural authorship. To the extent that this emerging model continues to reject intuition as a mystified source of architectural authority it should be welcomed. However, its parallel tendency to substitute highly technical processes as newly mystified generators of authority must be vigilantly critiqued. Such processes, and the forms they generate, remain signs to be interpreted critically and historically. Which is to say that now, as in the 1960s, the systems aesthetic is not an escape from the uncertainties of authorship and representation, but is itself a representation, in negative, of the particular uncertainties architecture faces in a digital age.

'Exoticising the Domestic': on New Collaborative Paradigms and Advanced Design Practices

Hélène Lipstadt

In a 1999 review of trends in architectural history, the architect and historian Beatriz Colomina celebrated the fact that the collaborative nature of architectural authorship was no longer one of architecture's "family secrets". In the span of two decades it had ceased to be one of those "things... that everybody knows" but that they never "acknowledge". Historians had finally come around to recognising a long list of collaborators in architecture: partners and associates; wives and mistresses; builders and engineers; photographers and critics; institutions such as magazines, museums and schools, "and even the client".[1] Today, the collaborative nature of architecture is more than merely acknowledged. The former family secret is now a subject on the agenda of members of what is often called "advanced practices". The advanced practices that espouse collaborative paradigms share a common investment (in both the economic and psychological sense) in the linking of technology to teamwork, up and down the line, from open source code sharing to the sharing of credit for publication. Those who call themselves "network practices" take collaboration further, for they combine in joint endeavours of self-styled "networks of network practices".[2] For these practices, collaboration has become an agenda in and of itself, an agenda for a new way of practicing a new form of architecture, one redefined and ready to meet and match the new social and cultural circumstances of a globalised economy and digital knowledge.

Collaborative models of architectural authorship are not new. William Morris's 'firm', a utopian and expressly anti-capitalist exercise in the reunification of architecture and crafts; Walter Gropius's The Architects' Collaborative, a design office based on teamwork; and the socially progressive community-based and transgressive anti-architectural design group interventions of the 1960s and 70s were conceived as collaborative alternatives to the standard model of the single master creator. But, as the editors of this volume argue, notwithstanding a long history of proposals to "dislocate" and "dissolve" the logic of authorship and the recent introduction of new digital technologies that have transformed those most authorial acts of design and drawing, the idea of the architect as the autonomous creator continues to dominate the professional identity of the architect. The belief in a unique creator not only survives, it thrives.

With regard to authorship, architecture therefore remains close to "traditional art history". According to Pierre Bourdieu, it continues to "succumb... without a fight" to what Walter Benjamin called the 'fetishism of the name of the master'. Bourdieu theorised an alternative social theory of authorship called the *sociology of the field of cultural production*.[3] Is it any wonder that proponents of the new paradigms of authorship, be they, to quote the editors' useful checklist, "collaborative, cybernetic, hybrid, open-source, transgenic or 'emergent' paradigms",[4] have taken up the questioning of traditional models of architectural authorship with a vision of reform so thorough-going that it is closer to that of Morris than of Gropius? That is, far from succumbing, they have come out fighting for collaboration and against fetishism.

The significance of the new collaborative paradigms' challenge to authorship cannot be underscored enough. To question this (or any) logic of authorship is to question the most fundamental shared value of an authorial discipline, its belief in itself as a game and in the stakes that make it a game that merits being played—one that is, furthermore, distinct from others. In cultural history, the logic of authorship is a representation, an "operation of classification and delineation that produces the multiple intellectual configurations by which reality is constructed in contradictory ways by various groups". [5] For the sociology of the field of cultural production, it is the *nomos*, the legitimate principle of vision and division that identifies a discipline as a field. The *nomos* is the ultimate stake for every field that counts itself as an art, and the heart of the *illusio*, the belief in the game. Bourdieu considers all definitions that differentiate legitimate and illegitimate practitioners as "'the founding point of view'" by which a *field*, or a universe or space of relations organised around specific logics and stakes, "is constituted as such". [6] The challenge puts into play nothing less than the redefinition of the nature of architecture as a field, the grounds on which the entry into the field is to be defined, and its place among the other fields—in short, control over the power to ascertain what is legitimately defined as 'Architecture' and to assert its status as an authorial work comparable to other works of cultural production. For the collaborative paradigms' challenge to succeed where other collaborative models have not, it needs to be posed with an energy and attention commensurate with its objectives. It is fair to argue that that the challenge needs to be able to withstand serious scrutiny.

This essay will attempt to undertake that scrutiny by studying and comparing two pairs of texts. The first pairing brings together articles by Dennis Kaspori and Christopher Hight in which a critique of authorship undergirds the case each makes for, respectively, open source and network practices. The second conjoins articles influenced by Bourdieu by Jean-Louis Violeau and Véronique Biau in which a study of ordinary practices reveals the undergirding logic of authorship. A comparison between the approaches of the two pairs of authors to the logic of authorship frames the essay, contrasting the first pair's concern with competing, in the everyday sense, and the second pair's concern with competitions in the sense of formally orchestrated and organised design contests. I will use the comparison to show the necessity of what French scholars call a *garde-fou*, literally, a safety railing and metaphorically, an epistemic and self-reflective protective cordon, for students of the logic of authorship. [7] I will argue that a reflexive analysis that I will call, following Bourdieu, the "exoticising of the domestic" introduces a Bourdieusien safety railing which can first transform and then redirect the rushing traffic in collaborative paradigms toward a new logic of authorship and a new practice of collaboration calibrated to today's transformed cultural conditions.

Bourdieu and Architecture

Bourdieu articulated his critique of the logic of authorship in his *sociology of the field of cultural production* and his social theory of the *'logic of practice'*—practice understood in the anthropological sense of what people do as a result of dispositions. He tested it in his many historical and large-scale empirical studies of writers, philosophers, poets, painters, and academics. Although he never studied architects, he did once propose a model for their use for their study of themselves. The "schema" to be deployed was the one he had developed for the study of literature, because architecture, like literature, was "in some respects a very intellectual or intellectualist art". By *intellectualist*, he meant it approaches artistic creation in the manner of the aesthetic tradition, which focuses on "the work as such, as *opus operatum*, [the] work of art already done" at the cost of knowing it as the "*modus operandi*", "manner of doing", "*métier*", "craftsmanship", or, to use Bourdieu's special vocabulary, the *habitus*, an embodied schema of perception and appreciation, a disposition. Intellectualism or the related "scholastic bias" prompts scholars to put a "scholar's mind" in every head, including those of artists, and to see everyday actions as the product of rational calculation. Their "*scholastic unconscious*" consists of a "prefabricated series of oppositions", such as "reflection vs. action" or "mind vs. body". These obscure, and even inhibit, an understanding that practice, in Bourdieu's anthropological sense of the term, is "a practical mastery without theory". [8]

Scholars of art, he told the architects, were in the best and worst position to take up the "very difficult" task of breaking with their scholastic bias and articulating the logic of practice. While as "professionals of reflection", they have the distance from the "practical experience of practice"—which includes artistic practice—needed to produce a reflection on the limits of scholarly thought, the same professional disposition of scholars predisposes them to a practice of theoretical reflection that has been historically allied with the "exaltation" of 'creation' and the concomitant "ignor[ing]" and "despis[ing]" of practical mastery. [9]

Véronique Biau, *L'architecture comme emblème municipal,* 1988. Cover design: Véronique Lemoine. Courtesy Plan Construction.

Bourdieu's proposal that architecture be studied as literature is consistent with his finding that all forms of cultural production are *homologous*, that is, that they posses structures that mirror each other. Bourdieu holds that they are all *symbolic goods* that possess a value that is incommensurate with their worth as a commodity. Such goods circulate in a *market of symbolic goods*, an inverted economy where an *anti-economic* logic of *disinterest* prevails. What remains of the logic of the right-side-up world of normal markets, such as competing, is retranslated there into upside-down terms. Competing is not disowned, but it is euphemised, or in psychological terms, denied. Cultural producers' disavowal of the *economicism* of other fields has historically earned them rights and liberties unimaginable in fields where economicism prevails, or a *greater*, albeit, *relative*, *autonomy* from those fields—the *political, economic, bureaucratic,* and *juridical* (legal and disciplinary) *fields* that together constitute the relational dynamic force field of *social space.* It secures them a degree of autonomy as well from the *power field*, a kind of meta-field that replaces the notion of the ruling class in Bourdieu's sociology. Their so-called 'interest in disinterest' gives them the "right and duty to ignore the demands and requirements of temporal powers, and even to combat them". [10]

While architecture is not reducible to the material realisations that go by that name, a materially realised architecture of any complexity and public presence requires a client. This architecture circulates in a right-side-up world of economic profitability; interest is openly avowed, and while there is an exceptional dependency on clients with regard to opportunities to create, there is also a privileged proximity to the field of power. As sociologists frequently note, the result is that the autonomy of the writer, the painter, or the poet is an "impossibility" for architects. [11] It is less frequently noted that the identification of a work as architecture increases the representational and historical value of the object so designated, bringing it into the realm of symbolic goods and enhancing its symbolic value for its owners and viewers. For Bourdieu, every work that is understood as art is the product of this kind of *transubstantiation.* In a sense, and an important one, Bourdieu's sociology of the field of cultural production is a collaborative paradigm, for the ultimate author is not any individual creator, but the field of cultural production itself. Not only does it, to use his formula, 'create the creator', it creates our faith in the creator's power to transubstantiate materiality into art and our and the public's belief in that object as one of art.

The "very difficult task" can be made less so by consulting *Homo Academicus*, 1984, Bourdieu's sociological study of the tenured professors of the academic field in Paris in the 1960s, including Bourdieu himself. Writing that book had demanded that Bourdieu work as an ethnologist or anthropologist, but in reverse. Studying his "own world in its nearest and most familiar aspect" obliged him to turn the ethnologist's "domesticat[ing of] the exotic" into the "exoticis[ing of] the domestic", or the "break[ing] with his initial relation of intimacy with modes of life and thought which remain opaque because... too familiar". The rupture enabled Bourdieu to bring to that familiar world the ethnologist's "detached scrutiny" as if, like the ethnologist, he was not "linked" to it by an "inherent complicity of being involved in its social game." That complicity constitutes for the scholar his or her *illusio*, the beliefs which "create the very value of the objectives of the game" and "the value of the game itself". Exoticising the domestic is a risky business, he warned, for "divulging tribal secrets... is also a kind of public confession". So much so that, like Li Zhi, the renegade Chinese whose book revealed the rules of the mandarin game, Bourdieu considered entitling his book, *A Book for Burning.* Bourdieu held the risks to be worth taking, for the author who objectifies his own social milieu undertakes a "*socio-analysis*", or the sociological version of a psychoanalysis, that can "offer a potential liberty" for others of the same milieu. Being subjects of the same "passions", they can participate practically in the endeavour. The American edition of *Homo Academicus* contained added instructions for transposing the "initiatory itinerary orientated toward the reappropriation of self" that he had designed for his "*homo academicus gaullicus*" to other academic worlds, making it extensible to architectural academia and thus to the site where the new paradigms originated and now flourish. [12]

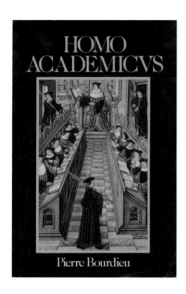

Pierre Bourdieu, *Homo Academicus*,
Stanford University Press/Polity edition,
1984. Courtesy Stanford University Press.

Pierre Bourdieu, *Acts of Resistance: Against
the Tyranny of the Market,* The New Press
edition, New York, 1998. Cover design: BAD,
Cover illustration from PhotoDisc. Courtesy
The New Press.

Re-domesticating Authorship

Dennis Kaspori makes the case for the open source or code sharing paradigm. Kaspori is unhappy with the current happy state of the architectural avant-garde in the Netherlands. Architects enjoy so many opportunities to be Dutch, to exercise their "pragmatic inventiveness", that they end up "try[ing] to rediscover the wheel with every new project." His example is NL Architects, an office that is "not doing a bad job in terms of media exposure", but who have nothing to show for it but "languishing" and "abandoned" projects. Kaspori suggest that Dutch inventiveness would be better off redirected to the reorganisation of practice, using a "collective (preferably interdisciplinary) approach".[13]

Kaspori draws on a number of current theorists of 'postproduction', but emphasises the distinction between the two software development organisational structures of the cathedral (i.e. Microsoft) and the bazaar (i.e. open source) theorised by the open source movement's "minister of propaganda", Eric S Raymond. Extending the distinction to architecture, Kaspori differentiates between the open and collective approach of the "bazaar model... based on cooperation" and the closed "cathedral model with the autonomous genius of the chief designer at the top of a strict hierarchy... based on competition". The bazaar's "network logic of an effective distribution of ideas" also turns the right of copyright and intellectual property, the legal protection of authorship, "on its head", by calling for its abandonment. Open source's potential as a generator of innovation is compared to the cathedral's record of competition, which produced innovation, but at the cost of "enormous fragmentation". Adoption of the open source paradigm is encouraged as "a process of growing awareness" and a way of radically transforming "the fundamental organizational principles of architectural practice". Although the proposal represents "a complete reversal of the existing organizational model of a discipline that is very keen on its autonomy", it does not do away with competing. In fact, for Kaspori the collective approach is a better form of competition. "An outward-looking practice offers far more scope for making the most of the opportunities.... Knowledge is the prime competitive advantage in the network society". In this vision of what he calls "A Communism of Ideas", design and knowledge are separated. Designers compete and construct, and knowledge providers "chart... developments and furnish... models to take advantage of [knowledge]".[14]

Although Raymond's metaphor was just that, a metaphor, it was an architectural one, and it therefore merits architectural verification if it is to serve as the ground for a paradigm of architectural authorship. In fact, Kaspori's description of the open source bazaar could work just as well as an account of the rise and spread of the French gothic cathedral. Of course, hierarchy was the rule in the 'age of the cathedrals'. But, it was also a time of collaborative architecture. Kaspori's open sourcing uses what he calls the "'swarm intelligence' of a large group of users and/or developers" who test and improve ideas.[15] So did the groups who developed the French gothic into regional and national gothic styles. French (and other) gothic cathedrals were the product of mostly anonymous authors who were organised in guilds unified by their common knowledge of a shared code, in the case of masons, their so-called 'secret'. Moreover, in the region around Paris where the French gothic reached its height (from the point of view of traditional art history), the qualities that made it 'the gothic' in plan, system, imagery, structural design, and structural logic were the result of what Kaspori could recognise as a collective 'swarm intelligence' and code sharing. As Erwin Panofsky famously argued, architects and clerics there shared an unconscious "mental habit" derived from the clerical client's philosophy of scholastism. By absorbing the model that organised all knowledge at the time in the schools run by scholastics, or by attending the public debates between scholastics that were the advanced performance media of the day, architects received, without necessarily being instructed to do so, the scholastic *modus operandi*, which in turn generated an architecture that resembled scholasticism and that we call the 'early' and 'high' gothic of the Ile-de-France.[16]

Kaspori has burdened his proposal with a *historical* blind spot that goes hand-in-hand with a *social* blind spot about competing. Hierarchy has not been abolished; rather it has been renewed and updated. If this is communism, it is not Marx's. In *Capital*, green (greenspace) development must be solved. While the country has big, important social problems, crying out as it were for intervention from architects and mediation from architecture, Dutch architecture continues to bask in the glory of international success. But this cannot go on much longer.

It is high time Dutch architects applied their famous pragmatic inventiveness not only to their designs but also to the organisation of their practice, and regained a significant role in spatial planning. In recent years, a great deal of effort has been expended on 'doing something different' within the narrow margins of the over-regulated Vinex housing task. The result is a practice in which architects try to rediscover the wheel with every new project. It is time to abandon this method and to look for alternative models for spatial design. This calls not for solo operations but a collective (preferably interdisciplinary) approach.

ACCORDINGLY, ARCHITECTURAL PRACTICE NEEDS TO BE TURNED INSIDE-OUT.

Architects should no longer look inwards in search of the essence of architecture. They should also cease harking back nostalgically to past times, when the architect was still a master builder. Architecture must look outwards and forwards, in search of the countless opportunities offered by these turbulent times of political and economic instability. The search for the essence of architecture will have to make way for the question of what architecture can mean for the contemporary network society. It is time for a collectively organised renewal of architectural practice.

after all, the main commodity of today's economy: 'Concepts, ideas and images – not things – are the real items of value in the new economy. Wealth is no longer vested in physical capital but rather in human imagination and creativity.'[16]

For an organisational renewal of architectural practice it is essential that knowledge be interwoven with every tier of the organisation and every step of the process. This is sometimes described as a learning organisation. Knowledge ensures that organisations stay alert to change.

THE LEARNING ORGANIZATION IS A MODEL FOR A SYSTEM THAT IS ABLE TO RESPOND TO DEVELOPMENTS, THAT CAN ADAPT AND COLLABORATE.

Using this model, an outward- and forward-looking practice can be developed. That is to say a practice that is open to external influences, that is capable of identifying developments at an early stage and responding accordingly.

From this perspective it is interesting to consider developments in other professional fields. It is worth noting that there are scattered undertakings which suggest interesting paths for renewal in architectural practice. Examples of collaborative practices can be found in fields as different as art and software engineering. Each of them offers an alternative model in which innovation is achieved through the active participation of all parties. Ideas and products are no longer developed in a closed production process organised around the autonomy of the artist or the company, but evolve out of the pragmatism of usage. That is the motor of innovation.

Nouveaux albums de
illustrent si besoin ét
socialement construi
entre travail de const
collectives, travail sc
de catégories, et trav
chacun opère dans la
la « jeunesse » est p
si l'on regarde attent
ses choix formels et
ses questionnements
ou moins manifeste
qui avaient pourtant

LES « PF
VOLONT
DE L'AR

par Jean-Louis Violeau*

Page layout. Dennis Kaspori, "Towards an Open Source Architectural Practice", in *What People Want: Populism in Architecture and Design,* edited by Michael Shamiyeh, 2005. Courtesy Birkhäuser.

famously, "what distinguishes the worst architect from the best of bees is this, that the architect raises his structure in imagination before he erects it in reality".[17] Here, one of the bees has bested the architects. Design drones erect in reality, while imagining is reserved for the collective queen bee. She, strangely, is able to propagate knowledge formations that give the drones a competitive edge without suffering any contamination to her program of openness.

Christopher Hight proposes a similar distinction of design and information in his recent review of three kinds of "so-called advanced practices". Hight sounds very much like Kaspori when he separates "networking of things for the production of knowledge" from the "design of buildings or cities". He distinguishes the pure architectural knowledge producers from the designers; and the members of network practices from upholders of autonomy and authorship. Like Kaspori, he proceeds from a base in current 'post' theory, that of post-cybernetics. The theories of Michel Foucault, Bruno Latour, and Friedrich Kittler enable Hight to claim that "mechanical-electronic reproduction and communication technologies engender different organizations of thought and practice". He, too, makes quick work of other avant-garde approaches. After showing that Manfredo Tafuri's 'autonomists' and 'new objectivists' of the historical avant-garde survive within certain advanced practices, he sets out to prove the greater promise of network practices.[18]

The new autonomists are represented by the "projective practices" of the "so-called new formalists" (i.e. Foreign Office Architects/Alejandro Zaera Polo and Farshid Moussavi); the *new* new objectivists, by practices that he characterised as "managerial practices" (i.e. OMA, SOM). He opposes both of these to the knowledge producing "new network practices". Contemplating the "new formalists'" use of computer-driven laborious processes, he points out that their displacing creation from the architect creator to machines or to codes and from control to cooperation, "actually implies... that one has [an] authority and expertise to surrender". Rather than criticise authorship and authorial autonomy, this paradigm "celebrate[s] and conserve[s] the idea of the creative subject by refracting the romantic myth of the genius through the economies of...

tectes
re
esse »,
ntités
aboration
e que
. Mais
u'un mot
arcours,
criture,
érêt plus
questions
és.

1967 et 1971 que l'on retrouve le plus de candidats². Nous sommes donc face à une classe d'âge qui a vu le jour autour des événements de 68 dont on sait l'importance qu'ils ont revêtus pour les architectes, accélérant la redéfinition de bon nombre des règles, des valeurs et des questionnements qui dominaient jusqu'alors leur univers. La génération en majesté, celle qui inventa notamment le «jeunisme institutionnel», voit donc symboliquement ses derniers enfants accéder à la reconnaissance à travers des formules promotionnelles dont elle encouragea la mise en place.

Avec cette composante de l'âge, a priori intangible, on voit pourtant déjà apparaître quelques clivages. Si l'âge moyen des candidats est donc de 31 ans et 4 mois, un peu plus élevé que l'âge moyen d'obtention du diplôme (29 ans), la moitié des membres des 16 équipes lauréates a pourtant moins de 30 ans (nés en 1972 ou après). Et en général, les mieux notés sont sensiblement plus jeunes que la moyenne. Plus anecdotique, mais pour autant pas insignifiant, les dossiers arrivés le plus tôt à l'IFA ont été mal

fokus från staden som objekt för arkitekturens geni till stadsbyggandet som firmans etiska modus operandi. Detta ger arkitekturen en ny position och låter den ta strid för den livskraftiga urbana "programvaran", som har förpisets på grund av vår nostalgi inför "stadens" hårdvara, vilket potentiellt förnyar arkitekturens sociala relevans.

En annan nätverkspraktik, Ocean North, och dess utlöpare Emergence and Design Group, undersöker de nya materialens möjligheter som ett annat sätt att omfördela arkitekturens kunskap i den vardagliga ingenjörskonstens transdisciplinära spektrum – det "sammanstrålande" av information och materia som bäddar in en ny nivå av intelligens i stadskroppen. Detta är väsentlig forskning, inte bara därför att den engagerar arkitekturens kunskap i arbetet med de utvecklande materiella informationsnätverk som omkonfigurerar vår förståelse och vår erfarenhet, utan också därför att den på nytt framställer den materiella och teknologiska forskningen som ett viktigt teoretiskt fält.

Hittills har galleriet utgjort den primära arbetsplatsen för det nätverk av nätverkspraktiker som växer fram. Detta måste förstås inom det sammanhang jag ovan beskrivit. Bruket av galleriet är inte en reträtt till objektets autonomi eller ett förkastande av objektets kris, utan ett sätt att gjuta nytt liv i arkitekturens agentskap genom att förnya dess verktyg, och därmed hantera de nya frågor det mediala rummet och dess sociala formationer väcker. Det är ett misstag att uppfatta sådana praktiker som en förlängning av neo-avantgardets formalistiska äventyr, trots att de själva ofta på nytt skriver in sin praktik i denna dikotomi. Deras arbete tog utgångspunkt i de "nya formalisterna" av den enkla anledningen att dessa var de första som försökte göra om arkitekturen från en tektonisk till en informationsmässig verksamhet genom att tillägna sig animationsprogramvara som utvecklats för Hollywoods syften. För den generationen förblir idéer som mångfald och nätverkande dock formella och organiserande begrepp, som handlar om hur man formger och förstår vad som förblir objekt för en traditionell arkitekturexpertis, hur

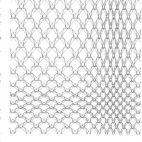

FIT FABRICS. ALGORITHMIC DIFFERENTIATION OF THE SKIN PANEL GEOMETRY.

for the emerging network of network practices. This needs to be understood in the above context. The use of the gallery is not a retreat to the autonomy of the object, or a rejection of the crisis of the object, but a reinvestment in the agency of architecture through its retooling to engage the emerging issues of media space and social formations. It is a mistake to see such practices as a continuation of the neo-avant-garde's adventures in formalism.

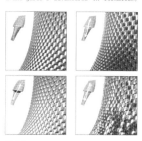

FIT FABRICS. SKIN PANEL ADAPTATION THROUGH CHANGES IN THE PANEL CURVATURE.

Page layout. Jean-Louis Violeau, "Les 'premiers collés' volontaires de l'architecture", in *AMC: Les Nouveaux albums des jeunes architectes* 2001/2002, 2002. Courtesy AMC-Le Moniteur Architecture.

Page layout. Christopher Hight, "Preface to the Multitude: The Return to the Network Practice in Architecture", in *01.AKAD— Experimental Research in Architecture and Design*, edited by Per Glembrandt, Katja Grillner and Sven Olof Wallenstein, 2005. Courtesy AKAD and Dekoder Design, Stockholm.

mass-customization and mediation". Hight's second paradigm of "managerial practices" is a derivation of the Koolhaasian notion that architecture can make the best of a bad capitalist situation, 'surfing its wave', in the now legendary formula, by mirroring its practices. While Hight opposes the "managerial practice's" model of "dissolution" of architectural expertise to the "new formalist's" "conserv[ational]" model, he also hints that the former shares the latter's "faith… [in] architecture's autonomy". Not so network practices (i.e. KRETS/AKAD, Oceans North/Emergence and Design Group, servo, and many more), he holds. They convert architectural questions into the "subject matter of architectural knowledge production" by transforming the objects of practice into the ground for a reconfiguration of practice itself. Network practices, like the new formalists, are ensconced in some of the most prestigious ivory towers and work with galleries and museums, at biennial exhibitions, and for publishers. To Hight's credit, he recognises that the role of the gallery and the space of cultural production as the primary site for the work of networked network practices brings them so close to the new formalists' domain that it puts his proposed distinction at risk. He gets network practices off the hook by describing their engagement with the gallery as "a reinvestment in the agency of architecture through its retooling to engage the emerging issues of media space and social formations".[19]

While Hight has valuably advanced the critique of traditional authorship by showing its recurrence in two types of advanced practices, I am still left wondering if the network practices' model of authorship is really so very different. Thus, Servo, we are told, is a distributed network in several cities on four continents that "recognizes and exploits the Internet". Thanks to this networked organisation, they produce "R&D product lines" rather than the "discrete projects" of "what humanists used to call 'authors'". Networking produces a "diversity and diffusion" that makes their "lattice urbanism… a business plan [that] shifts from the city as the object of the architectural genius to urbanism as the firm's ethical mode of operation".[20] It is possible that a schema that makes a "business plan" into an "ethical mode of operation" because its authors are from many nations and convene on the internet may count as a victory by redefinition. It is even more likely that a great number of questions are left begging by the differentiation of network practices' alliance with the gallery from new formalists' dependence on it on the ground that the first is a service rendered simultaneously to change in culture and society and to "architectural agency" (a universal that sounds suspiciously close to "what humanists used to call" authorship), while the second is a "retreat to the autonomy of the object".

What I do believe to be beyond any doubt is that both authors are differentiating theory from practice and practical mastery without theory and are proposing a euphemised form of competition. While the proponents of these collaborative paradigms concern themselves, and quite sincerely so, with modes of production, from the point of view of the logic of practice, they have not ceased to theorise practice in an intellectualist fashion. The theoretical mastery of knowledge production is divided off and held to be superior to design, the craft and métier of architecture. The 'prefabricated' oppositions have also reappeared in the form a renewed theory/practice, high/low, or, in architectural terms, architecture/building distinction, now become information/design. From the point of view of the sociology of the field of cultural production, competing has been transfigured into a claim on behalf of an interest of disinterest. We are back at our point of departure, at the ever present logic of authorship. Moreover, as intellectualism links architecture to the aesthetic tradition and the logic of authorship to the fetishism of the name of the master, we have also been returned to traditional art history.

"Exoticising the Domestic"

It is imperative to consider why our authors have been the surely unintentional re-activators of this particular return of the repressed. The reason becomes clear if the two authors' discourses on the historical and current avant-gardes are understood as examples, to use Bourdieu's terms, of the "*cumulativity*" and "irreversibility" of the history of fields of cultural production. He argues that all disciplines that recognise an authorship that is in accord with its particular logic are bound up with the history of its emergence as a relatively autonomous field, as that history is immanent in the products that are recognised as legitimate works of the discipline's authors. The more evolved a discipline and the more long-standing and deeply grounded its history of authorship, the more a knowledge of history is needed and the more peculiar to the discipline is that knowledge. Concomitantly, and, he admits, somewhat paradoxically, the works and views of aspiring revolutionaries or the avant-garde are the most liable to be beholden to history. An avant-garde that defines itself through its effort to surpass history is defined by the history of all previous surpassings of that history by earlier avant-gardes. The history that is part of the avant-garde's problem, and here, our problem, is also the key to the solution. Freedom from irreversibility and "*cumulativity*" is achieved through the 'social history' of the process by which that authorship and the relative autonomy of the field of which it is the expression came to be legitimate: "it is within history that the principle of freedom from history resides". As that social history must be free of "direct engagement" with current conditions and contexts, the exoticising of the domestic is a necessary first phase.[21]

Véronique Biau and Jean-Louis Violeau, who hold positions in the self-described French 'milieu' of architecture, the post May '68 universe of 'architect-intellectuals', researchers and educators, have both undertaken Bourdieu-inspired analyses of starchitects, marks of consecration, the signature, and France's all-pervasive competition system and the constitution of the milieu itself. They have thus surveyed conditions that are common to many architectural milieus, as well as with those that obtain especially in France.

Violeau studied publicly and privately sponsored promotional competitions in France for young architects under the age of 35. Although he notes that the inverted economy of the traditional art or literary field is most often absent in architecture, his analysis of promotional competitions suggest their logic is that of a field of cultural production. For example, they form a world apart and a closed circuit. Texts submitted along with the competition designs reveal that disinterest reigns among the competitors he studied, more or less in the manner of inverted economies. They describe their total submission to architecture, their obedience to it and the entailed sacrifices that are willingly endured. Promotional competitions lead to publications rather than to construction. The prevalence of promotional competitions in France has generated a group of successful designers whose name recognition is vastly disproportionate to any economic capital gained from realising buildings. They are known by a nickname that, significantly, has been borrowed from the limited circulation market for experimental and 'Indy' cinema: they are the *'architectes d'art et essai'*. The world of promotional competitions also resembles the world of experimental art in that it is one where youth is so valued as to be the object of clever redefinitions that keep certain artists forever young.[22]

With Biau, we accede to the world of the state-invited competition. She suggests, albeit tentatively, that one can speak of a French "'field of architecture'" which is manifested in the competition system that emerged after May '68 as a substitute for the "oligopolies" of state-consecrated architects (winners of the Grand Prix de Rome), their partners from the state engineering corps and the official state architects who held the monopoly on the state's representational architecture.[23] Her "competition architects", defined as architects who orient their efforts toward the obligatory competitions, whether or not they are successful, are part of her sample of 20 living French architects whose relationship to recognition and consecration she studied. The "competition architects" among these established practitioners share the same "model of canonical success" centred on the competition for public commissions of the younger aspirants studied by Violeau. Much like them, their "economic" and "symbolic strategies" are integrated in the pursuit of this goal. Although these established practitioners cannot permit themselves full-fledged explicit expressions of disinterest, that attitude appears, paradoxically, among the *most* successful of these competitors, as well as, naturally, among the *least* successful, who are kept socially young by their lack of success. The most successful, and these cases are rare, acquire an "aura" that frees them from the search for clients. They become state competition jurors, and serve as arbiters of quality in design and of taste for the general media, a role that they claim to pursue disinterestedly, to "'help' architecture as a whole". She comments on the homology of the architecture production field and the literary and artistic field, especially for those architects who have acquired the "emblematic 'signature'", the easily differentiated manner perceived by public clients as capable of consecrating their buildings. In this symbolic market of architecture, she concludes, it is possible for an architect's marketing strategies to show the "interest in disinterest" that for Bourdieu was the primary characteristic of the artist.[24]

In a separate study of several thousand architects who received some form of architectural "consecration" in the form of signs of sociological "distinction" between 1968 and 1995, Biau described the "aesthetic" or "cultural logic" shared by the "most legitimated architects": they believe that the profession is oriented as much toward original creations that enhance the environment aesthetically as it is toward the production of buildings determined by social needs or a profit motivation. This fundamentally "romantic" vision binds them to a constant search for clients who have embraced that logic and its corollary, that of the emblematic signature, and thus to public competitions. She concludes that there exists in architecture a power of the *signature* that is identical to the one Bourdieu found in the art market. This *"effect of a signature or trademark"* is "a power to consecrate objects or people (by publication, exhibition, etc.) and hence [one] of giving them value and of making profit from this operation".[25]

In these and other studies that focused on public clients, Biau has shown that the mayors who commission emblematic architecture and the representatives of public clients who sit on juries share the architects' aesthetic logic and interest in symbolic profits.[26] They acquire personal as well as institutional distinction from a stratification that puts them on the same plane as their architects. Needless to say, they acquire this distinction by ignoring the fact that they have collaboratively, that is to say collusively, assigned to the architect the power that they have themselves conceded, that it is they who have 'created the creator'. Their collusion is the counterpart of the *illusio*, the belief in the game. Violeau and Biau have shown that the *illusio* of the architect as creator remains undiminished in France, and that is dominated by the logic of authorship, which it itself subtended by romantic representations of artistic authorship. Disinterest is proclaimed, and the power of the name of the master remains undiminished.

Violeau and Biau have rendered the most familiar modes of French architectural "thought and life" less opaque, even while being part of the "world" and the "game" of architecture. They have, moreover, demonstrated the cost for architect, client, and discipline of the *illusio* that turns the right-side-up economic world into the upside-down. Because architecture exists in both worlds, this suspension of normal economic logic can lead to the granting of rights and privileges that would be otherwise unimaginable. But only for a small minority. For the majority of architects, there is unacknowledged and unacknowledgable disappointment. Biau and Violeau have also exoticised elements of the particular French architectural domestic that we recognise as the workings of our own architectural "world" and "game", like the signature.

A Bourdieusien Safety Railing

Hight and Kaspori's and Biau and Violeau's articles are, of course, very different. The first two are short essays with a programmatic, almost polemical, intent. The second two were lengthy reports of the results of extensive research of a sociological nature. They can nonetheless be usefully compared, and not only because of their aforementioned shared concern with competitive practices. All were written from within the discipline and milieu that they analysed, all four addressed the logic of authorship and all four demonstrated its tenacity, two of them wittingly, two of them unwittingly. All thus confirm the editors' observation about the pervasiveness of the notion of the architect as "solitary author". That observation is now amplified and extended to encompass the idea of the disinterested author and forms of lingering romanticism and persistent traditional avant-gardism. For reasons that we now understand to be inherent to the historical project of the critique of authorship, we can recognise the logic's capacity to smuggle itself into even the most sincere questioning of authorship. I conclude that we can agree on the defensive benefit of the kind of self-reflective epistemic vigilance that questions the belief in the game and its value, or what I have called a Bourdieusien safety railing of exoticising the domestic.

What of the promised liberatory benefits of socio-analysis and the social history of a field that generates a freedom from its history? I chose to emphasise epistemic vigilance not only because it could best be demonstrated in the space of one essay, but also because it was the one that could be transmitted in the form of an account of others' accounts of practice. A gloss, even the most faithful one, is incapable of expressing the logic of practice. A theory of practice can only be mastered by the practicing of it, by practically mastering it through its incorporation into one's own research disposition through practical appropriation. In socio-analysis, as in psychoanalysis, there are no surrogates, intermediaries or shortcuts. But, like Marx's architect, we can begin to 'raise the structure' of that appropriation, which is nothing other than the "difficult task", in our imagination.

Despite the blind spots described here, it is arguable that proponents of different types of collaborative paradigms are among the students of the logic of authorship who are best situated to use the exoticising of the domestic as a next step toward that task. First, they are acutely aware that the forces of misrecognition that kept the collaborative organisation of architectural practice hidden even from its historians cannot be dissipated by merely letting outsiders in on the family secret. It is, in short, not enough to argue that architecture is "collaborative, 'always already'"; its collaborative nature needs to be affirmed, time and again.[27] Secondly, they possess a home grown, indigenous insight into the workings and logic of professional practice that enabled them to identify lingering and current barriers to the transformation of practice, in Bourdieu's sense. For Kaspori, it is a collective academic unconscious inhabited by such national self-identities such as Dutch "pragmatic inventiveness". For Hight, it is the recognition that the misrecognition of one's own place in the always-present and ever-overtaking history of the avant-garde cannot be escaped. Thirdly, their proposed alternative of a transnational and denationalised communication between knowledge producers who collectively 'own' the modes of architectural production is both the legitimate offspring and the reaffirmation of the kind of authority that gained intellectuals the right to "combat the temporal powers" in the name of their own principles and norms.

At the same time, there is also a great urgency that they take up the exoticising of the parts of the architectural domestic that are currently engaged with hypercapitalism and neo-liberalism in the telecommunication and information sectors, in short, with outsourcing's cathedral. On the one hand, outsourcing and networked collaborative practices know their ambitions and power better than most for they work in close proximity with it. On the other, the proximity that has allowed some of them to be outspoken critics of hypercapitalism also puts them in danger of (mostly) inadvertently mimicking its way of thinking. Their distinction between information production and design bears a family resemblance to the media and information sector's formula that competition+technological progress=creativity, and that that creativity preempts and renders unnecessary traditional forms of cultural production.

If, however, they recognise that their close and historic relation with sites of traditional cultural production gives them the privileges of intellectuals much as it burdened them with the scholastic bias, then the Bourdieusien safety railing can also orient their reflection on new paradigms toward a more general and inclusive understanding of practice. There is space for architects in the largely collective project of the "*internationale of intellectuals* committed to defending the autonomy of universes of cultural production".[28] It is a collective far larger than their own networks, but like theirs, intent on the "denationalizing" of cultural creation.

In a keynote address to the meeting of the heads of the world's major media conglomerates in October 1999, Bourdieu told the "True Masters of the World":

> [You are] holders... of... [a] symbolic power, the power to make the world by imposing instruments for the cognitive construction of the world... [that] today... is being gathered in the hands of the few who control the large communications conglomerates, that is, the ensemble of the means of production and distribution of cultural goods.... Now, we know that it takes a long time to create creators, that is, for the partially autonomous social spaces of producers and consumers within which they can emerge, develop, and succeed.

Bourdieu cited examples from across the arts. Painting illustrated the course of the struggle for autonomy: five centuries for the right to paint in the colours of one's choice, two more to dissolve the subject of the painting altogether. The travails of independent film distributors facing the multiplexification of all cinemas under single ownership demonstrated the current threat of global control of media outlets. When, however, he sought a model for the kind of cultural resistance he envisaged, he turned to the example of an architect before his client.

> It is said that Michelangelo was so little concerned to respect the protocol of his day.... that the Pope [Julius II] had to hurry to sit himself down lest Michelangelo sit down before him.... One could say that I tried to perpetuate here, in a very modest but faithful manner, the tradition inaugurated by Michelangelo of the distance from the powers that be and especially from the new powers born of the conjugated forces of money and the media.[29]

A collaborative paradigm that can carry on the tradition inaugurated by Michelangelo within a network that resists the taking over of the means of cultural production will not only serve the members of advanced practices and the students they teach, but will also, by their initiative and example, inspire the many architects who are carrying on the everyday activities of design and building cities. For ordinary practice is also a collaboration.

Notes

Introduction

1 In *De re aedificatoria* (c. 1450) Leon Battista Alberti formulated a fundamental distinction between the architect and the 'workman' that draws upon the powers of preconception and of judgement: ''[T]o make something that appears to be convenient for use, and that can without doubt be afforded and built as projected, is the job not of the architect but of the workman. But to preconceive and to determine in the mind and with judgement something that will be perfect and complete in its every part is the achievement of such a mind as we seek.'' Alberti, Leon Battista, *On the Art of Building in Ten Books*, Joseph Rykwert, Robert Tavernor, Neil Leach trans., Cambridge, MA and London: MIT Press, 1988, IX, 10, p. 315.

2 The four architects, one architectural practice, and three buildings referred to here are all iconic within architectural discourse. Leon Battista Alberti wrote *De re aedificatoria*, ''On the Art of Building'' (c. 1450), which first defined the architect as an author, see above. On the basis of tradition, and very few documents, a corpus of famous Renaissance buildings is attributed to Alberti, who is interpreted as their author; for a recent study see Robert Tavernor, *On Alberti and the Art of Building*, New Haven and London: Yale University Press, 1998. The status of 'Le Corbusier's' chapel at Ronchamp as a definitive building of architectural modernism needs no defence, and the work is featured in Le Corbusier, *Oeuvre complete en 8 volumes*, Basel: Birkhäuser, 1999. Rem Koolhaas is perhaps the most famous architectural individual alive in the world today, as was Mies van der Rohe four years years after Le Corbusier's death in 1965. The Illinois Institute of Technology, and the Commons Building, which the recent project by the Office of Metropolitan Architecture redefines, are among Mies van der Rohe's most renowned post-war American works.

3 The habit of the patron's claim to the 'making' of monuments, for which they in part paid, was well established from the Italian Renaissance. The text in question is inlaid on the frieze that surmounts the facade of S Maria Novella in Florence, attributed to the Renaissance architect and humanist Leon Battista Alberti and paid for by the Florentine merchant Giovanni Rucellai. M[ARCUS].AGRIPPA. L[UCI].F[ILIUS].CO[N]S[UL].TERTIUM.FECIT is inscribed under the pediment of the Pantheon in Rome.

4 Barthes, Roland, ''The Death of the Author'' in Roland Barthes, *Image-Music-Text*, Stephen Heath trans. and ed., London: Fontana, 1977, pp. 142–148. Foucault, Michel, ''What is an author?'', in *Language, counter-memory, practice: Selected essays and interviews by Michel Foucault*, Donald F Bouchard ed., Donald F Bouchard and Sherry Siman trans., Ithaca: Cornell University Press, 1977, pp. 113–38.

5 Foucault, ''What is an author?'', p. 121.

6 Foucault, ''What is an author?'', pp. 124–138.

7 See Burke, Seán, *The Death and Return of the Author*, Edinburgh: Edinburgh University Press, 1992, reprinted 1999, p. 27.

8 See Donald E Pease, ''Author'' in *Critical Terms for Literary Study*, Frank Lentricchia and Thomas McLaughlin eds., London and Chicago: University of Chicago Press, 1990, pp. 105–117. Pease has proposed a genealogy of the author figure comprising three key personae (or figures)—the auctor, the modern author, and the Romantic genius. A contemporary account might add the closely-knit teamwork of collaborative authorship, such as occurs in cinematic and architectural authorship, and the dispersed, anonymous contributors to open source paradigms. For more on counter traditions to authorship, including post-humanist paradigms of autopoiesis and emergence, see the essay by Rolf Hughes in the present volume, ''The semi-living author: post-human creative agency''.

9 Burke, Seán, *Authorship: From Plato to the Postmodern*, Edinburgh: Edinburgh University Press, 1995, reprinted 2000, pp. 5–6.

10 ''On this view,'' Burke writes, ''the author renders reality objectively as an entirely receptive subject through whom impersonal truth is registered.'' See Burke, *Authorship*, p. 6.

11 See Dornbach, Marton, ''Timothy Clark. The Theory of Inspiration: Composition as a Crisis of Subjectivity in Romantic and Post-Romantic Writing'', in *Studies in Romanticism*, vol. 42, no. 2, 2003. Dornbach comments ''Inspiration… places the author in a precarious constellation with two forms of otherness: the dictating authority and the audience. The resultant 'crisis of subjectivity' explains the often ambivalent role played by inspiration in many writers' self-understanding.''

12 On the importance for Jurisprudence of the creation of the artist figure in the Italian Renaissance see Kantorowicz, Ernst, ''The Sovereignity of the Artist: A Note on Legal Maxims and Renaissance theories of Art'', in *Selected Studies by Ernst H Kantorowicz*, Locust Valley, NY: JJ Augustin, 1965, pp. 357–362, and Anstey, Tim, ''Authority and authorship in LB Alberti's De re aedificatoria'', *Nordiska Arkitekturforskning*, no. 4, 2003, pp. 19–25.

13 On the formation of the concept of the individual in eighteenth century Britain and the corresponding development of intellectual property and copyright law, see Rose, Mark, *Authors and Owners: The Invention of Copyright*, Cambridge, MA and London, England: Harvard University Press, 1993. For a discussion of contemporary copyright law, its origins in the nineteenth century Romantic understanding of the author as a solitary creative genius and contemporary social and cultural constructions of authorship, see Woodmansee, Martha and Jaszi, Peter, eds., *The Construction of Authorship: Textual Appropriation in Law and Literature*, Durham and London, Duke University Press, 1994. For an analysis of how the capitalist market has shaped modern idea of art and the aesthetic, see Woodmansee, Martha, *The Author, Art, and the Market: Rereading the History of Aesthetics*, New York: Columbia University Press, 1994.

14 See Gilbert, Sandra M, and Gubar, Susan, *The Madwoman in the Attic*, Chicago and London: Yale University Press, 1980. Gilbert and Gubar examine the struggle for authorship of nineteenth century women writers against the smothering patriarchal language that they must both use and transform.

15 See Locke, John, ''Of Identity and Diversity'', Book 2, Chapter XXVII, in *An Essay concerning Human Understanding*, Peter H Nidditch ed., Oxford: The Clarendon Press, 1975.

16 The rhetoric was most clearly advanced by Rayner Banham, see Whiteley, Nigel, *Rayner Banham: Historian of the immediate future*, Cambridge, MA and London: MIT Press, 2003 and Helena Mattsson, *Arkitektur och konsumtion: Rayner Banham och utbytbarhetens estetik*, Stockholm: Brutus Östlings Bokförlag Symposion, 2004.

17 On Cedric Price, see Mathews, Stanley, *From Agit-prop to Free Space: the Architecture of Cedric Price*, London: Black Dog Publishing, 2007, as well as Mathews' chapter on Price in this volume ''Cedric Price as anti-architect''.

18 The archives of Price's architectural office, including all the material relating to the ''Fun Palace'' are collected at the Canadian Centre for Architecture. The projects are represented in Price's own book on Cedric Price, *Works II*, London: Architectural Association, 1984, reprinted as *Cedric Price, The Square Book*, Chichester, West Sussex: Wiley-Academy, 2003.

19 For a development of this argument see the essay by Tim Anstey in this voume, ''Architecture and rhetoric: persuasion, context, action''.

20 Price, memorandum, (August, 1964), Fun Palace document folio DR1995:0188:526, Cedric Price Archives, Canadian Centre for Architecture, Montreal, cited in Mathews, ''Cedric Price as anti-architect''.

21 Barthes, ''The Death of the Author'', p. 146. See also Barthes, Roland, ''From Work to Text'' in *Image, Music, Text*, Stephen Heath trans. and ed., London: Fontana, 1977, pp. 155–164.

22 See for example Bernard Rudolfsky, *Architecture Without Architects—A short introduction to non-pedigreed architecture*, New York: Museum of Modern Art, 1964. In a publication such as this architectural history would be readily dismissed as amounting to ''little more than a who's who of architects who commemorated power and wealth; an anthology of buildings of, by, and for the privileged… with never a word about the houses of lesser people.'' Rudolfsky, *Architecture Without Architects*, p. 2.

23 In a figure such as Christopher Alexander we see, with the publication in 1964 of *Notes on a Synthesis of Form*, and later (1977) *A Pattern Language*, a characteristic convergence of both these interests. Christopher Alexander is discussed in Sean Keller's contribution to this volume, ''Systems Aesthetics, or How Cambridge solved Architecture''.

24 For further reference to and discussion of the works of these and related practices see for example Joseph Rosa, *Next Generation Architecture: Folds, Blobs, and Boxes*, Rizzoli Publications, 2003; Bart Lootsma, *Superdutch—New Architecture in the Netherlands*, London: Thames and Hudson, 2000; MVRDV, *Metacity Datatown*, Rotterdam: 010 Publishers, 1999.

25 For a discussion of the complexities involved in contemporary rhetoric of this nature, and the necessity of authorial responsibility in architecture, see Hélène

Lipstadt's essay in this volume, "'Exoticising the Domestic': on new collaborative paradigms and advanced design practices."

26 Powell, Kenneth, *Richard Rogers. Complete Works*, vol. 1, London: Phaidon, 1999, p. 13. The work of Norman Foster's practice work is recorded in the four volume *Norman Foster—Works*, David Jenkins ed., London: Prestel, 2003–2005.

27 This conscious shift to acknowledge the complexities of authorship within Foster and Partners is evident in recent interviews with and reviews of the practice. "Of course, in a practice with such a prolific turnover of projects, it would be unrealistic to expect one man to design each and every building the firm creates. Despite his talents, Norman Foster is no exception, and these days is content to oversee the work of his team and his senior partners." Cited at http://www.bbc.co.uk/dna/h2g2/A1087256 (accessed 25 April 2006). The footnote to this presentation article reads "For example, City Hall and 30 St Mary Axe were ostensibly designed by senior partner Ken Shuttleworth, and most of the Great Court at the British Museum by Spencer de Grey."

28 "The facades of Mies' building "bleed into Koolhaas' facades", wrote one journalist; Koolhaas has "literally (sic) screwed supports for his aluminium mullions into Mies' facade". Review article of the Student Centre at IIT by Rem Koolhaas, OMA, by Fred A Bernstein, "Fast Forward", *RIBA Journal*, vol. 110, no. 11, November 2003.

29 See Colomina, Beatrice, "Collaborations—The Private Life of Modern Architecture", in *Journal of the Society of Architectural Historians*, vol. 58, no. 3, pp. 413–471, esp. p. 414.

30 See for example Francesca Hughes' collection *The Architect Reconstructing her Practice*, Cambridge MA: MIT Press, 1996, pp. x–xvii, which follows a pragmatic strategy for incurring change by asserting both the (evident) presence of women architects (among these Agrest, Bloomer, Colomina, Diller, Ingraham, Richter) and requiring the acknowledgement of their various modes of practice as an integral part of the profession.

31 Servo, for example, was taken as a group name in 1999 by four graduates from the MA architecture programme at Columbia University: Marcelyn Gow, Ulrika Karlsson, Chris Perry and David Erdman for carrying out collaborative projects. This group have consciously promoted their work via their collaborative 'name', and there is an obvious fascination with the implications of branding in the titles of many of their projects (examples from Servo include names such as Speeline, Nurbia, Lattice Archipelogics, and most recently Spoorg). For more information on Servo see www.s-e-r-v-o.com (accessed 30 June 2006). See also article by Chris Hight, "Preface to the multitude—The return to the network practice in architecture" in *01.AKAD—Experimental Research in Architecture and Design—Beginnings*, Katja Grillner, Per Glembrandt, Sven-Olov Wallenstein eds., Stockholm: Axl Books, 2005, pp. 16–37; and Joseph Rosa Next Generation Architecture.

32 Hight, "Preface to the multitude", p. 17.

33 The members of Servo are careful to refer to their actions as actions by Servo, and they tend to present their different projects in terms not only of production and performance, but also of their critical objectives—one of these being repeatedly described as to question and destabilise traditional notions of authorial control in design. Projects that particularly engage directly with questions of authorship are the nurbline series (urban_toys, nurbia, and spee_toy) playing with notions of customisation and suggesting new relations between consumer and manufacturer in architectural design.

Affirmation

Architecture and Rhetoric: Persuasion, Context, Action

Tim Anstey

1 Generally, references to *De re aedificatoria* are given using the most recent English translation, *On the Art of Building in Ten Books*, Joseph Rykwert, Robert Tavernor, Neil Leach trans., Cambridge, MA, and London: MIT Press, 1988.

2 Alberti, *De re aedificatoria*, IX, 10.

3 The classic account of the changes in the status of the architect in the early Renaissance is to be found in Richard A Goldthwaite, *The building of Renaissance Florence. An Economic and Social History*, Baltimore and London: The John Hopkins University Press, 1980.

4 This case is put most eloquently by Francoise Choay, *The Rule and the Model*, Denise Bratton ed., Cambridge, MA, and London: MIT Press, 1997, pp. 65–135.

5 See Baxandall, Michael, *Giotto and the Orators. Humanist Observers of Painting in Italy and the Discovery of Pictorial Composition*, 1350–1450, Oxford: Oxford

University Press, 1971, esp. p. 38. See also Carroll William Westfall, *In This Most Perfect Paradise: Alberti, Nicholas V, and the invention of conscious urban planning in Rome, 1447–55*, University Park and London: The Pennsylvania State University Press, 1974; Christine Smith, *Architecture in the Culture of Early Humanism*, New York and Oxford: Oxford University Press, 1992. The texts most important of texts of Cicero for understanding the construction of the figure of the architect in Alberti's thesis are *On the Ideal Orator* (*De oratore*), James M May and Jakob Wisse trans., New York and Oxford: Oxford University Press, 2001; and *De officiis*, Walter Miller trans., TE Page et al ed., Loeb Classical Library, London: William Heinemann Ltd and Cambridge, MA: Harvard University Press, 1938.

6 Alberti's examples of the effectiveness of artistic compositions tend to be specifically advocational. Thus the praise of the art of painting made in *De pictura* (*On painting*, 1434)—"Rhodes was not burned down by King Demetrius lest a painting by Protagones be destroyed. So we can say that Rhodes was redeemed by a single picture"—is balanced by that of architecture, which "may even influence an enemy, by restraining his anger and so prevent the work from being violated". See Alberti, *De re aedificatoria*, VII, 3, p. 156, and Leon Battista Alberti, *On Painting*, Cecil Grayson trans., London: Penguin Books, 1991, II, 27, p. 62. Both eulogies are situated in positions of antagonism and persuasion and in both the artistic work effects a 'verdict' about future action. As scholars including Michael Baxandall and Christine Smith have emphasised, Alberti's own training which read the works of antique oratory through the lens of medieval jurisprudence, looms large in such formulations.

7 Alberti, *De re aedificatoria*, VII, 3, p. 156. The articulation of this sense is, Alberti maintains, the architect's primary aim: building is seen in *De re aedificatoria* as the medium through which beauty can be sensed. Alberti, *De re aedificatoria*, VII, 3, p. 156.

8 For a development of this argument see Tim Anstey, "Authority and authorship in LB Alberti's *De re aedificatoria*", *Nordiska Arkitekturforskning*, 4, 2003, pp. 19–25.

9 Alberti, *De re aedificatoria*, IX, 10, p. 315.

10 See Anstey, "Authority and Authorship".

11 See quote that begins this section, Alberti, *De re aedificatoria*, IX, 10.

12 Published in Rykwert, Joseph and Anne Engel eds., *Leon Battista Alberti*, Milan: Olivetti/Electa, pp. 456–462.

13 Alberti, *De re aedificatoria*, IX, 11, 318. A claim is being made in *De re aedificatoria* for the status of the designer's judgement which had existed before only in very particular circumstances. The architect is considered a personally celebrated figure in relation to acts of judgement that are his own, which are executed through work by other hands, and which pertain to the divine. In his treatise Alberti repeatedly cites Solomon as an exemplar for this figure; and at one level his model requires that the architect be King (or Queen—Alberti's other favourite exemplar is Seramis, the Assyrian Queen who 'built' the walls of Babylon). This, however, is specifically not the case; the architects Alberti is describing are, by definition, not absolute rulers.

14 Cicero, *On the Ideal Orator*, 3.53, p. 238: "Who is it who sends shivers down your spine? At whom do people stare in stunned amazement when he speaks?"

15 A beginning to this process can be witnessed, possibly, in the writings of Francesco di Giorgio Martini, which begin in the middle of his career when he is already established as ingeniere in Siena, but shortly before he moves into a wider, courtly, context. Directly one entertains the possibility that Francesco di Giorgio's texts helped establish his credentials in this new theatre, one is attributing a function to them similar to that outlined above.

16 In Cicero decorum was significant in two contexts. On one side, it had emerged with a moral dimension as an ideal of behaviour recommended to an errant Patrician class by an aging Cicero in *De officiis* (*On Duties*); on the other, in *De oratore* (*On the ideal orator*) Cicero identified decorum as an attribute of style in oratory.

17 The translation is first made in Vitruvius, who Alberti adapted in writing *De re aedificatoria* and who used decor as a term to describe a kind of beauty through propriety in buildings. For a description of Vitruvius' use of decorum and its relationship to the traditions of oratory and ethics, see John Onians, *Bearers of Meaning. The Classical Orders in Antiquity, the Middle Ages and the Renaissance*, Princeton, New Jersey: Princeton University Press, pp. 36–39.

18 See Onians, *Bearers of Meaning*, pp. 36–39. Vitruvius, *The Ten Books on Architecture*, Morris Hicky Morgan trans., New York: Dover Publications, 1960, I, 2, 6, p. 15.

19 Cicero, *De officiis*, I, XXXIX, p. 138.

20 Cicero, *De officiis*, I, XXXIX, p. 138.

21 This complexity is underlined in Cicero's work on oratory, see *De Oratore* 3.210, p. 290.

22 Architects after Alberti, conditioned one might argue by the set of limiting circumstances implied by the definitions of *De re aedificatoria*, began, in their re-reading of Vitruvius, to re-emphasise the significance of decorum. Decoro, in Serlio, for example, emphasises propriety, conformism, and respect for the context of tradition, all psychologically useful for building persuasive arguments endowed with a prosthetic authority. See Serlio, Sebastiano, *On Architecture* (*Tutte l'opere d'architettura et prospetiva*), Vaughan Hart and Peter Hicks trans., 2 vols., New Haven and London: Yale University Press, 1996, 2001. For a thorough discussion of Serlian decoro and the evolution of the theory of decorum in later Renaissance architectural treatises, see generally *Paper Palaces: the Rise of the Renaissance Architectural Treatise*, Vaughan Hart with Peter Hicks eds., New Haven and London: Yale University Press, 1998 and especially the introduction, Vaughan Hart, '"Paper palaces' from Alberti to Scamozzi", pp. 1–29.

23 It can be suggested that this condition impacts on the founding of learned societies to defend architects interests. Societies such as the Institute of British Architects (founded in 1835, granted its royal charter in 1837) sought to establish a role for the architect as ruling, with disinterested and authoritative judgement, over the administration of building contracts. This attempt to position the architect in a judge-like position can be read against the background of the very early definitions of the architect made in texts such as Alberti's (for which, it can be argued, the judge served as a specific ideal model of what the architect could be). That is to say, the attempt to reify the architects shadowy authority through the definition of a concrete role in the building process between patron or client and builder makes manifest a role for the architect that was already implicit in Alberti's ideal definition. On the model of the judge for Alberti's definition of the architect see Tim Anstey, "Authority and authorship", pp. 19–23.

24 On the repositioning of architectural education into the university, and an argument on the implications for 'design' resultant, see Adrian Forty, *Words and Buildings*, London: Thames and Hudson, 2000, pp. 138–141. Forty suggests that the establishment of architectural education as part of the university was revolutionary in that it allowed design to emerge as the central defining practice architects engaged in, and because it sealed the division between architect and builder. The arguments presented here suggest that this change should be read rather as the formalisation of a long-standing situation.

25 For the observations on Cedric Price in this article I am indebted to conversations with Stanley Mathews, Hobart and William Smith Colleges, Geneva, New York, and to the argument he presents in this book, "Cedric Price as anti-architect: the Fun Palace and the death of the architect" (see section 4). I am also indebted to Carola Ebert's arguments in relation to Rowe presented in her essay "Post-mortem: Architectural post-modernism and 'The death of the author'" (see below, section 1).

26 The situation was criticised acutely by Reyner Banham in *Theory and Design in the First Machine Age*, Oxford: Butterworth-Heinemann Ltd, (1960) 1994, which concentrated on the fall-out for the Modern Movement of the academic system of teaching in architecture. See also the essays collected in *A Critic Writes. Essays by Reyner Banham*, Berkeley, Los Angeles, London: University of California Press, 1996, particularly "1960—Stocktaking", pp. 49–63.

27 Price, memorandum, (August, 1964), Fun Palace document folio DR1995:0188:526, Cedric Price Archives, Canadian Centre for Architecture, Montreal, cited in Mathews, "Cedric Price as anti-architect".

28 See *The RIBA Journal*, vol. 88, no. 9, September 1981. The journal reports the RIBA conference from October 1980. It includes papers from Andrew Saint, "A History of Professionalism" and the contribution cited from Cedric Price, "An Alternative Voice" (pages unnumbered).

29 On the Fun Palace, see Mathews, "Cedric Price as anti-architect".

30 Banham, Reyner, article on the Fun Palace in the *New Statesman* (7 August, 1964), cited in *Cedric Price, Works II* (London, Architectural Association, 1984), repr. as *Cedric Price, The Square Book*, Chichester, West Sussex: Wiley-Academy, 2003, p. 59.

31 See Anstey, Tim, "Where is the project? Cedric Price on architectural action", in *Critical Architecture*, Mark Dorrian, Murray Fraser, Jonathan Hill, Jane Rendell, eds., London: Routledge, 2007.

32 The archive of material produced for this project is held in the Cedric Price archive at the Canadian Centre for Architecture, Montreal.

33 See Anstey, "Where is the project?".

34 On the development of the term context see Forty, *Words and Buildings*, pp. 132–135.

35 Rossi, Aldo, *L'architettura della città*, Padova: Marsilio, 1966; Rowe, Colin and Fred Koetter, "Collage City", *Architectural Review*, vol. 158, August 1975, pp. 66–91; revised and expanded as *Collage City*, Cambridge, MA, and London: MIT Press, 1978.

36 Rowe and Koetter's use of Rome and London as exemplars revealed how the experience of the city was conditioned by its growth according to ad hoc of ownership, and celebrated the collisions that resulted as positive. It can be argued that Rowe's interest was more formal and less historical than that of a figure such as Ernesto Rogers, who framed much of the continental European debate around context. Yet there in their sensitivity to the importance of organic urban patterns they remain similar, See Forty, *Words and Buildings*, 134–135.

37 Rowe and Koetter, "Collage City", p. 81.

38 See Forty, *Words and Buildings*, pp. 134–135.

39 See Price, "An alternative voice".

40 Rowe and Koetter, "Collage City", p. 83. "For, if planning can barely be more scientific than the political society of which it forms an agency, in the case of neither politics nor planning can there be sufficient information acquired before action becomes necessary. In neither case can performance await an ideal future formulation of the problem as it may, at last, be resolved; and, if this is because the very possibility of that future where such formulation might be made depends on imperfect action now, then this is only once more to intimate the role of bricolage which politics so much resembles and city planning surely should."

41 SHoP provide an account of much of the thinking that grounded their practice in *Versioning. Evolutionary Techniques in Architecture*, Christopher Coren and William Sharples, Kimberly Holden and Gregg Pasquarelli eds., Chichester: Wiley Academy, 2003. I would also like to thank Gregg Pasquarelli and Kimberly Holden for their help and advice in preparing this essay.

42 To an extent templates replicate the condition of 'shop-drawings', information produced within an organisation in which the question of authority is irrelevant and in which producer and reader are very closely linked.

43 SHoP Architects firm profile, quoted from http://www.dingaing.net/SHoP.htm, 31082006.

Architectural Creativity in Lewis Carroll's *The Vision of the Three T's*

Caroline Dionne

1 This first pamphlet was edited five times within the two following years. The third edition of 1872 bears the inscription "2nd thousand." The fourth and fifth edition came out in 1873 and, in 1874, both pamphlets were republished in the fourth section of *Notes of an Oxford Child*. According to Jean-Pierre Richard in his notice to the Oxford pamphlets, the successive reprints of the two texts suggest that they were widely circulated and well known within the context of both Christ Church and Oxford. See "Notes sur les pamphlets oxoniens," in Lewis Carroll, *Œuvres*, Paris: Gallimard, 1990, p. 1859.

2 The signature for the New Belfry is DCL—an anagram for Charles L Dodgson but also the acronym for *doctor civis legis* (Doctor of the Law), a title given at Oxford to the highest-ranking scholars. It seems very likely that in the context of Christ Church, Dodgson/Carroll's colleagues would have been aware of the fact that he was behind these pamphlets. See "Notes sur les pamphlets oxoniens", in Carroll, *Œuvres*, p. 1859.

3 Cardinal Thomas Wolsey was England's leading statesman, churchman and patron of the arts for a period of over fourteen years (1515–1529). He was the main consultant—and political educator—of King Henry VIII. His position of power led him to envision a series of building projects tied to his attempt at reforming the Church of England. His numerous commissions ranged from small individual houses to magnificent university colleges and bear the influence of the Italian Renaissance. This influence, coming both from the Italians and the French, is primarily visible in the programmatic choices (galleries, stacked lodging, individual domestic projects) and the iconography (stained glass, sculpture and painting, design of seals, etc.). Other Renaissance ideas permeate his work: the magnificence of architecture as a symbol of political and religious power, the utmost importance given to patronage in relation to the building, his emphasis on educational projects and the transmission of knowledge, the heightened presence of all the arts in the building project, and so on. In 1529, Wolsey fell from power as he refused to follow Henry VIII's position on the divorce issue. See *Cardinal Wolsey: Church, State and Art*, SJ Gunn and PG Lindley ed., Cambridge: Cambridge University Press, 1991.

4 See Tyack, Geoffrey, *Oxford An Architectural Guide*, Oxford; New York: Oxford University Press, 1998, p. 77.

5 See Sherwood, Jennifer and Nikolaus Pevsner, *The Buildings of England: Oxfordshire*, Harmondsworth: Penguin Books, 1974, pp. 110–112.

6 Sherwood and Pevsner agree in that sense.

It should be noted that the actual staircase to the Hall is an early nineteenth century addition (1805), by architect James Wyatt.

7 Dean Liddell was at the head of Christ Church College from 1855 to 1891. Carroll's *Alice's Adventures in Wonderland* was inspired by and dedicated to Liddell's second daughter Alice.

8 See Sherwood and Pevsner, *The Buildings of England: Oxfordshire*, p. 112. See also Tyack, *Oxford An Architectural Guide*, p. 77.

It is interesting that what Carroll is criticising in his architectural pamphlets is not the project as it was actually completed in 1879. Rather his critique is directed at an intermediary step of the building process. In that sense, the two architectural pamphlets are not intended solely at questioning the nature of architectural intervention per se but, instead, address the project as a whole: the programmatic basis of the intervention, the choice of the architects, the unfolding of the building process, its financial and political implications, and, finally, the aesthetic choices and stylistic nature of the intervention. Carroll's critique seems to imply an understanding of architecture that is broader and which encompasses all steps of the architectural project, from the artistic vision, to the design, to its completion.

9 To mention but a few, *The Hunting of the Snark* is written out as an epic poem that also emulates the work of the great Romantic poet Tennyson while *Sylvie and Bruno* is a novel organised around the world of "fairies". *Alice's Adventures in Wonderland* is no exception. Close examination of the narrative structure of the text reveals that Carroll is once again revisiting, and parodying, a literary *topoi* dear to writers of the late middle ages and early Renaissance, though in this case, there is no direct reference to a specific work or author. The tale of young heroine Alice roughly follows the model of the "allegorical dream" in a form that is not too dissimilar from Francesco Colonna's *Hypnerotomachia Poliphili*. Evidently, in all cases, Carroll's re-appropriation of a genre, which involves a high level of parody, led to something new, not only in terms of children's literature, but from a larger literary perspective as well. In the nineteenth century, caricatures and parody abound. Such modes of representation were praised for their way of expressing a profound verity by exaggerating the traits of a person, an idea or a work to such an extent that it would provoke laughter. In that sense, caricature is not simply a critique.

10 Carroll met Ruskin through his acquaintance with Dean Liddell. The two men apparently shared a concern for the arts, an interest in the Pre-Raphaelite Brotherhood, and a fascination with the Dean's second daughter Alice.

11 John Ruskin, "The Lamp of Obedience," in *The Seven Lamps of Architecture*, London: JM Dent & Sons, 1907, pp. 203–219.

12 Ruskin, "The Lamp of Obedience," p. 207. Already in the context of early humanism, writers on architecture drew this parallel. Alberti, for example, asserted that rhetoric had to serve as a guiding principle for all the arts, including architecture. In literary descriptions of buildings, beauty of style—i.e. careful construction according to the principles of rhetoric—was necessary to equal, if not surpass, the beauty and grandeur of the building itself as much as to convey its meaning. See Christine Smith, *Architecture in the Culture of Early Humanism: Ethics, Aesthetics, and Eloquence 1400–1470*, New York; Oxford: Oxford University Press, 1992, especially Part II, Chapter Five.

13 *The Compleate Angler, or the Contemplative Man's Recreation* was first published in 1653. The book was an immediate success and was reedited several times during its author's lifetime. It then fell into oblivion, until its rediscovery in the eighteenth century. Since then, some three hundred reprints have appeared—in the nineteenth century, it was one of the most widely circulated books. Walton (1593–1683) is also known for his biographical work. He wrote, among others, the *Lives* of, Sir Henry Wotton and John Donne (completing a version already begun by Wotton himself).

14 Though the culture of the Renaissance was a highly literate one in comparison to predominantly oral cultures such as those of Antiquity and the early middle ages, it nonetheless retained a high level of orality. The trend of the dialogue that developed at that time thus links it to rhetorical models reflecting more closely the rhythm of speech. On the transformations in the literary genre of the dialogue in the context of the Renaissance, see Virginia Cox, *The Renaissance Dialogue: Literary dialogue in its social and political contexts, Castiglione to Galileo*, Cambridge: Cambridge University Press, 1992.

15 Marc Fumaroli's thesis concerning the transformation, in the modern context, of one of the grounding principles of communication, rhetoric, is also insightful here. In his extensive study *L'âge de l'éloquence*, Fumaroli notes how ancient rhetoric was gradually transformed in the late eighteenth and early nineteenth century, systematised into a "rhétorique scolaire" and exhausted of its philosophical, political and oratory dimensions tied to eloquence (Aristotle). This systematisation eventually led to the abandonment of the teaching of rhetoric,

in the 1880s in France and a little earlier in the context of the English colleges (around 1850). This age-old discipline was, for the first time, viewed as empty and useless. Rhetoric was thus replaced, in school programs, by courses on the history of ancient and modern literatures. However, Fumaroli argues, this does not necessarily mean that rhetoric, as a guiding principle, a mode of regulating literary works, of giving them a specific—eloquent—shape, was abandoned. Rather, it manifests itself very well in the works of many literary writers who invent new, modern ways of framing language into compelling, effective literary works, discursive or fictional. In that sense, it can be said that nineteenth century writers have attempted to secure, through their work, the richness of ancient rhetoric, and succeeded in such a way that also contributed to render scholarly rhetoric irrelevant. Ancient rhetoric may have been reduced to a tropology, but this reduction remains incomplete. See Marc Fumaroli, *L'age de l'éloquence*, Paris: Albin Michel, 1994, especially pp. 1–16.

16 Threnodies, or elegies, are usually songs or poems for the dead, mourning the loss of a loved one, expressing nostalgia for bygone days.

17 Jeeby refers to the acronym GB—i.e. to Georges Bodley's initials.

18 Carroll, Lewis, "The Vision of the Three T's", *The Complete Illustrated Lewis Carroll*, Ware: Wordsworth, 1996, p. 1043.

19 Carroll, "The Vision of the Three T's", p. 1045.

20 Carroll, "The Vision of the Three T's", p. 1046. My emphasis.

21 Carroll, "The Vision of the Three T's", p. 1040.

22 "Builds castles up, then pulls them to the ground, Keeps changing round for square and square for round." Horace, Epistle I, 100. The subtext here is interesting. In this first epistle to his patron, Horace tells Maecenas that his views on poetry have changed, and that he wishes to devote himself to the pursuit of truth and beauty. Horace asks for his patron's indulgence, assuring him that his views may at first seem inconsequential, even insane, but that the patron, with all his wisdom and knowledge, will be able to discern the truth.

23 On Carroll's accounts of his writing process, see Lewis Carroll, "Sylvie and Bruno", *The Complete Works*, London: Nonesuch Press, 1939, p. 255.

24 On the distinctions between classical and Renaissance understandings of furor poeticus, and the Romantic and post-Romantic concepts of inspiration, see Timothy Clark, *The Theory of Inspiration: Composition as a crisis of subjectivity in Romantic and post-Romantic writing*, Manchester and New York: Manchester University Press, 1997.

25 Carroll, "The Vision of the Three T's", pp. 1051–1052.

26 Carroll. "The New Belfry of Christ Church, Oxford", *The Complete Illustrated Lewis Carroll*, Ware: Wordsworth, 1996, p. 1043.

27 Mark Dorian, "Ruskin's Theory of the Grotesque", in *Chora: Intervals in the Philosophy of Architecture*, vol. IV, Montreal: McGill Queens Press, 2004, p. 38.

28 See Dorian, "Ruskin's Theory of the Grotesque", p. 40.

29 The figure of the White Knight has often been associated by critics with the author himself. The character also evokes Cervantes' Don Quixote. See Lewis Carroll, "Through the Looking-Glass and What Alice Found There", in *The Annotated Alice*, intro and notes by Martin Gardner, New York: WW Norton & Company Inc, 2000, p. 243, note 2.

30 See Lewis Carroll, "Through the Looking-Glass and What Alice Found There", in *The Annotated Alice*, intro and notes by Martin Gardner, New York: WW Norton & Company Inc, 2000, pp. 207–220.

31 In his *Logic of Sense*, Gilles Deleuze discusses the philosophical implications of understanding sense, and nonsense, in relation to paradoxes, focusing his study on logic and the psychoanalytical implications of confronting one's mind to the pure *devenir-fou* that the paradox brings about. For Deleuze, Carroll represents a new type of writer within the modern literary tradition of the West; Carroll achieves—because he acknowledges and wants to conquer the paradoxical depth of surfaces themselves—the first great mise-en-scène of the paradoxes of sense. See Gilles Deleuze, *Logique du sens*, Paris: Minuit, 1969, Series two to six.

32 Nonsense is not be understood here as an absence of meaning but, rather, as a surplus, as the bringing together of opposite meanings.

33 "Le nonsense en tant que genre littéraire est l'expression de cette contradiction : il faut ordonner la langue, mais on peut jamais y parvenir ; il faut que le sujet locuteur soit maître de sa langue, mais il en peut en aucun cas l'être... Le nonsense campe aux frontières de la langue, là où le grammatical et l'agrammatical se rejoignent, là où l'ordre (toujours partiel) de la langue rejoint le désordre (jamais total) de son au-delà." See Jean-Jacques Lecercle, "Linguistic Intuitions: Lewis Carroll and 'Alice au pays des merveilles,'" *Europe-Revue littéraire mensuelle*, vol. 68, no. 736, 1990, p. 58, my translation.

Post-mortem: Architectural Post-modernism and the Death of the Author

Carola Ebert

1 Rowe, Colin, and Fred Koetter, *Collage City*, Cambridge, MA: MIT Press, 1976. An earlier version was published in *Architectural Review* in 1975. Tschumi, Bernard, *Architecture and Disjunction*, Cambridge, MA: MIT Press, 1994. The essays assembled in the book were initially published in the years 1975–1976 and 1981–1991.

2 Barthes, Roland, "The Death of the Author", *Image-Music-Text*, Stephen Heath trans., London: Fontana, 1977 (1968).

3 For an extensive discussion of Tschumi's use of contemporary French theory see: Martin, Louis, "Interdisciplinary Transpositions: Bernard Tschumi's Architectural Theory" in *de-, dis-, -ex-: The Anxiety of Interdisciplinarity*, Alex Coles and Alexia Defert eds., London: Black Dog Publishing, 1998.

4 Derrida, Jacques, interviewed by Eva Meyer, "Architecture Where Desire can live", *Domus*, no. 671, April 1986, p. 18.

5 Hollier, Denis, *Against Architecture: The writings of Georges Bataille*, Betsy Wing trans., Cambridge: MIT Press, 1989, p. 57.

6 Martin, "Interdisciplinary Transpositions…", p. 84.

7 Eagleton, Terry, *Literary Theory: An Introduction*, Oxford: Blackwell, 1983, p. 133. Tschumi, *Architecture and Disjunction*, p. 259.

8 Waldman, Diane, *Collage, Assemblage, and the Found Object*, London: Phaidon, 1992, pp. 264–265.

9 Bürger, Peter, *Theorie der Avant-Garde*, Frankfurt: Suhrkamp, 1974.

10 Nesbitt, Kate, "Introduction: The Pleasure of Architecture, Bernard Tschumi", in *Theorizing a New Agenda for Architecture: An Anthology of Architectural Theory 1965–1995*, Kate Nesbitt ed., New York: Princeton Architectural Press, 1996, pp. 530–531.

11 Tschumi, Bernard, *Advertisements for Architecture*, 1975. The *Advertisements for Architecture* were disseminated in form of posters and post cards. Tschumi appropriates the concept of combining photographs with printed texts whose meaning runs counter the expected meaning from artist Victor Burgin, who used it in his *What does possession mean to you?* (1976).

12 Tschumi, *Architecture and Disjunction*, p. 73.

13 Tschumi, *Architecture and Disjunction*, p. 205. Crossprogramming juxtaposes unexpected functions with inappropriate spaces, transprogramming mixes two incompatible programmes.

14 Tschumi, *Architecture and Disjunction*, p. 195.

15 Tschumi, Bernard, *The Manhattan Transcripts*, London: Academy Editions, 1994, p. 6.

16 Rowe, *Collage City*, p. 137.

17 Rowe, *Collage City*, p. 93.

18 Rowe, *Collage City*, p. 20.
Rowe, *Collage City*, p. 31.

19 Hill, Jonathan, *The Illegal Architect*, London: Black Dog Publishing, 1998, p. 26.

20 Lévi-Strauss, Claude, *The Savage Mind*, London: Weidenfeld & Nicholson, 1966, p. 16, quoted in Rowe, *Collage City*, p. 102.

21 Lévi-Strauss, *The Savage Mind*, p. 19, quoted in Rowe, *Collage City*, p. 103.

22 Lévi-Strauss, *The Savage Mind*, p. 22, quoted in Rowe, *Collage City*, p. 103.

23 Lévi-Strauss, *The Savage Mind*, p. 11, quoted in Rowe, *Collage City*, p. 139. Oechslin, Werner, "Working with Fragments—The Limitations of Collage", *Daidalos*, no. 16, June 1985, p. 19.

24 Poggi, Christine, *In Defiance of Painting: Cubism, Futurism, and the Invention of Collage*, New Haven: Yale University Press, 1992, p. 21.

25 Poggi, *In Defiance of Painting*, p. 45.

26 Rowe discussed the significance of Cubism for architecture in two essays written with Robert Slutzky, "Transparency: Literal and Phenomenal" (*Perspecta*, no. 8, 1963) and "Transparency: Literal and Phenomenal… Part II" (*Perspecta*, nos. 13/14, 1971).

27 Rowe and Koetter extract from the *beaux arts* concept *poché* a double function in which a building "acts both as a space occupier and a space definer, as positive figure and passive ground" (Rowe, *Collage City*, p. 79).

28 Tschumi, Bernard, "The Pleasure of Architecture" in Tschumi, *Architecture and Disjunction*. An earlier version of the text was published in *AD*: Tschumi, Bernard, "The Pleasure of Architecture", *Architectural Design*, March 1977. The title refers to the title of Roland Barthes' *Le Plaisir du Texte* (1973).

29 Tschumi, *Architecture and Disjunction*, pp. 195–196.

30 Nesbitt, Kate, "Introduction", in *Theorizing a New Agenda for Architecture*, Nesbitt ed., p. 35.

31 Tschumi, Bernard, "Disjunctions", in Tschumi, *Architecture and Disjunction*, originally printed as Tschumi, Bernard, "Disjunctions", *Perspecta: The Yale Architectural Journal*, no. 23, January 1987.
Tschumi, *Architecture and Disjunction*, p. 213.

32 "Collage City and The Reconquest of Time" chapter heading in Rowe, *Collage City*, p. 118.

33 For a detailed analysis of the critic and the author see: Burke, Seán, "Critic and Author?" in *The Death and Return of the Author*, Seán Burke, Edinburgh: Edinburgh University Press, 1992, pp. 158–162.

34 As Kate Nesbitt points out, "The term "contextualism" is not used by Rowe and Koetter, but was applied to their theory by [Thomas L] Schumacher in… 1971… Since then, contextualism has come to mean little more than "fitting in with existing conditions", according to Richard Ingersoll." Nesbitt, "Introduction", p. 54.

35 Heynen, Hilde, *Architecture and Modernity: a Critique*, Cambridge: MIT Press, 1999.

36 Heynen, *Architecture and Modernity*, pp. 10–13.

37 Heynen, *Architecture and Modernity*, p. 26.

38 Heynen, *Architecture and Modernity*, p. 13.

39 Heynen, *Architecture and Modernity*, p. 11.

40 Heynen, *Architecture and Modernity*, p. 13.
Rowe, *Collage City*, p. 45.

41 Rowe, *Collage City*, p. 2.

42 Hoesli, Bernard, "Kommentar zur Deutschen Ausgabe" in *Collage City*, Rowe, Colin, and Fred Koetter, Bernard Hoesli et al trans., Basel: Birkhäuser, 1994, p. 2 (my translation). The Swiss-German edition of *Collage City* can only be recommended—by way of its succinct wording, additional imagery and congenial layout—it is by far, as Colin Rowe himself put it, the superior edition.

43 Tschumi, *Architecture and Disjunction*, p. 176.

44 Tschumi's 'project' of disjunction aims to transform architecture. "Bataille, on the contrary, denounces… solutions…. To will the future…, to submit to planning and projects… is to lock oneself into a devalorised present…. "The project," according to Bataille, "is the prison. To want to get out of the labyrinth… is to close it, to close oneself inside it." Hollier, *Against Architecture*, p. 61.

45 Heynen, *Architecture and Modernity*, p. 11.

'In the Mind of the Architect': Representation and Authorship in Documentary Film

Naomi Stead

1 Sarris, Andrew, 'Notes on the Auteur Theory in 1962', first published in *Film Culture*, Winter 1962–1963, reprinted in Gerald Mast and Marshall Cohen eds., *Film Theory and Criticism: Introductory Readings*, New York: Oxford University Press, 1974, pp. 512–513.

2 See Pauline Kael 'Circles and Squares', first published in *Film Quarterly* in 1963, reprinted in Gerald Mast and Marshall Cohen eds., *Film Theory and Criticism: Introductory Readings*, New York: Oxford University Press, 1974, pp. 516–529. Wright Wexman, Virginia, 'Introduction', in *Film and Authorship*, Virginia Wright Wexman ed., New Brunswick: Rutgers University Press, 2003, p. 9. As Wexman writes, "During the medieval period… auctors (as authors were then called) were thought to derive their authority from the wisdom of the past and ultimately from God. The modern concept of originary authorship emerged in the early nineteenth century… [and] the auteurists drew on this formulation to position Hollywood directors as part of the pantheon of high culture."

3 For an important contemporary discussion of the issues see Virginia Wright Wexman ed., *Film and Authorship*, New Brunswick: Rutgers University Press, 2003, and David A Gerstner and Janet Staiger eds., *Authorship and Film*, New York: Routledge, 2003.

4 Wollen, Peter, "The Auteur Theory", excerpt from *Signs and Meaning in the Cinema*, reprinted in Gerald Mast and Marshall Cohen eds, *Film Theory and Criticism: Introductory Readings*, New York: Oxford University Press, 1974, p. 532.

5 Levison, Nancy, "Tall Buildings, Tall Tales: On Architects in the Movies", in Mark Lamster ed., *Architecture and Film*, New York: Princeton Architecture Press, 2000, p. 27.

6 Levison, Nancy, "Tall Buildings, Tall Tales: On Architects in the Movies", p. 27.

7 See http://www.abc.net.au/arts/architecture/about.htm

8 Coward, Rosalind, "Dennis Potter and the Question of the Television Author", in Robert Stam and Toby Miller eds., *Film and Theory: An Anthology*, Oxford: Blackwell Publishers, 2000, p. 10.

9 This was evidenced in an amusing exchange in the webchat following the third episode of the documentary, on 05/07/00 as follows: 'marcus', post id: 91: "When will the ABC do a series about Engineers? We are far more interesting than Architects, Lawyers or Medics." Followed by Sean Godsell [architect featured on the programme and panellist in the webchat] post id: 101: "... and clearly far more humble too !!!" Followed by 'Babar', post id: 108: "I'm an accountant and I find myself fascinating too". The humour in this rests in the knowing reference to and contrast between the stereotypical accountant, with all the connotations of its being an exacting, thorough, and careful, but also somewhat uncreative and rather dull profession, and the stereotypical architect, with many of the opposite traits. http://www2.abc.net.au/architecture/chat3/default.htm

10 Naremore, James, "Authorship", in Toby Miller and Robert Stam eds., A Companion to Film Theory, Oxford: Blackwell Publishers, 1999, p. 12.

11 Feldman, Allen, "Faux Documentary and the Memory of Realism", American Anthropologist, June 1998, vol. 100, no. 2, p. 495.

12 Feldman, Allen, "Faux Documentary and the Memory of Realism", American Anthropologist, June 1998, vol. 100, no. 2, p. 494.

13 Arthur, Paul, "Extreme Makeover: The Changing Face of Documentary", Cineaste, Summer 2005, vol. 30, no. 3, p. 21.

14 Arthur, Paul, "Extreme Makeover: The Changing Face of Documentary", Cineaste, Summer 2005, vol. 30, no. 3, p. 20.

15 Arthur, Paul, "Extreme Makeover: The Changing Face of Documentary", Cineaste, Summer 2005, vol. 30, no. 3, p. 20.

16 Rabiger, Michael, "Documentary Filmmakers Decide How to Present Compelling Evidence", Nieman Reports, Fall 2001, pp. 63–64.

17 Coward, Rosalind, "Dennis Potter and the Question of the Television Author", in Robert Stam and Toby Miller eds., Film and Theory: An Anthology, Blackwell Publishers, Oxford, 2000, p. 1.

18 Coward, Rosalind, "Dennis Potter and the Question of the Television Author", in Robert Stam and Toby Miller eds., Film and Theory: An Anthology, Blackwell Publishers, Oxford, 2000, p. 7.

19 The French auteurists were able to reconcile the fundamentally collaborative practice of filmmaking with their singular concept of authorship by recourse to the philosophy of existentialism. Jean-Luc Godard, for instance, wrote regarding Ingmar Bergman that "[t]he cinema is not a craft. It is an art. It does not mean teamwork. One is always alone on the set as before the blank page." Jean-Luc Godard, Godard on Godard, Jean Narboni and Tom Milne eds., New York: The Viking Press, 1972, p. 76; quoted by James Naremore, "Authorship", in Toby Miller and Robert Stam eds., A Companion to Film Theory, Oxford: Blackwell Publishers, 1999, p. 11.

20 Naremore, James, "Authorship", in Toby Miller and Robert Stam eds., A Companion to Film Theory, Oxford: Blackwell Publishers, 1999, p. 9.

21 Naremore, James, "Authorship", in Toby Miller and Robert Stam eds., A Companion to Film Theory, Oxford: Blackwell Publishers, 1999, p. 9.

22 This can be seen in the transcript of the 'webchat' discussion, for instance 'peter', on 21/06/00 at 22:02:28, post id: 178: "Please tell me why most architects shown tonight wore black and spoke in calm, almost hypnotic tones. Does this assist [sic] in persuading clients to follow their leads, or is it just a fashion thing, after all isnt architecture purely a fashion thing[?]" and 'Meryl', on 21/06/00 at 21:36:12, post id: 32: "Is there a particular requirement that architects speak in a languange [sic] of such density and artificial construction that mere mortals are left stunned and reaching for a nail gun or... did you just get lucky?"
'Lisa', on 8/07/00, at 11:19:20, post id: 265: "I thought [the documentary] was pretty slow moving and kind of trance like, as though we were being lulled into a receptive and compliant state of mind. As though we were supposed to be in awe of these architects. It was art documentary as anaesthetic."

23 For instance 'Mike', on 22/06/00, at 17:19:36, post id: 358: "Talk about footballers talking rubbish! Let the buildings speak for themselves—basta! Anyone who watched the show would realise what a bunch of rubbish comes out of architects mouths—perhaps they should get agents to do the talking for them! Anyway architects just seem to get in the way of the real people involved in the architectural professions—builders, tradesmen, producers of the materials and the occupiers—if you know what I mean?" and 'Steve Grey' on 21/06/00, at 22:33:15, post id: 319: "[…] This profession must come down to earth off their pedestals and make buildings for people to live in and stop making innapropriate [sic] Art Galleries to live out their fantasies at the communitie's [sic] expense. Perhaps then they might be asked to design more than 3% of our habitat."

24 In addition to this real-time feedback, there was an opportunity for guests to leave comments ('your stories') in an online guest book.

25 For instance 'Julia', on 22/06/00, at 9:26:23, post id: 346: "Can modern domestic architectual [sic] design permit disorder? After seeing the homes last night, it strikes me that it can't. Everything we saw was so squeaky clean and ordered. Was this just for the filming and everyone rushed around beforehand stuffing strewn clothes in cupboards, books on shelves, old newspapers in the recycle bin etc? After learning that in Godsell's building you are actually obliged to 'tidy' yourself by going into a cupboard to undress!—I fear there is no room for disorder in this modern world." Interestingly, the cupboard incident also galvanised the late Harry Seidler, one of the architects featured on the programme, who appeared to turn against the producer in the webchat discussions: "To protrait [sic] modern archtitecture [sic] as a place where you have to get dressed in a cupboard is libleous [sic] to the last eighty years of brilliant buildings in the Western World, of which we have hardly any in this, what is now confirmed as a provincial back water, of the western civilised world." Harry Seidler, on 5/07/00, at 22:11:39, post id: 170.

26 Corrigan, Tim, A Cinema Without Walls: Movies and Culture after Vietnam, New Brunswick: Rutgers University Press, 1991, p. 135.

27 See the Pritzker Prize website: http://www.pritzkerprize.com/2002annc.htm#about

28 http://www.pritzkerprize.com/2002annc.htm#about

29 Even in those cases where Murcutt does not work alone, for example in the recent Arthur and Yvonne Boyd Education Centre, this is either conveniently forgotten, or framed in terms of a collaboration of equals; of a group of privileged authors coming together, rather than anything so mundane as an employee.

30 Barthes, Roland, "The Death of the Author", in Image-Music-Text, trans. Stephen Heath London: Fontana Paperbacks, 1977, p. 148.

Dislocation

Nature's Lovers: Design and Authorship in the Eighteenth Century Landscape Garden

Katja Grillner

1 Pope, Alexander, "Epistle IV: To Richard Boyle, Earl of Burlington", in The Poems of Alexander Pope, Volume III ii—Epistles to several persons (Moral essays), John Butt, FW Bateson eds., lines 50–56, pp. 137–138.

2 For example, Capability Brown was trained as a gardener and, along with the painter William Kent, became one of the most celebrated 'heroes' of English landscape gardening.

3 With the publication of Thomas Whately's Observations on Modern Gardening in 1770 the theoretical debate concerning the landscape garden, its effects and its design, entered an intensive period. Between 1768 and 1777 the following publications were launched:
– Mason, George, Essay on Design in Gardening, London: 1768. (Second edition published in 1795, London: Benjamin and John White).
– Whately, Thomas, Observations on Modern Gardening, London: T Payne, 1770. (Facsimile edition published by Garland Publishing 1982).
– Walpole, Horace, A History of the Modern Taste in Gardening, London: 1771/80.
– Chambers, William, A Dissertation on Oriental Gardening, London: W Griffin, 1772.
– Watelet, Claude-Henri, Essai sur les Jardins, Paris: Prault, 1774. (Recently published in English translation as Essay on gardens: a chapter in the French picturesque translated into English for the first time, Samuel Danon ed., trans., Joseph Disponzio intro., Philadelphia: University of Pennsylvania Press, 2003.)
– Hirschfeld, Cristian Cajus Lorenz, Theorie der Gartenkunst, Leipzig: Weidmanns Erben und Reich, 1775. Extended from 1779–1785 into a five volume work with same title. (This longer version is published in English as Theory of Garden Art, Linda B Parshall trans., Philadelphia: University of Pennsylvania Press, 2001). The edition that will be referenced in this chapter is the 2001 English translation unless otherwise noted.
– Morel, Jean-Marie, Théorie des jardins, Paris: Pissot, 1776. (Facsimile edition Geneva: Minkoff, 1973).
– Girardin, René Louis le Marquis de, De la Composition des Paysages, Genève and Paris: PM Delaguette, 1777. (Published in English translation as Essay on Landscape; or, On the means of improving and embellishing the Country round our habitations, Daniel Malthus trans., London: J Dodsley, 1783. Republished in French in 1979, Paris: Éditions du Champ Urbain).
– Heely, Joseph, Letters on the Beauties of Hagley, Envil, and the Leasowes, London: R Baldwin, 1777.
Whately becomes the evident point of reference for most of these writers even

though no one, with the possible exception of Morel, borrow the ambitious treatise format of his *Observations*. They all aimed for an articulation of landscape gardening as an independent art form (one of the liberal arts) and shared a concern with design practice distinguishing them from the rest of the fast growing body of picturesque landscape observations and poetry.

4 An excellent example of research that enters into considerably more detail on the relation between these discursive formations and actual design practice is Joseph Disponzio's study of Jean-Marie Morel as presented in: "From Garden to Landscape—Jean Marie Morel and the Transformation of Garden History" in *AA-files*, 44, pp. 6–20; "Jean Marie Morel and the Invention of Landscape Architecture" in *Tradition and Innovation in French Garden Art*, John Dixon Hunt and Michel Conan eds., Philadelphia: University of Pennsylvania Press, 2002, pp. 135–159; and the catalogue of Morel's landscape designs published with an introduction by Disponzio in *Studies in the History of Gardens and Designed Landscapes*, vol. 21, no. 3–4, 2001. A thorough empirical study on the character, role and responsibilities of the eighteenth century gardener has been carried out on Swedish material by Åsa Ahrland in her PhD dissertation *Den osynliga handen—Trädgårdsmästaren i 1700-talets Sverige* [*The invisible hand—The gardener in 18th century Sweden*], Alnarp: SLU, 2005.

5 Foucault, Michel, "What is an Author?" in *Textual Strategies: Perpectives in Post-Structuralist Criticism*, Josué V Harari ed. and trans., Ithaca: Cornell University Press, 1979, pp. 141–160. The translation by JV Harari is based on Foucault's revised version of this lecture given at SUNY-Buffalo. The lecture was originally given for the Société Française de Philosophie and published in its Bulletin in 1969.

6 Roland Barthes' "The Death of the Author" was first published in 1967. In Roland Barthes, *Image-Music-Text*, Stephen Heath trans. and ed., London: Fontana, 1977, pp. 142–148.

7 "How can one reduce", Foucault asks rhetorically, "the great peril, the great danger with which fiction threatens our world? The answer is: one can reduce it with the author." Foucault, "What is an author?", p. 158.

8 Whately, Thomas, *Observations on Modern Gardening*, London: T Payne, 1770, p. 200.

9 Whately, *Observations*, Introduction, p. 1.

10 Whately, *Observations*, Introduction, pp. 1–2, on Woods, p. 25. The section on woods particularly underlines his emphasis on appearance: "an examination of the characteristic differences of trees and shrubs is necessary. I do not mean botanical distinctions; I mean apparent, not essential varieties." [Whately's emphasis].

11 Whately, *Observations*, Introduction, p. 2. "Nature, always simple, employs but four materials in the composition of her scenes, ground, wood, water, and rocks. The cultivation of nature has introduced a fifth species, buildings requisite for the accommodation of men."
Whately, *Observations*, ch. 2, p. 2. The geometrical language used here echoes the simplicity and straightforwardness of Euclid's *Elements of Geometry*, a common reference and disputed model for architectural treatises that preceded Whately's *Observations*. See Michele Sbacchi "Euclidism and Theory of Architecture", *Nexus Network Journal*, vol. 3, no. 3, Summer 2001 http://www.nexusjournal.com/Sbacchi.html (accessed 6 July 2006).

12 In his article "The French Garden in the Eighteenth Century: from Belle Nature to the landscape of time" RG Saisselin qualifies the French formal garden as 'outdoor architecture' in distinction to, not only the landscape garden, but also to the Italian formal gardens. Saisselin, RG, "The French Garden in the Eighteenth Century: from Belle Nature to the landscape of time" in *The Journal of Garden History*, vol. 5, no. 3, pp. 284–297 (p. 286).

13 This passage invokes the concepts used in theories and descriptions of the landscape garden at the time. The specific notion of buildings as 'ornaments' derives from Thomas Whately's discussion of buildings in *Observations*, p. 117.

14 Watelet, Claude-Henri, *Essai sur les Jardins*, Paris: Prault, 1774, pp. 108–109.

15 Whately describes the importance of planting trees with the future in mind, taking into account that while during the first years a more dense wood might be desired, as the trees grow the wood should be carefully cleared out. Whately, *Observations*, ch. 21, pp. 50–52.

16 William Chambers describes Kew Gardens as a disadvantageous site and proudly claims that "what was once a Desart is now an Eden" since judgement has employed art to "supply the defects of nature, and to cover its deformities", in William Chambers, *Plans, Elevations, Sections, and Perspective Views of the Gardens and Buildings at KEW in Surry, The seat o her Royal Highness The Princess Dowager of Wales*, London: J Haberkorn, 1763.

17 Morel, Jean-Marie, *Théorie des jardins*, Paris: Pissot, 1776, p. 90: "De tous les arts, le sien dois le moins s'écarter de la vérité; il n'étudie pas la Nature pour apprendre à l'imiter, mais pour la seconder".

18 The heavy emphasis on appearance finds its origin in the development of Lockean psychology, into the aesthetic sensationalism of, for example Addison, Burke, and Condillac. In the eighteenth century works of art that demand any kind of intellectual effort for their appreciation provoke impatience. Impressions of the beautiful should strike the imagination with immediate effect. For a comprehensive account of eighteenth century aesthetics see for example John Brewer, *The Pleasures of the Imagination*, London: Harper Collins Publishers, 1997.

19 The English painter Joshua Reynolds, whose *Discourses on Art* (delivered at the Royal Academy of Art from 1769–1790) were highly influential (translated at the time into Italian, French and German) pays very close attention to what it is that a painter does when imitating nature, and what qualifies the result as art. Reynolds, Joshua, *Discourses on Art*, Robert R Wark, ed., San Marino: Huntington Library, 1959. He emphasises that the mere skill of life-like imitation does not produce art: "The Art which we profess has beauty for its object… it is an idea that subsists only in the mind… residing in the breast of the artist… which he is yet so far able to communicate, as to raise the thoughts, and extend the views of the spectator" (p. 171). When the landscape designer is perceived to 'paint' (by trimming, planting etc.), the landscape with subtle revisions, one might argue that he adds nothing but this same 'idea of beauty' (ideal beauty), the idea that differentiates a mere life-like imitation (the random snap-shot in our days) from art. Reynolds is however very careful to differentiate the arts: "though they all profess the same origin… each has its own particular modes of imitating nature, and of deviating from it…. Also Gardening… is a deviation from nature…. Even though we define it, 'Nature to advantage dress'd' [Pope]… it is however, when so dress'd, no longer a subject for the pencil of a Landskip-Painter" (p. 240).
A philosophical complication, which caused some confusion in the case of landscape design was that the material that made up the model (the untouched landscape) was the same material that would be employed in its improvement (i.e. ground, woods, water, rocks etc.). Compare this with the more self-evident distinction between a painting of a tree and the tree itself, or likewise with a descriptive or ekphrastic poem.

20 Examples of specific text-places where these different titles are applied: Heely, *Letters*, p. 12, pp. 48–58; Whately, *Observations*, p. 2; Watelet, *Essai*, pp. 55–58, pp. 106–109; Morel, *Théorie*, p. 7; Hirschfeld, *Theory of Garden Art* (2001), vol. x, p. 339–346.

21 Morel, *Théorie*, p. 7, footnote 1: "Par Jardinier, j'entend l'Artiste de goût qui compose les Jardins, & non celui qui les cultive." All translations are, if not otherwise noted, by the author.

22 From 1804, Morel begins to be addressed by the title 'architecte-paysagiste', but it is not until Olmsted and Calvert Vaux in the 1860s that the title 'landscape architect' is coined and used in the English language. This chapter therefore applies the somewhat neutral term 'designer' or 'landscape designer', which was also in use at the time. For more on the history of landscape architecture as a profession, see John Dixon Hunt, *Greater Perfections*, Philadelphia: University of Pennsylvania Press, 1999, and Joseph Disponzio's essay (and particularly its appendix) "Jean Marie Morel and the Invention of Landscape Architecture", *Tradition and Innovation in French Garden Art*, John Dixon Hunt and Michel Conan eds., Philadelphia: University of Pennsylvania Press, 2002, pp. 135–159.

23 Girardin, René Louis le Marquis de, *Essay on Landscape; or, On the means of improving and embellishing the Country round our habitations*, Daniel Malthus trans., London: J Dodsley, 1783, p. 8–9. The corresponding passage in the original edition—De la composition (Geneva and Paris, 1777)—is found on p. 8: "Ce n'est donc ni en Architect, ni en Jardinier, c'est en Poète et en Peintre qu'il faut composer les paysages, afin d'intéresser tout à la fois l'oeil et l'esprit."

24 Watelet, *Essai*, p. 52. French original in Watelet, *Essai*, p. 107: "La précision du trait, la propreté des détails seront les recherches de l'Architecture; une certaine indécision pleine d'agrémens, cette negligence qui sied si bien à la Nature seront les finesses de l'Art des jardins."

25 Morel, *Théorie*, p. 6: "Entraîné par l'habitude de symmetriser les formes, de calculer les espaces, il voulut assujetir la Nature à ses méthodiques combinaisons & crut l'embellir; mais il la défigura."

26 The fact that similar transitions in aesthetic perception also affected architectural theory at the time, and that the architect and landscape designer were in reality often the very same person, did not in any way soften this oppositional rhetoric. For example Nicholas Le Camus de Mézières even dedicated *Le Génie de l'Architecture* to Claude Henri Watelet. For more on Nicholas Le Camus de Mézières, *Le Génie de l'Architecture*, Paris, 1780, see Louise Pelletier's chapter in this volume.

27 Morel, *Théorie*, p. 102. "Ici l'oeil & le sentiment, seuls juges des effets, en decident souverainement."

28 Nevertheless Morel complained that in spite of the uselessness of drawings and plans landowners would absolutely demand them. New and innovative modes of drawing topographical plans were also invented. Among the most interesting examples of these are the Swede Fredrik Magnus Piper's plans—for example of the Haga Park and the Drottningholm Park in Stockholm. They include delicate shading of hills and slopes, marked sightlines, and facade drawings of important buildings situated in their immediate surroundings. See further Piper, Fredrik Magnus, *Description of the Idea and General—Plan for an English Park Written during the years 1811 and 1812* by Fredrik Magnus Piper, Rebecka Millhagen, Magnus Olausson, John Harris eds., Stockholm: Byggförlaget in collaboration with the Royal Swedish Academy of Fine Arts, 2004.

29 Watelet, *Essay*, pp. 51–52. English translation slightly modified by the author ('decorateur' in the French original has been translated to 'developer of gardens' in the English publication. Instead 'decorator' is used in this version). French original in Watelet, *Essai*, p. 107. "D'aprés des intentions si différentes; les plans simples, les formes symmetrique, les proportions faciles a saisir, les masses régulieres seront préferées par l'Architecte; tandis que les plans mistérieux, les formes dissemblables, les effets plus apercus que leurs principes, les accidens qui combattent la regularité offriront les moyens les plus favourables au décorateur."

30 Watelet, *Essai*, pp. 107–108.

31 While the contrast set up by Watelet clearly repeats the simplistic caricatures of the insensitive architect mentioned above, the distinction made between a designer figure that imagines the possibility of original invention and acts on it, and one that essentially does not, is a significant one.

32 Whately clarifies this in relation to a discussion on the appropriateness of the 'interference of art' in the landscape garden, art then meaning either regularity (which poses a problem) or 'no more than merely' design (which is not a problem). Whately, *Observations*, p. 137.

33 Burke, Edmund, *A Philosophical Enquiry into the origins of our ideas of the Sublime and Beautiful*, Adam Phillips ed., Oxford: Oxford University Press, 1998, Part III, section 14. (Originally published in 1757).

34 Burke, *Philosophical Enquiry*, Part IV, section 23.

35 Heely, Joseph, *Letters on the Beauties of Hagley, Envil, and the Leasowes*, 2 vols. (London 1777), I, pp. 46–47.

36 Heely, *Letters*, vol. I, p. 46.

37 Delille, Jacques, *Les Jardins:—Ou l'Art d'Embellir les Paysages*, Paris and Rheims: 1783.

38 Delille, *Les Jardins*, Chant I, pp. 24-25: "Du haut de ces coteaux, de ces monts d'où la vue,/D'un vaste paysage embrasse l'étendue,/La Nature au Génie a dit: 'Écoute moi./Tu vois tous ces trésors, ces trésors sont à toi./Dans leur pompe sauvage et leur brute richesse,/Mes travaux imparfait implorent ton adresse.'/ Elle dit. Il s'élance; il va de tous côtés/Fouiller dans cette masses où dorment cent beautés/Des vallons aux côteaux, des bois à la prairie,/Il retouche en passant le tableau qui varie;/Il fait, au gré des yeux, réunir, détacher,/Éclairer, rembrunir, découvrir ou cacher./Il ne compose pas, il corrige, il épure,/Il acheve les traits qu'ébauche la nature./Le front des noirs rochers a perdu sa terreur;/La forêt égayée adoucit son horreur;/Un ruisseau s'égarait, il dirige sa course,/il s'empare d'un lac s'enrichit d'une source./Il veut, et des sentier courent de toutes parts,/Chercher, saisir, lier, tous ces membres épars,/Qui, surpris, enchantés du noeud qui les rassemble,/Forment de cent détails un magnifique ensemble."

39 Pope, "Epistle IV", lines 57–58, 63–64, pp. 138–139.

40 With the Romantic genius in literature the traditional significance of the term 'genius' as denoting an artist of exceptional skill and sensitivity faded (or, one might argue, was dramatically radicalised). The term became now explicitly connected to what had previously been referred to as divine frenzy or madness (*furore divina*)—that is exceptional divine inspiration, and thus effected a release of authorial control. It depended, however, still on the poet to serve as a 'vessel' or 'channel' for an external force.

41 Darby Lewes, *Nudes from nowhere: Sexual Utopian Landscapes*, Oxford: Rowman and Littlefield Publishers, 2000, pp. 43–65.

42 Heely, *Letters,* vol. II, pp. 85–86.

43 In her article "Transplantation of the Picturesque: Emma Hamilton, English landscape, and redeeming the picturesque" in *Gender and Landscape—Renegotiating morality and space*, L Dowler, et al eds., London: Routledge, 2005, pp. 55–74, Shin-ichi Anzay gives the account of Emma Hamilton, mistress and later wife of Sir William Hamilton. Her husband and herself, residing in Naples, developed a type of picturesque performance where she posed publicly in what they called different "attitudes" imitating famous paintings, sometimes sitting in a box to represent the frame. She would then be portrayed by artists/tourists passing by. In caricatures of the time the act of drawing her is frequently perverted into an imagined sexual act.

44 Bohl, Elizabeth A, *Women Travel Writers and the Language of Aesthetics 1716–1818*, Cambridge: University of Cambridge Press, 1995.

45 Bohl, *Women Travel Writers*, p. 5.

46 For reference, a number of important critical studies of landscape and ideology should be mentioned here in addition to the above cited works by Darby Lewes and Elizabeth A Bohl: Bermingham, Ann, *Landscape and Ideology*, Berkeley: University of California Press, 1986; Labbe, Jacqueline M, *Romantic Visualities—Landscape, Gender and Romanticism*, New York: MacMillan Press, 1998; Barrell, John, *The Dark Side of Landscape*, Cambridge, University of Cambridge Press, 1980; Mitchell, WJT ed., *The Power of Landscape*, Chicago: University of Chicago Press, 1994; Pugh, Simon, *Garden, Nature, Art*, Manchester: Manchester University Press, 1988.

47 Kittler, Friedrich, *Discourse Networks, 1800/1900*, Stanford: Stanford University Press, 1990.

48 Kittler, *Discourse*, pp. 27–39.

49 Herder quoted in Kittler, *Discourse*, p. 73. From Herder "Uber die Wirkung der Dichtkunst auf die Sitten der Völker in alten und neuen Zeiten" Sämtliche Werke, in Bernard Suphan ed., Berlin: 1877–1913, VIII, p. 339.

50 Morel, *Théorie*, pp. 89–90. "Celui, au contraire,/.../sans cesse aux pieds de la Nature, la contemple, l'interroge, l'examine avec curiosité, il la suit pas-à-pas, & n'est content de lui-même que lorsqu'il a saisi la pureté de ses contours, qu'il la copié les formes avec la plus scrupuleuse exactitude, & rendu ses effets dans toute leur verité."

51 Kittler, *Discourse*, pp. 53–69, pp. 127–131.

52 Lower forms such as letter-writing, diaries or travel accounts were considered more appropriate genres for the female writer. Kittler, *Discourse*, p. 127.

53 In my articles "Experience as Imagined" and "Re-writing Landscape" I develop this argument in detail drawing on detailed readings on particularly Thomas Whately's and Joseph Heely's techniques of landscape description. Grillner, Katja, "Experience as imagined—Writing the Landscape garden", presented at the conference *Experiencing the Garden in the 18th Century*, March 2004. Published in *Experiencing the Garden in the 18th Century*, ML Calder ed., Bern: Peter Lang Publishers, 2006; and "Re-writing Landscape—Description as Theory in the 18th Century Landscape Garden" in *Nordic Journal of Architectural Research*, no. 4, 2003. In "Re-Reading the Eighteenth-Century English Landscape Garden" Stephen Bending emphasises the importance of the text, the guidebook and the description, as a coercive force to render designed landscapes a shared public meaning. Bending, Stephen, "Re-Reading the Eighteenth-Century English Landscape Garden" in *Huntington Library Quarterly*, vol. 55, 1992, pp. 379–399. Peter de Bolla's book *The Education of the Eye*, studies in particular the demand for 'educating' the eye in the 'regime of the eye' which he argues is replacing the 'regime of the picture' from the 1760s. de Bolla, Peter, *The Education of the Eye—Painting, Landscape and Architecture in Eighteenth Century Britain*, Stanford: Stanford University Press, 2003.

54 Whately, *Observations*, ch. 48.

55 Whately, *Observations*, ch. 49, p. 151.

56 Whately, *Observations*, ch. 50, p. 153.

57 Whately, *Observations*, ch. 50, p. 156.

58 Kittler, *Discourse*, p. 3.

59 The writers and publications I refer to are those listed above in note 3. For a more detailed discussion on the 'writing of landscape' see my articles 'Experience as Imagined', and 'Re-Writing Landscape' cited above.

60 I am referring here first to critical regionalism as the position advanced by Kenneth Frampton in the 1980s; secondly to developments from the 1990s in urban design with leading protagonists such as Rem Koolhaas and his OMA office, but also lately Kenneth Frampton again. In his lectures "Mega-form as Urban Landscape" (The 1999 Wallenberg lecture, Ann Arbour: The University of Michigan, 1999) and 'The Catalytic City: Between Strategy and Intervention' (unpublished MS) Frampton suggests that the current predicament of urbanisation calls for interventions that reach beyond the scale of the architectural project. By returning to the notion of megaform and to projects such as Atelier 5's low-rise high-density housing Frampton points the contemporary architect and planner toward strategies of catalytic intervention—hoping to inject urban sprawl with civic form "capable not only of sustaining a sense of place but also of serving as an effective catalyst for the further development of the region" (Frampton, "Megaform", p. 15). Thirdly I am referring to Christian Norberg-Schulz furthering in the 1970s the notion of genius loci which became very influential, in particular in Scandinavia. Fourthly, to landscape critics and architects such as James Corner, Sébastien Marot, Christophe Girot and Georges Descombes.

61 One could argue that Kenneth Frampton expresses these conflicting positions within his own body of work, if one compares his earlier critical regionalist

position with his more recent call for a reconsideration of megaforms (see footnote above).

62 Whately, *Observations*, p. 170.

63 Whately, *Observations*, p. 171.

64 Pope, "Epistle IV", see note 1.

65 Norberg-Schulz, Christian, *Genius Loci—Towards a Phenomenology of Architecture*, London: Academy Editions, 1980, p. 40.

66 The construction of the English landscape garden as a 'landscape of liberty' was pursued as part of Whig politics. Its most efficient document is perhaps Horace Walpole's *History of the Modern Taste in Gardening* (1771/1780) which constructs a wholly chauvinistic account of the progressive development of the English garden, representative of the liberal system of government. See further Leslie, Michael, "History and Historiography in the English Landscape Garden" in *Perspectives on Garden History*, Michel Conan, ed., Washington DC: Dumbarton Oaks, 1999, pp. 91–106; and Bending, Stephen "Horace Walpole and Eighteenth Century Garden History" in *Journal of the Courtauld and Warburg Institutes*, vol. 57, 1994, pp. 209–226.

Interior/Image: Authorship and the Spatialities of Domestic Life

Charles Rice

1 "interior", "interior decoration", in The Oxford English Dictionary, 2nd edn., Oxford: Clarendon Press, 1989.

2 The concept of interior decoration gave rise to a profession that, by the late nineteenth century, had emerged in its own right and largely seized control of the interior's treatment. See Peter Thornton, *Authentic Décor: the Domestic Interior, 1620–1920*, New York: Viking, 1984, pp. 10–12. For the impact of the interior's emergence in the context of literary description, see Charlotte Grant, "Reading the House of Fiction: From Object to Interior, 1720–1920", *Home Cultures*, vol. 2, no. 3, 2005, pp. 233–49.

3 See, for example, Charles Baudelaire, "The Twofold Room" (1862), in *The Poems in Prose*, with La Fanfarlo, Francis Scarfe ed. and trans., London: Anvil Press, 1989, pp. 36–39; and Xavier de Maistre, "A Journey Around My Room" (1794), and "A Nocturnal Expedition Around My Room" (1825), in *A Journey Around My Room*, Andrew Brown trans., London: Hesperus, 2004.

4 Vidler, Anthony, *The Architectural Uncanny: Essays in the Modern Unhomely*, Cambridge, MA: MIT Press, 1992.

5 Evans, Robin, "The Developed Surface: An Enquiry into the Brief Life of an Eighteenth-Century Drawing Technique", in *Translations from Drawing to Building and Other Essays*, London: Architectural Association, 1997, pp. 200–203.

6 Evans, "The Developed Surface", pp. 210–214, 222. In terms of the occupation of such rooms, Evans suggests that "The peripheral ring of chairs in particular was a long-established formation. In Daniel Marot's well-known designs for the furnishing of a palace, published in the 1690s, a ring of chairs is to be found in nearly every room. With Chippendale, Hepplewhite and Adam furniture, the seventeenth century bulk is quite gone, allowing de facto freedom to escape this arcane arrangement, but the magnet of convention is still strong. When the room is empty, the furniture reverts to the wall. During the last three decades of the eighteenth century, a brief equilibrium was achieved between house planning, the method of representing interiors, and the distribution of furniture" (p. 214).

7 The adequacy of representation was not necessarily measured in an architectural sense. In Evans' argument, adequacy relates primarily to the interior being able to be represented as an entire spatial ensemble. As Evans suggests, "Insufficient by itself, incapable (because of the extremity of its flatness) of incorporation with perspective, the developed surface was now a positive hindrance to comprehension." Evans, "The Developed Surface", p. 222.

8 Evans, "The Developed Surface", p. 219. Emphasis in original.

9 Gere, Charlotte, *Nineteenth Century Interiors: An Album of Watercolours*, London: Thames and Hudson, 1992.

10 Evans, Robin, "Rookeries and Model Dwellings", in *Translations from Drawing to Building*, p. 112.

11 Kerr, Robert, *The Gentleman's House, or How to Plan English Residences from the Parsonage to the Palace; with Tables of Accommodation and Cost, and a Series of Selected Plans*, 3rd revised ed., London: John Murray, 1871 [1864].

12 Evans, Robin, "Rookeries and Model Dwellings", p. 101.

13 Donzelot, Jacques, *The Policing of Families*, Robert Hurley trans., Baltimore: Johns Hopkins University Press, p. xxiv.

14 Foucault, Michel, *The History of Sexuality Volume 1: An Introduction*, Robert

Hurley trans., London: Allen Lane, 1978, pp. 120–131.

15 Foucault, *The History of Sexuality*, p. 47.

Foucault, *The History of Sexuality*, p. 46.

16 Freud, Sigmund "The Interpretation of Dreams", in *The Standard Edition of the Complete Psychological Works of Sigmund Freud*, James Strachey ed. and trans., 24 vols., London: The Hogarth Press, 1953–1974, vol. 5, p. 346.

17 Freud, "The Interpretation of Dreams", p. 214, n. 2.

Freud, "The Interpretation of Dreams", p. 354.

18 Freud, "Introductory Lectures on Psychoanalysis. Lecture XIX: Resistance and Repression", in *The Standard Edition*, vol. 16, pp. 295–296.

19 Freud, "Fragment of an Analysis of a Case of Hysteria", in *The Standard Edition*, vol. 11.

20 Benjamin, Walter, "Paris, Capital of the Nineteenth Century (exposé of 1939)", in *The Arcades Project*, Howard Eiland and Kevin McLaughlan trans., Cambridge, MA: The Belknap Press of Harvard University Press, 1999, pp. 19–20.

21 See the discussion of Freud's consulting rooms in Diana Fuss, "Freud's Ear", in *The Sense of an Interior: Four Writers and the Rooms that Shaped Them*, London: Routledge, 2004, pp. 71–105.

22 Benjamin, "Paris, Capital of the Nineteenth Century", p. 20.

23 Loos, Adolf, "The Poor Little Rich Man", in *Spoken Into the Void: Collected Essays. 1897–1900*, Jane O Newman and John H Smith trans., Cambridge, MA: MIT Press, 1982, p. 125.

24 Van Duzer, Leslie, and Kent Kleinman, "The Subjects of the Raumplan", in *Villa Muller: A Work of Adolf Loos*, New York: Princeton Architectural Press, 1994, pp. 38–43.

25 Kerr, *The Gentleman's House*, p. 61.

26 Loos, Adolf, "Architecture", in *On Architecture*, Michael Mitchell trans., Riverside, CA: Ariadne Press, 2002, pp. 73–85.

27 One should also recognise that spatial manipulation is not simply a Modernist novelty, nor does it happen because the question of decoration is refused. For example, Victor Horta's Maison Horta exhibits spatial effects resonant with the Raumplan even as it is caught within an Art Nouveau moment. Loos' early manipulations of domestic spaces borrow heavily on contemporary developments in English domestic architecture, and his materially rich internal surfaces, along with Le Corbusier's polychromy, certainly play in the spatial effects they developed. On the idea of surface effects, and in relation to Loos in particular, see Andrew Benjamin, "Surface Effects: Borromini, Semper, Loos", *The Journal of Architecture*, vol. 11, no. 1, 2006, pp. 1–36.

28 Banham, Reyner, "Design by Choice", in *A Critic Writes. Essays by Reyner Banham*, Berkeley: University of California Press, 1996, p. 77. In light of the preceding discussion, it is important to understand the rise of a consumer culture in relation to domestic goods through the turn-of-the-century debates in the Germanic world around the reform of design, and especially the establishment of the German Werkbund. See Fredric Schwartz, *The Werkbund: Design Theory and Mass Culture before the First World War*, New Haven: Yale University Press, 1996. Loos' critique of the Werkbund turns on the issue of the role architects and architecture should have in the design and provision of industrially produced domestic goods. See especially Adolf Loos, "Surplus to Requirements", in *Ornament and Crime: Selected Essays*, Michael Mitchell trans., Riverside, CA: Ariadne Press, 1998, pp. 154–156.

29 Lavin, Sylvia, *Form Follows Libido: Architecture and Richard Neutra in a Psychoanalytic Culture*, Cambridge, MA: MIT Press, 2004.

30 Deleuze, Gilles, "Postscript on the Societies of Control", in *Rethinking Architecture: A Reader in Cultural Theory*, Neil Leach ed., London: Routledge, 1997, p. 312.

31 Lavin, *Form Follows Libido*, pp. 3–9.

32 Riley, Terence, *The Un-Private House*, New York: Museum of Modern Art, 1999.

33 Virilio, Paul, "The Last Vehicle", in *Looking Back on the End of the World*, Dietmar Kamper and Christoph Wulf, eds., New York: Semiotext(e), 1989, p. 114.

Sweet Garden of Vanished Pleasures: Derek Jarman at Dungeness

Jonathan Hill

1 The name derives from the nearby Denge Marsh and the Old Norse term 'nes', meaning headland.

2 Left behind when a railway company closed the station built to transport shingle excavated from the headland.

3 A few miles north-east of Dungeness, on a Ministry of Defence site at Denge,

three concrete "acoustic mirrors", each a parabolic reflector, face out to sea. One is a 60 metre-long curved wall; the others are curved dishes, respectively nine and six metres in diameter. Built between 1928 and 1930 as an experimental early warning system to detect incoming aircraft at sea they were ineffective and made obsolete by the invention of radar in 1932.

4 The best way to approach Dungeness is a 13 mile journey at 25mph. Following the coast, through woodland and marsh, past caravan parks and back gardens, the Romney, Hythe and Dymchurch Railway was founded in 1927.

5 Run by the Royal Society for the Protection of Birds (RSPB).

6 Jarman, Derek, *Derek Jarman's Garden*, London: Thames and Hudson, 1995, p. 15.

7 Jarman, quoted in Keith Collins, "Preface", *Derek Jarman's Garden*, p. 5.

8 Jarman, *Derek Jarman's Garden*, p. 65.

9 Jarman, *Derek Jarman's Garden*, p. 65.

10 Jarman, Derek, *Modern Nature: The Journals of Derek Jarman*, London: Century, 1991, p. 71 (Saturday 29 April 1989).

11 Jarman later extended the cottage.

12 Jarman, *Derek Jarman's Garden*, p. 66.

13 Jarman, *Derek Jarman's Garden*, p. 66.

14 Jarman, *Modern Nature*, p. 276 (Friday April 1990).

15 Jarman, *Derek Jarman's Garden*, p. 11.

16 Jarman, *Modern Nature*, p. 10.

17 Jarman, *Derek Jarman's Garden*, p. 12.

18 Jarman, *Modern Nature*, p. 3.

19 Jarman excavated shingle to create a planting hole, filled it with manure from a nearby farm and restored the shingle surface around the plant.

20 Lloyd created the nearby garden at Great Dixter, East Sussex, which Jarman admired.

21 Lloyd, Christopher, "The Jarman Garden Experience", in *Derek Jarman: A Portrait. Artist, Film-maker, Designer*, Roger Wollen ed., London: Thames and Hudson, 1996, p. 152.

22 Jarman refers to William Blake (1757–1827). Jarman, *Modern Nature*, p. 25 (Tuesday 28 February 1989).

23 Jarman, Derek, *Kicking the Pricks*, London: Vantage, 1996, p. 136. First published in 1987 as *The Last of England*.

24 The genius loci is a concept with classical origins important to the picturesque and Romanticism.

25 Locke, John, *Essay concerning Human Understanding*, Peter H Nidditch ed., Oxford: Clarendon Press, 1975.

26 Hume, David, "Of the Standard of Taste", in *Selected Essays*, pp. 133–154, Oxford: Oxford University Press, 1993, pp. 136–137.

27 Liberty, however, was limited to the learned and prosperous.

28 Thomas Whately distinguishes between the emblematic gardens of the early eighteenth century picturesque, which require careful analysis and understanding, and the expressive gardens of the late eighteenth century picturesque, which emphasise immediate and intuitive experience, and he favours. Whately, Thomas, "From Observations on Modern Gardening'", in *The Genius of the Place: The English Landscape Garden 1620-1820*, John Dixon Hunt and Peter Willis eds., London: Elek, 1975, p. 38. First published in 1770.

29 Pevsner, Nikolaus, "The Genius of the Place", in *Pevsner on Art and Architecture: The Radio Talks*, Stephen Games ed., London: Methuen, 2002, p. 232.

30 Pevsner, Nikolaus, *The Englishness of English Art: An Expanded and Annotated Version of the Reith Lectures Broadcast in October and November 1955*, London: Architectural Press, 1956.

31 In 1960 Jarman enrolled for a BA in English, History and History of Art. In the face of fierce criticism Pevsner promoted the picturesque as a means to cast Modernist architecture in an English light, an idea that is less relevant to Jarman although he comments positively on some twentieth century buildings and went on walking tours with Pevsner. Pevsner, Nikolaus, "Twentieth-Century Picturesque: An Answer to Basil Taylor's Broadcast", *Architectural Review*, vol. 115, no. 688, April 1954, pp. 228–229. Jarman, *Modern Nature*, pp. 193–195.

32 Jarman, *Kicking the Pricks*, pp. 136–138.

33 Jarman, Derek, dir., *The Last of England*, Anglo International Films for British Screen, Channel 4 and ZDF, 1987.

34 Jarman, Derek, *Know What I Mean*, an interview preceding *A Night with Derek*, Channel 4 Television, 16 July 1994.

35 Jarman, *Kicking the Pricks*, p. 245.

36 Hunt, John Dixon, *Gardens and the Picturesque: Studies in the History of Landscape Architecture*, Cambridge, MA, and London: MIT Press, 1992, p. 237.

37 Peake, Tony, *Derek Jarman*, London: Little, Brown and Company, 1999, p. 25.

38 For example, *Far From the Madding Crowd*, 1874, and *Tess of the d'Uirbervilles*, 1891. The town depicted in *The Mayor of Casterbridge*, 1886, is

39 Jarman, Derek, dir., *The Angelic Conversation*, BFI, 1985.

40 Jarman, Derek, "The Papers of Derek Jarman", quoted in Peake, *Derek Jarman*, p. 39.

41 Jarman started a Diploma in Fine Art at the Slade in 1963, with painting and drawing as his major subject and stage design as his subsidiary subject.

42 Jarman, *Kicking the Pricks*, p. 41.

43 Coleridge composed *The Rime of the Ancient Mariner*, 1797, and *Kubla Khan*, 1798. Together Coleridge and William Wordsworth produced the *Lyrical Ballads*, 1798. Dorothy Wordsworth wrote the Alfoxden Journal, 1797–1798, which was not intended for publication.

44 Jarman, *Modern Nature*, p. 68.

45 Hinkley Point A is a Magnox reactor built between 1957–1965; Hinkley Point B is an Advanced gas-cooled reactor, built between 1967–1975.

46 Jarman, *Derek Jarman's Garden*, p. 41; Jarman, *Modern Nature*, p. 15.

47 Jarman, *Kicking the Pricks*, pp. 239–240.

48 Jarman, *Derek Jarman's Garden*, p. 66.

49 From Burke developed the principle that the arts should attempt to replicate not natural forms but sensations of the sublime found in the experience of nature.

50 Burke, Edmund, *Philosophical Enquiry into the Origin of our Ideas of the Sublime and Beautiful*, Oxford: Oxford University Press, 1998, p. 36.

51 Price refers to the late eighteenth century picturesque, which was more expressive and less allegorical than the early eighteenth century picturesque. Price, Uvedale, "From An Essay on the Picturesque", in John Dixon Hunt and Peter Willis eds., *The Genius of the Place: The English Landscape Garden 1620–1820*, London: Elek, 1975, p. 354.

52 Peake, *Derek Jarman*, p. 366.

53 Jarman, Derek, *At Your Own Risk: A Saint's Testament*, London: Vintage, 1993, p. 4.

54 Jarman, *Derek Jarman's Garden*, p. 12.

55 Jarman, *Kicking the Pricks*, p. 151.

56 Jarman, *Modern Nature*, p. 30 (Tuesday 7 March 1989).

57 As quoted in Jarman, *Derek Jarman's Garden*, p. 117.

58 Ruskin reserved praise for ageing due to the effects of use and weather rather than the appearance of ageing, as in the newly fabricated picturesque ruin, and regretted the effects of industrialisation. Rather than acknowledging the passage of time, conservation policy may lead to the denial of change. In 1877, delighting in the effects of time on buildings and influenced by Ruskin, William Morris founded the Society for the Protection of Ancient Buildings on the premise that, instead of returning a building to its original state, each layer of history should be retained. Ruskin, John, *The Seven Lamps of Architecture*, New York: Farrar, Straus and Giroux, 1984, ch. VI, X, p. 177. First published in 1849.

59 Jarman, *Derek Jarman's Garden*, p. 130.

60 Jarman, "The Papers of Derek Jarman", quoted in Peake, *Derek Jarman*, pp. 405, 407.

61 Jarman, *Modern Nature*, p. 310 (Wednesday 1 August 1990).

62 Jarman died on 19 February 1994, bequeathing Prospect Cottage to his partner, Keith Collins.

63 Peake, *Derek Jarman*, p. 2.

64 Jarman, *Derek Jarman's Garden*, p. 81. Extract from an untitled poem.

65 Birksted, Jan, "The Prospect at Dungeness: Derek Jarman's Garden", in Jan Birksted ed., *Relating Architecture to Landscape*, London and New York: E and FN Spon, 1999, p. 256.

66 In the eighteenth century, picturesque gardens proliferated in conjunction with parliamentary land enclosures, which transformed open land into regular fields defined by hedges and walls, creating larger estates.

67 Jarman, "Interview with Derek Jarman", in Chris Lippard, ed., *By Angels Driven: The Films of Derek Jarman*, Trowbridge: Flicks Books, 1996. p. 167.

68 Jarman, *Kicking the Pricks*, p. 54.

69 Jarman, *Kicking the Pricks*, p. 54.

70 Jarman, Derek, dir., *The Garden*, Basilisk in association with Channel 4, British Screen, ZDF and Uplink, 1990.

71 O' Pray, Michael, *Derek Jarman: Dreams of England*, London: British Film Institute, 1996, p. 179.

72 O' Pray, *Derek Jarman: Dreams of England*, p. 178.

73 O' Pray, *Derek Jarman: Dreams of England*, p. 38.

74 *The Garden* is "an AIDS-related film but AIDS was too vast a subject to 'film' ". Jarman, *Derek Jarman's Garden*, p. 91.

75 Jarman, *Modern Nature*, p. 296 (Saturday 23 June 1990).

76 The most noted example is the primitive hut—a frame of timber branches finished in mud—described by the Roman architect Vitruvius. Vitruvius, *The Ten Books on Architecture*, Morris Hicky Morgan trans., New York: Dover, 1960, pp. 38–39. First published as *De Architectura* in the first century BC

77 Fletcher, Banister, *A History of Architecture on the Comparative Method*,

London: BT Batsford, 1924, 7th edition, p. 1.
78 Freud quotes from a dictionary, Daniel Sanders, *Wörtenbuch der Deutschen Sprache*, 1860, Freud, Sigmund, ''The 'Uncanny' '', Alix Strachey trans., *The Standard Edition of the Complete Psychological Works of Sigmund Freud*, vol. 17, James Strachey ed., Toronto: Clarke Irwin, 1955, p. 223.
79 The uncanny is a perception, not a property of a space.
80 Jarman, *Derek Jarman's Garden*, pp. 68–69.

Translation

Genius, Fiction and the Author in Architecture

Louise Pelletier

1 Blondel, Jacques-François, *Cours d'architecture*, 9 vols., Piere Patte ed., Paris, 1771–1779, vol. IV, pp. xl–lii.
2 Diderot, *Encyclopédie; ou, Dictionnaire raisonné des sciences, des arts et des metiers*, Paris: Briasson, 1751–1780, vol. 7, p. 582.
3 Diderot, *Encyclopédie*, vol. 7, p. 582.
4 Diderot, *Encyclopédie*, vol. 7, p. 582.
5 This is a complex issue that I develop in more details in chapter one of my book entitled *Architecture in Words*, London: Routledge, 2006.
6 Denis Diderot, *Oeuvres esthétiques*, Pierre Vernière ed., Paris: Garnier Frères, 1968, p. 533.
7 For a more detailed comparison between Le Camus de Mézières's treatise and Bastide's *La petite maison*, see Pelletier, *Architecture in Words*, chapter 9.
8 Nicolas Le Camus de Mézières, *Le génie de l'architecture: ou, L'analogie de cet art avec nos sensations* [Paris: B. Morin, 1780], Geneva: Minkoff Reprint, 1972, pp. 44–45; translated by El-Khoury in his introduction to Jean-François de Bastide, *The Little House: An Architectural Seduction*, New York: Princeton Architectural Press, 1995, p. 31.
9 Bastide, *The Little House*, p. 75.
10 Nicolas Le Camus de Mézières, *The Genius of Architecture; or, the Analogy of That Art With Our Sensations*, David Britt trans., Santa Monica, CA: The Getty Center, 1992, p. 128.
11 Le Camus de Mézières, *The Genius of Architecture*, pp. 116–118.
12 Le Camus de Mézières, *The Genius of Architecture*, p. 176.
13 Boullée's epigraph at the beginning of his *Architecture, Essai sur l'art* reads: ''Ed io anche son pittore''.
14 Le Camus de Mézières, *The Genius of Architecture*, p. 175.
15 Le Camus de Mézières, *The Genius of Architecture*, pp. 93–94.
16 Quoted by Joan Gadol, *Leon Battista Alberti: Universal Man of the Early Renaissance*, Chicago and London: The University of Chicago Press, 1969, pp. 111–112.

Cultures of Display: Exhibiting Architecture in Berlin, 1880–1931

Wallis Miller

1 Joachimides, Alexis, ''Die Schule des Geschmacks. Das Kaiser-Friedrich-Museum als Reformprojekt'', *Museumsinszenierungen. Zur Geschichte der Institution des Kunstmuseums. Die Berliner Museumslandschaft 1830–1990*, Joachimides, Alexis, Sven Kuhrau, Viola Vahrson, and Nikolaus Bernau eds., Dresden and Basel: Verlag der Kunst, 1995, p. 145.
2 Architekten-Verein zu Berlin, ''Preis-Aufgabe zum Schinkel-Fest 1905. Auf dem Gebiete der Architektur. Entwurf zu einem Museum für Architektur und Architekturplastik in Berlin'', Berlin, 1903, p. 1 (Technische Universität Berlin, Universitätsbibliothek, Plansammlung).
3 Architekten-Verein zu Berlin, ''Bericht des Beurteilungs-Ausschusses für die zum Schinkelfest 1905 eingegangenen Wettbewerbentwürfe auf dem Gebiete der Architektur'', Berlin, n.d. [1904?], p. 30. (Technische Universität Berlin, Universitätsbibliothek, Plansammlung).
4 F, ''Von der Jubiläums-Ausstellung der Kgl. Akademie der Künste zu Berlin'', *Deutsche Bauzeitung*, vol. 20, no. 41, 22 May 1886, pp. 244–246.
5 For examples of the Academy Catalogues, please see the reprints in *Die Katalog der Berliner Akademie Ausstellungen 1786–1850* (3 vols.), Helmut Börsch-Supan ed., Berlin: Hessling, 1971.
6 For example, see Schliepmann, Hans, ''Die Architektur auf der diesjährigen Grossen Berliner Kunstausstellung'', *Berliner Architekturwelt*, no. 4, 1902, pp. 114–123.
7 Bauausstellungen, Johannes Cramer and Niels Gutschow eds., Stuttgart: Kohlhammer, 1984, p. 12.
8 Schmarsow, August ''The Essence of Architectural Creation'' (1893), *Empathy, Form, and Space. Problems in German Aesthetics, 1873–1893*, Harry Francis Mallgrave and Eleftherios Ikonomou trans., Santa Monica, CA: Getty Center for the History of Art and the Humanities, 1994, p. 286. Originally published as *Das Wesen der architektonischen Schöpfung*, Leipzig: Karl W Hirsemann, 1894. Inaugural lecture given at the University of Leipzig on 8 November 1893.
9 Mallgrave, Harry Francis and Eleftherios Ikonomou, introduction to *Empathy, Form, and Space. Problems in German Aesthetics, 1873–1893*, p. 59.
10 Schwarzer, Mitchell W, ''The Emergence of Architectural Space: August Schmarsow's Theory of Raumgestaltung'', *Assemblage*, no. 15 (August 1991), pp. 50–53 and Mallgrave and Ikonomou, introduction, p. 64.
11 Schwarzer, ''The Emergence of Architectural Space'', p. 54.
12 Architekten-Verein zu Berlin, ''Preis-Aufgabe zum Schinkel-Fest 1905'', p. 2. For a history of the Crystal Palace and the Fine Arts Courts, see Piggott, JR, *Palace of the People. The Crystal Palace at Sydenham 1854-1936*, Madison: The University of Wisconsin Press, 2004, pp. 67–121.
13 von Bode, Wilhelm, ''Das Kaiser Friedrich-Museum in Berlin. Zur Eröffnung am 18. Oktober 1904'', *Museumskunde*, vol. 1, 1905, pp. 12–13. For a thorough discussion of von Bode and the confrontations over display strategies see, for example, Joachimides, ''Die Schule des Geschmacks. Das Kaiser-Friedrich-Museum als Reformprojekt'', pp. 142–156.
14 Schalles, Hans-Joachim, ''Rezeptionsgeschichtliche Nachlese zum Pergamonaltar'', in Wolfgang Schindler, *Modus in Rebus*, Berlin: Gebr Mann, 1995, p. 189.
15 Bernau, Nikolaus and Nadine Riedl, ''Für Kaiser und Reich. Die Antikenabteilung im Pergamonmuseum'', *Museumsinszenierungen*, p. 175. For an extensive discussion and documentation of the competitions see Waetzoldt, Stephan, *Pläne und Wettbewerbe für Bauten auf der Berliner Museumsinsel 1873–1896*, (*Jahrbuch der Berliner Museen*, vol. 35, supplement), Berlin: Gebr. Mann, 1993.
16 Bilsel, SM Can, 2003, *Architecture in the Museum: Displacement, Reconstruction and Reproduction of the Monuments of Antiquity in Berlin's Pergamon Museum*, vol. 1, PhD diss., Princeton University, p. 139.
17 Königliche Museen zu Berlin, *Führer durch das Pergamon-Museum*, Berlin: Georg Reimer, 1902, p. 5.
18 See Can Bilsel, *Architecture in the Museum*, p. 139. Along with the attention to the detail of the Altar in the museum, a sketch of its reconstruction depicted opposite the title page of the guidebook suggests that there was some ambivalence about how visible it should be.
19 Bilsel, *Architecture in the Museum*, p. 152.
20 Bernau and Riedl, ''Für Kaiser und Reich. Die Antikenabteilung im Pergamonmuseum'', p. 174.
21 Bilsel, *Architecture in the Museum*, pp. 157–160.
22 Bilsel, *Architecture in the Museum*, pp. 149–150.
23 Bilsel, *Architecture in the Museum*, p. 163.
24 Bilsel, *Architecture in the Museum*, pp. 215–217.
25 Rave, Paul Ortwin, *Das Schinkel-Museum und die Kunst-Sammlungen Beuths*, Berlin: Ernst Rathenau, 1931, p. 43.
26 Rave, *Das Schinkel Museum*, p. 36.
27 For a detailed study of *The Dwelling of Our Time* please see Miller, Wallis 1999, *Tangible Ideas: Architecture and the Public at the 1931 German Building Exhibition in Berlin*, PhD diss., Princeton University.
28 *Die Form*, vol. 6, no. 6, 15 June 1931 and vol. 6, no. 7, 15 July 1931.
29 ''Deutsche Bau-Ausstellung Berlin 1931'', *Bau-Rundschau*, vol. 21, no. 12, 25 June 1930, p. 261.
30 Ausstellungs-, Messe- und Fremdenverkehrs-Amt der Stadt Berlin, *Deutsche Bauausstellung Berlin 1931. Amtlicher Katalog und Führer*, Berlin: Bauwelt-Verlag/Ullsteinhaus, 1931, p. 175.
31 *Deutsche Bauausstellung Berlin 1931. Amtlicher Katalog und Führer*, pp. 160–177.
32 Tegethoff, Wolf, ''From Obscurity to Maturity: Mies van der Rohe's Breakthrough to Modernism'', *Mies van der Rohe: Critical Essays*, Franz Schulze, ed., New York: The Museum of Modern Art, 1989, p. 70; Pommer, Richard and Christian Otto, *Weissenhof 1927 and the Modern Movement in Architecture*, Chicago: University of Chicago Press, 1991, p. 33.
33 Miller, *Tangible Ideas*, pp. 109–111.
34 Miller, *Tangible Ideas*, pp. 91–94, 108.
35 Miller, *Tangible Ideas*, pp. 108–109, 116–117.
36 Mies van der Rohe, ''Zum Thema: Ausstellungen'', *Die Form*, vol. 5, no. 4 (1928), p. 121.

The Inhuman One: the Mythology of Architect as Réalisateur

Renée Tobe

1 *L'Inhumaine*, dir. L'Herbier, perf. Georgette Leblanc and Jaque Catelain, France, 1924.
2 Mac Orlan, Pierre, *L'Inhumaine*, Paris: Gallimard, 1925.
3 *Last Year in Marienbad*, dir. Resnais, perf. Delphine Seyrig, Giorgio Albertazzi, and Sacha Pitoeff, France, 1961.
4 Becherer, Richard, "Picturing Architecture Otherwise: the voguing of the Maison Mallet-Stevens," *Art History*, vol. 23, Issue 4, November 2000, pp. 559–598.
5 Becherer, "Picturing Architecture Otherwise".
6 Mallet-Stevens, Robert, "Le Cinéma et les arts, l'architecture," *Les Cahiers du Mois*, nos. 16 and 17, 1925, p. 96.
7 Colomina, Beatriz, *Privacy and Publicity, Architecture as Mass Media*, London: MIT Press, 1994, p. 47.
8 Pinchon, Jean-Francois, *Rob. Mallet-Stevens: Architecture, Furniture, Interior Design*, Cambridge: MIT Press, 1990, p. 95.
9 Colomina, *Privacy and Publicity*, p. 312.
10 Becherer, "Picturing Architecture Otherwise".
11 Colomina, *Privacy and Publicity*, p. 306.
12 Klein, Richard, *Robert Mallet-Stevens; La Villa Cavrois*, Paris: Editions A et J Picard, 2005.
13 Mallet-Stevens, Robert, *Dessins 1921 pour une cité moderne*, Paris: Gallerie Fanny Giullon-Laffaille, 1986.
14 Colomina, *Privacy and Publicity*, p. 297.
15 A film enthusiast, Noailles also financed Jean Cocteau's first film *Le Sang d'un poète*, 1946 and Buñuel's *L'Age d'or*, 1930.
16 *Les Mystères du château du Dé*, dir. Man Ray, France, 1928.
17 Vaillant, Odile, "Robert Mallet-Stevens—Architecture, Cinema and Poetics," *Melies, Mallet-Stevens and Multi-Media*, Francois Penz and Maureen Thomas, ed., London: BFI, 1998, p. 28–33.
18 Just as Leblanc suggested the use of Modernism for *L'Inhumaine*, Gloria Swanson suggested Nelson design sets reflecting Modernist sensibilities in her film *What a Widow*, 1930, directed by Alan Dwan. Albrecht, Donald, *Designing Dreams; modern architecture in the movies*, Santa Monica: Hennessey and Ingalls, 2000, p. xiv.
19 Mallet-Stevens, "Le Cinéma et l'architecture".
20 Wiser, William, *The Crazy Years; Paris in the Twenties*, Great Britain: Thames and Hudson, 1983, p. 145.
21 For example, the lounge of the Maison Mallet-Stevens built in Paris in 1927, was duplicated by Richard Day for a 1927 film, *The Kiss*, 1929 directed by Jacques Feyder, that includes the symmetrical bookshelves and Paul and Sonia Delauney painting. Becherer, "Picturing Architecture Otherwise".
22 Green, Christopher, *Léger and the Avant-Garde*, London: Yale University Press: 1976, p. 295.
23 Mallet-Stevens, Robert, *Le Décor moderne au cinema*, Paris: Charles Massin, 1928.
24 Turvey, Malcolm, "The Avante-Garde and the 'New Spirit'; the Case of *Ballet Mécanique*," *October*, vol. 102, Fall 2002, pp. 35–58.
25 Vaillant, Odile, "Robert Mallet-Stevens—Architecture, Cinema and Poetics".
26 Mallet-Stevens designed a home for Poiret, but when the couturier declared bankrupt, the Maison Poiret remained unfinished until purchased by an actor sometime later. The original plans were published in a special De Stijl edition of *L'Architecture Vivante*, Spring/Summer 1924. Albrecht, *Designing Dreams*, p. 45.
27 Gronberg, Tag, *Designs on Modernity; Exhibiting the City in 1920s Paris*, Manchester, Manchester University Press: 1998, p. 28.
28 Turvey, "The Avant-Garde and the 'New Spirit'", p. 41.
29 Alberto Cavalcanti also directed many films including *Went the Day Well*, 1942 and *Dead of Night*, 1945.
30 *La Roue*, dir. Abel Gance, France, 1922.
31 *Metropolis*, dir. Fritz Lang, Germany, 1927.
32 Deleuze, Gilles, *Cinema 1: The Movement-Image*, Hugh Tomlinson and Barbara Habberjam trans., London: The Athlone Press, 1992, p. 72.
33 Shanahan, Maureen, *Indeterminate and Inhuman: Georgette Leblanc in L'Inhumaine*, Institute for European Studies, 2003.
34 Shanahan, *Indeterminate and Inhuman*.
35 Shanahan, *Indeterminate and Inhuman*.
36 Mallet-Stevens' Villa Cavrois, for many years in abandoned disrepair until recently named a National Historic Monument, appeared in a 1980s *bande dessinée*. Three figures fly over the villa and land on its terrace in Yves Cheraqui

and Ted Benôit's *Histoire Vraies*, Paris: Les Humanoïdes Associés, 1982.
37 Mallet-Stevens, 'Le Cinéma et les Arts L'Architecture,' *Intelligence du Cinématographe*, Marcel L'Herbier, ed. Paris: Editions Correa, 1948.
38 Gadamer, Hans-Georg, *Truth and Method*, London: Ward and Sheed, 1993, pp. 60–64.
39 Cowie, Elizabeth, *Representing the Woman: Cinema and Psychoanalysis*, London: Macmillan Press Ltd, 1997, pp. 72–102.
40 The First World War firmly established the Machine Age with its optimism and looming threats as well. It also returned the focus to home and the family, the values that the soldiers were told they were fighting for, and Modernism in film began to lose its glamorous appeal. With the fears from the Second World War the bright whites of 1930s Modernism melted into the shadows of 1940s Film Noir.

The Allegorical Project: Architecture as 'Figurative Theory'

Penelope Haralambidou

1 Fletcher, Angus, *Allegory: The Theory of a Symbolic Mode*, Ithaka and New York: Cornell University, 1965, p. 2.
2 Frye, Northrop, *Anatomy of Criticism: Four Essays*, Harmondsworth: Penguin, 1990, p. 89.
3 For a discussion of Lyotard's notion of the figure see, Jay, Martin, *Downcast Eyes: The Denigration of Vision in Twentieth-Century French Thought*, Berkeley: University of California, 1994, pp. 563–573.
4 Fineman, Joel, "The Structure of Allegorical Desire", in Stephen J Greenblatt, ed., *Allegory and Representation: Selected Papers from the English Institute, 1979–80*, Baltimore and London: Johns Hopkins University, 1981, p. 47.
5 MacQueen, John, *Allegory*, in series ed., Jump, John D., *The Critical Idiom*, no. 14, London: Methuen, 1976.
6 Examples include a passage from *Phaedrus* where the soul is compared to a charioteer driving two steeds, the spiritual and the sensual element in man, and a series of allegories in different styles on the subject of love from the *Symposium*. See MacQueen, *Allegory*, p. 7.
7 Whitehead, Christiania, *Castles of the Mind: A Study of Medieval Architectural Allegory*, Cardiff: University of Wales, 2003.
8 MacQueen, *Allegory*, p. 54.
9 Cowan, Bainard, "Walter Benjamin's Theory of Allegory", *New German Critique*, no. 22, Special Issue on Modernism, (Winter, 1981), p. 110.
10 Cowan, "Walter Benjamin's Theory of Allegory", p. 110.
11 Mâle, Emile, *The Gothic Image: Religious Art in France of the Thirteenth Century*, trans. by Dora Nussey, London and Glasgow: Collins, 1961. Quoted in McQueen, *Allegory*, p. 40.
12 For an analysis of my allegorical project, *The Fall*, see, Haralambidou, Penelope, 'The Fall: The Allegorical Architectural Project as a Critical Method', in Jane Rendell, Jonathan Hill, Murray Fraser and Mark Dorrian, eds., *Critical Architecture*, London: Routledge, 2007
13 Fineman, "The Structure of Allegorical Desire", p. 26.
14 Rem Koolhaas, Ben Nicholson and Jonathan Hill have studied at the AA, while Michael Webb was connected by approximation through other Archigram members. For over 15 years Jonathan Hill has been running a successful diploma unit at the Bartlett, where Ben Nicholson is an external examiner and frequent lecturer alongside Michael Webb.
15 Koolhaas, Rem, *Delirious New York: A Retroactive Manifesto for Manhattan*, Rotterdam: 010, 1994, p. 293.
16 Webb, Michael, *Temple Island: A Study*, London: Architectural Association, 1987, drawing 02 0, n. pag.
17 Nicholson, Ben, *Appliance House*, Chicago and Cambridge: Chicago Institute for Architecture and Urbanism and MIT, 1990, p. 37.
18 Nicholson, *Appliance House*, p. 12.
19 Fletcher, *Allegory*, p. 23.
20 Hill, Jonathan, *Actions of Architecture: Architects and Creative Users*, London: Routledge, 2003, p. 130.
21 Nicholson, Ben, *The World: Who Wants It?*, London: Black Dog Publishing, 2004.
22 Homer's two poems reflect these two literary modes: *Iliad* is the narration of a battle and *Odyssey* recounts a series of adventures linked by a journey.
23 Hill, *Actions of Architecture*, p. 130.
24 Hill, *Actions of Architecture*, p. 131.
25 Webb, *Temple Island*, n. pag.

26 Owens, Craig, "The Allegorical Impulse: Toward a Theory of Postmodernism", *October*, nos. 12 and 13, 1980, p. 74.

27 Hill, *Actions of Architecture*, pp. 130–131.

28 Hill identifies in the "montage of gaps" an underlying structure governing the design of his book.

29 Nicholson, *Appliance House*, p. 12.

30 Fineman, "The Structure of Allegorical Desire", pp. 51–52.

31 Koolhaas, Rem, *Delirious New York: A Retroactive Manifesto for Manhattan*, New York: Oxford University Press, 1972, p. 247.

32 Although the claim on Kafka's novels as allegory is often contested, many critics discuss them in allegorical terms, including Fletcher and Bainard Cowan, who states that "if new chapters in the history of allegory are to be written, the inquiry ought to start with two German-language Jewish writers: Kafka, of whom Benjamin once commented that his work was like 'the rumor about the true things (a sort of theological whispered intelligence dealing with matters discredited and obsolete)'—and Benjamin himself". See Fletcher, *Allegory*, pp. 14–15, and Cowan, "Walter Benjamin's Theory of Allegory", p. 122.

33 Fletcher, *Allegory*, p. 174.

34 Owens, "The Allegorical Impulse", p. 70.

35 See http://www.renaissancesociety.org/site/Publications/Details.0.41.0.0.0.html (last visited 29 August 2006).

36 Nicholson, *Appliance House*, p. 23.

37 The original publication of *Delirious New York* by Oxford University Press includes images not featuring in the recent publication by 010. See image *Flagrant délit*, by Madelon Vriesendorp, in Koolhaas, *Delirious New York*, 1972, pp. 134–135.

38 Koolhaas, *Delirious New York*, 1972, p. 252.

39 Lyotard, Jean-François, *Discours, figure*, Paris: Klincksieck, 1985. For more on Lyotard's complex definition of discourse and figure, see Crome, Keith and James Williams, *The Lyotard Reader and Guide*, Edinburgh: Edinburgh University, 2006; Dews, Peter, "The Letter and the Line: Discourse and Its Other in Lyotard", *Diacritics*, vol. 14, no. 3, 1984; and Jay, Martin, *Downcast Eyes: The Denigration of Vision in Twentieth-Century French Thought*, Berkeley: University of California, 1994.

40 Katja Grillner offered the term "lens" in her comments on the first draft of this paper.

Dissolution

The Semi-living Author: Post-human Creative Agency

Rolf Hughes

1 Shelley, Mary, *Frankenstein*, Harmondsworth: Penguin Classics, 2003, p. 8.

2 von Kleist, Heinrich "On the Marionette Theatre", 1810 trans. Idris Parry in *Essays on Dolls* trans. Idris Parry and Paul Keegan, Harmondsworth: Penguin Books, 1994.

3 Langton, Christopher "Artificial Life" in *Artificial Life*, ed. Christopher Langton. Santa Fe Institute Studies in the Sciences of Complexity, vol. 6, Reading, MA: Addison Wesley, 1989), p. 5. Cited by Whitelaw, Mitchell *Metacreation: Art and Artificial Life*, Cambridge, MA and London: MIT Press, 2004, p. 7.

4 See Shiff, Richard "Originality", pp. 145–159 in Nelson, Robert S and Shiff, Richard, eds., *Critical Terms for Art History*, Chicago and London: University of Chicago Press, 2003.

5 The term autopoiesis was originally coined by Chilean biologist Humberto Maturana in 1972 to describe the biological "self-making" of living creatures. It was subsequently adapted for social systems by German sociologist Niklas Luhmann. See Maturana, Humberto and Varela, Francisco, *Autopoiesis and Cognition: The Realization of the Living*, Boston Studies in the Philosophy of Science, vol. 42, Dordrecht, Holland: D Reidel, 1980 and Luhmann, Niklas, *Essays in Self-Reference*, New York: Columbia University Press, 1990.

6 This is what Luhmann deemed the "decisive conceptual innovation" (*Essays*, p. 3) of autopoiesis theory in biology in the 1970s. Manturana and Varela developed the implications of the concept in *Autopoiesis and Cognition* where Manturana describes his decision to treat "the activity of the nervous system as determined by the nervous system itself, and not by the external world; thus the external world would have only a triggering role in the release of the internally-determined activity of the nervous system". Maturana, Humberto and Varela, Francisco, *Autopoiesis and Cognition*, p. xv. Cited by Hayles, N Katherine in *How We Became Posthuman*, London: University of Chicago, 1999, p. 136. Noting that Manturana's key insight is to realise that if the behaviour of the nervous system

is determined by its organisation, this results in a circular, self-reflexive dynamic, Hayles comments: "A living system's organization causes certain products to be produced, for example, nucleic acids. These products in turn produce the organization characteristic of that living system. [...] Building on this premise of autopoietic closure, Manturana developed a new and startlingly different account of how we know the world."

7 A caption to a series of portraits undertaken by MEART and exhibited at Spaceworks Gallery, The Tank, New York City, July 2003, concluded as follows: "This installation is dedicated to the memories of Dish #4080 & Dish #4821 who sadly passed away shortly after completing these artworks. (July 17, 2003)."

8 As Whitelaw remarks, "Distinctions between natural and artificial, born and made, become unsupportable. Technoscience seems to have an ever increasing command of living matter, and in an era of global capital, life is reshaped according to logics that are principally commercial." *Metacreation*, p. 4.

9 For a discussion of author figures, see the Introduction to the present volume.

10 Noting that scientific authorship, while largely neglected by scholarly and philosophical discourse, remains the cause of great professional concern among scientists, Mario Biagioli & Peter Galison comment, "The assignment of credit in large-scale biological, computer science, and physics collaborations is a major issue for young scientists; it hits every aspect of their career trajectories, from thesis writing to hiring and promoting. Physicists have long been debating what the Nobel Prize means in an age when two thousand scientists sign a single paper. The hundreds of authors listed in the byline of a biomedical paper reporting the result of a large clinical trial ask the same questions about the meaning and definition of authorship. And so do the editors of the journals who review those manuscripts, and the academic committees, departmental chairs, and deans who have to make hiring or tenure decisions based on CVs listing those publications. For all these reasons, the authorship debate in science has been entirely practical, and has generated thousands of administrative memos, policy statements, guidelines, articles, editorials, reports, and heated letters to the editor." Biagioli, Mario and Galison, Peter, eds., *Scientific Authorship: Credit and Intellectual Property in Science*, New York and London: Routledge, 2003, p. 2.

11 Klein, Julie Thompson "Interdisciplinarity and complexity: An evolving relationship", in *E:CO*, Special Double Issue vol. 6 nos. 1–2, 2004, p. 8.

12 Klein, "Interdisciplinarity and complexity", p. 4.

13 See Ortony, Andrew, ed., *Metaphor and Thought*, 2nd edition, London: Cambridge University Press, 1993.

14 Rosenberg, Martin E, "Constructing Autopoiesis: The Architectural Body in Light of Contemporary Cognitive Science" in *Interfaces* 21/22 (2003), p. 163.

15 "MEART—The Semi Living Artist" was developed by SymbioticA Art and Science Collaborative Research Lab in collaboration with The Potter Lab. SymbioticA Research Group: Guy Ben-Ary, Philip Gamblen, Iain Sweetman, Prof. Stuart Bunt & Oron Catts. The Potter Lab: Dr. Steve M Potter, Douglas Bakkum.

16 I am grateful to Guy Ben-Ary for clarifying these details in a private email dated 6 October 2006.

17 Cited in article "Cybernetic artist gives culture new meaning", *Technique Magazine* Friday March 3, 2006. Available online: http://www.fishandchips.uwa.edu.au/project/press/Technique030306MEART.pdf (accessed 29 September 2006).

18 Vanouse, Paul, "Contemplating Meart—The Semi-Living Artist", 2006, Available on project web site: http://www.fishandchips.uwa.edu.au/project/publications.html (accessed 29 September 2006).

19 Project website: http://www.fishandchips.uwa.edu.au/project.html (accessed 29 September 2006). On the Artbots website, the project is articulated via a set of discursive oppositions such as "unpredictability" and "temperament", "dependent" and "independent": "MEART—The Semi Living Artist is a geographically detached, bio-cybernetic project exploring aspects of creativity and artistry in the age of biological technologies and the future possibilities of creating semi living entities. It investigates our abilities and intentions in dealing with the emergence of a new class of beings (whose production may lie far in the future) that may be sentient, creative and unpredictable. Meart takes the basic components of the brain (isolated neurons) attaches them to a mechanical body through the mediation of a digital processing engine to attempt and create an entity that will seemingly evolve, learn and become conditioned to express its growth experiences through "art activity". The combined elements of unpredictability and "temperament" with the ability to learn and adapt, creates an artistic entity that is both dependent, and independent, from its creator and its creator's intentions."
Source: Artbots website http://artbots.org/2003/participants/MEART/ (accessed 29 September 2006).

20 Whitelaw, 2004, p. 228.

21 Writing on human imagination, physicist and theorist David Bohm comments, "The power to imagine things that have not been actually experienced has, on the one hand, commonly been regarded as a key aspect of creative and intelligent thought. On the other hand, this power of imagination has equally commonly been regarded as a rather passive and mechanical capacity to arrange and order the images of thought arising associatively out of memory, with the aid of which the mind may at best make routine sorts of adjustments, and at worst contrive to deceive itself in such a way as may be conducive to its own pleasure, comfort, and superficial satisfaction." Bohm, David, "The Range of Imagination", chapter 3 of *On Creativity*, Abingdon and New York: Routledge, 1996, reprinted in Routledge Classics, 2004, p. 50.

22 A parallel debate concerns the authorial identity of network design practices such as Servo. For more information on Servo see www.s-e-r-v-o.com (Accessed 29 September 2006). See also article by Chris Hight, "Preface to the multitude —The return to the network practice in architecture" in *01.AKAD— Experimental Research in Architecture and Design—Beginnings*, Katja Grillner, Per Glembrandt, Sven-Olov Wallenstein eds., Stockholm: Axl Books, 2005, pp. 16–37; and Hélène Lipstadt's essay which ends the present collection, "'Exoticising the domestic': on new collaborative paradigms and advanced design practices."

23 At the same time, the project team themselves question the market logic of art, as Emma McRae reports; "During previous exhibitions they have given MEART's drawings to people not in exchange for money but for whatever the recipient felt the drawing was worth, as a means of eliciting responses to and opinions of their work. They received things as varied as a pot plant, a hug, a PhD thesis dedication, and an abstract drawing by an eight year old girl, all of which indicate differing methods and degrees of valuation as responses to the experience of interacting with MEART." Emma McRae, "A report on the practices of SymbioticA Research Group in their creation of MEART—the semi-living artist". Available on project web site: http://www.fishandchips.uwa.edu.au/project/publications.html (accessed 29 September 2006).

24 Project web site: http://www.fishandchips.uwa.edu.au/project.html (accessed 29 September 2006).

25 Rosenberg, Martin E, "Constructing Autopoiesis: The Architectural Body in Light of Contemporary Cognitive Science" in *Interfaces* 21/22 (2003), p. 182.

26 Eisenman, Peter "Post-Functionalism", in *Oppositions 6*, Fall 1976, reprinted in K Nesbitt, ed., *Theorizing a New Agenda for Architecture: An Anthology of Architectural Theory*, New York: Princeton Architectural Press, 1996, pp. 80–81. John Frazer has defined emergent architecture as "a property of the process of organizing matter rather than a property of the matter thus organised"—i.e. a "process-driven architecture" which emerges "on the very edge of chaos, where all living things emerge, and it will inevitably share some characteristics of primitive life forms." He extends the analogy of architecture as living system in his definition of what he calls "evolutionary architecture" which will exhibit "metabolism" and enjoy "a thermodynamically open relationship with the environment in both a metabolic and a socio-economic sense" while "using the processes of autopoiesis, autocatalysis and emergent behaviour to generate new forms and structures". Here the emphasis on a "symbiotic relationship" between model and environment, the suggestion that architecture may be capable of a form of artificial life, an "organism" capable of responding to its surroundings and inhabitants, and modifying its structures accordingly ("Not a static picture of being, but a dynamic picture of becoming and unfolding—a direct analogy with a description of the natural world."), clearly suggests that we have come a long way from the paradigm of architect as author, whose design intentions are seamlessly realised and expressed in built form. Frazer, John, *An Evolutionary Architecture*, London: Architecture Association, 1995, p. 103.

27 See, for example, Ascott, Roy, 1990, "Is There Love in the Telematic Embrace?", *Art Journal*, New York: College Arts Association of America, 49:3, pp. 241–247. These terms appear on p. 241.

28 Wilson, Stephen, "Artificial Life and Genetic Art", *Information Arts: Intersections of Art, Science, and Technology*, Cambridge, MA: MIT Press, 2002, p. 364.

29 See Williams, Sam, "Unnatural Selection" in *Technology Review*, February 2005, p. 56.

30 de Landa, Manuel, "Deleuze and the Use of the Genetic Algorithm in Architecture", 2001. Available at: http://boo.mi2.hr/~ognjen/tekst/delanda2001.html

31 See Ashby, WR, "Can a mechanical chess-player outplay its designer?", *British Journal for the Philosophy of Science*. 3, 1952, pp. 44–57. Reprinted in *Mechanisms of Intelligence: Ross Ashby's Writings on Cybernetics*, R Conant ed., Intersystems Publications, Salinas, California, 1981.

32 Thompson, Adrian, Layzell, Paul and Zebulum, Ricardo Salem, "Explorations in Design Space: Unconventional Electronics Design Through Artificial Evolution,"

IEEE Transactions on Evolutionary Computation 3, no. 3, 1999, pp. 167–196. Available online at: http://www.cogs.susx.ac.uk/users/adrianth/cacm99/paper.html (accessed 29 September 2006).

33 Pablo Miranda explains the appeal of Pask's experiments as follows: "Pask's devices are fascinating for a number of reasons: they belong to a tradition of cybernetics which employs machines as rhetorical arguments, with early examples such as Norbert Wiener's self-steered 'moth-bug' robot or Ross Ashby's 'homeostat' from 1940. In the openness of its operations, the chemical computer combines morphological, material and informational processes in mutually affecting, circular causal relations. Lastly, the chemical computer addresses the epistemological limitations of computation as symbol manipulation and proposes a strategy for transcending them by allowing free connections and mappings between the symbolic and the material world." Miranda, Pablo "Out of Control: The media of architecture, cybernetics and design" in *Material Matters*, ed., Katie Lloyd-Thomas, London: Routledge, 2007, p. 158.

34 See Cariani, Peter, "To evolve an ear: epistemological implications of Gordon Pask's electrochemical devices" in *Systems Research*, 1993; 10 (3): pp. 19–33. Available online at: http://homepage.mac.com/cariani/CarianiWebsite/PaskPaper.html (accessed 6 December 2006).

35 Statement on Miranda's home page http://www.armyofclerks.net/ (accessed 4 December 2006).

36 See Occular Witness home page: http://smart.tii.se/smart/projects/occular/index_en.html (accessed 4 December 2006).

37 Private communication, April 2006. As in MEART's extreme Cartesian mind-body dualism, the humour here, if intentional, is somewhat deadpan.

38 Klein, "Interdisciplinarity and complexity", p. 2.

39 For a Bourdieu-influenced reading of open source and other contemporary paradigms of design, see Hélène Lipstadt's essay which concludes this section, "Exoticising the domestic", on new collaborative paradigms and advanced design practices.

40 Hayles, *How We Became Posthuman*, p. 225.

41 Bateson, Gregory, *Steps to an Ecology of Mind*, London: Paladin, 1973, p. 428.

42 Norbert Wiener, discussing the necessity of difference in information theory, writes, "the more probable a message, the less information it gives. Clichés, for example, are less illuminating than great poems." Wiener, Norbert, *The Human Use of Human Beings: Cybernetics and Society*, London: Eyre and Spottiswoode, 1954, p. 21.

43 See Hayles, N Katherine, "Narratives of Artificial Life", in *Future Natural*, ed. George Robertson, Melinda Mash, Lisa Tickner, Jon Bird, Barry Curtis, and Tim Putnam, London: Routledge, 1996. See Whitelaw, "Emergence" (Chapter 7) in *Metacreation*, pp. 206–237. Mitchell Whitelaw, in his outline of the history of emergence as a concept, traces the first technical use of the term to the English philosopher and literary critic George Henry Lewes in his *Problems of Life and Mind*, 1875. Lewes uses the term emergent to describe an effect involving several causes that cannot be reduced or traced back to those component causes. His definition is part of a discussion on causality which was earlier addressed by the philosopher John Stuart Mill in *A System of Logic*, 1843, in which Mill also discusses cases where multiple causes produce a single effect, but distinguishes between cases where the effect is a simple accumulation of multiple causes (for example, the vectoral composition of force will always move the same object the same distance under successive applications) and cases where the effect is irreducible to those causes (certain chemical compounds—water, for example, cannot be reduced to simply hydrogen plus oxygen; it is a new substance with properties very different from those of its components. It is these properties that Lewes labels "emergent.") Mill argues that regardless of how well we know the individual elements of the living body, "it is certain that no mere summing up of the separate actions of those elements will ever amount to the living body itself." Furthermore, he predicts that such "irreducible effects" will be discovered in many more areas, suggesting that this complex causality "will be found equally true in the phenomena of mind; and even in social and political phenomena." In other words, Mill anticipates the field now known as complex systems science (*Metacreation*, p. 209). The following comments derive from Whitelaw's discussion in this chapter.

44 *Metacreation*, p. 226.

45 *Metacreation*, p. 226.

46 In *At Home in the Universe: The Search for the Laws of Self-Organization and Complexity*, Stuart Kauffman, a theoretical biologist and one of the leading figures in complexity studies, asks what is common to "the teeming molecules that hustled themselves into self-reproducing metabolisms, the cells coordinating their behaviours to form multi-celled organisms, the ecosystems and even economic and political systems". He answers: "The wonderful possibility... is

that on many fronts, life evolves toward a regime that is poised between order and chaos. The evocative phrase that points to this working hypothesis is this: life exists at the edge of chaos. Borrowing a metaphor from physics, life may exist near a kind of phase transition. (…) *Networks in the regime near the edge of chaos—the compromise between order and surprise—appear best able to coordinate complex activities and best able to evolve as well.*" (my emphasis). Kauffman, Stuart, *At Home in the Universe: The Search for the Laws of Self-Organization and Complexity*, New York: Oxford University Press, 1995, p. 26. Cited by Mark Taylor in *The Moment of Complexity: Emerging Network Culture*, Chicago and London: The University of Chicago Press, 2005, pp. 24–25.

47 See Taylor, Mark, *The Moment of Complexity*, p. 25.

48 See Moeini, S Iradj, "Architecture's Inspirations from the Information Age" in *The Four Faces of Architecture: On the Dynamics of Architectural Knowledge*, ed. Lena Wilner and Abdellah Abarkan, Stockholm: School of Architecture/Royal Institute of Technology, 2005, p. 123.

49 Klein, 2004, p. 3.

50 Burke, Seán, *Authorship: From Plato to the Postmodern*, Edinburgh, Edinburgh University Press, 1995, reprinted 2000, Preface, x.

51 Paul Watson "Critical approaches to Hollywood cinema: authorship, genre and stars", in Nelmes, Jill, ed., *An Introduction to Film Studies* (Third Edition), London and New York: Routledge, 1996; 3rd edition reprinted 2003, p. 141.

52 Paul Watson "Critical approaches to Hollywood cinema: authorship, genre and stars", in Nelmes, Jill, ed., *An Introduction to Film Studies* (Third Edition), London and New York: Routledge, 1996; 3rd edition reprinted 2003, p. 141.

53 In *The Work of Art in the Age of Mechanical Reproduction*, Walter Benjamin describes what is at stake when mechanical reproduction strips an artefact of its aura of "authenticity": "The authenticity of a thing is the essence of all that is transmissible from its beginning, ranging from its substantive duration to its testimony to the history which it has experienced. Since the historical testimony rests on the authenticity, the former, too, is jeopardized by reproduction when substantive duration ceases to matter. And what is really jeopardized when the historical testimony is affected is the authority of the object." Benjamin, Walter, "The Work of Art in the Age of Mechanical Reproduction", trans. Harry Zohn in *Illuminations*, London: Fontana, 1992, p. 215.

54 Vanouse, Paul, "Contemplating Meart—The Semi-Living Artist", 2006, Available on project web site: http://www.fishandchips.uwa.edu.au/project/publications.html (accessed 29 September 2006). The phrase "realities that emerge from handwork" is taken from a Rainer Maria Rilke 1903 letter to Lou Andreas-Salomé: "Somehow I too must come to make things; not plastic, but written things—realities that emerge from handwork. Somehow I too must discover the smallest basic element, the cell of my art, the tangible, immaterial means of representation for everything…" Quoted in "Introduction", Rainer Maria Rilke, *New Poems: The Other Part*, trans., Edward Snow, 1908, reprint, New York: North Point Press, 1998, ix.

Cedric Price as Anti-architect

Stanley Mathews

1 Price, memorandum, August, 1964, Fun Palace document folio DR1995:0188:526, Cedric Price Archives, Canadian Centre for Architecture, Montreal. Rem Koolhaas has also suggested the same role for the architect: "Bigness is impersonal: the architect is no longer condemned to stardom…. Beyond signature, Bigness means surrender to technologies; to engineers, contractors, manufacturers; to politics; to others. It promises architecture a kind of post-heroic status—a realignment with neutrality." Rem Koolhaas, "Bigness—the Problem of Large", *S, M, L, XL*, New York: Monacelli Press, 1995, pp. 513–514.

2 Price, quoted in James Burns, *Arthropods*, London, Academy Editions, 1972, p. 58.

3 Roland Barthes, "The Death of the Author", *Image-Music-Text*, New York, Hill and Wang, 1977, pp. 142–147.

4 Barthes, pp. 142–143.

5 Barthes, p. 146.

6 Roland Barthes, *Image-Music-Text*, New York, Hill and Wang, 1977.

7 Barthes, p. 142.

8 Barthes, p. 143.

9 Barthes, p. 148.

10 Barthes, p. 142.

11 Barthes, p. 148.

12 The unbridled optimism towards technology of the time may also have blinded Price and Littlewood to the more sinister aspects of cybernetics and systems theories, for the objectification of people as information quanta held serious political implications. The most egregious example of abuse was the case of Stafford Beer. A member of the Fun Palace Cybernetics Committee, Beer moved to Chile in the 1970s to serve the Pinochet Allende government as a consultant on the application of cybernetics and systems theories as means of social control and repression.

13 The social plight of East London had been the subject of numerous books and articles, but had failed to attract widespread public attention until the publication of Sir Walter Besant's 1882 novel *All Sorts and Conditions of Men: An Impossible Story*, London, Chatto and Windus, 1900. Although the novel itself is a relatively insignificant Victorian period piece, it represented a significant work of amateur social criticism and theory. In the book, Besant describes a "People's Palace"—an educational and recreational facility for the disadvantaged of London's East End. After a groundswell of public support, Besant eventually established a foundation to promote the idea of the People's Palace, and it was actually built in 1887 on Mile End Road, and continued to operate until 1953.

14 Barthes, p. 148.

Ernst Neufert's Architect's Data: Anxiety, Creativity and Authorial Abdication

Gernot Weckherlin

1 Nietzsche, Friedrich, "Belief in Inspiration", in *Human, All Too Human, A Book for Free Spirits*, (*The Complete Works of Friedrich Nietzsche*, vol. 3), trans. with an Afterword by Gary Handwerk, Stanford University Press, 1995, pp. 118–119.

2 Aalto, Alvar, "The Trout and the Stream", in Göran Schildt, ed., *Aalto in his own words*, New York: Rizzoli International Publications, 1997, pp. 107–109.

3 Reichlin, Bruno, "Den Entwurfsprozess steuern–eine fixe Idee der Moderne?", in *Daidalos 71*, 1999, pp. 6–21.

4 Many German architects refuse to admit the use of this book. Surprisingly, however, it can be found in almost every architectural studio.

Ernst Neufert was born in 1900 in Freyburg, Unstrut. He died in 1986 in Bugneaux sur Rolle, Switzerland.

5 Neufert, Ernst: *Architects' Data*, 2nd English Edition, Jones, Vincent ed., London, Toronto, Sidney, New York: Granada-Halsted Press, 1980, p. XI. (The first English edition was published ten years earlier: Neufert, Ernst: *Architects' Data*, Rudolf Herz ed. and rev., GH Berger, Sonia P Dell et al trans., London: Lockwood, 1970).

6 To mention only one American example of a similar popular bestseller of this genre: Ramsey, Charles, George Sleeper, Harold Reeve, *Architectural Graphic Standards for Architects, Engineers, Decorators, Builders and Draftsmen*, New York: J Wiley and Sons, 1932.

7 The latest 38th edition, 2005, was revised and updated by the architect Johannes Kister, editor for the "Neufert Foundation".

8 Several unauthorised reprints are on the market—for example, a Vietnamese edition.

9 Anonymous author, "Im Medaillon", *Bauwelt*, 11, 1960, p. 294.

10 The first Spanish translation of Neufert's "Bauentwurfslehre" dates back to 1942, *Arte de proyectar en arquitectura: Fundamentos, normas y prescripciones; Consultor para arquitectos, constructores, propietarios y estudiantes*, Versión de la 8. ed. orig. von Company, Manuel, Barcelona, Gili, 1942. NN, "Im Medaillon", *Bauwelt*, 11, 1960, p. 294.

11 His major projects were Dyckerhoff cement works and headquarters Amöneburg, Dyckerhoff cement works, Lengerich, Schott Glas works, Mainz, Linde refrigerator assembly shed, Mainz-Kostheim, Eternit works Leimen, (fibre cement board industry), Quelle mail-order house headquarters, Nürnberg, and Hoesch tube-rolling mill, in Hamm.

12 Klopfer, Paul, "Ernst Neufert. Ein Architekt unserer Zeit. Zu seinem fünfzigsten Geburtstag beglückwünscht von Paul Klopfer", in *Neue Bauwelt*, 11, 1950, pp. 41–52.

13 Hegemann, Werner, "Das dänische Handbuch der Bauindustrie", in *Wasmuths Monatshefte für Baukunst*, Berlin, 6, 1931, pp. 272–274.

14 For more details on Neufert's pictorial language see the author's forthcoming publication, *Zur Systematisierung des architektonischen Wissens am Beispiel Ernst Neufert*.

15 Neufert Ernst, *Bauentwurfslehre, Grundlagen, Normen, Vorschriften, über Anlage, Bau, Gestaltung, Raumbedarf, Raumbeziehungen, Maße für Gebäude, Räume, Einrichtungen, Geräte mit dem Menschen als Maß und Ziel; Handbuch für den Baufachmann, Bauherrn, Lehrenden und Lernenden*. Berlin, Bauwelt-Verlag, 1936.

16 Neufert, Ernst, unpublished typescript, dated 1976, Neufert-Archive, Weimar-Gelmeroda.

17 See Gropius, Walter, "Der große Baukasten", in *Das neue Frankfurt*, 2, 1926, pp. 20–30.

18 For a brilliant overview on contemporary concepts of architectural education see: Wolsdorff, Christian, "Kann man bauen lernen ohne zu Bauen? Architekturausbildung in Deutschland 1918–1931", in *Das andere Bauhaus. Otto Bartning und die Staatliche Bauhochschule Weimar, 1926–1930*. Bauhaus-Archiv Berlin, ed., Berlin: Kupfergraben-Verlag, 1997, pp. 81–93.

19 Neufert, Ernst, (attributed) manuscript without title on architectural education, Staatliche Bauhochschule Weimar, 2.12.1926, NAI, archive Van Eesteren, A-2-12-27, quoted by Wolsdorff "Kann man bauen lernen ohne zu Bauen?", p. 87.

20 See Alain Pottage, "Architectural Authorship: The Normative Ambitions of Le Corbusier's Modulor", *AA-files*, (31), 1996, pp. 64–70.

21 Dörte, Nicolaisen, ed., Bauhaus-Archiv Berlin, *Das andere Bauhaus. Otto Bartning und die Staatliche Bauhochschule Weimar, 1926-1930*, Berlin, Kupfergraben-Verlag, 1997.

22 Gotthelf, Fritz, *Ernst Neufert. Ein Architekt unserer Zeit*, Berlin, Frankfurt, and Wien: Ullstein-Fachverlag, 1960, p. 12.

23 Durand, Jean-Nicolas-Louis, "Précis des Leçons d'Architecture Donées à l'École Royale Polytechnique", Paris, 1819.

24 Gotthelf, *Ernst Neufert*, p. 12.

25 Durand, Jean-Nicolas-Louis, "Précis des Leçons d'Architecture Donées à l'École Royale Polytechnique", Paris, 1819.

26 Neufert, Ernst, *Bauentwurfslehre*, 3rd ed. 1936, p. 22.

27 One example of this literary genre is Wolf, Gustav, *Die Grundriß-Staffel. Eine Sammlung von Kleinwohnungsgrundrissen der Nachkriegszeit mit einem Vorschlag folgerichtiger Ordnung und Kurz-Bezeichnung von Professor Gustav Wolf. Beitrag zur Grundrißwissenschaft*, München: Callwey, 1931.

28 Neufert, Ernst, *Bauentwurfslehre, Grundlagen, Normen, Vorschriften, über Anlage, Bau, Gestaltung, Raumbedarf, Raumbeziehungen, Maße für Gebäude, Räume, Einrichtungen, Geräte mit dem Menschen als Maß und Ziel; Handbuch für den Baufachmann, Bauherrn, Lehrenden und Lernenden*, Berlin: Bauwelt-Verlag, 1936, p. 34.

29 Neufert, Ernst, *Bauentwurfslehre*, Braunschweig, Wiesbaden, Vieweg, 1984, p. V.

30 Neufert, Ernst, "Ausbildung der schöpferischen Fähigkeiten des Architekten", *Der Architekt im Zerreisspunkt. Vorträge, Berichte und Diskussionsbeiträge der Sektion Architektur auf dem Internationalen Kongress für Ingenieurausbildung (IKIA) in Darmstadt 1947*, Darmstadt: Eduard Roether Verlag, 1948, pp. 75–91.

31 The sharpest criticism of Neufert's research into modular and technological standardisation can be found in Hugo Häring's "Neues Bauen" in *Baukunst und Werkform*, 1, 1947, pp. 30–36.

32 Leowald, Georg, "Sinn und Grenzen der Normung. Eine nachgeholte Auseinandersetzung mit Neuferts "Bauordnungslehre", in *Baukunst und Werkform*, 1, 1947, pp. 52–79.

33 "Meinungen zur Maßordnung—Ein Bericht und eine Umfrage" in *Neue Bauwelt*, 39, 1948, p. 610.

Systems Aesthetics, or how Cambridge Solved Architecture

Sean Keller

1 Wigley, Mark, "Network Fever", *Grey Room*, 4, 2001, p. 84.

2 March, Lionel, "Modern Movement to Vitruvius: Themes of Education and Research", *Royal Institute of British Architects Journal*, 81, 1972, p. 109.

3 March, Lionel, Marcial Echeñique, and Peter Dickens, eds., "Models of Environment", *Architectural Design*, 41, 1971, p. 275.

4 Grabow, Stephen, *Christopher Alexander: The Search for a New Paradigm in Architecture*, Stocksfield, England, Oriel Press, 1983, p. 31.

5 Alexander, Christopher, "The Synthesis of Form: Some Notes on a Theory", PhD dissertation, Harvard University, 1962; and Alexander, Christopher, *Notes on the Synthesis of Form*, Cambridge, MA, Harvard University Press, 1964.

6 Alexander, *Notes on the Synthesis of Form*, pp. 137–142.

7 Alexander, *Notes on the Synthesis of Form*, preface to the 1971 edition.

8 Alexander, *Notes on the Synthesis of Form*, preface to the 1971 edition.

9 March, Lionel, "The Logic of Design and the Question of Value", *The Architecture of Form*, Lionel March, ed., Cambridge: Cambridge University Press, 1976, p. 21.

10 March, Lionel, "The Logic of Design and the Question of Value", p. 18.

11 March, Lionel, "The Logic of Design and the Question of Value", pp. 21–22.

12 For more on this point see my "Fenland Tech: Architectural Science in Post-war Cambridge", *Grey Room*, 23, 2006, pp. 40–65.

13 "Discord Over Harmony in Architecture: The Eisenman/Alexander Debate," *Harvard Graduate School of Design News*, 2, 1983, p. 12.

14 Eisenman, Peter, "Towards an Understanding of Form in Architecture", *Architectural Design*, 33, 1963, pp. 457–458.

15 Eisenman, Peter, "The Formal Basis of Modern Architecture", PhD dissertation, University of Cambridge, 1963, reprinted by Lars Müller, 2006, p. 1.

16 Eisenman, Peter, "Post-Functionalism", *Oppositions*, 6, 1976, pp. i–iii.

17 Eisenman, Peter, "The Formal Basis of Modern Architecture", p. 4.

18 Eisenman, Peter, "The Formal Basis of Modern Architecture", p. 6.

19 Martin, Leslie, Ben Nicholson, and Naum Gabo, eds., *Circle: International Survey of Constructive Art*, London: Faber and Faber, 1937.

20 March, Lionel, "Research and Environmental Studies", *Cambridge Review*, 2 February 1973, p. 85.

21 Cooke, Catherine, "The Town of Socialism", PhD dissertation, University of Cambridge, 1974.

22 March, Lionel, foreword to *The Architecture of Form*, Lionel March, ed., Cambridge: Cambridge University Press, 1976, p. vii.

23 Colin Rowe paraphrasing Clinton Rossiter in Colin Rowe, *As I Was Saying: Recollections and Miscellaneous Essays*, Alexander Caragonne, ed., Cambridge: MIT Press, 1996, vol. 1, p. 131.

24 March, Lionel, foreword to *The Architecture of Form*, p. ix.

25 Allen, Stan, talk given for "Five Architects and After", Harvard University Graduate School of Design, session 4 of the series "The 70's: the Formation of Contemporary Architectural Discourse", presented by the Harvard University Graduate School of Design and Cornell University Department of Architecture, 2000–2001. Video recording available at Visual Resources, Loeb Library, Harvard Graduate School of Design.

'Exoticising the Domestic': on New Collaborative Paradigms and Advanced Design Practices

Hélène Lipstadt

1 Colomina, Beatriz, "Collaborations: The Private Life of Modern Architecture", *Journal of the Society of Architectural Historians*, vol. 58, no. 3, September 1999, pp. 462 & 464.

2 Hight, Christopher, "Preface to the Multitude: The Return to the Network Practice in Architecture", in *01.AKAD—Experimental Research in Architecture and Design—Beginnings*, Katja Grillner, Per Glembrandt, et al, eds., Stockholm: Axl Books, 2005, pp. 16–37.

3 Bourdieu, Pierre, *The Rules of Art: Genesis and Structure of the Literary Field*, Susan Emanuel, trans., Stanford: Stanford University Press, 1996, cites Benjamin, without giving a source on p. 229. Bourdieu's conceptual terminology is italicised when introduced.

4 Tim Anstey, Katja Grillner, Rolf Hughes, *Call For Papers: Architecture and Authorship*, 2005, On H-ARTHIST, www.arthist.net or www.auctor.se (accessed 3 August 2005).

5 Chartier, Roger, *Cultural History Between Practices and Representations*, Lydia G Cochrane, trans., Ithaca: Cornell University Press, 1988, p. 9.

6 Bourdieu, *Rules of Art*, pp. 223 & 224.

7 Sapiro, Gisèle," Pourquoi le monde va-t-il de soi? De la phénoménologie à la théorie de l'habitus", in *Sartre, une écriture en acte. Cahiers RITM 24*, Geneviève Idt, ed., Nanterre: Publidix, 2001, p. 178.

8 Bourdieu, Pierre, "Habitus", in *Habitus: A Sense of Place*, Jean Hillier and Emma Rooksby, eds., Aldershot: Ashworth, 2002, pp. 32–33.

9 Bourdieu, "Habitus", p. 33.

10 Bourdieu, *Rules*, p. 221.

11 Montlibert, Christian de, *L'impossible autonomie de l'architecte*, Strasbourg: Presses universitaires de Strasbourg, 1995.

12 Bourdieu, Pierre, *Homo Academicus*, Peter Collier, trans., Stanford: Stanford University Press, 1988, pp. xi–xii, 5.

13 Kaspori, Dennis, "A Communism of Ideas: Towards an Architectural Open Source Practice", *Archis*, 2003, www.archis.org/archis_old/english/archis_art_e_2003/art_3b_2003e.html (accessed 24 August 2005). For an expanded version, see Kaspori, Dennis, "Toward an Open-Source Architectural Practice", in *What*

People Want: Populism in Architecture and Design, Michael Shamiyeh, ed., Basel: Birkhäuser, 2005, pp. 324–333.

14 Kaspori, "A Communism of Ideas".

15   Kaspori, "A Communism of Ideas".

16 Panofsky, Erwin, *Gothic Architecture and Scholasticism: An Inquiry Into the Analogy of the Arts, Philosophy and Religion in the Middle Ages*, New York: World Publishing, 1951.

17 Marx, Karl, *Capital: A Critique of Political Economy*. vol. 1, Frederick Engels, ed., Ernest Untermann, trans., Chicago: Charles H Kerr and Co, Cooperative, 1909, p. 198.

18 Hight, "Preface to the multitude", pp. 16–37.

19 Hight, "Preface to the multitude", p. 33.

20 Hight, "Preface to the multitude", p. 32.

21 Bourdieu, *Rules*, pp. 242–248.

22 Violeau, Jean-Louis, "Les "premiers collés" volontaires de l'architecture", *AMC: Les Nouveaux albums des jeunes architectes 2001/2002, Hors Séries, 2002*, pp. 8–15, 85–87 and "A la recherche de la 'qualité' architecturale: les formules promotionelles au miroir des incertitudes", in *Droits d'entrée*, Gérard Mauger, ed., Paris: Editions de la MSH, 2002, pp. 64–95.

23 Biau, Veronique, "New Professional Context and New Symbolic Elites Among French Architects", in *Professional Identities in Transit: Cross-Cultural Dimensions*, Inga Hellberg, Mike Saks, et al, eds., Gothenberg: Almqvist and Wiksell, 1998, p. 382.

24 Biau, Véronique, "Professional Positioning Among French Architects", in *Professions, Identity, and Order in Comparative Perspective*, Vittorio Olgiati, Louis Orzack, et al, eds., Oñati: Oñati International Institute for the Sociology of Law, 1998, pp. 42–43, 50, 47, 52, 49, 52.

25 Biau, "New Professional", pp. 382, 378, 380, 381.

26 Biau, Véronique, *L'architecture comme emblème municipal: les grands projets des maires*, Paris-La Défense: Plan Construction et architecture, 1992.

27   I adapt the formulation and notion from Tim Anstey, personal communication, 29 March 2006.

28 Bourdieu, *Rules*, p. 344.

29 Bourdieu, Pierre, "Some Questions for the True Masters of the World", Loïc Wacquant, trans., Berkeley Journal of Sociology, vol. 46, 2002, pp. 170, 174, 176, translation modified.

Bibliography

Introduction

Alberti, Leon Battista, *On the Art of Building in Ten Books*, Joseph Rykwert, Robert Tavernor, Neil Leach, trans., Cambridge, MA and London: MIT Press, 1988.

Anstey, Tim, "Authority and authorship in LB Alberti's *De re aedificatoria*", *Nordiska Arkitekturforskning*, no. 4, 2003.

Barthes, Roland, *Image-Music-Text*, Stephen Heath, trans. and ed., London: Fontana, 1977.

Bernstein, Fred A, "Fast Forward", *RIBA Journal*, vol. 110, no. 11, November 2003.

Burke, Seán, *Authorship: From Plato to the Postmodern*, Edinburgh: Edinburgh University Press, 1995, reprinted 2000.

Burke, Seán, *The Death and Return of the Author. Criticism and subjectivity in Barthes, Foucault and Derrida*, Edinburgh, Edinburgh University Press, 1992, reprinted 1999.

Colomina, Beatrice, "Collaborations—The Private Life of Modern Architecture", in *Journal of the Society of Architectural Historians*, vol. 58, no. 3.

Dornbach, Marton, "Timothy Clark. The Theory of Inspiration: Composition as a Crisis of Subjectivity in Romantic and Post-Romantic Writing", in *Studies in Romanticism*, vol. 42, no. 2, 2003.

Foucault, Michel, "What is an Author", in *Language, counter-memory, practice: Selected essays and interviews by Michel Foucault*, Donald F Bouchard, ed., Sherry Siman, trans., Ithaca: Cornell University Press, 1977.

Gilbert, Sandra M, and Susan Gubar, *The Madwoman in the Attic*, Chicago and London: Yale University Press, 1980.

Grillner, Katja, Per Glembrandt, Sven-Olov Wallenstein, eds., *01.AKAD—Experimental Research in Architecture and Design—Beginnings*, Stockholm: Axl Books, 2005.

Hughes, Francesca, ed, *The Architect Reconstructing her Practice*, Cambridge, MA: MIT Press, 1996, reprinted 1998.

Jenkins, David, ed., *Norman Foster—Works*, 4 vols., London: Prestel, 2003–2005.

Kantorowicz, Ernst, *Selected Studies by Ernst H. Kantorowicz*, Locust Valley, NY: JJ Augustin, 1965.

Le Corbusier, *Oeuvre complete en 8 volumes*, Basel: Birkhäuser, 1999.

Lentricchia, Frank and Thomas McLaughlin, eds., *Critical Terms for Literary Study*, London and Chicago: University of Chicago Press, 1990.

Locke, John, *An Essay concerning Human Understanding*, Peter H Nidditch, ed., Oxford: The Clarendon Press, 1975.

Lootsma, Bart, *Superdutch—New Architecture in the Netherlands*, London: Thames and Hudson, 2000.

Mathews, Stanley, *From Agit-prop to Free Space: the Architecture of Cedric Price*, London: Black Dog Publishing, 2007.

Mattsson, Helena, *Arkitektur och konsumtion: Rayner Banham och utbytbarhetens estetik*, Stockholm: Brutus Östlings Bokförlag Symposion, 2004.

MVRDV, *Metacity Datatown*, Rotterdam: 010 Publishers, 1999.

Powell, Kenneth, ed., *Richard Rogers. Complete Works*, 3 vols. London: Phaidon, 1999–2006.

Rosa, Joseph, *Next Generation Architecture: contemporary digital experimentation + the radical avant-garde*, London: Thames and Hudson, 2003.

Rudofsky, Bernard, *Architecture Without Architects—A short introduction to non-pedigreed architecture*, New York: Museum of Modern Art, 1964.

Tavernor, Robert, *On Alberti and the Art of Building*, New Haven and London: Yale University Press, 1998.

Whiteley, Nigel, *Rayner Banham: Historian of the immediate future*, Cambridge, MA and London: MIT Press, 2003.

Affirmation

Architecture and Rhetoric: Persuasion, Context, Action

Tim Anstey

Alberti, Leon Battista, *On Painting*, Cecil Grayson, trans., London: Penguin Books, 1991.

Alberti, Leon Battista, *On the Art of Building in Ten Books*, Joseph Rykwert, Robert Tavernor, Neil Leach trans., Cambridge MA and London: MIT Press, 1988.

Anstey, Tim, "Authority and authorship in LB Alberti's *De re aedificatoria*", *Nordiska Arkitekturforskning*, 4, 2003.

Anstey, Tim, "The ambiguities of *disegno*", *Journal of Architecture*, vol. 10, no. 3, June 2005.

Banham, Rayner, *A Critic Writes. Essays by Rayner Banham*, Berkeley, Los Angeles, London: University of California Press, 1996.

Banham, Rayner, *Theory and Design in the First Machine Age*, Oxford: Butterworth-Heinemann Ltd, (1980) 1994.

Baxandall, Michael, *Giotto and the Orators. Humanist Observers of Painting in Italy and the Discovery of Pictorial Composition, 1350–1450*, Oxford: Oxford University Press, 1971.

Choay, Francoise, *The Rule and the Model*, Denise Bratton, ed., Cambridge, MA and London: MIT Press, 1997.

Cicero, *De officiis*, Walter Miller, trans., TE Page et al eds., Loeb Classical Library, London: William Heinemann Ltd and Cambridge, MA: Harvard University Press, 1938.

Cicero, *On the Ideal Orator (De oratore)*, James M May and Jakob Wisse trans., New York and Oxford: Oxford University Press, 2001.

Dorrian, Mark, Murray Fraser, Jonathan Hill, Jane Rendell, eds., *Critical Architecture*, London: Routledge, 2007.

Forty, Adrian, *Words and Buildings*, London: Thames and Hudson, 2000.

Hart, Vaughan and Peter Hicks, eds., *Paper Palaces: the Rise of the Renaissance Architectural Treatise*, New Haven and London: Yale University Press, 1998.

Onians, John, *Bearers of Meaning. The Classical Orders in Antiquity, the Middle Ages and the Renaissance*, Princeton, New Jersey: Princeton University Press.

Price, Cedric, "An Alternative Voice", *The RIBA Journal*, vol. 88, no. 9, September 1981.

Price, Cedric, *The Square Book*, Chichester, West Sussex: Wiley-Academy, 2003.

Rossi, Aldo, *L'architettura della città*, Padova: Marsilio, 1966.

Rossi, Aldo, *The Architecture of the City*, Diane Ghirardo and Joan Ockman, trans., Cambridge, MA and London, MIT Press, 1982.

Rowe, Colin and Fred Koetter, "Collage City", *Architectural Review*, vol.158, August 1975.

Rowe, Colin and Fred Koetter, *Collage City*, Cambridge, MA and London: MIT Press, 1978.

Saint, Andrew, "A History of Professionalism", *The RIBA Journal*, vol. 88, no. 9, September 1981.

Serlio, Sebastiano, *On Architecture (Tutte l'opere d'architettura et prospetiva)*, Vaughan Hart and Peter Hicks, trans., 2 vols., New Haven and London: Yale University Press, 1996, 2001.

Smith, Christine, *Architecture in the Culture of Early Humanism*, New York and Oxford: Oxford University Press, 1992.

Vitruvius, *The Ten Books on Architecture*, Morris Hicky Morgan, trans., New York: Dover Publications, 1960.

Westfall, Carroll William, *In This Most Perfect Paradise. Alberti, Nicholas V, and the invention of conscious urban planning in Rome, 1447-55*, University Park and London: The Pennsylvania State University Press, 1974.

Architectural Creativity in Lewis Carroll's *The Vision of the Three T's*

Caroline Dionne

Carroll, Lewis, *Lewis Carroll The Complete Works*, London: Nonesuch Press, 1939.

Carroll, Lewis, *The Complete Illustrated Lewis Carroll*, Ware: Wordsworth, 1996.

Carroll, Lewis, *The Annotated Alice*, intro and notes by Martin Gardner, New York: WW Norton & Company Inc, 2000.

Clark, Timothy, *The Theory of Inspiration: Composition as a crisis of subjectivity in Romantic and post-Romantic writing*, Manchester and New York: Manchester University Press, 1997.

Cox, Virginia. *The Renaissance Dialogue: Literary dialogue in its social and political contexts, Castiglione to Galileo*, Cambridge: Cambridge University Press, 1992.

Deleuze, Gilles, *Logique du sens*, Paris: Minuit, 1969.

Dorrian, Mark, "Ruskin's Theory of the Grotesque," in *Chora: Intervals in the Philosophy of Architecture*, vol. IV, Montreal: McGill Queens Press, 2004.

Fumaroli, Marc, *L'age de l'éloquence*, Paris: Albin Michel, 1994.

Gunn, SJ, and PG Lindley, eds., *Cardinal Wolsey: Church, State and Art*, Cambridge: Cambridge University Press, 1991.

Horace, Epistle I, 100.

Lecercle, Jean-Jacques, "Linguistic Intuitions: Lewis Carroll and 'Alice au pays des merveilles,'" *Europe-Revue littéraire mensuelle*, vol. 68, no. 736, 1990.

Richard, Jean-Pierre, *Lewis Carroll, Oeuvres*, Paris: Gallimard, 1990.

Ruskin, John, *The Seven Lamps of Architecture*, London: JM Dent and Sons, 1907.

Sherwood, Jennifer and Nikolaus Pevsner, *The Buildings of England: Oxfordshire*, Harmondsworth: Penguin Books, 1974.

Smith, Christine, *Architecture in the Culture of Early Humanism: Ethics, Aesthetics, and Eloquence 1400-1470*, New York and Oxford: Oxford University Press, 1992.

Tyack, Geoffrey, *Oxford An Architectural Guide*, Oxford and New York: Oxford University Press, 1998.

Walton, Isaak, *The Compleate Angler*, Jonquil Bevan, ed., Oxford: Clarendon Press, 1983.

Post-mortem: Architectural Post-modernism and the Death of the Author

Carola Ebert

Barthes, Roland, *Image-Music-Text*, Stephen Heath, trans., London: Fontana, 1977.

Bürger, Peter, *Theorie der Avant-Garde*, Frankfurt: Suhrkamp, 1974.

Burke, Seán, *The Death and Return of the Author*, Edinburgh: Edinburgh University Press, 1992.

Coles, Alex and Alexia Defert, eds., *de-, dis, -ex-: The Anxiety of Interdisciplinarity*, London: Black Dog Publishing, 1998.

Derrida, Jaques, interviewed by Eva Meyer, "Architecture Where Desire can live", *Domus*, no. 671, April 1986.

Eagleton, Terry, *Literary Theory: An Introduction*, Oxford: Blackwell, 1983.

Heynen, Hilde, *Architecture and Modernity: a Critique*, Cambridge, MA: MIT Press, 1999.

Hill, Jonathan, *The Illegal Architect*, London: Black Dog Publishing, 1998.

Hollier, Denis, *Against Architecture: The writings of Georges Bataille*, Betsy Wing, trans., Cambridge, MA: MIT Press, 1989.

Lévi-Strauss, Claude, *The Savage Mind*, London: Weidenfeld & Nicholson, 1966.

Nesbitt, Kate, ed., *Theorizing a New Agenda for Architecture: An Anthology of Architectural Theory 1965-1995*, New York: Princeton Architectual Press, 1996.

Oechslin, Werner, "Working with Fragments—The Limitations of Collage", *Daidalos*, no. 16, June 1985.

Poggi, Christine, *In Defiance of Painting: Cubism, Futurism, and the Invention of Collage*, New Haven: Yale University Press, 1992.

Rowe, Colin and Fred Koetter, *Collage City*, Bernard Hoesli et al, trans., Basel: Birkhäuser, 1984.

Rowe, Colin, and Fred Koetter, *Collage City*, Cambridge, MA: MIT Press, 1978.

Rowe, Colin and Robert Slutzky, "Transparency: Literal and Phenomenal", *Perspecta*, no. 8, 1963.

Rowe, Colin and Robert Slutzky, "Transparency: Literal and Phenomenal... Part II", *Perspecta*, nos. 13/14, 1971.

Tschumi, Bernard, *Architecture and Disjunction*, Cambridge, MA: MIT Press, 1994.

Tschumi, Bernard, "The Pleasure of Architecture", *Architectural Design*, no. 3, 1977.

Waldman, Diane, *Collage, Assemblage, and the Found Object*, London: Phaidon, 1992.

'In the Mind of the Architect': Representation and Authorship in Documentary Film

Naomi Stead

Arthur, Paul, "Extreme Makeover: The Changing Face of Documentary", *Cineaste*, Summer 2005, vol. 30, no. 3.

Australian Broadcasting Commission, *In the Mind of the Architect* www.abc.net.au/arts/architecture/about.htm

Barthes, Roland, *Image-Music-Text*, trans., Stephen Heath, London: Fontana, 1977.

Corrigan, Tim, *A Cinema Without Walls: Movies and Culture after Vietnam*, New Brunswick: Rutgers University Press, 1991.

Feldman, Allen, "Faux Documentary and the Memory of Realism", *American Anthropologist*, June 1998, vol. 100, no. 2.

Gerstner, David A and Janet Staiger, eds., *Authorship and Film*, New York, Routledge, 2003.

Lamster, Mark, ed., *Architecture and Film*, New York: Princeton Architecture Press, 2000.

Mast, Gerald and Marshall Cohen, eds., *Film Theory and Criticism: Introductory Readings*, New York: Oxford University Press, 1974.

Miller, Toby and Robert Stam, eds., *A Companion to Film Theory*, Oxford: Blackwell Publishers, 1999.

Pritzker Foundation, Pritzker Prize www.pritzkerprize.com/2002annc.htm#about

Rabiger, Michael, "Documentary Filmmakers Decide How to Present Compelling Evidence", *Nieman Reports*, Fall 2001.

Stam, Robert and Toby Miller, eds., *Film and Theory: An Anthology*, Oxford: Blackwell Publishers, 2000.

Wexman, Virginia Wright, ed., *Film and Authorship*, New Brunswick: Rutgers University Press, 2003.

Dislocation

Nature's Lovers: Design and Authorship in the Eighteenth Century Landscape Garden

Katja Grillner

Ahrland, Åsa, *Den osynliga handen—Trädgårdsmästaren i 1700-talets Sverige [The invisible hand—The gardener in 18th century Sweden]*, Alnarp: SLU, 2005.

Barthes, Roland, *Image-Music-Text*, Stephen Heath trans. and ed., London: Fontana, 1977.

Bending, Stephen, "Re-Reading the Eighteenth-Century English Landscape Garden" in *Huntington Library Quarterly*, vol. 55, 1992.

Bohl, Elizabeth A, *Women Travel Writers and the Language of Aesthetics*

1716-1818, Cambridge: University of Cambridge Press, 1995.

Bolla, Peter de, *The Education of the Eye–Painting, Landscape and Architecture in Eighteenth Century Britain*, Stanford: Stanford University Press, 2003.

Brewer, John, *The Pleasures of the Imagination*, London: Harper Collins Publishers, 1997.

Burke, Edmund, *A Philosophical Enquiry into the origins of our ideas of the Sublime and Beautiful*, Adam Phillips, ed., Oxford: Oxford University Press, 1998, Part III, section 14. (Originally published in 1757).

Chambers, William, *A Dissertation on Oriental Gardening*, London: W Griffin, 1772.

Delille, Jacques, *Les Jardins: – Ou l'Art d'Embellir les Paysages*, Paris and Rheims, 1783.

Disponzio, Joseph, "From Garden to Landscape—Jean Marie Morel and the Transformation of Garden History" in *AA-Files*, 44.

Dixon Hunt, John and Michel Conan, eds., *Tradition and Innovation in French Garden Art*, Philadelphia: University of Pennsylvania Press, 2002.

Dowler, L et al, eds., *Gender and Landscape—Renegotiating morality and space*, London: Routledge, 2005.

Foucault, Michel, *Textual Strategies: Perpectives in Post-Structuralist Criticism*, Josué V Harari, ed. and trans., Ithaca: Cornell University Press, 1979.

Girardin, René Louis le Marquis de, *De la Composition des Paysages*, Geneva and Paris, PM Delaguette, 1777. Republished in French in 1979, Paris: Éditions du Champ Urbain.

Girardin, René Louis le Marquis de, *Essay on Landscape; or, On the means of improving and embellishing the Country round our habitations*, Daniel Malthus, trans., London: J Dodsley, 1783.

Grillner, Katja, *Experiencing the Garden in the 18th Century*, ML Calder, ed., Bern: Peter Lang Publishers, 2006.

Heely, Joseph, *Letters on the Beauties of Hagley, Envil, and the Leasowes*, London: R Baldwin, 1777.

Hirschfeld, Cristian Cajus Lorenz, *Theorie der Gartenkunst*, Leipzig: Weidmanns Erben und Reich, 1775. Extended from 1779–1785 into a five volume work with same title.

Hirschfeld, Cristian Cajus Lorenz, *Theory of Garden Art*, Linda B Parshall, trans., Philadelphia: University of Pennsylvania Press, 2001.

Hunt, John Dixon, *Greater Perfections*, Philadelphia: University of Pennsylvania Press, 1999.

Kittler, Friedrich, *Discourse Networks, 1800/1900*, Stanford: Stanford University Press, 1990.

Lewes, Darby, *Nudes from nowhere: Sexual Utopian Landscapes*, Oxford: Rowman and Littlefield Publishers, 2000.

Mason, George, *Essay on Design in Gardening*, London, 1768. (Second edition published in 1795, London: Benjamin and John White).

Morel, Jean-Marie, *Théorie des jardins*, Paris: Pissot, 1776. (Facsimile edition published Geneva: Minkoff, 1973).

Norberg-Schulz, Christian, *Genius Loci—Towards a Phenomenology of Architecture*, London: Academy Editions, 1980.

Piper, Fredrik Magnus, *Description of the Idea and General-Plan for an English Park Written during the years 1811 and 1812 by Fredrik Magnus Piper*, Rebecka Millhagen, Magnus Olausson, John Harris, eds., Stockholm: Byggförlaget in collaboration with the Royal Swedish Academy of Fine Arts, 2004.

Pope, Alexander, *The Poems of Alexander Pope, Volume III ii—Epistles to several persons (Moral essays)*, John Butt, FW Bateson, eds.

Reynolds, Joshua, *Discourses on Art*, Robert R Wark, ed., San Marino: Huntington Library, 1959.

Saisselin, RG, "The French Garden in the Eighteenth Century: from Belle Nature to the landscape of time" in *The Journal of Garden History*, vol. 5, no. 3.

Walpole, Horace, *A History of the Modern Taste in Gardening*, London, 1771/80.

Watelet, Claude-Henri *Essai sur les Jardins*, Paris: Prault, 1774.

Watelet, Claude-Henri, *Essay on gardens: a chapter in the French picturesque translated into English for the first time*, Samuel Danon, ed., trans., Joseph Disponzio intro., Philadelphia: University of Pennsylvania Press, 2003.

Whately, Thomas, *Observations on Modern Gardening*, London: T Payne, 1770. (Facsimile edition published by Garland Publishing, 1982).

Interior/Image: Authorship and the Spatialities of Domestic Life

Charles Rice

Banham, Reyner, *A Critic Writes. Essays by Reyner Banham*, Berkeley: University of California Press, 1996.

Baudelaire, Charles, *The Poems in Prose, with La Fanfarlo*, Francis Scarfe, ed. and trans., London: Anvil Press, 1989.

Benjamin, Andrew, "Surface Effects: Borromini, Semper, Loos", *The Journal of Architecture* vol. 11, no. 1, 2006.

Benjamin, Walter, *The Arcades Project*, Howard Eiland and Kevin McLaughlan, trans., Cambridge, MA: The Belknap Press of Harvard University Press, 1999.

de Maistre, Xavier, *A Journey Around My Room*, Andrew Brown, trans., London: Hesperus, 2004.

Donzelot, Jacques, *The Policing of Families*, Robert Hurley, trans., Baltimore: Johns Hopkins University Press, 1979.

Evans, Robin, *Translations from Drawing to Building and Other Essays*, London: Architectural Association, 1997.

Foucault, Michel, *The History of Sexuality Volume 1: An Introduction*, Robert Hurley, trans., London: Allen Lane, 1978.

Freud, Sigmund, *The Standard Edition of the Complete Psychological Works of Sigmund Freud*, James Strachey, ed. and trans., 24 vols., London: The Hogarth Press, 1953–74.

Fuss, Diana, *The Sense of an Interior: Four Writers and the Rooms that Shaped Them*, London: Routledge, 2004.

Gere, Charlotte, *Nineteenth Century Interiors: An Album of Watercolours*, London: Thames and Hudson, 1992.

Grant, Charlotte, "Reading the House of Fiction: From Object to Interior, 1720-1920", *Home Cultures*, vol. 2, no. 3, 2005.

Kamper, Dietmar and Christoph Wulf, eds., *Looking Back on the End of the World*, New York: Semiotext(e), 1989.

Kerr, Robert, *The Gentleman's House, or How to Plan English Residences from the Parsonage to the Palace; with Tables of Accommodation and Cost, and a Series of Selected Plans*, 3rd revised ed., London: John Murray, 1871 [1864].

Lavin, Sylvia, *Form Follows Libido: Architecture and Richard Neutra in a Psychoanalytic Culture*, Cambridge, MA: MIT Press, 2004.

Leach, Neil, ed., *Rethinking Architecture: A Reader in Cultural Theory*, London: Routledge, 1997.

Loos, Adolf, *Ornament and Crime: Selected Essays*, Michael Mitchell, trans., Riverside, CA: Ariadne Press, 1998.

Loos, Adolf, *On Architecture*, Michael Mitchell, trans., Riverside, CA: Ariadne Press, 2002.

Loos, Adolf, *Spoken Into the Void: Collected Essays. 1897–1900*, Jane O Newman and John H Smith, trans., Cambridge, MA: MIT Press, 1982.

Riley, Terence, *The Un-Private House*, New York: Museum of Modern Art, 1999.

Schwartz, Fredric, *The Werkbund: Design Theory and Mass Culture before the First World War*, New Haven: Yale University Press, 1996.

Thornton, Peter, *Authentic Décor: the Domestic Interior, 1620-1920*, New York: Viking, 1984.

Van Duzer, Leslie, and Kent Kleinman, *Villa Muller: A Work of Adolf Loos*, New York: Princeton Architectural Press, 1994.

Vidler, Anthony, *The Architectural Uncanny: Essays in the Modern Unhomely*, Cambridge, MA: MIT Press, 1992.

Sweet Garden of Vanished Pleasures: Derek Jarman at Dungeness

Jonathan Hill

Birksted, Jan, ed., *Relating Architecture to Landscape*, London and New York: E and FN Spon, 1999.

Burke, Edmund, *Philosophical Enquiry into the Origin of our Ideas of the Sublime and Beautiful*, Oxford: Oxford University Press, 1998.

Dixon Hunt, John and Peter Willis, eds., *The Genius of the Place: The English Landscape Garden 1620–1820*, London: Elek, 1975.

Fletcher, Banister, *A History of Architecture on the Comparative Method*, London: BT Batsford, 1924, 7th edition.

Freud, Sigmund, *The Standard Edition of the Complete Psychological Works of Sigmund Freud, vol. 17*, James Strachey, ed., Alix Strachey, trans., Toronto: Clarke Irwin, 1955.

Hume, David, *Selected Essays*, Oxford: Oxford University Press, 1993.

Hunt, John Dixon, *Gardens and the Picturesque: Studies in the History of Landscape Architecture*, Cambridge, MA and London: MIT Press, 1992.

Jarman, Derek, *Derek Jarman's Garden*, London: Thames and Hudson, 1995.

Jarman, Derek, dir., *The Angelic Conversation*, BFI, 1985.

Jarman, Derek, *At Your Own Risk: A Saint's Testament*, London: Vintage, 1993.

Jarman, Derek, dir., *The Garden*, Basilisk in association with Channel 4, British Screen, ZDF and Uplink, 1990.

Jarman, Derek, *Kicking the Pricks*, London: Vantage, 1996.

Jarman, Derek, *Know What I Mean*, an interview preceding *A Night with Derek*, Channel 4 Television, 16 July 1994.

Jarman, Derek, dir., *The Last of England*, Anglo International Films for British Screen, Channel 4 and ZDF, 1987.

Jarman, Derek, *Modern Nature: The Journals of Derek Jarman*, London: Century, 1991.

Locke, John, *Essay concerning Human Understanding*, Peter H Nidditch, ed., Oxford: Clarendon Press, 1975.

O'Pray, Michael, *Derek Jarman: Dreams of England*, London: British Film Institute, 1996.

Peake, Tony, *Derek Jarman*, London: Little, Brown and Company, 1999.

Pevsner, Nikolaus, *The Englishness of English Art: An Expanded and Annotated Version of the Reith Lectures Broadcast in October and November 1955*, London: Architectural Press, 1956.

Pevsner, Nikolaus, *Pevsner on Art and Architecture: The Radio Talks*, Stephen Games, ed., London: Methuen, 2002.

Pevsner, Nikolaus, "Twentieth-Century Picturesque: An Answer to Basil Taylor's Broadcast", *Architectural Review*, vol. 115, no. 688, April 1954.

Ruskin, John, *The Seven Lamps of Architecture*, New York: Farrar, Straus and Giroux, 1984. First published in 1849.

Vitruvius, *The Ten Books on Architecture*, Morris Hicky Morgan, trans., New York: Dover, 1960. First published as *De Architectura* in the first century BC.

Wollen, Roger, Lloyd, ed., *Derek Jarman: A Portrait. Artist, Film-maker, Designer*, London: Thames and Hudson, 1996.

Translation

Genius, Fiction and the Author in Architecture

Louise Pelletier

Bastide, Jean-François de, *The Little House: An Architectural Seduction*, trans. and introduction by Rodolphe el-Khoury, preface by Anthony Vidler, New York: Princeton Architectural Press, 1995.

Bastide, Jean-François de, *La petite maison* [1758, 1763], ed. and introduction by Michel Delon, Paris: Editions Gallimard, 1995.

Blondel, Jacques-François, *Cours d'architecture, ou, Traité de la décoration, distribution & construction des bâtiments contenant les leçons données en 1750 & les années suivantes par JF Blondel*, 9 vols., ed. Pierre Patte, Paris: Desaint, 1771–1779.

Diderot, Denis, *Encyclopedie; ou, Dictionnaire raisonne des sciences, des arts et des metiers/par une Societe de gens de lettres; mis en ordre & publie par M. Diderot…; quant a la partie mathematique par M. D'Alembert…*, 17 vols. [Paris: Briasson, 1751–1780], New York: Pergamon Press, 1969.

Diderot, Denis, *Oeuvres esthétiques*, ed. Pierre Vernière, Paris: Garnier Frères, 1968.

Gadol, Joan, *Leon Battista Alberti: Universal Man of the Early Renaissance*, Chicago and London: The University of Chicago Press, 1969.

Le Camus de Mézières, Nicolas, *Le genie de l'architecture: ou, L'analogie de cet art avec nos sensations* [Paris: B. Morin, 1780], Geneva: Minkoff Reprint, 1972.

Le Camus de Mézières, Nicolas, *The Genius of Architecture; or, the Analogy of That Art With Our Sensations*, D Britt, trans., introduction by Robin Middleton, Santa Monica, CA: The Getty Center, 1992.

Pelletier, Louise, *Architecture in Words*, London: Routledge, 2006.

Cultures of Display: Exhibiting Architecture in Berlin, 1880–1931

Wallis Miller

Ausstellungs-, Messe- und Fremdenverkehrs-Amt der Stadt Berlin, *Deutsche Bauausstellung Berlin 1931. Amtlicher Katalog und Führer*, Berlin: Bauwelt-Verlag/Ullsteinhaus, 1931.

Bau-Rundschau, vol. 21, no. 12, 25 June 1930.

Bilsel, SM Can, *Architecture in the Museum: Displacement, Reconstruction and Reproduction of the Monuments of Antiquity in Berlin's Pergamon Museum*, vol. 1, PhD diss., Princeton University, 2003.

Börsch-Supan, Helmut ed., *Die Kataloge der Berliner Akademie Ausstellungen 1786-1850* (3 vols.), Berlin: Hessling, 1971.

Cramer, Johannes and Niels Gutschow, eds., *Bauausstellungen*, Stuttgart: Kohlhammer, 1984.

Die Form, vol. 6, no. 6, 15 June 1931 and vol. 6, no. 7, 15 July 1931.

Joachimides, Alexis, Sven Kuhrau, Viola Vahrson, and Nikolaus Bernau, eds., *Museumsinszenierungen. Zur Geschichte der Institution des Kunstmuseums. Die Berliner Museumslandschaft 1830-1990*, Dresden and Basel: Verlag der Kunst, 1995.

Königliche Museen zu Berlin, *Führer durch das Pergamon-Museum*, Berlin: Georg Reimer, 1902.

Mies van der Rohe, Ludwig, "Zum Thema: Ausstellungen", *Die Form*, vol. 5, no. 4, 1928.

Miller, Wallis, *Tangible Ideas: Architecture and the Public at the 1931 German Building Exhibition in Berlin*, PhD diss., Princeton University, 1999.

Piggott, JR, *Palace of the People. The Crystal Palace at Sydenham 1854-1936*, Madison: The University of Wisconsin Press, 2004.

Pommer, Richard and Christian Otto, *Weissenhof 1927 and the Modern Movement in Architecture*, Chicago: University of Chicago Press, 1991.

Rave, Paul Ortwin, *Das Schinkel-Museum und die Kunst-Sammlungen Beuths*, Berlin: Ernst Rathenau, 1931.

Schindler, Wolfgang, *Modus in Rebus*, Berlin: Gebr Mann, 1995.

Schliepmann, Hans, "Die Architektur auf der diesjährigen Grossen Berliner Kunstausstellung", *Berliner Architekturwelt*, no. 4, 1902.

Schwarzer, Mitchell W, "The Emergence of Architectural Space: August Schmarsow's Theory of *Raumgestaltung*", *Assemblage*, no. 15 August 1991.

Schulze, Franz, ed., *Mies van der Rohe: Critical Essays*, New York: The Museum of Modern Art, 1989.

Vischer, Robert, Conrad Fiedler, Heinrich Wölfflin, Adolf Göller, Adolf Hildebrand, August Schmarsow *Empathy, Form, and Space. Problems in German Aesthetics, 1873-1893*, Harry Francis Mallgrave and Eleftherios Ikonomou, trans., Santa Monica, CA: Getty Center for the History of Art and the Humanities, 1994.

"Von der Jubiläums-Ausstellung der Kgl. Akademie der Künste zu Berlin", *Deutsche Bauzeitung*, vol. 20, no. 41, 22 May 1886.

von Bode, Wilhelm, "Das Kaiser Friedrich-Museum in Berlin. Zur Eröffnung am 18. Oktober 1904", *Museumskunde*, vol. 1, 1905.

Waetzoldt, Stephan, *Pläne und Wettbewerbe für Bauten auf der Berliner Museumsinsel 1873-1896, Jahrbuch der Berliner Museen*, vol. 35, supplement, Berlin: Gebr. Mann, 1993.

The Inhuman One: the Mythology of Architect as Réalisateur

Renée Tobe

Albrecht, Donald, *Designing Dreams; modern architecture in the movies*, Santa Monica: Hennessey and Ingalls, 2000.

Becherer, Richard, "Picturing Architecture Otherwise: the voguing of the Maison Mallet-Stevens," in *Art History*, vol. 23, Issue 4, November 2000.

Cheraqui, Yves and Benôit Ted, *Histoire Vraies*, Paris: Les Humanoïdes Associés, 1982.

Colomina, Beatriz, *Privacy and Publicity, Architecture as Mass Media*, London: MIT Press, 1994.

Cowie, Elizabeth, *Representing the Woman: Cinema and Psychoanalysis*, London: Macmillan Press Ltd, 1997.

Deleuze, Gilles, *Cinema 1: The Movement-Image*, Hugh Tomlinson and Barbara Habberjam, trans., London: The Athlone Press, 1992.

Dwan, Alan, dir., *What a Widow*, perf. Gloria Swanson, USA, 1930.

Gadamer, Hans-Georg, *Truth and Method*, London: Ward and Sheed, 1993.

Gance, Abel, dir., *La Roue*, France, 1922.

Green, Christopher, *Léger and the Avant-Garde*, London: Yale University Press, 1976.

Gronberg, Tag, *Designs on Modernity; Exhibiting the City in 1920s Paris*, Manchester: Manchester University Press, 1998.

Klein, Richard, *Robert Mallet-Stevens; La Villa Cavrois*, Paris: Editions A et J Picard, 2005.

L'Herbier, Marcel, dir., *L'Inhumaine*, perf. Georgette Leblanc and Jaque Catelain, France, 1924.

L'Herbier, Marcel, ed., *Intelligence du Cinematographe*, Paris: Editions Correa, 1948.

Lang, Fritz, dir., *Metropolis*, perf. Brigitte Helm, Rudolf Klein-Rogge, Germany, 1927.

Léger, Fernand, dir., *Ballet Mécanique*, perf. Kiki de Montparnasse, Katherine Murphy, France, 1924.

Mac Orlan, Pierre, *L'Inhumaine*, Paris: Gallimard, 1925.

Mallet-Stevens, Robert, "Le Cinéma et les arts, l'architecture," in *Les Cahiers du Mois*, nos. 16 and 17, 1925.

Mallet-Stevens, Robert, *Le Décor moderne au cinema*, Paris: Charles Massin, 1928.

Mallet-Stevens, Robert, *Dessins 1921 pour une cité moderne*, Paris: Gallerie Fanny Giullon-Laffaille, 1986.

Man Ray, dir., *Les Mystères du château du Dé*, France, 1928.

Penz, Francois, and Maureen Thomas, eds., *Melies, Mallet-Stevens and Multi-Media*, London: BFI, 1998.

Pinchon, Jean-Francois, *Rob. Mallet-Stevens: Architecture, Furniture, Interior Design*, Cambridge, MA: MIT Press, 1990.

Resnais, Alain, dir., *Last Year in Marienbad*, perf. Delphine Seyrig, Giorgio Albertazzi, and Sacha Pitoëff, 1961.

Shanahan, Maureen, *Indeterminate and Inhuman: Georgette Leblanc in L'Inhumaine*, Institute for European Studies, 2003.

Turvey, Malcolm, "The Avante-Garde and the 'New Spirit'; the Case of *Ballet mécanique*," in *October*, vol. 102, Fall 2002.

Wiser, William, *The Crazy Years; Paris in the Twenties*, Great Britain: Thames and Hudson, 1983.

The Allegorical Project: Architecture as 'Figurative Theory'

Penelope Haralambidou

Cowan, Bainard, "Walter Benjamin's Theory of Allegory", *New German Critique*, no. 22, Special Issue on Modernism, Winter, 1981.

Crome, Keith and James Williams, *The Lyotard Reader and Guide*, Edinburgh: Edinburgh University, 2006.

Dews, Peter, "The Letter and the Line: Discourse and Its Other in Lyotard", *Diacritics*, vol. 14, no. 3, 1984.

Fletcher, Angus, *Allegory: The Theory of a Symbolic Mode*, Ithaka and New York: Cornell University, 1965.

Frye, Northrop, *Anatomy of Criticism: Four Essays*, Harmondsworth: Penguin, 1990.

Greenblatt, Stephen J, ed., *Allegory and Representation: Selected Papers from the English Institute, 1979–80*, Baltimore and London: Johns Hopkins University, 1981.

Hill, Jonathan, *Actions of Architecture: Architects and Creative Users*, London: Routledge, 2003.

Jay, Martin, *Downcast Eyes: The Denigration of Vision in Twentieth-Century French Thought*, Berkeley: University of California, 1994.

Jump, John D, ed., *The Critical Idiom*, no.14, London: Methuen, 1976.

Koolhaas, Rem, *Delirious New York: A Retroactive Manifesto for Manhattan*, New York: Oxford University Press, 1972.

Koolhaas, Rem, *Delirious New York: A Retroactive Manifesto for Manhattan*, Rotterdam: 010, 1994.

Lyotard, Jean-François, *Discours, figure*, Paris: Klincksieck, 1985.

Nicholson, Ben, *Appliance House*, Chicago and Cambridge: Chicago Institute for Architecture and Urbanism and MIT, 1990.

Nicholson, Ben, *The World Who Wants It?*, London: Black Dog Publishing, 2004.

Owens, Craig, "The Allegorical Impulse: Toward a Theory of Postmodernism", *October*, nos. 12 and 13, 1980.

Webb, Michael, *Temple Island: A Study*, London: Architectural Association, 1987.

Whitehead, Christiania, *Castles of the Mind: A Study of Medieval Architectural Allegory*, Cardiff: University of Wales, 2003.

Dissolution

The Semi-living Author: Post-human Creative Agency

Rolf Hughes

Bateson, Gregory, *Steps to an Ecology of Mind*, London: Paladin, 1973.

Benjamin, Walter, *Illuminations*, Harry Zohn, trans., London: Fontana, 1992.

Biagioli, Mario and Peter Galison, eds., *Scientific Authorship: Credit and Intellectual Property in Science*, New York and London: Routledge, 2003.

Bohm, David, *On Creativity*, Abingdon and New York: Routledge, 1996, reprinted by Routledge Classics, 2004.

Boyle, Robert, *Selected Philosophical Papers of Robert Boyle*, MA Stewart, ed., New York: Manchester University Press, 1979.

Burke, Seán, *Authorship: From Plato to the Postmodern*, Edinburgh: Edinburgh University Press, 1995, reprinted 2000.

Frazer, John, *An Evolutionary Architecture*, London: Architecture Association, 1995.

Hayles, N Katherine, *How We Became Posthuman*, London: University of Chicago, 1999.

Kauffman, Stuart, *At Home in the Universe: The Search for the Laws of Self-Organization and Complexity*, New York: Oxford University Press, 1995.

Klein, Julie Thompson, "Interdisciplinarity and complexity: An evolving relationship", in *E:CO* Special Double Issue, vol. 6, nos. 1–2, 2004.

Langton, Christopher, ed., *Artificial Life*, Santa Fe Institute Studies in the Sciences of Complexity, vol. 6, Reading, MA: Addison Wesley, 1989.

Latour, Bruno, "Why Has Critique Run out of Steam? From Matters of Fact to Matters of Concern", *Critical Inquiry*, vol. 30, no. 2.

Lloyd-Thomas, Katie, ed., *Material Matters*, London: Routledge, 2007.

Luhmann, Niklas, *Essays in Self-Reference*, New York: Columbia University Press, 1990.

Maturana, Humberto and Francisco Varela, *Autopoiesis and Cognition: The Realization of the Living*, Boston Studies in the Philosophy of Science, vol. 42, Dordrecht, Holland: D Reidel, 1980.

Nelmes, Jill, ed., *An Introduction to Film Studies*, London and New York: Routledge, 1996, 3rd edition reprinted 2003.

Nesbitt, K, ed., *Theorizing a New Agenda for Architecture: An Anthology of Architectural Theory*, New York: Princeton Architectural Press, 1996.

Ortony, Andrew, ed., *Metaphor and Thought*, London: Cambridge University Press, 1993, 2nd edition.

Rosenberg, Martin E, "Constructing Autopoiesis: The Architectural Body in Light of Contemporary Cognitive Science" in *Interfaces* 21/22, 2003.

Speaks, Michael, "Theory was interesting... but now we have work", *arq* 6/2, "perspective," June 26, 2002.

Taylor, Mark, *The Moment of Complexity: Emerging Network Culture*, Chicago and London: The University of Chicago Press, 2005.

Thompson, Adrian, Paul Layzell and Ricardo Salem Zebulum, "Explorations in Design Space: Unconventional Electronics Design Through Artificial Evolution," *IEEE Transactions on Evolutionary Computation 3*, no. 3, 1999.

von Kleist, Heinrich, *Essays on Dolls*, Idris Parry and Paul Keegan, trans., Harmondsworth: Penguin Books, 1994.

Whitelaw, Mitchell, *Metacreation: Art and Artificial Life*, Cambridge, MA and London: MIT Press, 2004.

Wiener, Norbert, *The Human Use of Human Beings: Cybernetics and Society*, London: Eyre and Spottiswoode, 1954.

Williams, Sam, "Unnatural Selection" in *Technology Review*, February 2005.

Wilner, Lena and Abdellah Abarkan, eds., *The Four Faces of Architecture: On the Dynamics of Architectural Knowledge*, Stockholm, School of Architecture/Royal Institute of Technology, 2005.

Wilson, Stephen, *Information Arts: Intersections of Art, Science, and Technology*, Cambridge, MA: MIT Press, 2002.

Cedric Price as Anti-architect

Stanley Mathews

Barthes, Roland, *Image-Music-Text*, New York: Hill and Wang, 1977.

Besant, Sir Walter, *All Sorts and Conditions of Men: An Impossible Story*, London: Chatto and Windus, 1900.

Burns, James, *Arthropods*, London: Academy Editions, 1972.

Koolhaas, Rem, *S, M, L, XL*, New York: Monacelli Press, 1995.

Mathews, Stanley, *From Agit Prop to Free Space: the Architecture of Cedric Price*, London: Black Dog Publishing, 2007.

Ernst Neufert's Architect's Data: Anxiety, Creativity and Authorial Abdication

Gernot Weckherlin

Aalto, Alvar, *Aalto in his own words*, Göran Schild, ed., New York: Rizzoli International Publications, 1997.

Anonymous, "Im Medaillon", in *Bauwelt*, no. 11, 1960.

Durand, Jean-Nicolas-Louis, *Précis des Leçons d'Architecture Donées à l'Ècole Royale Polytechnique*, Paris, 1819.

Gotthelf, Fritz, *Ernst Neufert. Ein Architekt unserer Zeit*, Ullstein-Fachverlag, Berlin, Frankfurt, Wien, 1960.

Gropius, Walter, "Der große Baukasten", in *Das neue Frankfurt*, 2, 1926.

Häring, Hugo, "Neues Bauen" in *Baukunst und Werkform*, 1, 1947.

Hegemann, Werner, "Das dänische Handbuch der Bauindustrie", in *Wasmuths Monatshefte für Baukunst*, Berlin, 6, 1931.

Klopfer, Paul, "Ernst Neufert. Ein Architekt unserer Zeit. Zu seinem fünfzigsten Geburtstag beglückwünscht von Paul Klopfer", in *Neue Bauwelt*, 11, 1950.

Leowald, Georg, "Sinn und Grenzen der Normung. Eine nachgeholte Auseinandersetzung mit Neuferts ,Bauordnungslehre', in *Baukunst und Werkform*, 1, 1947.

Neufert, Ernst, *Bauentwurfslehre, Grundlagen, Normen, Vorschriften, über Anlage, Bau, Gestaltung, Raumbedarf, Raumbeziehungen, Maße für Gebäude, Räume, Einrichtungen, Geräte mit dem Menschen als Maß und Ziel; Handbuch für den Baufachmann, Bauherrn, Lehrenden und Lernenden*, Berlin, 1936.

Neufert, Ernst, *Bauordnungslehre*, Albert Speer, ed., Berlin: Volk und Reich-Verlag, 1943.

Neufert, Ernst, "Ausbildung der schöpferischen Fähigkeiten des Architekten" in *Der Architekt im Zerreisspunkt. Vorträge, Berichte und Diskussionsbeiträge der Sektion Architektur auf dem Internationalen Kongress für Ingenieurausbildung (IKIA) in Darmstadt 1947*, Darmstadt: Eduard Roether Verlag, 1948.

Neufert, Ernst, *Architects' Data*, Vincent Jones, ed., London, Toronto, Sidney, New York, 1980, p. XI, 2nd English edition.

Nicolaisen, Dörte, ed., Bauhaus-Archiv Berlin, *Das andere Bauhaus. Otto Bartning und die Staatliche Bauhochschule Weimar 1926-1930*, Berlin: Kupfergraben-Verlagsgesellschaft, 1996.

Nietzsche, Friedrich, *Human, All Too Human, A Book for Free Spirits*, (The Complete Works of Friedrich Nietzsche vol. 3), translated with an Afterword by Gary Handwerk, Stanford University Press, 1995.

Pottage, Allain, "Architectural Authorship: The Normative Ambitions of Le Corbusier's Modulor" in *AA-Files*, 31, 1996.

Prigge, Walter, ed., *Ernst Neufert. Normierte Baukultur im 20. Jahrhundert*, Frankfurt and New York: Campus, 1999.

Ramsey, Charles George, Harold Reeve Sleeper, *Architectural Graphic Standards for Architects, Engineers, Decorators, Builders and Draftsmen*, New York: J Wiley and Sons, 1932.

Reichlin, Bruno, "Den Entwurfsprozess steuern–eine fixe Idee der Moderne?" in *Daidalos 71*, 1999.

Weilbier, Rudolf, "Triumph der Gleichform und des Zusammenpassens" in *Bauwelt*, 1944.

Wolf, Gustav, *Die Grundriß-Staffel. Eine Sammlung von Kleinwohnungsgrundrissen der Nachkriegszeit mit einem Vorschlag folgerichtiger Ordnung und Kurz-Bezeichnung von Professor Gustav Wolf. Beitrag zur Grundrißwissenschaft*, Munich: Callwey, 1931.

Systems Aesthetics, or how Cambridge Solved Architecture

Sean Keller

Alexander, Christopher, *Notes on the Synthesis of Form*, Cambridge, MA: Harvard University Press, 1964.

Alexander, Christopher, "The Synthesis of Form: Some Notes on a Theory", PhD diss., Harvard University, 1962.

Allen, Stan, talk given for "Five Architects and After", Harvard University Graduate School of Design, session 4 of the series "The 70's: the Formation of Contemporary Architectural Discourse", presented by the Harvard University Graduate School of Design and Cornell University Department of Architecture, 2000-1. Video recording available at Visual Resources, Loeb Library, Harvard Graduate School of Design.

Cooke, Catherine, "The Town of Socialism", PhD diss., University of Cambridge, 1974.

"Discord Over Harmony in Architecture: The Eisenman/Alexander Debate," *Harvard Graduate School of Design News*, 2, 1983.

Eisenman, Peter, "Post-Functionalism", *Oppositions*, 6, 1976.

Eisenman, Peter, "The Formal Basis of Modern Architecture", PhD diss., University of Cambridge, 1963.

Eisenman, Peter, "Towards an Understanding of Form in Architecture", *Architectural Design*, 33, 1963.

Grabow, Stephen, *Christopher Alexander: The Search for a New Paradigm in Architecture*, Stocksfield, England: Oriel Press, 1983.

Keller, Sean, "Fenland Tech: Architectural Science in Postwar Cambridge", *Grey Room*, 23, 2006.

March, Lionel, ed., *The Architecture of Form*, Cambridge: Cambridge University Press, 1976.

March, Lionel, "Modern Movement to Vitruvius: Themes of Education and Research", *Royal Institute of British Architects Journal*, 81, 1972.

March, Lionel, "Research and Environmental Studies", *Cambridge Review*, 2 February 1973.

March, Lionel, Marcial Echeñique and Peter Dickens, eds., "Models of Environment", *Architectural Design*, 41, 1971.

Martin, Leslie, Ben Nicholson, and Naum Gabo, eds., *Circle: International Survey of Constructive Art*, London: Faber and Faber, 1937.

Rowe, Colin, *As I Was Saying: Recollections and Miscellaneous Essays*, Alexander Caragonne, ed., Cambridge, MA: MIT Press, 1996.

Wigley, Mark, "Network Fever", *Grey Room*, 4, 2001.

'Exoticising the Domestic': on New Collaborative Paradigms and Advanced Design Practices

Hélène Lipstadt

Biau, Véronique, *L'architecture comme emblème municipal: les grands projets des maires*, Paris-La Défense: Plan Construction et architecture, 1992.

Bourdieu, Pierre, "Some Questions for the True Masters of the World", Loïc Wacquant, trans., *Berkeley Journal of Sociology*, vol. 46, 2002.

Bourdieu, Pierre, *Homo Academicus*, Peter Collier, trans., Stanford: Stanford University Press, 1988.

Bourdieu, Pierre, *The Rules of Art: Genesis and Structure of the Literary Field*, Susan Emanuel, trans., Stanford: Stanford University Press, 1996.

Chartier, Roger, *Cultural History Between Practices and Representations*, Lydia G Cochrane, trans., Ithaca, Cornell University Press, 1988.

Colomina, Beatriz, "Collaborations: The Private Life of Modern Architecture", *Journal of the Society of Architectural Historians*, vol. 58, no. 3, September 1999.

Grilllner, Katja, Per Glembrandt et al, eds., *01.AKAD—Experimental Research in Architecture and Design—Beginnings*, Stockholm: Axl Books, 2005.

Hellberg, Inga, Mike Saks et al, ed., *Professional Identities in Transit: Cross-Cultural Dimensions*, Gothenberg: Almqvist and Wiksell, 1998.

Hillier, Jean and Emma Rooksby, eds., *Habitus: A Sense of Place*, Aldershot: Ashworth, 2002.

Idt, Geneviève, ed., *Sartre, une écriture en acte. Cahiers RITM 24*, Nanterre: Publidix, 2001.

Kaspori, Dennis, "A Communism of Ideas: Towards an Architectural Open Source Practice", *Archis*, 2003, www.archis.org/archis_old/english/archis_art_e_2003/art_3b_2003e.html

Marx, Karl, *Capital: A Critique of Political Economy*. vol. 1, Frederick Engels, ed., Ernest Untermann, trans., Chicago: Charles H Kerr and Co Cooperative, 1909.

Mauger, Gérard, ed., *Droits d'entrée*, Paris: Editions de la MSH, 2002.

Montlibert, Christian de, *L'impossible autonomie de l'architecte*, Strasbourg: Presses universitaires de Strasbourg, 1995.

Olgiati, Vittorio, Louis Orzack et al, ed., *Professions, Identity, and Order in Comparative Perspective*, Oñati: Oñati International Institute for the Sociology of Law, 1998.

Panofsky, Erwin, *Gothic Architecture and Scholasticism: An Inquiry Into the Analogy of the Arts, Philosophy and Religion in the Middle Ages*, New York: World Publishing, 1951.

Shamiyeh, Michael, ed., *What People Want: Populism in Architecture and Design*, Basel: Birkhäuser, 2005.

Violeau, Jean-Louis, "Les 'premiers collés' volontaires de l'architecture", *AMC: Les Nouveaux albums des jeunes architectes 2001/2002*, Hors Séries, 2002.

Contributors

Tim Anstey is an architect and researcher. He holds a PhD in the History and Theory of Architecture and is a Lecturer at the University of Bath in England, and Guest Senior Lecturer at the School of Architecture, Royal Institute of Technology, Stockholm. He is a member of the research project Architecture and its Mythologies and combines studio teaching with research interests that span between architectural theory and technology. He is currently working on a book about the construction of the figure of the architect in the fifteenth century, with a special focus on the architectural treatise of Leon Battista Alberti, *De re aedificatoria*.

Caroline Dionne holds a PhD in the History and Theory of Architecture from McGill University, 2005. In the recent years, her published contributions include essays in *Spirale, Inter Art Actuel, ETC Montréal, Chora 4 Intervals in the philosophy of Architecture*, as well as artists' exhibition catalogues for Gallerie Articule and Gallerie B 312, in Montreal, and The Or Gallery in Vancouver. She participated in the research project, "Theatrical Space as a Model for Architecture: An Annotated Bibliography on Ephemeral Structures, Theatrical Urban Space, and the Architecture of the Stage in Modern Europe", sponsored by the Institut du Recherche en l'Histoire de l'Architecture (IRHA), from 2000 to 2001, and was a research assistant at the CCA Study Centre in Montréal, from 2004 to 2005. She lives and works in Lausanne, Switzerland.

Carola Ebert, Dipl. Ing. Architect MSc, runs a small, thriving practice for residential projects in Berlin, Germany. She has been a visiting critic and lecturer at various universities in Berlin and London and has presented her research on composite practices in architecture, architectural ideologies, and the 1960s at different architecture conferences in Estonia, Finland, Germany, the UK etc.. She studied architecture at the Bartlett School of Architecture, University College London, and the Technical University Berlin, 1998, and holds a Master in Architectural History, 2001, from the Bartlett, where she is currently investigating the 1960s modernist Bungalow in West Germany as an MPhil/PhD candidate.

Katja Grillner, M.Arch, PhD, is an architect and critic based in Stockholm, Sweden. She is a Senior Lecturer at the Department of Architecture, Royal Institute of Technology, Stockholm, where she is the director of research and PhD studies, and the director of AKAD. She is a member of the board of the Swedish Architecture Museum. Among her book publications are her PhD dissertation *Ramble, linger and gaze – philosophical dialogues in the landscape garden*, Stockholm: KTH, 2000, and as main editor, *01.AKAD—Experimental Research in Architecture and Design*, Stockholm: AxlBooks, 2005. Her research on architecture and landscape combines theoretical, historical and literary strategies of investigation.

Dr Penelope Haralambidou is a designer, researcher and Lecturer in Architecture at the Bartlett, UCL. Her work investigates cultural constructs of spatial perception, imagination and representation, she sees architectural drawing as a critical method, and her projects have been distinguished in international competitions and exhibited in Europe and the US, most notably DomoBaal, London, 2006 and 2007; Slade Galleries, London, 2004; Museum of Contemporary Art, Athens, 2002; and 7th Biennale of Architecture, Venice, 2000. She was a founding member of Tessera, a collaborative architectural practice addressing issues of contemporary public space, which designed the exhibition 'Athens-Scape', RIBA, London, 2003.

Jonathan Hill, an architect and architectural historian, is Professor of Architecture and Visual Theory and Director of the MPhil/PhD by Architectural Design programme at the Bartlett School of Architecture, University College London. He is the author of *The Illegal Architect*, 1998, *Actions of Architecture*, 2003, and *Immaterial Architecture*, 2006. Jonathan is the editor of *Occupying Architecture*, 1998, *Architecture—the Subject is Matter*, 2001, and the 'Research by Design' issue of *The Journal of Architecture*, 2003. He is co-editor of *Critical Architecture*, 2007. Galleries where he has had solo exhibitions include the Haus der Architektur, Graz, and Architektur-Galerie am Weissenhof, Stuttgart.

Rolf Hughes is a writer, researcher and critic. He holds a PhD in Creative and Critical Writing from the University of East Anglia and has co-edited (with John Monk) *The Book of Models: Essays on Ceremonies, Metaphor and Performance*, 1998, reprinted 2003, and *Hybrid Thought*, 2003. *Second Nature: Reproduction and the Artificial in Art, Science and New Media*, co-edited with Jenny Sundén, is due in 2007. His scholarly research has been published in *The Journal of Architecture*, *OASE*, *Critical Architecture*, and elsewhere. A researcher in the projects *Architecture and its Mythologies* and *Autopoiesis and Design* at the KTH Royal Institute of Technology, both funded by the National Research Council, Hughes teaches at the Department of Interdisciplinary Studies at Konstfack, Stockholm, and is a member of the board of The Academy for Practice-Based Research in Architecture and Design (www.akad.se).

Sean Keller is a visiting lecturer in the Department of the History of Art at Yale University. His article "Fenland Tech: Architectural Science in Postwar Cambridge" appeared in the spring 2006 issue of *Grey Room*. An essay on the work of Peter Eisenman is forthcoming in the catalogue for *From Diagram to Code: The Computational Turn of Contemporary Architecture*, an exhibition at the Maison de l'Architecture et de la Ville, Marseille, December 2006–February 2007. His PhD dissertation for Harvard University, "Systems Aesthetics: Architectural Theory at the University of Cambridge, 1960-75," was completed in 2005.

Hélène Lipstadt is a cultural historian of architecture whose specialisation is in architectural authorship. She has taught at the Université de Montréal and the Massachusetts Institute of Technology. A founding Director of the US chapter of the international preservation organisation, DOCOMOMO, she is the Secretary of its Board and serves as its co-executive director. Her studies include historical and theoretical examinations of the illustrated architectural journal, exhibitions and publishing, architect-intellectuals, architectural competitions, and, through the study of national memorials, architects and the state and memory. She writes and lectures extensively on the application of Pierre Bourdieu's sociology to architecture, and is preparing a book on the subject to be published by the Pennsylvania State University Press.

Wallis Miller is the Charles P Graves Associate Professor of Architecture at the University of Kentucky. She is the author of several articles on architecture exhibitions and museums including, "Mies and Exhibitions" for the 2001 exhibition *Mies in Berlin*, held at the Museum of Modern Art, New York, and, most recently, "Circling the Square" for *OM Ungers. Kosmos der Architektur*, held in 2006 at the New National Gallery in Berlin. She is currently working on *Berlin's Architecture Museum*, a book about collecting and exhibiting architecture in Berlin during the nineteenth and early twentieth centuries.

Stanley Mathews is a professor of architectural history and design at Hobart and William Smith Colleges in New York State. His pioneering doctoral work at Columbia University with Robin Middleton, Kenneth Frampton, and Mary McLeod helped to establish Cedric Price as a major contributor to contemporary architectural discourse. Mathews has published articles on Price's work in *AD, A+U, Journal of Architectural Education*, and *Journal of Technoetic Arts*. The first volume of his two-volume book on Price, *From Agit Prop to Free Space: The Architecture of Cedric Price*, is published by Black Dog Publishing, 2007.

Louise Pelletier is an architect. She is a professor at the School of Design at the Université du Québec à Montréal in the program of Design of the Environment and in the graduate program in Design of Events. She was awarded a PhD in the History and Theory of Architecture by McGill University in 2000. She is the author of *Architecture in Words: Theatre, Language and the Sensuous Space of Architecture* published by Routledge in 2006. She co-authored *Architectural Representation and the Perspective Hinge*, 1997, with A Pérez-Gómez. She also led a major research project on architecture and theatre that resulted in the publication of *Theatrical Space as a Model for Architecture*, McGill University Digital Collections, 2003. Her current research is on *The Material Imagination of the Event*.

Charles Rice is a Senior Lecturer in the School of Architecture at the University of Technology, Sydney. He has also taught in histories and theories at the Architectural Association School of Architecture, London. He is author of *The Emergence of the Interior: Architecture, Modernity, Domesticity*, 2006. His recent work is also published in the anthologies *Negotiating Domesticity: Spatial Constructions of Gender in Modern Architecture*, 2005, *Walter Benjamin and History*, 2005, and *Capitales de la modernité: Walter Benjamin et la ville*, 2005, and in journals including *The Journal of Architecture* and *Home Cultures*.

Naomi Stead is a Senior Lecturer in architectural theory, philosophy and cultural studies at the University of Technology, Sydney. She holds a Bachelor of Architecture from the University of South Australia, and a PhD from the University of Queensland. She writes architectural criticism for a number of professional journals in Australia, and is a contributing editor to *Architecture Australia*. Her scholarly research has been published in *The Journal of Architecture*, *OASE*, and the *Open Museums Journal*. Her research interests include concepts of authorship in architecture, the history and theory of museums, architectural criticism, representations of architecture and the metropolis, and queer space.

Renée Tobe is head of History and Theory and Senior Lecturer at Sheffield Hallam University. She studied architecture at the Architectural Association and has a PhD from Cambridge University. Her research covers architecture in film, graphic novels, and television. Current publications include: "Both Frightening and Familiar" in *Visual Culture and Tourism*, 2003, "Architectural Grounding in Miller's *Elektra*: Temporality and Spatiality in the Graphic Novel" in *ImageText*, "Port Bou and Two Grains of Wheat: In Remembrance of Walter Benjamin", in Architectural Theory Review, Summer 2005, and "Where We Are Now" in *Robert Maciejuk; Day for Night*, 2006.

Gernot FA Weckherlin is a Lecturer in architectural history at the Bauhaus University in Weimar. He is a chartered architect in Berlin, and a critic writing for architectural magazines such as *Bauwelt, Deutsches Architektenblatt, Baumeister, Thesis—Wissenschaftliche Zeitschrift der Bauhaus-Universität Weimar, Graz Architecture Magazine*. His recent publications include articles entitled "The Architecture Machine or: The Theory of Architecture, an Applied Science?", "Die Angst des Architekten vor dem leeren Blatt: Architekturhandbücher als Medien im künstlerischen Prozess", and "Architekturführer Thüringen 2: Vom Bauhaus bis heute." Weckherlin is currently engaged in a research project on architectural manuals: "Ernst Neufert's Manuals: The Order of Architectural Knowledge."

Index

Edited by Tim Anstey, Katja Grillner, Rolf Hughes

Designed by Matthew Pull

Cover image taken from "Invisible Cities: Location Study 007", Photograph, Jonas Dahlberg, 2004, exhibited as part of *Invisible Cities* by Jonas Dahlberg at the São Paulo Biennale, 2004 and at Moderna Museet, Stockholm, 2005, courtesy of Jonas Dahlberg and Galerie Nordenhake Berlin/Stockholm.

Black Dog Publishing Limited
Unit 4.4 Tea Building
56 Shoreditch High Street
London
E1 6JJ

Tel: +44 (0)20 7613 1922
Fax: +44 (0)20 7613 1944
Email: info@blackdogonline.com

www.blackdogonline.com

British Library Cataloguing-in-Publication Data.

A CIP record for this book is available from the British Library.

ISBN 10: 1 904772 74 9
ISBN 13: 978 1 904772 74 3

Black Dog Publishing is an environmentally responsible company. *Architecture and Authorship* is printed on Fedrigoni Symbol Freelife Satin, an environmentally friendly, wood-free paper, with 50 per cent virgin fibres, 40 per cent recycled pre-consumer wood free fibres, and ten per cent recycled, post-consumer, de-inked fibres.

architecture art design
fashion history photography
theory and things

black dog
publishing

www.blackdogonline.com